Strategic Manufact
for Competitive Advantage

Strategic Manufacturing for Competitive Advantage

Transforming operations from shop floor to strategy

STEVE BROWN
University of Brighton and
Baruch College, City University, New York

PRENTICE HALL
LONDON • NEW YORK • TORONTO • SYDNEY • TOKYO
SINGAPORE • MADRID • MEXICO CITY • MUNICH

First published 1996 by
Prentice Hall Europe
Campus 400, Maylands Avenue
Hemel Hempstead
Hertfordshire, HP2 7EZ
A division of
Simon & Schuster International Group

Typeset in Stone, 9½/12pt
by Photoprint, Torquay

Printed and bound in Great Britain by
Hartnolls Limited, Bodmin, Cornwall

Library of Congress Cataloging-in-Publication Data

Brown, Steve.
Strategic manufacturing for competitive advantage: transforming operations from shop floor to strategy / by Steve Brown.
p. cm.
Includes bibliographical references and index.
ISBN 0–13–184508–X
1. Strategic planning. 2. Manufactures. I. Title.
HD30.28.B7823 1996 95–25503
658.4'012--dc20 CIP

British Library Cataloguing in Publication Data

A catalogue record for this book is available from the British Library

ISBN 0–13–184508–X

1 2 3 4 5 00 99 98 97 96

This book is dedicated to my mother and to my father –
Charles Edward Brown, whose memory lives on

There is more creativity in manufacturing than in most other jobs. The only limitations are in people's minds. (Ferry, 1993, p.127)

Manufacturing must become a, if not the, primary marketing tool in the firm's arsenal. Quality, maintainability, responsiveness . . . flexibility, and the length of the innovation cycle (for both incremental improvement of current products and major new product development) are all controlled by the Factory.

(Peters, 1987, p.159)

The factory is no longer a place of dirty floors and smoking machines, but rather an environment of ongoing experimentation and continuous innovation.

(Kenney and Florida, 1993, p.65)

Contents

Acknowledgements xiii
Introduction xv

1 *Strategic issues in manufacturing* 1

1.1 Introduction 1
1.2 The value chain 7
1.3 Focus, core competence and distinctive capabilities 9
1.4 The scope of strategic decision-making activities 10
1.5 The company in relation to the industry/market 13
1.6 Stakeholders and strategy 17
1.7 The strategic planning process 19
1.8 Strategic options 22
1.9 The use of matrices in strategic decision-making 29
1.10 Evaluating strategic decisions 33
Conclusion 35
Summary 37
Case BMW, Honda and Rover 38

2 *Manufacturing strategy* 40

2.1 Introduction 40
2.2 The national importance of manufacturing 44
2.3 The problems of past attitudes to manufacturing 52
2.4 Reasons for the continued image problem of production/operations 56
2.5 Present-day developments of production/operations' image 58
2.6 Key reasons for having a manufacturing strategy 59
2.7 Formulating a manufacturing strategy 64
2.8 Market forces and manufacturing: from craft to strategic manufacturing 71
2.9 The need for holistic management 73
2.10 Evaluating the success of manufacturing strategies 75
Conclusion 75
Summary 79
Case Manufacturing strategy at Compaq 80

3 *Issues in new product development* 83

3.1 Introduction 83
3.2 A brief overview of reasons for new product launches 86
3.3 The strategic importance of new product development 87
3.4 The role of R&D in new product development 93
3.5 New product developments and related industries 100
3.6 Types of new product development 102
3.7 The failure factor in product innovation 104
3.8 Basic considerations in new product development 106
3.9 The process of new product developments 108
3.10 Organizational considerations in new product development 111
3.11 Computer-aided design 123
3.12 Indications of design effectiveness 125
3.13 Modular design 127
Conclusion 128
Summary 130
Case Ford 130

4 *Manufacturing investment, process choice and strategy* 133

4.1 Introduction 133
4.2 Basic layout types 136
4.3 Overview of process choice 139
4.4 Process choice and strategy 143
4.5 Process choice and marketing strategy 147
4.6 Factory focus 150
4.7 Process choice and the product lifecycle 151
4.8 Flexible manufacturing systems (FMS) 152
4.9 Group technology and factory focus 159
4.10 Overview of automation 160
4.11 Computer-integrated manufacturing (CIM) 164
4.12 The scope of investment in manufacturing technology 165
4.13 Types of automation 165
4.14 The debate on investment in process technology 168
4.15 Failures with automation 171
Conclusion 172
Summary 174
Case IBM's manufacturing plant in Scotland 175

5 *Quality as a strategic factor* 177

5.1 Introduction 177
5.2 Quality as part of the mission statement 179
5.3 Defining quality 179
5.4 The strategic importance of quality 185

5.5 The evolution from inspection to TQM 189
5.6 Total quality management (TQM) 189
5.7 The cost of quality 192
5.8 The evidence and real cost of quality failure 194
5.9 Human factors in quality management 197
5.10 *Kaizen* 201
5.11 Quality awards 202
5.12 Tools and techniques 203
5.13 TQM and work study 210
5.14 Total productive maintenance (TPM) 217
5.15 Implementing the process of quality management 218
Conclusions 219
Summary 221
Case TQM at Motorola 222

6 The strategic importance of inventory management 224

6.1 Introduction 224
6.2 The scope of materials management 226
6.3 Tactical/functional roles in materials management 228
6.4 The competitive importance of materials management 228
6.5 Stock-holding 230
6.6 ABC analysis 231
6.7 The economic order quantity (EOQ) model 232
6.8 The development towards a strategic/holistic approach 235
6.9 MRP – where operational and strategic levels begin to meet 236
6.10 Overview of just-in-time 244
6.11 Electronic data interchange (EDI) 251
6.12 The strategic development of buyer–supplier relationships 251
6.13 The development from adversarial to partnership relationships 254
6.14 The reduction and consolidation in the number of suppliers 260
6.15 Suppliers and innovation 261
6.16 The transplant suppliers 264
6.17 The transfer of Japanese practices to Japanese transplants in the West 265
Conclusions 267
Summary 267
Case Sun Microsystems 268

7 Strategic human resource management 271

7.1 Introduction 271
7.2 An overview of key areas in the firm's human resource audit 273
7.3 The importance of human involvement in production/operations 274
7.4 Three major manufacturing eras and their effect upon human resources 277

7.5 Relevant human resource theories for production/operations management 280
7.6 Motivation theories 281
7.7 Charismatic leadership or company-wide effort? 286
7.8 Remuneration for production/operations staff 287
7.9 International comparisons of hours and wages 290
7.10 Organizational factors 290
7.11 Training 297
7.12 Organizational learning 302
7.13 Collaboration 308
Conclusions 310
Summary 311
Case General Motors 312

8 *World-class strategic manufacturing* 316

8.1 The current position 316
8.2 Overview of markets 319
8.3 The importance of globalization 319
8.4 The strategic response to markets 322
8.5 Describing the current manufacturing era 326
8.6 World-class manufacturing 327
8.7 Is lean manufacturing sufficient? 330
8.8 Defining strategic manufacturing 334
8.9 Becoming strategic: linking corporate, marketing and manufacturing strategies 338
Conclusions 341

Bibliography 344
Index 356

Acknowledgements

I have many people to thank for this book. First to my colleagues at the Brighton Business School at the University of Brighton, in particular to Colin Harris who, in addition to being a first-class colleague, has also become a very dear friend. My thanks go to him, Tracey Taylor, Alex and Tom.

I would like to thank Robert Griffith-Jones, John Bareham and the Director of the University of Brighton, David Watson, who all agreed that I could go to the United States for a year as part of a professorship exchange. This was a fruitful experience and much research was undertaken there which formed a considerable part of the content for this book.

I would like to thank colleagues at Baruch College, City University of New York where I am a visiting professor, in particular Professor George Schneller, Professor David Dannenbring, Professor Steve Savas, Professor Julian Freedman and my good friend, Professor Alvin Booke. The drive into New York from New Jersey with Professor Booke was a time of learning and good humour.

My thanks go to other academic colleagues who over the years have encouraged me in one way or another: Professor Richard Lamming at the University of Bath, Professor John Bessant at the University of Brighton and Professor Terry Hill at the London Business School.

I learned much from my years working in industry and the public sector. My thanks go to the former management team of the 'Beryl B' platform in the North Sea. Memories of my time working there remain dear to me and the team taught me more than they probably realized. My thanks go to George O'Hara whose wise insight and good humour taught me much.

Tom Mullen provided useful notes and Christine Williams' input was invaluable in reading and commenting upon draft chapters. John Yates' support at Prentice Hall UK was appreciated throughout the project.

I am indebted to friends outside of the business and academic world. Jennifer Smith and Jon and Jane Humberstone are precious friends. I thank Gary Numan for the opportunity to have been part of the music world, a truly wonderful experience. I also thank Julia Fordham who, as well as being probably the best female singer–songwriter on earth is also one of the funniest, sanest and most wonderful people I have ever talked to.

My time in the United States was made pleasurable by the kindness of a number of people there, especially John and Marianne Nordgren, Andrew and Ruth Markoe, and the Eide family.

Thanks to V.M. for everything.

Introduction

This book is offered in the hope that it will be of use both for students and management practitioners alike. In my position as an academic in a Business School, I am totally committed to providing the best possible service that I can for my students and to industry. To my mind, the business academic must be fully up to date and should see his/her role as one of service. As well as gaining student feedback in the classroom, another vitally important response that a business academic should actively seek is from industry. It is vital that we provide strong academic grounding; it is equally important that this is useful and applicable in the real world.

The last few years have seen dramatic declines in the manufacturing capability and performance of many firms in key industries in the West. This is particularly true of Britain, where the manufacturing base has been eroded to a large degree. This is tragic in many ways, particularly for the highly skilled men and women who cannot find jobs in manufacturing. The reasons for this decline are many, but one common theme underpinning this decline seems to be the inability of many manufacturing firms to see their core activity, manufacturing, in terms of strategic importance. The tone throughout this book is that manufacturing must be seen in terms of *strategic* rather than mere *functional* importance. After all, any organization will largely fall under one of two distinct types of business sectors, manufacturing or services. It would seem logical that corporate decisions should be aimed at improving the long-term manufacturing capability so that the organization can successfully compete in its chosen markets.

The phrase, 'long-term' here is significant; a long-term attitude, manifested in a commitment to winning in market segments, has been at the core of Japanese thinking in manufacturing. Short-term profitability has been sacrificed for longer term commitment to winning market share and customer loyalty. Investment in manufacturing in all aspects, including process technology, long-term supplier relationships and development of human resources, including training, provides one of the biggest distinctions between traditional Western and enlightened Japanese approaches to manufacturing.

Clearly, there needs to be a change to the approach which currently dominates much of Western manufacturing and which manifests itself in two distinct and dangerous outcomes for the firm:

1. An obsession with short-termism so that financial criteria (especially short-term profitability) are seen as the sole means of judging performance. This also means that investment in process technology will be sacrificed in order for financial ratios such as return on assets to appear to be strong. In short, the ratio will look good because the plant is often old and incapable of competing against other, world-class, strategically minded competitors.

2. Firms become pulled into different market segments, sometimes by over-zealous marketing or corporate managers, into business areas in which the firm cannot compete. This comes about by a lack of understanding of production/operations capability, or incapability. This lack of understanding is because a strategic audit of manufacturing processes and technology has been omitted from the decision-making process at corporate level.

This book does not intend to criticize other areas of the firm, such as human resource management, marketing or finance. Rather, it is meant to highlight one of the common areas of corporate mismanagement in many Western firms, namely the omission of production/operations, contribution from the decision-making process at corporate level. The involvement of senior manufacturing personnel in corporate strategic planning and implementation will not by itself guarantee success. However, the omission of competent managers able to link the required awareness of manufacturing capability with sound business acumen will typically prove fatal for the manufacturing firm.

This book is meant for both students and practising managers in the area of manufacturing. It is my hope that it will provide a different view of manufacturing from the more mathematical, technique-driven approaches, which emphasize only the short-term aspects of manufacturing. Such an approach is taught in some business schools and more alarmingly is practised within some manufacturing firms.

The manufacturing manager must be good at managing a number of important areas:

- People skills in managing a key resource of the firm – human resources.
- A commitment to meeting customer requirements.
- Forming long-term relationships with other organizations, such as suppliers and any other type of alliance that the firm might have to support manufacturing.
- Managing a large proportion of the firm's assets, including fixed (process technology) and current (materials and bought-in components).

I have had the pleasure of working in, and consulting for, world-class companies; equally exciting has been working with manufacturing companies which are intent on becoming world-class by continuously improving everything that they do.

My hope is that this book will add to our understanding of the vital importance of manufacturing. I warmly recommend manufacturing management as a career which provides wonderful opportunities to use the very best of management skills. Possession of these skills is a requirement to compete in a business world full of world-class, strategic manufacturing firms.

1 Strategic issues in manufacturing

1.1 Introduction

This book is concerned with manufacturing. The question might be asked, Why have a chapter on corporate strategy in a text which is devoted to manufacturing? After all, there are many well-written books on corporate strategy. For example, Whittington (1993) estimates that there are thirty-seven books with the title *Strategic Management* and these books offer some good insight into the nature, scope and complexity of strategic management. The reason for including a chapter on corporate strategy in a book on manufacturing is twofold:

1. The books on corporate strategy tend to ignore the *strategic* importance and contribution of production/operations in corporate decisions.
2. Books written on production/operations – with rare exceptions – also ignore the strategic importance of production/operations in corporate decisions. The standard texts on manufacturing – as good as some of these are – concentrate on tools and techniques of the day-to-day running of operations.

As stated in the introduction, the tone throughout this book is to emphasize the strategic importance of production/operations. This chapter examines basic strategic options available to a company and their relevance for manufacturing firms, and discusses some of the literature which pertains to strategic planning and implementation. It is clear that some works treat corporate strategy as an elitist activity, determined by senior managers only, without any bottom-up involvement or consideration. Also, the identity of the strategic decision-makers is a mystery; any discussion on what qualifies a person to make strategic decisions in a *manufacturing* firm is a glaring omission from texts and articles on corporate strategy.

The tone, particularly before 1980, was that strategy was devised at the highest levels of the firm and simply passed down. This view has changed to some degree, to where the strategy process in some firms involves various functional areas and more than just the most senior levels of the firm.

Strategic management calls for the very best of managerial skills. Strategic planners must guide the company in the most beneficial way and at the same time have to do so with the awareness of stakeholders' interests, which include shareholders, employees, the government, suppliers and distributors. Strategic management is not simply concerned with satisfying short-term requirements of shareholders and other financial institutions; strategy is concerned with providing competitive advantage for the firm.

Part of the problem for strategists is in having to satisfy so many different and sometimes conflicting factors. Kanter (1989a) points to some of the dichotomies facing corporate planning and strategy

> Get 'lean and mean' through restructuring – while being a great company to work for and offering employee-centred policies, such as job security.
>
> Encourage creativity and innovation to take you in new directions – and 'stick to your knitting'.
>
> Communicate a sense of urgency and push for faster execution, faster results – but take more time to deliberately plan for the future.
>
> Decentralize to delegate profit and planning responsibilities to small, autonomous business units. But centralize to capture efficiencies and combine resources in innovative ways. (p.21)

Clearly, strategic management is a difficult role; awareness of the implications of a particular decision have to be known and evaluated. There is no evidence to suggest that the more planning a firm does, the more it will succeed. On the other hand, if the firm does no planning it may well flounder.

1.1.1 Successful strategy and production/operations

One major problem is that successful strategies are really only known *after* the event. Even then, it is difficult to assess why a particular strategy was successful or even if the outcome was the same as that anticipated by the company. For example, we know that Honda has been enormously successful in the motorcycle industry, but the reasons why they have been successful are difficult to determine. As Kay (1993) states, there are two accounts of Honda's success – one by the Boston Consulting Group, which suggests that this success was the result of an intense and deliberately planned pursuit of the market; another account by Pascale (1984) suggests that it was more to do with good fortune. Neither account can be fully proven to be the truth. Kay (1993) is right to say that Pascale's good fortune view of Honda's success might be more convincing had Honda not been so successful in its other endeavours; it is stretching credibility to put this all down to good fortune. What is clear from both accounts is that manufacturing capability is described without being seen as one of the key factors behind Honda's success. Indeed, as we shall see, much of the literature on strategy glosses over the vital importance of production/operations in providing competitive advantage. In the case of Honda, a major factor was their manufacturing capability in providing low cost, reliable, quality motorcycles (through production/operations capability) which allowed them to win against other competitors.

Later on (as we shall see in chapter 8) they were able to fend off Yamaha's challenge by this same capability.

In this text it is argued that production/operations capability must be in place in the manufacturing firm. Without this capability, the firm cannot hope to gain any sustainable competitive advantage and efforts in marketing or other areas of the firm will be wasted. The reasons why a particular firm is successful may be difficult to assess; underpinning the success of manufacturing firms, however, will be world-class production/operations capability. Whether success comes from extensive corporate planning, or by good fortune or by clever exploitation of a particular opportunity, or by a combination of all three possibilities, success for manufacturing firms is dependent to a large degree upon production/operations capability and competence.

1.1.2 Definitions of strategy

Various definitions of the term strategy are offered in the literature on corporate strategy. For example in his classic work on strategy, Chandler (1962) defined strategy as

> the determination of the basic long-term goals and objectives of an enterprise, and the adoption of courses of action and the allocation of resources necessary for carrying out these goals. (p.16)

Evered (1983) defines strategy as:

> the broad program for defining and achieving an organization's objectives and implementing its missions. (p.57)

Wheelan and Hunger (1989) add that strategy:

> includes the determination and evaluation of alternative paths to achieve an organization's objectives and mission and, eventually, a choice of the alternative that is to be adopted. (p.5)

From the above – which are quite representative of the types of definitions on corporate strategy – a number of factors begin to emerge:

- Strategy is concerned with decisions which tend to have a long-term impact (this is discussed later in the chapter) and not just short-term, quick-fix solutions.
- Strategy is formed by senior managers, although other levels may be involved.
- Strategy serves to focus the organization's aims – these can then be part of its mission statement.
- Strategy is about generating possible options (planning) which will then become narrowed down to specific choices (actions for implementation).

1.1.3 The origin of strategy

The term strategy as used in the corporate or business strategy sense clearly has strong associations with the military terminology from which it is derived, where plans and timescales were devised in order to outmanoeuvre the opposition. This does not mean that there is complete destruction of one company by another, although this is sometimes the case. What can happen, though, is that one firm attacks another in a relatively small market segment without wiping out the competitor. To take the military analogy further, we may think of strategy in terms of planning and devising an attack or strike in a particular market segment where the enemy – the other players in the market – are either weak or not paying sufficient attention. This lapse in attention from other players may be related to their unsuccessful positioning of current products, or quality problems of existing products, or their inability to meet other competitive factors such as delivery speed and reliability, flexibility and rapid product innovation. A lapse in attention may be in the competitors' inability to exploit export opportunities or other market factors. For example, Apple attacked IBM by focusing on two market segments – education and home-users – which were largely ignored by IBM, who paid much more attention to the business sectors. Similarly, General Motors lost market share to both US and foreign competitors, who attacked by creating or concentrating on existing smaller segments such as turbos, four-wheel drive cars and minivans. If we are to use this analogy of businesses as attacking other competitors, then Table 1.1 is applicable.

1.1.4 Time horizons in strategic decisions

A distinguishing feature of strategic decisions is that they tend to be long term, relating to where the business is likely to be in five or more years from the decision-making process. Operational or tactical decisions have much shorter time horizons. This time factor still holds true despite the increasingly volatile nature of markets and their propensity to continuously fragment into smaller market segments. A number of companies in the petroleum industry, for example, will create long-term scenarios for the future; Shell has a Central Planning Group whose job it is to 'plan the future' for the company. Pharmaceutical companies also tend to have long-term strategic planning groups.

The factor of time has relevance for production/operations in a number of ways. If we take capacity, for example, we can say that a *strategic* capacity decision would relate to long-term investment regarding new plant, new facilities and the like, which Muhlemann *et al.* (1992) would call 'potential capacity', whereas *short-term* capacity decisions would be examining capacity that is typically available within a twelve-month period. The strategic capacity decision would have far-reaching consequences in terms of long-term financial commitment to fixed assets. Factors such as additional capacity through creating a new plant, or investment in process technology of existing plants, or commitment to continuous improvement and total quality programmes are all directly related to long-term investments in manufacturing. The Japanese transplants in the United Kingdom and United States are examples of potential capacity decisions.

Where investment in fixed assets take place, this will either support the company and allow it to compete (a vital asset), or the firm will be stuck with a fixed liability which will disable the company in terms of competing against other world-class firms.

1.1.5 The ultimate decision-making responsibility

In addition to timing in strategic decision-making, another factor concerns the role of the ultimate decision-makers. Whilst there are an increasing number of companies where the process of strategic decision-making includes all levels of the hierarchy and cross-functional teams work together to shape strategy, the ultimate decisions still tend to rest with senior managers, as stated by Johnson and Scholes (1988):

> Corporate objectives are usually formulated by senior members of the board or even the chairman or chief executive. They are more likely to be

Table 1.1 Key points for successful strategy

- The firm must know where it will specifically attack in a market (by product, by region and so on) and must then focus its resources and capabilities to succeed
- The firm must anticipate and be prepared for retaliation from other competitors once it has made its attack on a particular market segment
- Equally, the firm must know where it will *not* attack and to stay out of dangerous areas in which it cannot hope to compete
- Everybody in the organization must know and understand the strategy, feel that they own any changes that will be made and be committed to them
- A sense of timing is vital – a long-term strategy does not mean neglecting short-term urgency. In many markets, especially high-tech manufacturers, speed is vital both for delivery speed of *existing* products and rapid product innovations
- Alliances are an invaluable means of providing competitive advantage for the manufacturing firm. They allow the firm to concentrate on what it does best rather than being involved in areas in which it does not have particular expertise. Alliances with other manufacturing firms provide excellent means of organizational learning. Alliances also act as a means of combining a cluster of firms with the capability of competing against other clusters of firms

> handed down to, rather than formulated by, lower levels of management. (p.135)

This has been challenged to some degree by two issues:

1. The cross-functional Japanese model of strategy undoubtedly includes bottom-up, as well as top-down approaches and this has been copied by some firms in the West.
2. The levels of management hierarchy have been drastically reduced in many firms.

However, the ultimate decision-making responsibility for strategic decisions still tends to remain at the highest levels of the firm. Each level will have particular responsibilities and some of these may be strategic in nature. The main levels of responsibility tend to be in the areas shown in Table 1.2.

If the ultimate decision-makers know little or nothing about manufacturing, then not surprisingly the nature of decisions could be detrimental to the manufacturing firm. The criteria might shift to being purely financial in nature, where short-term approaches might override long-term investment in new processes, plant and technology. For manufacturing firms, there would seem to be two alternatives:

1. The ultimate decision-makers must be senior managers who are themselves knowledgeable about manufacturing as well as other business considerations.
2. The ultimate decision-makers themselves might not necessarily know a great deal about manufacturing but will involve those personnel within the com-

Table 1.2 Decision-making levels in an organization

Strategy level	*Primary responsibility*	*Areas of focus*
Corporate	CEO, other key executives	Directing a portfolio of business units; long-term investment decisions; reviewing/revizing/unifying major strategic approaches
Strategic business Units (SBU's)	General managers	Determining areas of competitive advantage; forming responses to external changes; seeking opportunities
Functional strategies	Functional managers	Determining strategies for key areas such as production/marketing/finance/human resources/R&D
Operating strategies	Unit leaders	More time-specific strategies aimed to support the broader strategies of senior managers

pany who do – thus allowing the manufacturing managers to be a key input into shaping and deciding corporate strategy for the manufacturing firm.

1.2 The value chain

Porter's (1985) value chain model has direct relevance for manufacturing firms. He states that:

> Value is the amount buyers are willing to pay for what a firm provides them . . . creating value for buyers that exceeds the cost of doing so is the goal of any generic strategy. Value, instead of cost, must be used in analyzing competitive position. (p.38)

To this end, all activities within the firm form part of the value chain. The task for the manufacturing firm is to analyze those activities which it does best and to focus on these. This means focusing on its core strengths and using this capability to provide added value for the firm's customers. In doing so, the firm must then become reliant upon partnerships with other firms in order to provide value in those areas and activities which the manufacturing firm has now subcontracted. Porter (1985) divides these activities into *primary* and *support* activities. Primary activities are cited as:

1. *Inbound logistics*. These are all inputs to the product including inventory control.
2. *Operations*. All activities related to transforming inputs into final product.
3. *Outbound logistics*. Collecting, storing and distributing the product to buyers.
4. *Marketing and sales*. Providing the means for buying the product, as well as the inducement to do so (advertising, selling, distribution, pricing and promotion).
5. *Service*. Enhancing the value of a product, e.g. installation, training, repair and maintenance.

Support activities are cited as:

1. *Procurement*. Purchasing raw materials, supplies and other company assets.
2. *Technology development*. Developing know-how, procedures and technological input.
3. *Human resource management*. Selection, appraisal, training and development.
4. *Firm infrastructure*, including all general management activities and support systems.

Clearly, procurement and technology development directly relate to production/operations. In addition, human resource management ties in with production/operations since, in a manufacturing firm, the majority of employees are often involved in the transformation process. Also, the firm's infrastructure directly impacts upon and is in turn influenced by production/operations, because decisions about the supplier base, the amount of subcontracting to be undertaken, and the basic choice of manufacturing process to be used, fall under the heading of 'firm infrastructure'. An essential part of the firm's strategy, then, is to combine all of these activities in such a way as to provide value and not simply cost to the customer.

In order to compete at all in some industries, low cost is a requirement. However, other competitive requirements provide value too, so the firm needs to be able to satisfy delivery speed and reliability, flexibility and any other customer requirements. Achieving these customer requirements will largely fall under the responsibility of production/operations. The problem with the concept of the value chain, in terms of world-class manufacturing practice, is that, by its very nature, the chain tends to be seen in terms of links, arranged in series from raw materials to end customer. As the model stands – helpful as it is – there is no sense of interlinking between the various players within the overall value chain. Indeed, each link in the chain seems to be a stand-alone factor; there does not appear to be any sense of interrelationships of a *strategic* nature involving all links in the overall value chain (Figure 1.1).

Figure 1.1 The value chain.

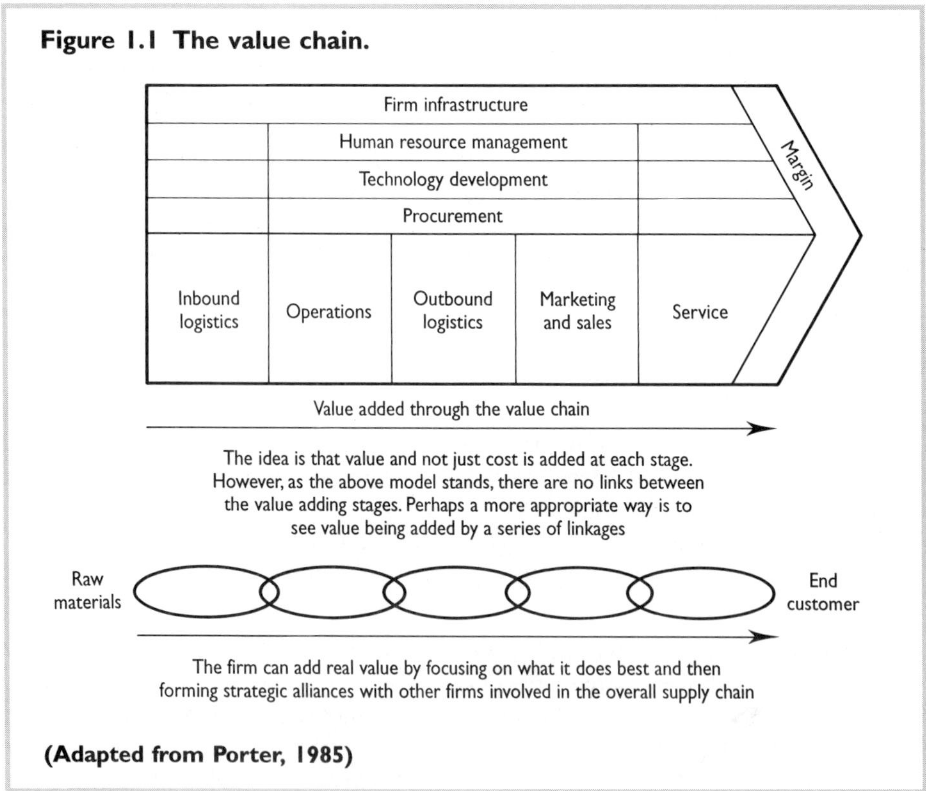

(Adapted from Porter, 1985)

Admittedly, Porter (1985) speaks in terms of value systems, as a fleet of interlinking value chains, but even here each stage is seen as a separate entity. It is clear from Porter's 'five forces model' (discussed in Section 1.5.1) that the buyer–supplier relationship is couched in terms of win/lose scenarios where the winner (buyer or supplier) is determined by a number of constituent factors – notably size – which act as threatening devices which may be used to enhance power against either party. This may well hold true to some degree in Western manufacturing, but does not appear to be the norm in Japanese manufacturing, where buyer–supplier relationships are viewed as strategic and mutually beneficial (this is discussed in Chapter 6). In the 1990s and beyond, therefore, we must view manufacturing companies as part of a fluid, interactive, mutually beneficial series of relationships between raw materials and end customer (vertical linkages), and also joint ventures between companies (horizontal linkages), as shown in Figure 1.2.

1.3 Focus, core competence and distinctive capabilities

Throughout this book emphasis is made on the firm's need to focus, rather than being pulled in different directions. A company can be unfocused in two ways:

1. Competing in markets without undertaking a manufacturing audit. This means that there is a mismatch between the targeted market and the firm's technology, skills capabilities and other key resources. Such an audit must be made before attacking new markets.
2. By being involved in activities which fall outside of the firm's core competence. This is particularly true of manufacturing firms which feel the need to

Figure 1.2 Strategic alliances – horizontal and vertical.

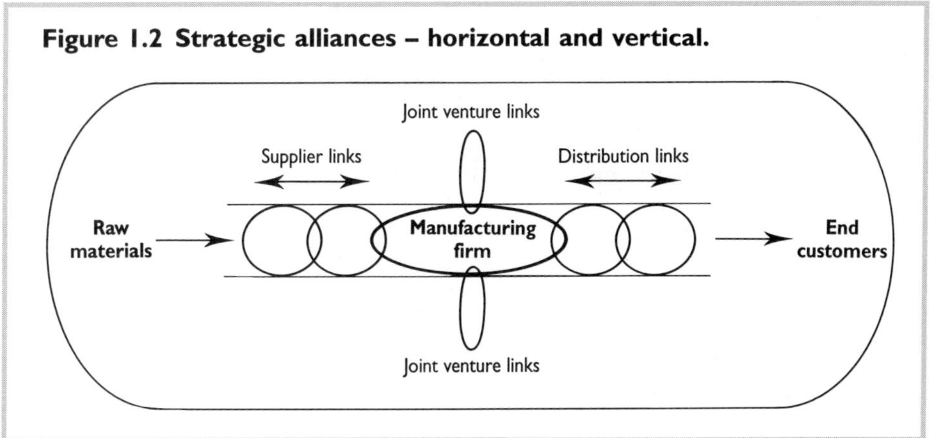

backwardly integrate and own suppliers. This often moves the manufacturer into entirely new manufacturing processes in which it might have no expertise.

The emphasis on focus ties in with two other important strategic concepts – core competences (Hamel and Prahalad, 1994) and distinctive capabilities (Kay, 1993). These two are quite similar – both emphasize the need to focus and build upon those capabilities that the firm has which might provide competitive advantage. Throughout the book, we will allude to the fact that in manufacturing firms the production/operations capability must form part of the firm's core competence or distinctive capabilities. No amount of effort from other areas of the firm can possibly compensate for poor production/operations performance. This capability or competence can bring rapid new product development, low-cost production (not dependent on large volume), and assured reliability of delivery and improved delivery speed. Such factors are key to competitive advantage. As Corsten and Will (1994) suggest:

> Production is the key area for forming competitive advantage for a company. Therefore the aim of strategic production management is to provide competitive advantage by creating an optimal coordination between competitive strategy and production strategy. (p.111)

As we shall see, the link between competitive and production strategy is often not well made. Production strategies are often an afterthought, once corporate decisions have already been made.

1.4 The scope of strategic decision-making activities

Johnson and Scholes (1993) provide a useful list of factors involved in strategic decisions: all firms will have to make decisions based on certain areas as set out in Table 1.3.

This list provides the essential ingredients. However, to arrive at particular

Table 1.3 Factors in strategic decision-making

- The scope of an organization's activities
- Matching those activities with the organization's environment
- Matching activities with the resource capabilities
- Allocation of resources
- Values, expectations and goals of those influencing strategy
- The direction that the organization will move in the long term
- Implications for change *throughout* the organization

Adapted from Johnson and Scholes (1993)

decisions, there is a balancing act which comes into play. Johnson and Scholes (1993) see the scope of activities embracing three, interactive key elements:

Strategic analysis
⇙ ⇘
Strategic choice ⇔ Strategic implementation

1. **Strategic analysis** In terms of resource awareness, environmental audits and appreciation of corporate expectations.
2. **Strategic choice** Generating and evaluating options and then choosing from them
3. **Strategic implementation** Organizational structuring and planning resources required to carry out strategy.

Strategy therefore has to be a process of continuous information gathering and awareness where analysis, choice and implementation, together with feedback mechanisms, work together to position the firm at its most competitive standpoint. The strategy process also has to include an appreciation of the capabilities and limitations of the firm's resources, together with an awareness of the responsibilities that a firm has to all its stakeholders. Johnson and Scholes (1993) also speak in terms of the strategic fit that has to take place between the firm and the decisions it makes about strategy.

This idea is discussed by Thompson and Strickland (1989), who state that the strategy process involves creating a series of 'tight fits':

> Between strategy and organization structure; between strategy and what the organization's skills and competencies give it the ability to do; between strategy and budget allocations; between strategy and internal policies, procedures and support systems; between strategy and reward structure; between strategy and corporate culture. (p.133)

In a manufacturing company, much of this 'fit' has to do with the linkage between market requirements and manufacturing capability; these two elements must match, otherwise the firm will suffer.

Hax and Majluf (1991) offer six key variables in their assessment of the process of strategic decisions. To them strategic decisions should:

1. Be a coherent, unifying and integrative process.
2. Determine long-term objectives, action programmes and resource allocation priorities.
3. Plan and select the businesses the organization is in or should be in and *should not* be in.
4. Attempt to achieve a long-term sustainable advantage by responding to opportunities and threats in the firm's environment and strengths and weaknesses of the firm's organization.
5. Engage all hierarchical levels of the firm, not just senior management levels.
6. Define the contributions (both economic and non-economic) to the firm's stakeholders.

This list adds to our understanding and shows developments that have taken place between the 1960s and today of the strategy process. First, the need to focus and in consequence to stay *out* of certain markets, contrasts with the common approach of diversification in the 1960s, 1970s and, to a lesser degree, the 1980s. Second, engaging all hierarchical levels of the firm and not just senior management levels is, perhaps, the single most important of present-day strategic planning which owes much to the Japanese style of management.

The list offered by Hax and Majluf provides further clues to the importance of production/operations at senior levels of the firm, in particular, long-term objectives and resource allocation where production/operations will account for at least 60 per cent of fixed assets use. Also, the 'attempt to achieve a long-term, sustainable advantage' has everything to do with production/operations ability to compete on low cost, delivery, flexibility or other competitive requirements. With this in mind, it is strange indeed that many corporate decisions are made without senior manufacturing personnel being involved in the decision-making process. The reasons for this are discussed further in Chapter 2.

1.4.1 Strategic fit versus strategic stretch

A logical, linear approach to formulating strategy would be simply to match a firm's existing capability with a particular marketing segment which best exploited this existing capability. Such an approach might be termed as a strategic fit between resources (particularly production/operations capability) and targeted markets. Alternatively, a firm might be more lateral or visionary in thinking when planning strategy. This might involve future scenarios that went beyond mere matching to stretching resources, in other words, by providing ways of stretching the firm beyond its current resource base (Hamel and Prahalad, 1994). This may come in a number of ways, for example, forming alliances with other firms which allows the organization to remain focused rather than blurred in its corporate vision. Being restrained by current resources is almost designed to bring failure. Similarly, being bound by short-term financial criteria as a basis for strategic planning is short-sighted and dangerous. The move away from strategic fit to strategic stretch is well summarized by Verdin and Williamson (1994):

> Basing strategy on existing resources, looking inwards, risks building a company that achieves excellence in providing products and services that nobody wants . . . market-based strategy, with stretching visions and missions, can reinforce and complement competence or capability-based competition. And that successful strategy comes from matching competences to the market. (p.10)

We should take special note here, with the greatest respect to marketing personnel, that market-based strategy is not always the same as marketing-department-based strategy. External markets set the criteria, not the power of one department over another within an organization.

Figure 1.3 Porter's five forces model.

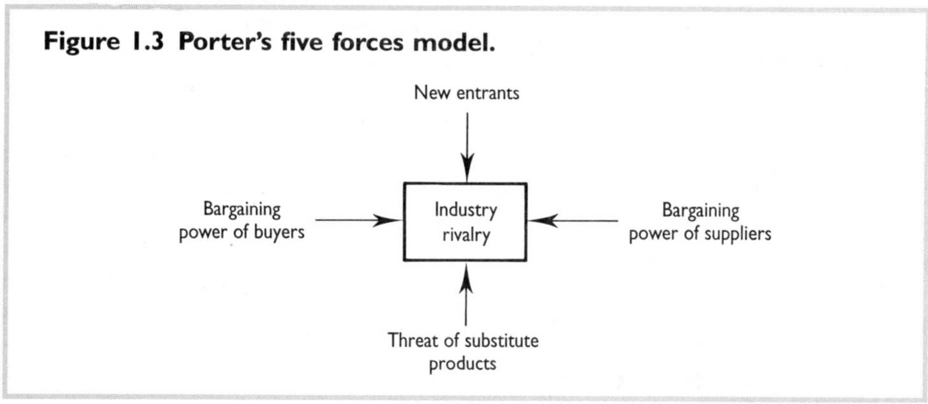

1.5 The company in relation to the industry/market

1.5.1 Porter's five forces model

Porter (1985) provides a model of industry structure (Figure 1.3). From this, a firm is able to determine its present position in order to plot its strategy.

Porter's five forces model is of explicit relevance to manufacturing firms for the following reasons

1. **The threat of new competitors** According to Porter, the ability to compete at all is dependent upon some perceived sustainable advantage either through cost (which clearly is a major factor for manufacturing) or differentiation (again a major factor, since this will depend upon production/operations' capability to actually produce the product which is perceived to be differentiated). Relatively new entrants in the automobile industry (for example, Hyundai and Kia) have seen their own manufacturing capability as a key factor to entry. The Japanese entrance into many industries such as steel, processors, consumer electronics and automobiles, was achieved by having world-class manufacturing capability at the centre of their attack on these markets.
2. **Rivalry between industry competitors** This will be enhanced by the number of players and the extent of rivalry in a particular market segment.
3. **Threats of substitute products** The launch of new or substitute products is only possible if production/operations' capabilities can satisfy market requirements including cost, flexibility, delivery and product quality. The transition from prototype to volume manufacture is also a crucial production/operations task.
4. and 5. **Bargaining power of suppliers** and **bargaining power of buyers** In manufacturing settings, this has more to do with buyer/supplier relationships (the buyer being the manufacturer) within the overall supply chain. The

balance and relationship between these two are critical. For example, Intel is a supplier of microchips to the likes of IBM and others in personal computer (PC) manufacture, so any breakthroughs in their research and development will have immediate impact on the buyer (manufacturer). Increasingly, the buyer–supplier relationship is one of collaboration, rather than confrontation. This win/win relationship is well developed in a number of buyer–supplier relationships in the car, computing and telecommunication industries. It must be said, though, that when Porter (1980) discussed the buyer–supplier relationship, he couched the relationships in terms of confrontation and conflict where one of the 'sides' would be stronger and would exert power over the other. As we shall see in Chapter 6, this idea has now changed and has been developed into mututally beneficial buyer–supplier relationships. The partnership is formed in order to compete against other such buyer–supplier relationships in an industry.

1.5.2 Competitive analysis and competitors' response

The assessment that a company makes of itself is essentially one of comparison with the company's competitors. A firm will generate strategic ideas following an analysis of the market, then plan its competitive move. The manufacturing firm has to anticipate competitive responses. When undertaking a current analysis, a number of competitive variables may be used, each of which will be judged in comparison to competitors and may include the indicators listed in Table 1.4.

Porter (1980) provides a framework for competitor analysis, shown in Figure 1.4.

The comparison with other firms is not merely an information-gathering exercise on competitors' strengths and weaknesses. In formulating a plan, part of the process has to include likely competitive responses to actions and strategies made by the firm. The military analogy cited earlier is applicable here; a firm makes a particular move, hopefully as a result of matching external market opportunities with internal core skills and capabilities (including production/

Table 1.4 Points of competitive analysis between firms

- Important distinctive competencies of a firm
- Existing strong market share and sustained market growth
- A distinctive, pacesetting strategy, renowned in the industry
- Market visibility
- Products are in fastest-growing market segments
- Strongly differentiated products or services in terms of quality, technical superiority, value for money or strong customer support service
- Sustainable cost advantages which are unlikely to be matched
- Profitability against the industry average or some other profit comparison
- Strong technological and innovational capability in processes or products

Figure 1.4 Porter's competitor analysis framework.

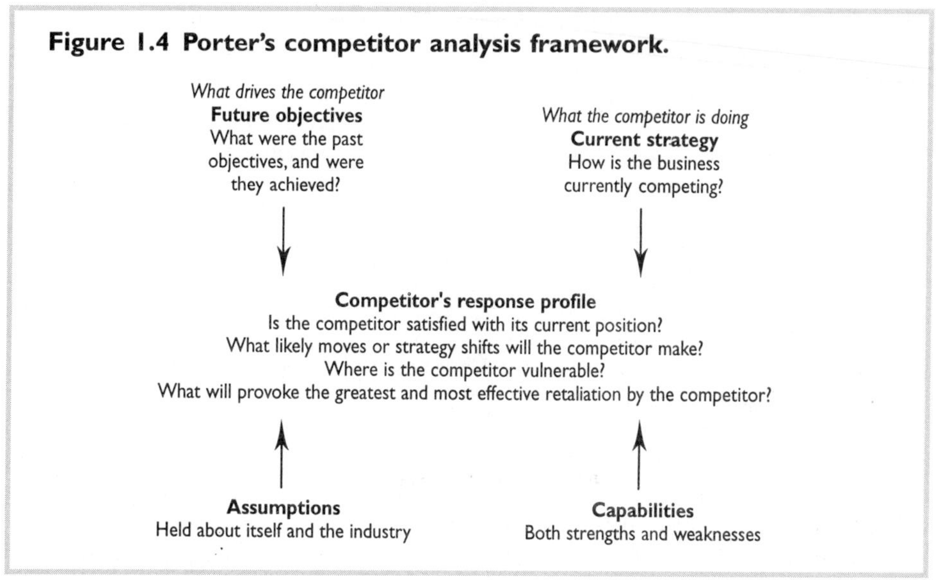

operations); the move may provoke a competitive response which can be defensive or aggressive in nature. The firm then faces a choice to further react to competitors' responses. A firm's planned move may come from aligning its internal strengths with external opportunities; such an analysis can come from a SWOT analysis which we will now discuss.

1.5.3 SWOT analysis

When a firm undertakes a SWOT (strengths, weaknesses, opportunities, threats) analysis, it is vital that the list of strengths and weaknesses are specific and clear. Each category must be mutually exclusive, since no factor can be both a strength and a weakness at the same time. Key headings in relations to production/ operations include:

- **Technology** Strength of R&D expertise, production process capability and rapid new product introduction.
- **Manufacturing** Low-cost production, process and product quality (fewer defects and repairs), high use of fixed assets (especially in capital intensive/ high fixed-cost industries), low-cost plant locations, skilled and trained labour force, high productivity, low-cost design (which has massive effect upon overall costs) and flexibility in terms of the range and volumes of products.
- **Human Resources** Superior competencies, quality control abilities, ability to develop products from R&D phase to market sooner than competitors; all of these come from human resource capability.

Table 1.5 A typical listing of a firm's strengths and weaknesses

Strengths	*Weaknesses*
• Distinctive competencies	• No clear direction
• Financial resources	• Obsolete plant
• Acknowledged as a market leader	• Poor track record of strategic implementation
• Insulation from competition	• A too narrow product line
• Cost leaders	• Weak market image
• Product innovation skills	• Weak distribution network
• Superior technological know-how	

General headings under strengths and weaknesses are shown in Table 1.5.

A typical list of opportunities and threats is shown in Table 1.6.

One factor which is often overlooked in a SWOT analysis is the role of time. Strengths and weaknesses are *internal* considerations which tend to relate to past and present capabilities. Opportunities and threats are *external* considerations which relate to present and future possibilities as Table 1.7 shows.

A successful SWOT analysis, therefore, is one which matches present internal strengths with external opportunities and avoids threats which may be manifested as a result of present weaknesses. Again, it is clear that in a manufacturing firm the contribution that production/operations can make is both central and vital. Key headings such as technological capability, industrial relations, flex-

Table 1.6 Indicative headings under opportunities and threats

Opportunities	*Threats*
• Additional customer groups	• Entry of low-cost competitors
• Enter new markets or market segments	• Substitute products
• Expand product line	• Slow market growth
• Related product diversification	• Adverse exchange rate conditions
• Falling trade barriers in foreign markets	• Changing buyer needs and tastes
• Faster market growth	• Adverse demographic changes

Table 1.7 The time factor in SWOT analysis

Heading	*Internal/external*	*Time factor*
Strengths	Internal	Past and present
Weaknesses	Internal	Past and present
Opportunities	External	Present and future
Threats	External	Present and future

ibility, delivery speed and reliability and product innovation hinge around the capability of production/operations' performance. If capability exists, all of these features will fall under strengths; if capability does not exist, then they will come under weaknesses. These competitive factors, largely under the umbrella of production/operations capabilities, will to a large degree shape the evaluation of opportunities and threats.

1.5.4 *Business forces/environmental factors*

As part of its competitive analysis, the firm must be aware of macro factors that have relevance. They include a PEST analysis (political, economic, social, technological), as well as the roles of demographics, labour, ecology, competitors, government and the relative balance of power between buyers and suppliers. These have direct relevance for the manufacturing firm, in particular developments in technology, awareness of competitive strengths and relationships with suppliers.

Essential macro factors would include general economic growth, inflation rates, unemployment levels and disposable incomes. Where a firm is involved in exporting, it must make constant reviews of foreign markets and foreign exchange rates. Analysis must be made of the industry and competitors and these have to be matched with the strengths and weaknesses that are evident in the firm.

Johnson and Scholes (1993) offer a model for the process in environmental analysis, which forms Figure 1.5.

This analysis is not made in isolation, but serves to feed into other considerations which in total will determine the strategy of the firm. To make strategic plans without an awareness of pertinent environmental factors is short-sighted and dangerous for the firm. Like all of the other inputs into the strategic formulation process, an environmental audit has to be an ongoing process.

The point of undertaking the environmental analysis is to be aware of opportunities and threats (from a vast array of headings) and to tie these to the strengths and weaknesses of the firm. In doing so, the firm should be able to successfully target appropriate market segments and to avoid others. This gelling of external markets and production/operations capability in areas such as low cost, flexibility and innovation is again central in achieving this success.

1.6 Stakeholders and strategy

A major consideration that has to be faced is the impact of a particular strategy upon the stakeholders. The stakeholders can include shareholders, customers, employees, suppliers, distributors and governments. Each of these would have a particular interest and these might be in opposition to each other. Essential measures of success for each type of stakeholder are shown in Table 1.8

Figure 1.5 Johnson and Scholes' environment analysis model.

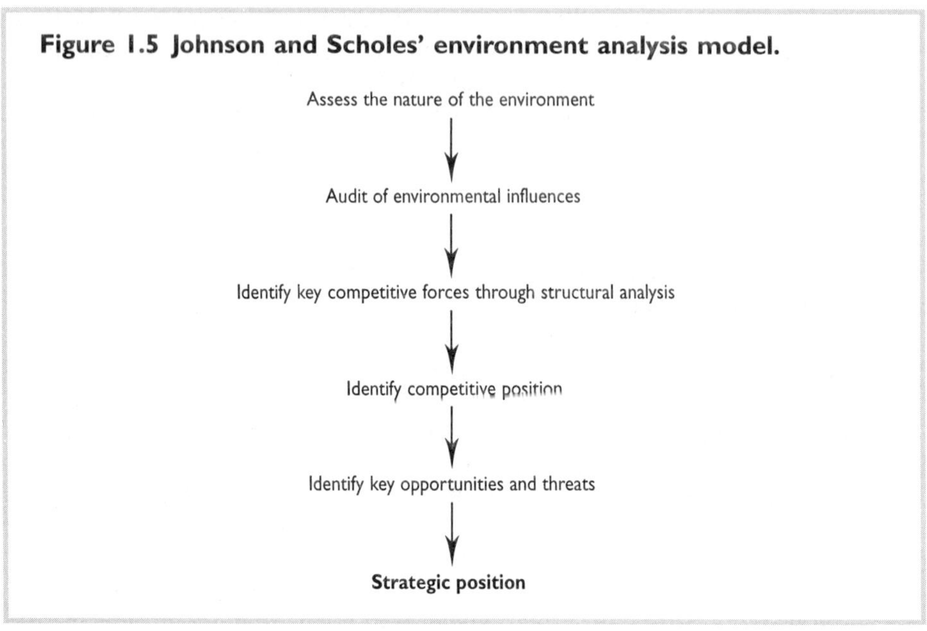

Each stakeholder is relevant for manufacturing firms; the problem is in trying to satisfy the balance between various stakeholder interests. Unfortunately, man-

Table 1.8 Stakeholders and their criteria of success

Stakeholder	*Measure of success*
Shareholders	Return on equity, liquidity, increase in value/equity of the firm, increase in stock value of the firm
Employees	Job satisfaction, job security, remuneration, training
Suppliers	On-time payments, long-term stable relationships (especially JIT)
Customers	Quality products, perceived fair pricing, value
Local community	Healthy factory practices, especially in toxic handling and emission, purchases from local vendors
Financiers	Timely interest and loan repayments
Distributors	On-time, reliable deliveries
General public/government	Fair pricing, increasing technology, fair competition, taxes, pollution controls, safety, adherence to laws and regulations

ufacturing firms in the West have often concentrated on satisfying short-term interests (shareholders and other financial interests), rather than on strategic areas – such as long-term supplier relationships, ongoing employee development and new plant investment.

1.7 The strategic planning process

1.7.1 How strategy is developed

Strategy has a process flow which develops from initial planning through to the implementation and monitoring of strategic decisions. We contrast two models offered by Thompson and Strickland (1989, 1992) and Argenti (1980) in Table 1.9.

The lists are not cited as a means of comparison – one is not better than the other – and neither is offered as a formula for success. However, in both approaches the following is evident: an understanding of internal, key competencies which might allow the firm to compete at all; the need to be aware of external factors; setting objectives and targets; formulating an explicit plan after generating options; implementing the plan; monitoring the plan through shorter, control-type devices, such as budgets.

To this end the process flowchart (Figure 1.6) offered by Wheelan and Hunger (1993) is most pertinent: they speak of the strategic 'audit' that takes place and determine the process as having 'eight interrelated steps' (p.47).

Table 1.9 Contrasting two models of strategy formulation

Thompson and Strickland	*Argenti*
1. The organizational mission: Where the firm declares the business it is currently in and if this will change in the future	1. Target setting: Clarify corporate objectives; set target levels
2. Performance objectives: This will include both short- and long-term objectives	2. Gap analysis: Forecast future performance on current strategies. Identify gaps between forecasts and targets
3. The strategic plan: Where the explicit plan is made known	3. Strategic appraisal: External and internal appraisal; identify competitive advantages
4. Strategic implementation: Where the full range of managerial activities associated with the chosen plan is made clear and known	4. Strategic formulation generic strategic options: Evaluate and take strategic decision
	5. Strategic implementation: Draw up action plans and budgets; monitor and control

The process flows offered by Argenti (1980), Wheelan and Hunger (1993) and others only serve to clarify the process of strategic planning. All of the above are academic models of understanding and as Hofer and Schendel (1989) observe:

> In practice (these steps) are interactive, recycle and repeat themselves and do not move forward in sequence as neatly as described here. (p.23)

This sentiment is endorsed by Quinn (1980) when he writes:

> Executives managing strategic change . . . do not . . . follow highly formalized text-book approaches in long-range planning, goal generation, and strategy formulation. Instead they artfully blend formal analysis, behavioral techniques, and power politics to bring about cohesive, techniques towards end . . . which are then constantly refined and reshaped as new information appears. (p 16)

The process, although having separate entities, will have simultaneous activities taking place in terms of internal awareness and external analysis. The process will

Figure 1.6 Hunger and Wheelan's strategy formulation model.

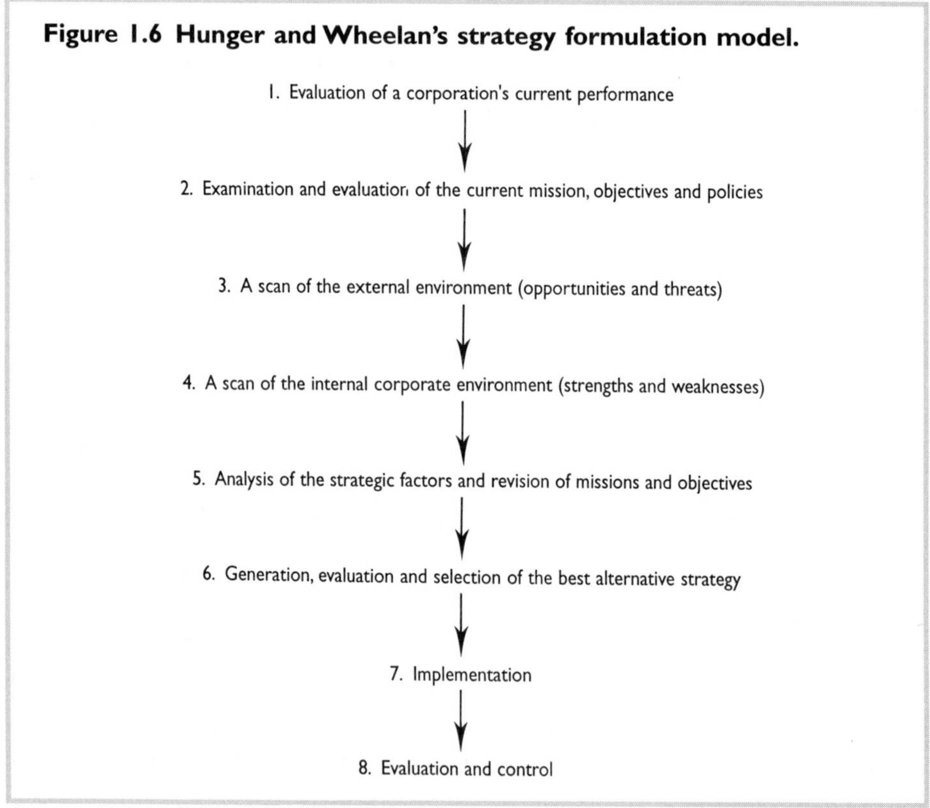

involve linear and lateral thinking, sensing new opportunities and threats and evaluating strengths and weaknesses. The process is a mixture of hard approaches, where financial analysis techniques will be used and attitudes toward risk will be discussed, and soft issues (corporate culture and organizational change).

Debate continues on the value of strategic planning. For example, in 1980 two contradictory statements were made by leading academics on the worth of planning:

> My data suggest that when well-managed major organizations make significant changes in strategy, the approaches they use frequently bears little resemblance to the rational, analytical systems so often described in the planning literature. (Quinn, 1980, p.14)

Porter (1980) by contrast stated:

> there are significant benefits to gain through an explicit process of formulating strategy, to insure that at least the policies (if not the actions) of functional departments are coordinated and directed at some common set of goals. (p.xiii)

It is absurd to speak in terms of whether one of the writers is right or correct in their assessment. They are cited because, in doing so, it becomes clear just how complex the process and implementation of strategic decisions can be. For some firms the planning process is very formal and static in approach, following a checklist of points to be assessed. For other firms, the business world is seen as too complex and changing for exhaustive planning to be seen as useful. They might argue that, by the time the planning has been undertaken, the opportunity might have passed by and so, for these companies, the planning process is more fluid, ad hoc and dynamic. Mintzberg and Waters (1985) provide useful discussion on a range of strategies including 'deliberate', 'adaptive', 'planning' and 'emerging'.

The problem with most strategic planning models is the fact that production/operations' capability and contribution to the strategic process is at best only implied. Hamel and Prahalad's (1994) comments are pertinent here – they warn of the need to use capability as a means of creating future strategy:

> To get to the future first, top management must either see opportunities not seen by other top teams or must be able to exploit opportunities, by virtue of pre-emptive and consistent capability-building, that other companies can't. (p.78)

Often, production/operations' contribution, in terms of its capability, is ignored until *after* strategic plans have been already formulated by an elite planning group, whose understanding of production/operations' contribution may be very limited indeed.

1.8 Strategic options

1.8.1 Generic choices

Every firm has to choose from a number of generic options available and the choice of the option or group of options is the essence of strategic management. Johnson and Scholes (1988) offer a useful model of strategic possibilities which forms Table 1.10.

What a particular firm chooses to do will depend to a large extent upon the following information:

Table 1.10 Strategic options

	Development methods		
Direction	*Internal*	*Acquisition*	*Joint Ventures*
'Do nothing'	–	–	–
Withdraw	Liquidate	Complete sell-out Partial divestment Management buyout	Licensing Subcontracting
Consolidation	Grow with market, increase quality, productivity, marketing Capacity reduction	Buy and shut down	Technology transfer subcontracting
Market penetration	Increase quality, productivity, marketing	Buy market share Industry rationalization	Collaboration
Product/service development	R&D Modifications Extensions	Buy-in products	Licensing, franchising Consortia Lease facilities
Market development	Extend sales area Export New segments New uses	Buy competitors	New agents Licensing Consortia
Integration: Backward Horizontal Forward Unrelated Diversification	Switch 'focus' New units Create subsidiaries	Minority holdings Buy subsidiaries	Technology sharing Exclusive agreements Tied arrangements Franchising Consortia

From Johnson and Scholes (1988)

- The market size.
- The scope of competitive rivalry.
- The market growth rate.
- The number of competitors and their relative size and power.
- The number of buyers and their relative sizes.
- The ease of entry and exit from a particular industry – high barriers protect positions of existing firms in the market; low entry allows new entrants in much more easily (Porter, 1980).
- The pace of technological change in both new product development and process technology.
- The differentiation evident in the markets being served and/or targeted.
- The presence of economies of scale in manufacturing, transportation or mass marketing – other firms may be able to leapfrog over competitors, especially in relation to reducing costs.
- The capacity utilization needed to achieve low-cost production efficiency – a surplus will push up prices and drive profits down; a shortage pushes them up.
- The importance (or not) of a strong learning/experience curve.
- The amount of backward and forward integration.

1.8.2 Generic competitive choices

Porter (1980) argues that a company has to decide whether it is to compete on cost or differentiation. These, he argues, are the two generic strategies open to the firm and a company has to choose one or the other, otherwise it risks being stuck in the middle. Porter states that a company has to be focused in its efforts. Whilst this serves as a point of clarity and does indeed help to focus the firm, in reality companies in the 1990s have to be both low cost and differentiated in particular market segments. Thus, although there is clearly a price war in certain segments within the car industry, each company is offering perceived differentiation – however small – for their products as well. One of the problems with this is that perceived differentiation is often very easily copied – for example, features such as airbags in cars – and, therefore, the perceived differentiation is lost after relatively short periods of time. Porter (1980) argues that success, either in low-cost or differentiation strategies, will depend upon how sustainable the advantage is in a market segment. In the 1990s and beyond, however, it becomes increasingly difficult to simply choose one or other strategy and to believe that this is the formula for success. Other, equally important, competitive factors are more prominent now than ever before and provide the biggest indication of production/operations' contribution, in particular, flexibility, delivery speed and reliability and product innovation.

Porter (1980) acknowledges that there are dangers with pursuing either a low-cost or differentiation strategy:

- **Cost** An overemphasis on low-cost efficiency can cause a firm to be out of touch with the changing requirements of customers; in a commodity market, being second or third behind the cost leader brings no competitive advantages; low-cost production is relatively easy to copy and as industries mature, the concept of the experience curve becomes invalid.
- **Differentiation** If the perceived distinction is easily imitated, then rivalry will quickly switch to cost factors; costs incurred in providing differentiation might not be paid back by prices which are unattractive to customers; broad-based differentiators may be outmanoeuvred by specialist firms which target one particular segment.

1.8.3 Growth strategies

If a company wishes to expand its business, then typical strategies for this would include:

1. Developing existing markets by more intensive marketing, distribution or product improvement and innovation.
2. Entering new markets within the same country.
3. Exporting either through a new outlet or through extension to new national markets.
4. Widening the product range within the existing market.
5. Diversification into unrelated fields.

Factors that have to be taken into consideration when a company wishes to expand its business would include:

- **Growth potential** In terms of the size of the market (measured in money), the potential to realize target revenue figures, anticipated competitive situation and response, competitive power and the anticipated time to achieve targets.
- **Profitability** Sales margins, value added for the firm and profit targets.
- **Marketability** Durability of market (e.g. product lifecycles), scope and breadth of market, opportunities for segmentation and segment leadership, sustainable product differentiation possibilities, quality–price relationship, seasonal trends, rate of technological change, global potential, effect on existing strategies including company culture, the relationship of expansion with existing products, enhancement of company image, promotional and advertising needs, distribution channels and speed of potential market entry.

Implications for production/operations

A growth strategy has clear implications for production/operations. The question facing firms is to what extent production/operations are involved in shaping the growth decision. The myopic view of production/operations' task, largely as a result of corporate-level ignorance, is that all production/operations managers have to do is to provide low-cost manufacture (gained, supposedly, through scale economies). Such a narrow view will undoubtedly deprive the firm of other important competitive weaponry gained through production/operations efforts. Flexibility, innovation and delivery speed and reliability are key attributes, which owe little to growth being achieved. Growth will impact on capacity, manufacturing processes, the supply base and possibly alliances with other companies in order to achieve the growth target.

The problem with growth strategies. The problem for a number of companies, formerly successful, now struggling, was that their strategy was to concentrate on high volume within large market segments. In doing so, they neglected smaller but profitable segments, obsessed instead with ongoing growth.

Drucker (1974) provides a few pertinent words on growth

> There is no virtue in a company getting bigger. The right goal is to become better. Growth to be sound, should be the result of doing the right things. By itself, growth is vanity and little else. (p.772)

The obsession with growth was often reflected in the equally obsessive trend for purchasing other companies in order to buy market share. Growth through purchasing another company can often change the complexion of the buying company. For example, IBM's purchase of Lotus in 1995 focused the company further toward software and was aimed to compete against Microsoft.

1.8.4 Divestment

Divestment includes selling subsidiaries or withdrawing single or a range of similar products from the market. There are good reasons for doing so: a product or group of products may be at the end of the product lifecycle; the products may be demanding a disproportionate amount of management time and effort in order to keep them viable; sentiment and emotion may be blurring the actual performance of a product which will ultimately be detrimental to the firm; new processes may be in place which best suit new products; the products themselves may no longer be produced at a profit for the firm; the firm cannot meet increased market requirements of lower cost, added differentiation, delivery speed and delivery reliability or any other competitive variable.

Implications for production/operations

From a production/operations viewpoint, divestment can often provide an opportunity to release capacity, particularly where old products have been manufactured on inappropriate processes. It is clear and essential that a firm should be customer-driven in all that it does; it is also clear and equally essential for firms to divest products that do not link to process capability and to offer instead products which do. Of course companies must invest in process technology to mirror the changing needs of product innovation.

Divesting is not an indication of management failure; in fact, appropriate withdrawal of products will indicate management expertise in being proactive in decision-making and allowing manufacturing resources to be better used on products and activities which will serve to enhance the image and better the profitability of a firm. For example, *Business Week* (5 September 1994) reported how Ford, Chrysler and General Motors had all divested non-core businesses to suppliers, including seat assembly (Ford), fabric covers (Chrysler) and electric motors (General Motors).

1.8.5 Diversification

Diversification can be seen as a means of spreading risk and is best understood in terms of strategic choice, which includes changes in technology, additional products/services, geographic markets, customer segments, distribution, internal developments or acquisitions. There are a number of ways of diversifying:

1. Where a number of markets are served by a single product. Diversification here is largely one of positioning (distribution) into additional market segments.
2. Where there is an increase in the number of different industries served and not just different market segments within a particular industry.
3. Diversification may occur when a firm positioned in one type of industry provides goods which are classified under a different industry.
4. Firms entering new markets with new products.

Implications for production/operations

A diversification strategy will typically affect the method of manufacturing, either by increasing volume of existing products or in terms of adding to the existing product range. Both factors could influence plant capacity, in addition, the type of manufacturing process used might be changed (a discussion of process choice is in Chapter 4).

1.8.6 Integration and alliance strategies

Until the 1980s, much of the acquisition activity in the United States took place in vertical integration – the ownership of firms throughout the supply chain – both forward (distribution, warehousing, marketing activities) or backward (raw materials and components). From the mid-1980s, this has become less of an issue, since more companies are involved in strategic alliances throughout the supplier chain. Where integration does occur, however, this can affect supplier and distribution channels. However, a specific choice facing a manufacturing company is in 'vertigration'. The possibilities include:

1. **Backward integration** Where the company will own raw material or component suppliers, machine manufacturers, designers and possibly transportation. Clearly, purchasing fixed assets as part of the ownership of the supply chain can cause the company to be involved in owning assets in which it has

no experience or expertise – Ford's former ownership of steel mills highlights the problem; the processes and, indeed, the business itself were entirely different. Later, Ford wisely divested this ownership.

2. **Horizontal integration** Where the company will buy competitors both in terms of competitive products and complementary products. Much discussion has taken place regarding merger and acquisition activity. Problems occur in terms of how to measure successful mergers and acquisitions: Is success measured purely in terms of returns to shareholders, or as a strategy to buy the competition? An aggressive growth strategy is to purchase market share. What becomes clear is that acquisitions *per se* are not the problem. The problem is in purchasing unrelated companies. As Hamill (1991) states, 'diversifying acquisitions have a low success factor' (p.28). From a manufacturing point, unrelated may include other companies which, although placed in the firm's overall supply chain, are unrelated in terms of manufacturing choice and infrastructure. BMW's purchase of Rover is an example of horizontal integration within the car industry.
3. **Forward integration** Where the company might choose to own distribution outlets, repairs and servicing activities, marketing companies and transportation outlets. The mismatch discussed in backward integration applies to forward integration as well.

However, in the last ten years there has been a move away from ownership of either end of the supply chain in which the manufacturing company is placed. Instead, a whole range of alliance strategies have come into play. The range of alliances will include those listed in Table 1.11

Alliances demand long-term commitment, mutual trust and the belief that such an alliance is a win–win situation for both parties. Ohmae (1985) offers guidelines to facilitate joint ventures and alliances:

- At least one key top management sponsor on each side of the venture should be present, each convinced that the undertaking is of benefit to their respective companies.
- These sponsors should be responsible for the alliance.
- Ensure active cross-fertilization and frequent 'face-to-face' communications at all levels.
- The venture should be one of communication, rather than control.

Table 1.11 Types of strategic alliances

• Licensing agreements	• Marketing agreements/dual marketing
• Joint ventures	• Franchising
• Buyer–seller relationships (particularly in just-in-time production)	• Consortia between companies
• Research and development alliances	• Joint access to technology and markets

Strategic alliances – as opposed to ownership – can be a very powerful approach and as Devlin and Bleackley (1988) observe:

> Strategic alliances take place in the context of a company's long-term strategic plan and seek to improve or dramatically change a company's competitive position. (p.20)

The above authors cite the tie-up between Generale d'Electricité and ITT which, 'produced a new manufacturing alliance capable of serving global markets and challenging its existing global competitors' (p.21). However, as Datta (1988) observes:

> Joint ventures, while offering the promise of economic and other benefits, often entail significant costs in their implementation. Shared decision making makes them much more difficult to manage and, consequently, joint ventures tend to be fragile relationships with a high failure rate. (p.79)

This is endorsed by research by Beamish (1985) and Reynolds (1984), who speak in terms of a 45–50 per cent failure rate of alliances and joint ventures. However, alliances are common in many industries. This is due to a large extent to two factors:

1. There are fewer companies which have the resources which enable them to enter into mergers and acquisitions than was the case in the relatively cash-rich days of the 1960s and 1970s.
2. Merger and acquisitions have not proved to be successful for many companies and the alternative is to form alliances with other players in the market and form strong buyer–supplier relationships throughout the supply chain. An excellent in-depth analysis of buyer–supplier relationships is offered by Lamming (1993).

   For manufacturing firms, alliances provide massive benefits: first, they allow the firm to concentrate on core manufacturing activities and second, they become a means of organizational learning. In Rover's alliance with Honda, an exchange took place: Rover gained access to know-how of Japanese technology and practices; Honda gained access to British and European car markets.

   A major reason for alliances is that many firms cannot go it alone in R&D activity and it makes sense to collaborate in R&D activity with other partners; as Dussauge *et al.* (1992) observe:

   > Not all alliances are technology-based but in a majority of cases, technology is a key element ... about two-thirds of all strategic alliances can be considered as technology-based. (p.127)

1.8.7 Summarizing strategic options for the manufacturing firm

In manufacturing companies there is a range of strategic options and decisions to be made. They include backward and forward integration (or forming alliances with other companies within the supply chain) and related or unrelated diversification (again either by purchasing companies or by forming alliance strategies), as shown in Figure 1.7.

1.9 The use of matrices in strategic decision-making

Like all models, their relevance will depend upon the understanding of the applications and limitations of the model. The matrices are essentially a means of providing a snapshot of where the company is. This may be in terms of assessing its current product portfolio (the Boston matrix discussed below) or in terms of mapping the firm's current competitive position. These matrices have been severely criticized (Slatter, 1980; McDonald, 1993). One major problem is that they tend to encourage keeping a portfolio of products which may well be

Figure 1.7 Strategic options for manufacturing companies.

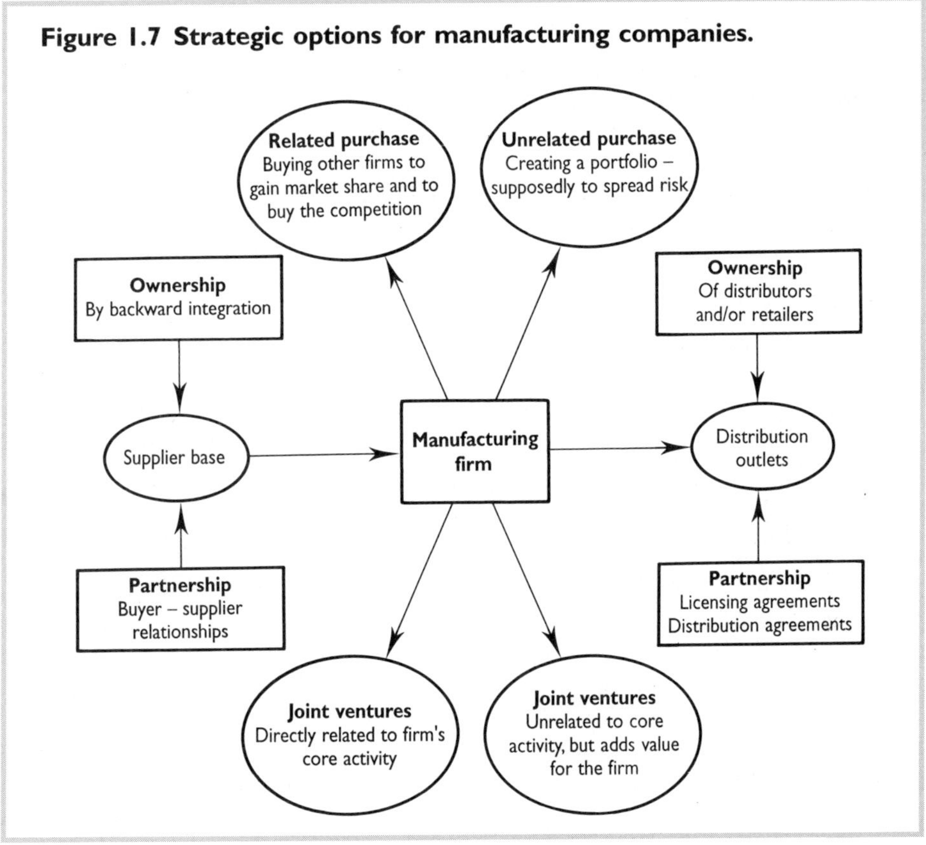

Table 1.12 Shell's directional policy matrix

Company's competitive position	*Prospects for market sector profitability*		
	Unattractive	*Average*	*Attractive*
Weak	Disinvest	Phased withdrawal	Double or quit
Average	Phased withdrawal	Proceed with care	Try harder
Strong	Cash generator	Growth	Leader

unrelated. This clashes with ideas of focusing and concentrating on what the company does best. Each of these matrices seeks to evaluate the product portfolio of the firm and to suggest courses of action. We will now examine some of the matrices and assess their use for manufacturing firms.

1.9.1 Shell directional policy matrix

One of the strategic tools is the Shell directional policy matrix. One major role this has is to determine how resources should be allocated according to product performance and potential. It compares two variables as shown in Table 1.12:

1. Prospects for market sector profitability.
2. The company's competitive position.

The terms used in Table 1.12 can be defined as follows:

- Disinvestment: These products should be withdrawn from the market.
- Phased withdrawal: These are products with unattractive market prospects; resources should be used elsewhere.
- Cash generator products are typically those moving toward the end of the product lifecycle. Cash from these should be used to generate new, replacement products.
- Double or quit products are R&D projects with the best prospects; these should be selected for full backing and the rest should be abandoned or phased out.
- Try harder are products which, backed with further resources, could be moved toward the 'leader box'. However, these resources might be in excess of what the product can generate for itself.
- Leader products should seek to maintain the present position; resources may be needed to expand capacity.
- Growth products should grow with the market and should be self-financing.
- Proceed with care: These are products where some investment may be justified, but where major investment is discouraged.

1.9.2 The BCG matrix (the Boston Box)

The Boston Consulting Group offer a model by which the firm's product portfolio can be determined and four categories come into play here:

1. **Star**. Where a product enjoys high market share in a market which itself is growing. Stars represent the best opportunities for profit and investment.
2. **The cash cow**. Products here enjoy high market share in a mature market where growth is not necessarily increasing. Large cash surpluses are normally generated by cash cows and are, therefore, vital to the firm.
3. **The question mark**. These products do not have a high market share but are in a market which is itself increasing. Further investment in these products is often required; alternatively divestment will take place.
4. **Dogs**. This is the worst scenario, where there is a low market share in a market which is declining. Such products are often a cash drain and may use up disproportionate resources. Divestment is often the strategy here. The actual matrix is shown in Table 1.13

Table 1.13 The BCG matrix

Market growth rate	*Market share*	
	High	*Low*
High	Star	Question/problem child
Low	Cash cow	Dog

This portfolio analysis is important because it reveals the balance of products across the organization. It is vital that the firm has some products which will generate sufficient cash (cash cows) in order to provide for the future of the business (question marks and stars). The application of the BCG matrix is in determining strategy; four strategic choices are offered by Hax and Majluf (1991) and are set out in Table 1.14.

1.9.3 General Electric's nine-cell portfolio matrix

Another commonly used matrix is General Electric's nine-cell portfolio matrix. Here the two variables are

1. **Long-term industry attractiveness** Factors here include market size and growth rate; industry profit margins; competitive intensity; seasonality; economies of scale; technology and capital requirements; social, environmental, legal and human impacts; emerging opportunities and threats; barriers to entry and exit.

Table 1.14 Hax and Majluf's adaptation of the BCG matrix

Quadrant	*Strategic choice*	*Profitability*	*Required investment*	*Cash flow*
Star	Hold/increase market share	High	High	Zero to negative
Cash cow	Add market share	High	Low	Very positive
Problem child	Increase market share or divest	None or negative	Very high	Negative or positive (divest)
Dogs	Divest/liquidate	Low/negative	Disinvest	Positive

2. **Business strength/competitive position** Factors for consideration would include relative market share; profit margins relative to competitors; knowledge of customer and market; ability to compete on price and quality; competitive strengths and weaknesses; technological capability.

The matrix is shown in Table 1.15.

Table 1.15 General Electric's nine-cell matrix

Long-term industry	*Business strength/competitive position*		
attractiveness	*Strong*	*Average*	*Weak*
High	Investment and growth	Selective growth	Selectivity
Medium	Selective growth	Selectivity	Harvest/divest
Low	Selectivity	Harvest/divest	Harvest/divest

1.9.4 A critique of matrices

Each of the above matrices clearly conflict with any idea of focus. At best, the above matrices are tools in managing a portfolio of products, some of which are more profitable/beneficial than others. By contrast, it could be argued that a firm should focus on what it does best, rather than run the risk of being stuck in the middle. At best the matrices offer a mere snapshot of the range of products whose success is measured purely by short-term profitability. Problems with using matrices are discussed by Slatter (1980). They include:

1. **Defining the relevant market** The arbitrary definitions of markets can be a problem; if, for example, a market segment is too narrowly defined, then a firm's supposed presence in that market may be cited as high – in reality it

could be much smaller if seen within a wider, truer picture. Slatter (1980) offers pharmaceuticals and breweries as two examples where segmentation becomes very difficult.

2. **Using the product lifecycle** Particular care has to be paid in writing off products too early, presuming that they are in a stage of decline, whereas they may enjoy another take-off.
3. **Divesting the 'dogs'** Instantly divesting the 'dog' products is not as easy as it might sound. As Slatter (1980) states, 'The practical reality for many managers is that they have to manage not just a dog, but a whole "kennel of dogs"!' (p.20). The fact is that exiting a market can carry considerable costs. Of course, it is not suggested that a firm sticks with low contribution products. The point is that exiting is more difficult than implied in these matrices.
4. **Market stability** In high-technology markets, the cash benefits which are supposedly gained when a market slows down cannot be applied; new products are required on an ongoing basis and the growth rate of existing products may not have declined. The matrices assume a stability period – when major cash benefits are gained – followed by a period of new product introduction when cash gained from the cash cow is used to fund the new product. Such a static view of markets is at best irrelevant and more likely dangerous.

Lastly, every matrix discussed above is an internal, closed system, where funds derived from successful cash-cows are used to develop other products. In reality, funding is forthcoming from external sources and not just internal generation of income.

None of the matrices cited above attempts to see the firm holistically and there is no sense of how the firm links with other stakeholders. In typical myopic fashion, there is no acknowledgement of the role of production/operations. There is also no sense of timing here and no clues as to how sustainable advantage might be realized through, for example, further investment in process technology. The criterion running through the matrices is short-term finance, rather than long-term sustainable advantage – this short-termism is the very approach which has cost the West dearly in manufacturing capability and performance in key industries.

1.10 Evaluating strategic decisions

A number of key factors can be used to determine the degree of success, or otherwise, of strategic decisions. Some of these will be couched in financial measures. The list provided by Hax and Majluf (1991) in Table 1.16 serves as a useful guideline.

However, financial criteria must not be the only ones and in fact some of the indicators can be misleading. Return on investment (ROI), for example, is often

Table 1.16 Financial performance measurements

Performance variable	*Key areas*
Size	Sales, assets, profits, market value, number of employees
Growth	Sales, assets, profits, market value, number of employees
Profitability	Profit margin, return on assets, return on equity
Capital markets	Dividend yield, return to investors, price/earning ratio, market to book value ratio, payout dividend, price per share, book value per share
Liquidity	Current ratio, quick ratio, cash position, working capital
Leverage	Debt-to-equity ratio, short versus long-term debt
Turnover	Total assets turnover, inventory turnover
Other financial	Bond rating, beta, cost of debt

Adapted from Hax and Majluf (1991)

cited but has disadvantages: it is very sensitive to depreciation policy – depreciation write-off variances between divisions affect ROI performance; ROI is sensitive to book value and older plants can enhance ROI artificially; where one division sells to another (transfer pricing) and it operates in favourable conditions it will look better than the other division; by its accounting nature, the time horizons are short-term and other long-term performance measures must be used to balance the impression of performance. A further, salient point is offered by Chandler (1992) when he states:

> statistical evaluations of ROI too often failed to incorporate complex non-quantifiable data as to the nature of specific product markets, changing production technology, competitor's activities and internal organizational problems ... Top management decisions were becoming based on numbers, not knowledge. (p.278)

Over and above the financial indicators there are other measurements which should be determined from other functional areas as in Table 1.17.

Whilst the financial ratios are useful, the functional areas offered, together with excellent marketing skills, are those factors which serve to make the firm competitive; the financial ratios are historic indicators *after* the event. However, a firm's ability to provide excellent quality products at competitive costs and meet customers' delivery requirements, together with all other specific needs, are the competitive variables which enable a firm to win in the marketplace. The approach, therefore, has to be both holistic and focused; holistic, in terms of calling upon the whole organization to win in the marketplace and focused in terms of the direction in which the company must concentrate (Figure 1.8).

Table 1.17 Non-financial measurements of performance

Functional area	*Key areas*
Technology	rate of technology innovation, R&D productivity, rate of return in R&D investment, resources allocated to R&D, rate of new product development, cycle times of product development, royalties on sales of technology
Procurement	Cost, service, quality, vendor relationships
Manufacturing	Cost, delivery, quality, flexibility, new product introduction

Conclusion

The scope, implications and responsibilities in strategic planning and implementation are massive. Questions that are asked have to go beyond those offered in some of the literature which, starkly, border on the philosophical (Where are we? Where do want to be?) to precise and specific boundaries. These questions will home into one essential question, namely, What business are we in? This is a critical statement because, it will focus the firm in its efforts and form the main mission of the firm.

Clearly, the contents of the strategic plan have to include the following: a mission and vision of where the firm wishes to be; an analysis of internal factors, especially in realizing the firm's competencies which can be turned into opportunities; a clear understanding of macro environmental factors, both as opportunities and threats; a focused list of plans with specific time-frames for each; feedback and control mechanisms to monitor strategic implementation. The list serves as a feedback loop as shown in Figure 1.9.

Strategic planning calls for the best of management skills: linear thinking in terms of plotting in a logical manner the implications of a proposed plan; lateral thinking in terms of possible, tangential, knock-on effects of a particular decision; an attention to detail in all pertinent information; providing specific time-frames in which all stages of the plan should be implemented; involving all those who are affected by the strategy and gaining their acceptance and ownership of the plan, ideally at early stages, rather than after the event; empowering employees in terms of leadership style and resources to enable them to carry out strategy.

Once strategy has been determined the organizational structure, leadership and communication styles have to reflect this strategy. In manufacturing firms, to be fully effective, each functional area then has to create its own strategy which will serve to support the firm in its mission and will allow it to compete in its chosen market. The frameworks discussed earlier only make sense – as far as their application in manufacturing industries is concerned – if senior production/operations staff are active in the planning and shaping of the firm's mission, objectives and strategies in order to win in markets.

However, in the West, production/operations is largely viewed as a function, rather than being in an area of strategic importance. It is argued throughout this book that production/operations must be seen in terms of strategic importance and that essentially the key areas of production/operations – human resources, materials management, new product development, investment in manufacturing processes, managing quality – are, in themselves, *strategic* in nature.

The role that an explicit manufacturing strategy can have in corporate strategy forms the basis of Chapter 2.

Figure 1.8 Choosing appropriate market segments.

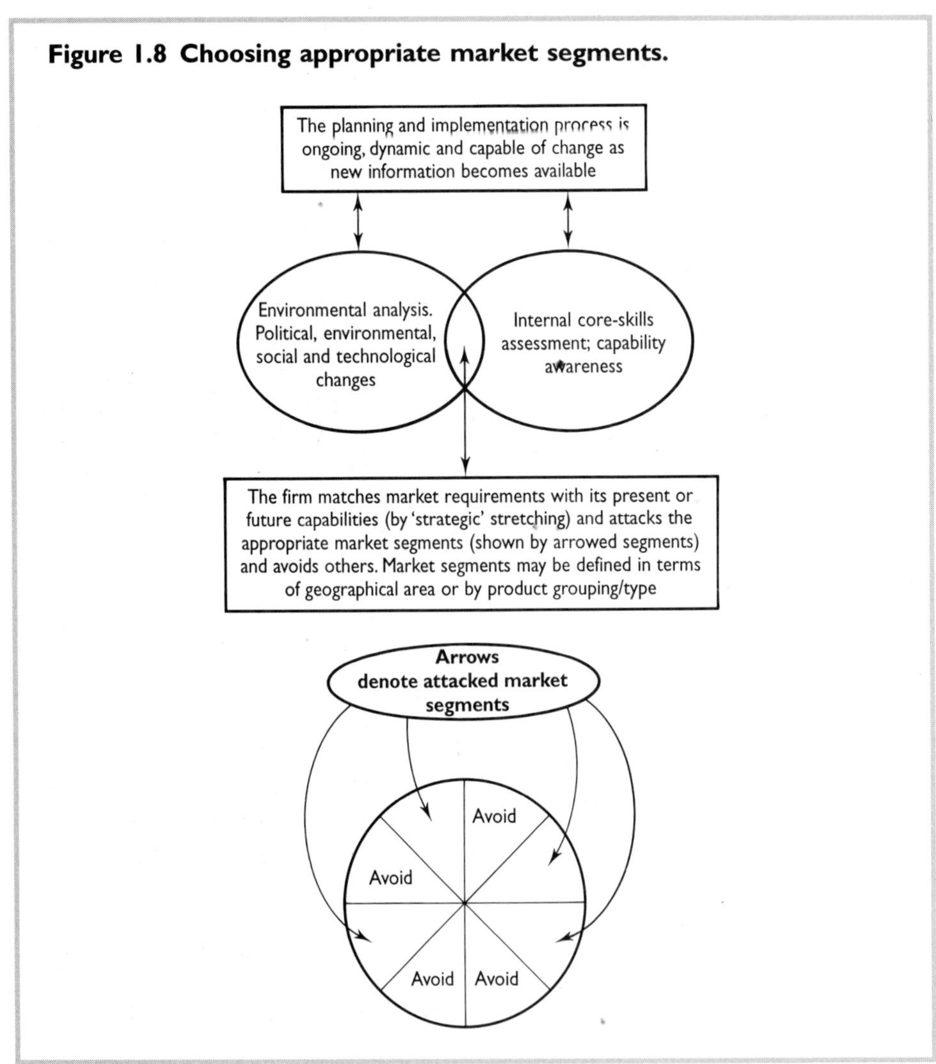

Figure 1.9 The strategy planning and implementation loop.

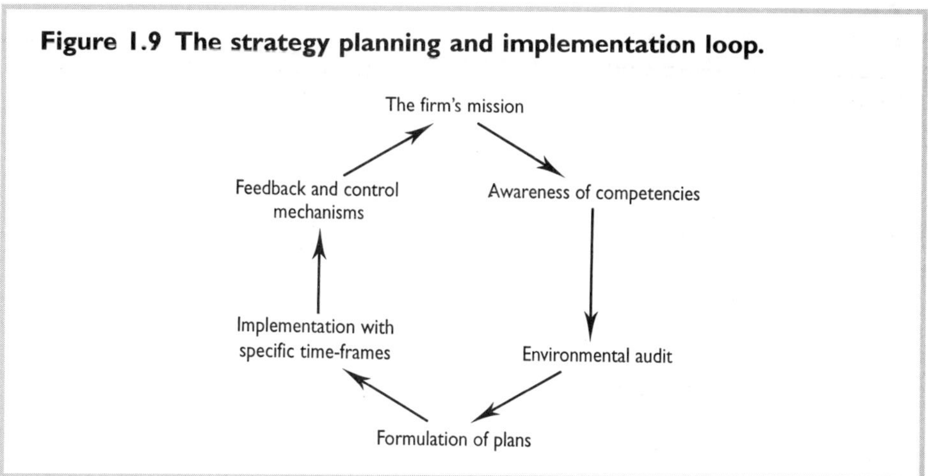

Summary

- **Strategy includes the following activities: analysis of the business and competitive environment in which a firm is placed; planning, generating options and deciding on a particular course or direction in which the firm will go.**
- **Strategic decisions tend to be long-term – or at least, to have long-term implications as a result. However, a sense of urgency and timing needs to be in place in order to accomplish targets. This urgency includes short-term implementation issues.**
- **Strategic planning can involve various departments and levels within the firm.**
- **Typically the ultimate decision-making authority tends to be at most senior levels within the firm. The question has to be asked, however, Who are the best qualified people to make strategic decisions for a manufacturing firm?**
- **Financial criteria are only one of many factors which need to be considered prior to deciding on a particular strategy for the firm.**
- **Part of the planning process is the awareness of various stakeholders' interests in the firm.**
- **Decisions should be aimed at providing a competitive advantage for the firm.**
- **The scope of decision-making includes the extent of vertical and horizontal integration.**
- **Increasingly, alliances (both vertical and horizontal) are entered into as**

a preferred alternative to integrating – by buying other firms – especially in the supply chain.

- **Everybody needs to understand the strategic plan and to have a sense of ownership.**

CASE BMW, Honda and Rover

At the beginning of 1994, a decision was made that provides much insight into attitudes toward manufacturing in Britain; Rover was sold to a competitor car company, BMW, for £800 million. By the time of the sale, Rover had enjoyed a remarkable turnaround in its manufacturing capability, in the main due to the learning that it had gained from the strategic partnership with Honda which began in 1979. For many years prior to this partnership, Rover had performed poorly, losing millions of pounds. As part of British Leyland, Rover had managed to survive only because vast sums had been injected by successive UK governments each year.

Rover had learned much from Honda; the high quality ratings of Rover's 200, 400 and 800 series owed a great deal to the adoption of world-class manufacturing techniques gained from Honda. This learning was not restricted to manufacturing practice (important as this was), but included actual design of cars as well. The Rover 800 was based on Honda's Acura Legend, the 600 on the Accord and the 200/400 on the Honda Concerto.

From BMW's viewpoint, the deal allowed them to gain access to Rover models such as the Land Rover range (which had continued to steadily increase in exports over recent years), and the Mini and Metro saloons. BMW–Rover would now have premium products in the upper niches of each segment in the car market. These are the segments where profit margins are largest. The deal meant a combined output capability of over one million cars per year. At the same time, BMW gained access to production capacity in relatively low-cost Britain. From a marketing viewpoint, BMW captured Rover's share of the market in Britain, estimated at 13.4 per cent in 1995 and nearly 7 per cent of the European market with a wider product range than some bigger rivals. (source: Author's interviews)

The combined effort of BMW–Rover fell short of that which could have developed had the proposed Volvo–Renault agreement been completed. However, the latter would have been more of an alliance, rather than the outright purchase of one car company by another, as in the case of BMW and Rover. Alliances and mergers are common practice in many industries – the likelihood is that other European players will seek to form further alliances or to merge in order to compete in the intensely competitive European car market. Another major consideration for European car makers is that Japanese transplants in the United Kingdom are aiming towards output of around one million cars per annum by the year 2000, by which time all limits to exporting to other countries in the European Union will have ceased. For the United Kingdom, the worst possible future scenario is that, if unemployment continues to be a problem in Germany, Rover cars could be made in a German manufacturing base in later years. This would also mean providing jobs in Germany for all of the support activities, including the supplier base. Another scenario could be that cars will continue to be made in the United Kingdom but, over a period of time, the supply base for the cars will be German. At the very least, BMW has purchased manufacturing capability and know-how gained over a fifteen-year period from Rover's alliance with Honda.

A number of other options could have been pursued if there had been any serious intent to keep the manufacturing plant British-owned: a management buy out was suggested and rejected by the owners, British Aerospace (BAe); closer links could have been formed with Honda (Honda and Rover already had 20 per cent stakes in each other's company as a goodwill sign of commitment); other UK financial packages could have been put together. However, none of these, or any other propositions, were accepted and the United Kingdom lost its only mass-producer of cars to a rival. For BAe, the deal was a good one, freeing the company from its diversification attempt and allowing it to concentrate on its core business – aerospace. It also provided the firm with large profits gained from the sale to BMW – BAe had bought Rover for £150 million in 1988.

From the above a number of key points can be related to the issues raised in Chapter 1:

- BMW focused on a growth strategy.
- It did so by acquiring another competitor: horizontal integration.
- The Rover–Honda alliance had played a key role in Rover's turnaround.
- Stakeholders' interests are noticeable; the proposed management buy out by senior Rover management was waived by the major stakeholder (BAe as owner) in favour of another stakeholder's interest: BMW (a competitor). Another stakeholder (the British Government) remained outside, refusing to intervene.
- Divestment was evident from the sell-off by BAe of one of its businesses.

Not surprisingly, the Japanese reaction to this sale was one of shock and anger; Honda, like many Japanese companies, saw such an alliance in terms of strategic importance, a long-term, mutually beneficial arrangement for both parties. With the sale of Rover by BAe, this alliance became severely damaged in the short term and will probably be terminated in the longer term. In addition, this could possibly damage further initiatives for British–Japanese joint ventures and alliances in various industries.

2 Manufacturing strategy

2.1 Introduction

This chapter examines the importance of having an explicit manufacturing strategy which feeds into, and forms part of, the overall corporate strategy. Too often, however, production/operations is seen as a function, rather than in terms of strategic importance for the company. The reasons for this are explored and 'traditional' and 'enlightened' views of manufacturing are offered. It is argued, though, that in a complex, dynamic and volatile business world where markets continue to fragment and new entrants compete from all over the globe, it is simplistic to speak in terms of one best practice, since the criteria for this will be subject to constant change. Instead, a paradigm is offered for *minimum* requirements in order to compete in markets, on the understanding that the firm must always seek to improve every area of its performance as an ongoing, continuous pursuit of meeting customer requirements.

It is not suggested that production/operations managers should take the lead in terms of targeting customer groups and other market requirements. It is argued though that production/operations' involvement at early stages of key activities such as targeting new market segments, changing the mix of current product volumes and new product development is vital if success is to be gained in these areas. Not all business is good business for the firm and there has to be a match between operational capability and market requirements (as discussed in Chapter 1, this is not always the same as the marketing departments' requirements). It is proposed, for manufacturing companies, that there has to be a threefold approach; a company must be:

1. **Strategically oriented** In Chapter 1 it was argued that for a decision to be strategic, it must include the following features: it will typically be made by top management; it must be long term in time horizons; it should be a means of identifying and exploiting opportunities to gain advantage over other competitors.
2. **Focused** The term here is used in the following ways: focused in terms of the firm's targeted market segments – knowing what the customer requirements are and constantly matching and if appropriate *exceeding* the customer re-

quirements; focused in terms of arranging plants into a number of focused areas of operations dedicated to particular customers, products or processes.

3. **Holistic** In terms of the firm's decision-making, involving all functions in shaping the corporate vision and strategy; making the vision and mission explicit and clearly understood by all. Holistic also refers to an approach which has sight of other stakeholders in the manufacturing firm – in particular the firm's suppliers. As we shall see, having an holistic view which includes a strategic view of suppliers in a mutually beneficial relationship is often difficult for manufacturing firms to establish.

These three factors interface with each other, as shown in Figure 2.1.

2.1.1 Manufacturing strategy in corporate strategy literature

The phrase 'manufacturing strategy' is noticeable by its absence in mainstream literature on strategy. As we saw in Chapter 1, the importance of a production/ operations strategy to an organization is implicit, for example in Porter (1985) as part of the discussions on the value chain and technology strategy. The idea of the value chain is that value (and not just cost) is added throughout the range of activities from inbound logistics to end customer. In manufacturing, it is clear that costs will be added at each stage of activity; the task for would-be world-class manufacturers is to ensure that value is added at each stage as well.

However, the actual phrase 'manufacturing strategy' is not explicitly used and the tone, sentiment, and language from Porter – and indeed from other writers on corporate strategy – is that manufacturing, if it has a strategy in a company at all, should be placed in a more reactive, tactical and functional arena, rather than as an integral part of the corporate level planning process. For some companies the possibility that there might be a manufacturing strategy comes as a surprise.

Figure 2.1 The required three-factor view for manufacturing companies.

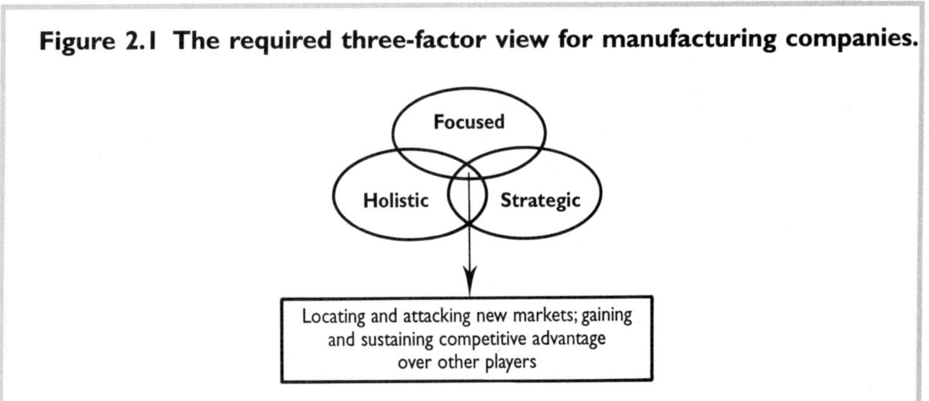

2.1.2 Manufacturing strategy in production/operations literature

In manufacturing literature, the actual explicit term 'manufacturing strategy' is relatively new and can be traced back to Skinner (1969) who used the term in his *Harvard Business Review* article.

The term has been used in manufacturing literature since and in the last ten years the term 'manufacturing strategy', has become increasingly common. However, the terms 'manufacturing strategy' and 'operations strategy' often become blurred. Samson (1991) sees manufacturing strategy as a subset of operations strategy, whilst Dilworth (1992) sees production and operations as interchangeable terms. In addition, there seems to be confusion over the distinction between strategy and tactics.

With all this confusion, it is hardly surprising that many American and European manufacturers' performance bears little resemblance to any strategy they have supposedly adopted. That is not to say, of course, that failure in manufacturing is wholly to do with attitudes to manufacturing strategy – failure to invest in technology, training and education, organizational factors and commitment to quality are other central issues.

2.1.3 An overview of manufacturing strategy

Clearly, a sense of timing has to form part of strategy, both in terms of overall time horizons and the distinct stages of implementation. Strategy can be seen as a long-term master plan of how the company will pursue its mission, so if we are to think of manufacturing having a strategy, we therefore have to consider longer time horizons than have traditionally been associated with manufacturing. We need also to formulate manufacturing strategy in such a way that it will support, or even help to define, the mission of the company. This has much to do with the factor of time, as shown in Figure 2.2.

Although a long-term strategic vision is important for the firm, there must also be time-specific alignment in place, so that the corporate vision ties together marketing and production/operations. To do otherwise is illogical and this misalignment is almost *designed* to ensure that implementation will fail. To have a long-term strategic plan which does not include production/operations from formulation to implementation is myopic and foolish. Clearly, the recent renewed success of Ford in the United States, particularly with the Ford Taurus, owes much to the holistic approach, whereby corporate, marketing and production/operations areas were linked together from product concept to launch. Other major players in the auto industry – Toyota especially – have this approach which for many companies in the West is not the case.

If production/operations is not to be seen in terms of strategy then the tactical decisions should nonetheless be consistent with corporate strategy. Any strategy has to take into account the 'strategic triangle' – the customer, the competition and the company itself (Ohmae, 1983). The traditional view is that the customer and competition factors are essentially tied to marketing activities and that the

Figure 2.2 The factor of time in manufacturing strategy.

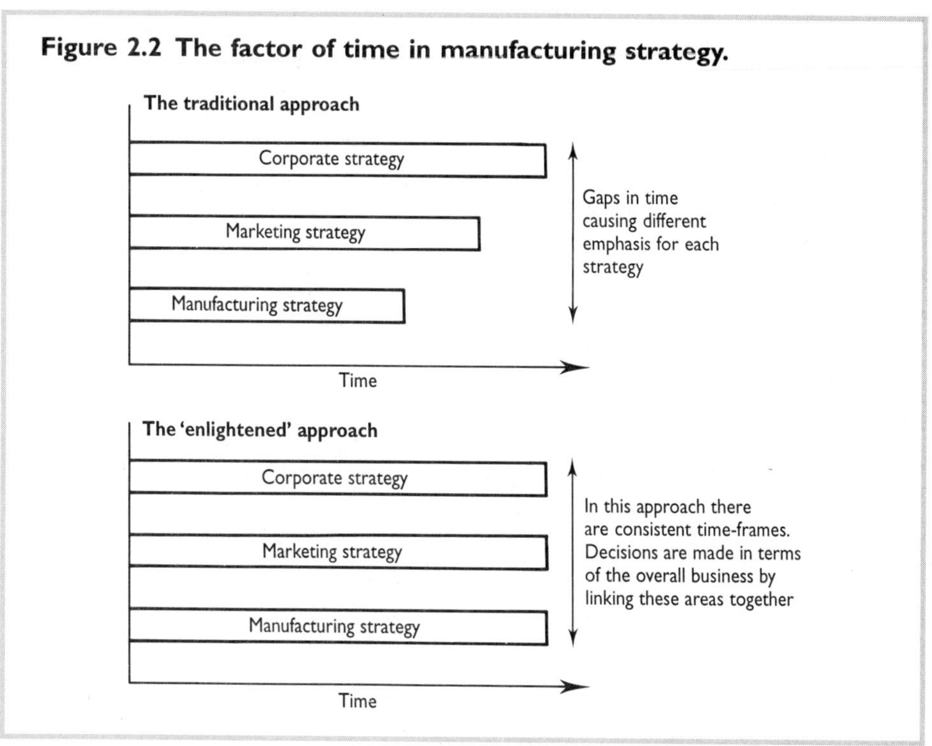

company involves all activities, including production/operations, whose job it is to simply react to marketing plans. However, such an approach is dangerous; decisions by marketing departments might be made in key areas such as volume, flexibility and delivery that might not be possible or achievable by existing manufacturing processes. The net result is that, by this approach, the company will fail in its plans. Marketing departments' myopia can pull the company into areas, and even whole markets, to which the firm is not suited. Hill (1990) is critical of marketing departments' 'functional indulgence' in their 'perceived role of creating ideas' and urges that external markets, rather than marketing departments within companies themselves, should form the basis of company strategy. An holistic approach is therefore required whereby the match between internal capabilities and external markets is achieved. Old approaches need to be replaced by an integrated strategy, as shown in Figure 2.3.

Figure 2.3 Linking corporate, marketing and manufacturing strategies.

Traditional model

Created by an 'elite' group whose criterion is essentially financial, rather than long-term strategy (*cf* Japanese approach). Often little or no manufacturing presence, expertise or knowledge at corporate level

Strategy is 'passed down' from corporate level – marketing strategy is now to determine new products, new market segments, pricing and distribution policies in order to satisfy corporate strategy

A 'second-hand' message is presented to production who now react to plans already in place. Production here is viewed as a 'tactical' function that responds to company strategy, rather than having involvement in shaping corporate strategy. Planning centres around areas such as scheduling, materials handling and day-to-day activities

Enlightened model

This is clearly the approach taken by world-class manufacturers. Time horizons are long term for corporate, manufacturing and marketing strategies and plans are made in an holistic approach by jointly agreeing internal capabilities and matching these to market opportunities. The firm is now focused and clear in its mission. Such an approach allows the company to avoid targeting markets in which it cannot succeed. Market requirements of cost, flexibility, delivery speed and reliability, together with quality requirements, are clearly understood by all and resources are allocated to meet these requirements

2.2 The national importance of manufacturing

2.2.1 Overview

The national importance of manufacturing is argued by Dilworth (1992), who states that manufacturing will be responsible for the improvement or decline of entire nations. It seems clear that manufacturing is central to the prosperity of nations yet, in the West – and in particular, the United States and United Kingdom – there has been an abandonment of manufacturing's role in favour of service industries. Services are important, of course, but cannot be seen as a replacement for manufacturing. As Cohen and Zysman, (1987) write:

> Manufacturing is critical to the health of the economy; lose manufacturing and you will lose – not develop – high-wage service jobs. (p.xiii)

and

> Exports of services are simply too small to offset the staggering deficits we (USA) are running in industrial goods...a decisive band of high-wage service exports are linked to mastery and control of manufacturing. Services are complements – not substitutes or successors – to manufacturing. (p.4)

Admittedly, invisible earnings are important sources of income, but the poor performance of manufacturing firms, when added together in a particular country, causes a national deficit; in simple terms, if a particular country buys more than it sells, it will suffer a trade deficit. This deficit can only be serviced in two ways:

1. By borrowing money.
2. By drawing on the country's own savings or reserves.

2.2.2 *Indications of national performance in manufacturing*

Figure 2.4 shows the comparative trade figures of six countries. A number of Western countries import more than they export, so their reserves are at risk and the amount of borrowed money has increased, particularly since the 1970s. Williams in *Management Today* warned of the problems facing the United Kingdom if it continues its decline in manufacturing:

> De-industrialisation matters for trading nations like Britain . . . manufactures are internationally tradable in a way that services are not . . . Exports of services just can't fill the gap left by the run-down of industry. (24 January 1994, p.38)

The performance of the UK's trade figures are shown in Figure 2.5. In each case, the UK imports more than it exports to the countries shown in Figure 2.5. What has happened in the United Kingdom is that over a number of years the manufacturing base has been eroded. The decline in manufacturing jobs in the United Kingdom is revealing, as shown in Table 2.1.

Not surprisingly, this decline has affected the UK's Gross Domestic Product, as shown in Figure 2.6.

The figures are revealing in themselves. However, the underlying trend over a number of years is a better indicator, rather than a snapshot of performance in

Figure 2.4 1994 trade figures.

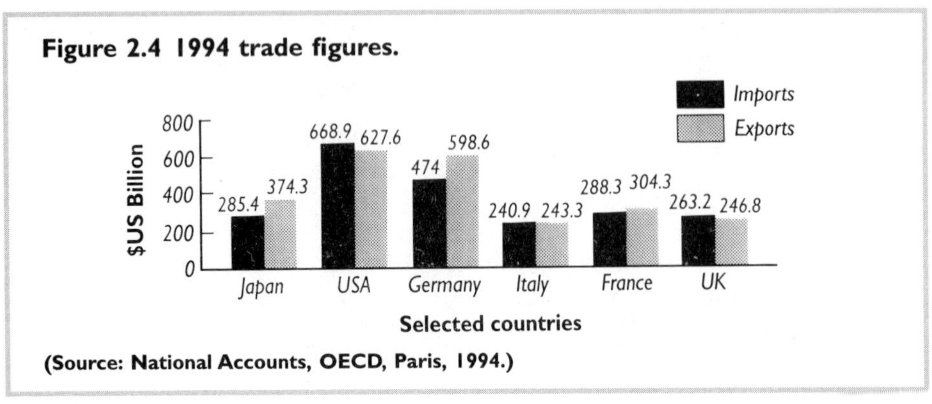

(Source: National Accounts, OECD, Paris, 1994.)

Figure 2.5 UK's imports and exports figures: 1993.

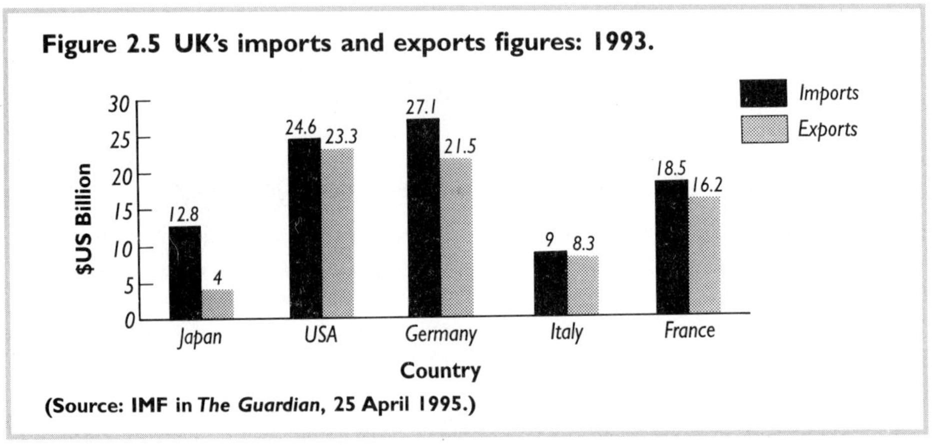

(Source: IMF in *The Guardian*, 25 April 1995.)

Table 2.1 Change in manufacturing employment: 1964–90 (%)

Britain	–31.7
France	–13.8
Germany	–14.7
Japan	+42.6
USA	–25.7

Source: OECD figures in *Management Today*, January 1994

Figure 2.6 Gross Domestic Product: 1993.

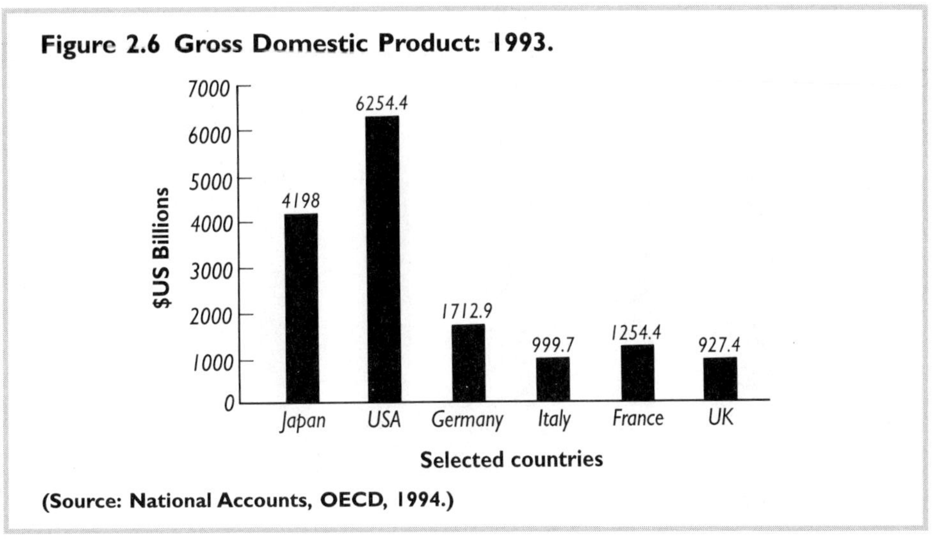

(Source: National Accounts, OECD, 1994.)

one particular year. Table 2.2 shows the relatively poor contribution of manufacturing to Britain's Gross Domestic Product (GDP) between 1973 and 1990.

Figure 2.7 shows how Britain's decline in employment in manufacturing between 1985 and 1994 has been matched by its decline in manufacturing output. In fact, there seems to be an interesting correlation between decline in employment and decline in output during this period.

The decline in manufacturing employment during this period poses questions about one of the major performance indicators used (in short-term criteria) – that of productivity ratios. In short, Britain's productivity looked very impressive during the 1980s, simply because fewer and fewer people were being employed in manufacturing jobs during this period. This is summarized by Hamel and Prahalad (1994):

Table 2.2 Manufacturing and Gross Domestic Product indicators

	Manufacturing as % of GDP: 1990	*GDP Growth 1973–90 (% p.a.)*
Britain	19.8	1.6
France	21.1	2.2
Germany	30.4	2.3
Japan	31.3	3.9
USA	22.5	2.4

Source: OECD figures in *Management Today*, January 1994

Figure 2.7 International comparisons of industrial output: 1994.

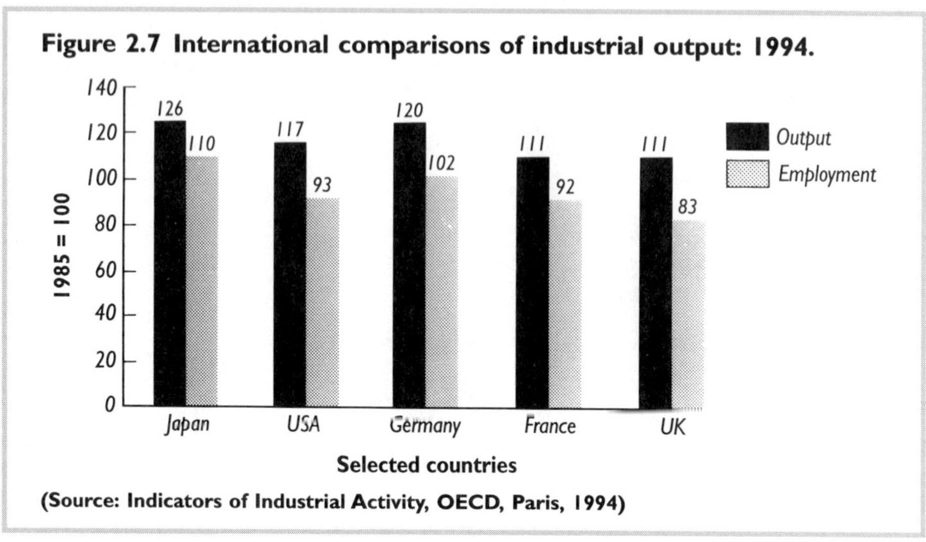

(Source: Indicators of Industrial Activity, OECD, Paris, 1994)

> Between 1969 and 1991, Britain's manufacturing output . . . went up by a scant 10% in real terms. Yet over this same period, the number of people employed in British manufacturing . . . declined by 37% . . . during the early and mid 1980s . . . UK manufacturing productivity increased faster than any other major industrialized country except Japan . . . British companies were, in fact, surrendering global market share. (p.9)

Two questions might be asked here. First, why did Britain's productivity only increase by 10 per cent? Second, what happened to the 37 per cent no longer required? This improvement through productivity was also apparent in the United States where, as Dertouzos *et al.* (1989) write:

> There is a dark side to these developments, however. A significant fraction of the productivity gains in manufacturing were achieved by shutting down inefficient plants and by permanently laying off workers at others. Employment in U.S. manufacturing industry declined by 10 percent between 1979 and 1986, and that loss of jobs accounted for about 36 percent of the recorded improvements in labor productivity. (p.31)

2.2.3 *The short-term obsession*

Short-term criteria, particularly with volatile and erratic market indicators in both Wall Street and The City in London have been seen as the criteria for performance of manufacturing firms. Long-term, strategic commitment has often given way to short-term profitability, where non-strategic, quick-fix measures are rewarded by increases in financial indicators. These indicators say very little about manufacturing performance and, when they do, the indicators are only for the very immediate past and future – Japan, by contrast, sees commitment to, and measurement of, manufacturing performance in terms of decades. This is clearly described by Dertouzos *et al.* (1989):

> The competitive advantage associated with longer time horizons is particularly strong in rapidly growing markets. Japanese firms have been willing to take on high levels of debt in order to invest in new production capacity and marketing infrastructure ahead of the growth in demand. (p.55)

2.2.4 Manufacturing and national R&D expenditure

One of the interesting indicators in long-term investment is that of R&D expenditure. Again, the relative lack of investment in the United Kingdom and United States, as a percentage of GDP is revealing, as shown in Table 2.3.

Interestingly the relatively small percentages of R&D expenditure by some countries is linked to the decline in their manufacturing base. This factor is highlighted by Dertouzos *et al.* (1989):

> A related fact is that manufacturing firms account for virtually all of the research and development done by American industry. They thus generate most of the technological innovations adopted both inside and outside their own industry. High technology manufacturing industries account for about three-quarters of all funding for research and development, and the other manufacturing industries account for most of the rest. (p.40)

In other words, although a relatively large part of a nation's R&D expenditure is aimed at manufacturing, this investment has decreased as the manufacturing base has itself decreased.

Table 2.3 National comparisons of R&D expenditure

	R&D Expenditure 1990 (% of GDP)	*R&D Investment 1986–91 (% of GDP)*
Britain	2.21	17.6
France	2.40	22.2
Germany	2.81	20.8
Japan	2.88	26.8
USA	2.80	14.2

Source: OECD figures in *Management Today*, January 1994

2.2.5 *Manufacturing and national prosperity*

The fact is that the decline in manufacturing in some Western countries has been such that the future prosperity of these nations is at stake. As Finniston (in Bignell, 1985) states:

> The importance of manufacturing to Britain's prosperity, and hence to the welfare and living standards of her people, cannot be over stressed. (p.9)

and

> Britain is now poorer than many of the countries she formerly out-performed . . . both the roots of that relative decline and the seeds of the future recovery lie with the performance of her manufacturing industries. (p.14)

Bessant (1991) provides clear indications of the decline in British manufacturing and the dramatic decline in exports:

> Whereas in 1900 Britain made 60% of the world's shipping, she now accounts for less than 3%. In 1948 the UK was the largest steel producer, yet she now only just manages tenth place . . . over 50% of cars and 98% of motorcycles are imported. (p.1)

Bessant places the US performance in much the same light and contrasts both the US and UK experience with Japan and Germany.

This is supported by Skinner (1985), who states:

> By the late 1970s it was clear that the United States had lost its century-old dominance in manufacturing in dozens of industries. Our competitive edge was destroyed by lower costs, better quality, and product and process technologies of global competitors. Imports were surging into the country from Japan, Korea, Singapore, Taiwan, and many countries of Western Europe. (p.vii)

The conclusion to all of this as far as the United States is concerned is clear:

> Unless the United States gets its manufacturing operations back in shape – and fast – it could lose any hope of maintaining the foundation on which tomorrows' prosperity rests. (Evans *et al.*, 1990, p.5)

Samson (1991) recognizes the national importance of manufacturing for Australia, when he asks:

> Would Australia have the same difficulties of declining wealth and high debt if it had a set of large, wonderfully competitive manufacturing companies? (p.17)

The Australian Manufacturing Council (1990) also endorsed the national importance of manufacturing:

> businesses, not countries, are the primary vehicle for industrial com-

> petitiveness; Boeing, not the USA, leads the world in commercial aircraft and IBM in computers; and it is BHP, not Australia, that has a strong position in exporting coated steel. (in Samson, 1991, p.17)

2.2.6 *The Japanese approach to manufacturing*

The Japanese success in manufacturing is well documented. In the 1960s and 1970s Japan's labour productivity increased at a rate three to four times faster than that of the United States. (Garvin, 1992). By the 1980s, the comparative failure rates of products in semiconductors, cars, air conditioners and televisions showed that Japan's product reliability greatly out-performed the United States. Japanese firms are aggressive in their pursuit of targeted markets. The ability to do so is clearly summarized by Hayes and Pisano (1994):

> Japanese companies began in the late 1970s to assault world markets in a number of industries with increasing ferocity. Their secret weapon turned out to be sheer manufacturing virtuosity. Most were producing products similar to those offered by West companies and marketing them in similar ways. What made these products attractive was not only their cost but also their low incidence of defects, their reliability, and their durability. (pp.80–1)

One of the key factors behind Japan's success is that companies have a clear, interlinked and holistic view, especially between marketing and production/operations areas which is not typically the case in the West. Part of the problem is that both the United Kingdom and United States have much shorter time-frames. This attitude has shown itself in terms of investment in advanced manufacturing technology. In the West short-term, an accounting view of the business pervades, where accounting ratios such as return on investment (ROI) or return on net assets (RONA) are used as the criteria for investment decisions. This is clearly not the case in Japan. As Hobday (1989) states:

> Japanese companies, often with Government co-ordination and support through the Ministry of Trade and Industry (MITI) have invested heavily . . . heavy investment in SC (Semi-conductors) R&D is one of the most crucial factors in their market success. (p.71)

This serves to support the view that Japanese companies see this investment as part of their strategy and that manufacturing for them is indeed of strategic, long-term importance, which accounts to a large degree for their success in these markets at the expense of their Western competitors. This point is supported by Skinner (1985) who states that despite the need to change factories by appropriate investment, progress in the United States is slow, 'surprisingly cautious' and 'disappointing'.

What also emerges is that both Europe and the United States trail behind Japan in terms of national developments in manufacturing; the key requirements in Europe and America seem to be on quality, while the Japanese are primarily concerned with low cost and flexibility. That is not to say that Japan sees quality as something which is now completed – they are obsessed with continuous improvement in process and product quality. The message here though is that high levels of process and product quality are consistently reached in Japanese manufacturing and it is almost assumed and that the objective for Japanese manufacturers has now developed and indeed moved on.

The biggest indictment against US performance is offered by Hayes *et al.* (1988), when they say that lessons that manufacturing managers are learning from Japan are lessons that:

> American managers developed, taught the rest of the world, and then, their attention directed elsewhere, forgot. (p.31)

This is particularly noticeable in the area of quality. While it would be naive to state that Japan's quality performance is due totally to American gurus, such as Deming and Juran, we can say that their involvement and teaching were central. Unfortunately, the area of quality has been neglected in many companies in the West until recently and the gurus were largely ignored in the United States. Hayes and Wheelwright (1984) endorse this criticism when they state:

> There seems to have been a tacit agreement between firms in . . . manufacturing industries over the past 15–20 years to compete on dimensions other than manufacturing ability. (p.20)

2.3 The problems of past attitudes to manufacturing

2.3.1 The exclusion from corporate merger and acquisition decisions

There have been a number of publications on ill-fated merger and acquisition activity in the United States during the 1970s and 1980s. It is clear that much of the activity in mergers and acquisitions took place with little or no thought given to an exhaustive operations audit prior to purchasing another firm, and decisions were made without regard to operational compatibility.

Many of the problems concerning inappropriate merger and acquisition deals which were so common in the United States in the 1970s and 1980s were that the decision-makers themselves had no operations experience and little manufacturing-specific knowledge or expertise. Consequently, corporate decisions were made in terms of vertical and horizontal integration, as well as diversification strategies which added little value to the company. Much of the synergy which was envisaged by these acquisitions simply did not take place. Acquiring other companies will undoubtedly have a major impact on manufacturing in terms of processes and infrastructure. The firm may well be ill-equipped to manage the new acquisition, whose processes and technology might be alien to the existing focus and capability in production/operations. This is particularly true of vertical integration which in certain industries has been replaced by enhanced buyer–supplier relationships. Fortunately, the former trend in the 1970s and 1980s for asset growth and ownership of organizations involved in the supply chain in which the manufacturing company is placed has declined. Reasons for acquiring another company are often centred around financial considerations and, under the traditional approach, therefore, such a decision would be made at corporate level without production/operations input or presence at this level. Even if some sort of short-term financial achievement is realized, this is hardly the basis of sustainable competitive advantage and as Love and Scouller (1990) state:

> It is a basic tenet of the Western concept of enterprise that companies exist to maintain and, if possible, increase the wealth of their owners. This may or may not be a rather narrow objective on which to base the organisation of productive activity (significantly the Japanese view of enterprise is different). (p.5)

2.3.2 The exclusion from internal investment decisions

Whereas production/operations has tended to be excluded from corporate debates concerning *external* mergers and acquisitions – often resulting in decisions incompatible with operations – it would also appear that *internal* investment decisions in technology have often taken place without production/operations' involvement either. Decisions have shifted from merger and acquisition activity to technological investment decisions, but the common link is that these decisions have been made by specialists – financial in merger decisions, high-tech engineers in technology, but production/operations input seems to be missing in the corporate debates on decisions involving vast sums of investment.

More alarmingly, investment decisions involving billions of dollars have proven to be of no competitive benefit to some companies, General Motors, for example. However, the joint venture between Toyota and General Motors – the NUMMI project – has relatively little technology, but has been successful. From Toyota's view, the venture has served as part of their ongoing, organizational learning.

In their study of companies adopting advanced manufacturing technology, Beatty and Gordon (1991) found that the planning process and implementation was 'often haphazardly planned, if at all' whilst Hayes and Jaikumar (1988) conclude that advanced technology is installed with little overview of how it might allow the company to be more effective. With no competitive advantage having been gained by these investment decisions in process technology, companies 'go on with life as before'.

Decisions concerning manufacturing investment, in terms of new processes or technology, have to be made on long-term manufacturing advantage and not narrow financial criteria such as ROI or immediate cost savings.

It is clear that some CEOs/MDs have made the decision to buy in technology without any great appreciation as to how this might enhance – or inhibit – the firm's presence in the market. As is often the case, the scale of making the wrong decision – either in terms of technological investment decisions or entering inappropriate markets – is known only after the event. Inappropriate targeting of markets and failed investments in process technology have both been menacing factors to some Western firms. Meyers (1969) narrates the disaster which faced Babcock and Wilcox after the decision was made to shift from fossil-fuel to nuclear power vessels. The same manufacturing processes were assumed to be appropriate for both types of products, although one product needed to be made in a 'flow line'; the other – nuclear vessels – had to be made in a 'job shop' process. Because the manufacturing resources were neglected prior to winning orders, the scale of the mistake was devastating to Babcock and Wilcox, resulting in poor quality, late deliveries and massive financial penalties. The vital importance of investment in technology and process choice is discussed in Chapter 4.

2.3.3 The perceived lack of strategic importance of production/operations

Hayes and Wheelwright (1984) contend that there are three management practices which have resulted in the decline of US industry:

1. An emphasis on analytical detachment over hands-on experience and well-managed line operations.
2. A focus on short-term results rather than long-term goals.
3. Managerial emphasis on marketing and financial areas at the expense of manufacturing and technological resources.

This is endorsed by Hill (1985), who states that corporate performance is typically based on ROI and shareholder responsibilities. Moreover, attitudes to risk are largely risk-averse and top management's inexperience in manufacturing provides an 'unreceptive climate in which to consider strategic process investment' (p.19).

With such a short-sighted approach, companies rob themselves of undertaking a full resource audit – for example as part of a SWOT analysis, discussed in Chapter 1 – because production/operations' input is not made at developmental, exploratory stages of new product introduction, attacking new markets and other vital areas. Skinnner (1969) had said much the same thing before, but at this stage manufacturing for many companies could not be couched in terms of strategy and business planning, other than as a reactive function.

This short-term view of the business is maintained because, as Lazonick (1993) argues, there is sometimes a vested interest to do so from the decision-makers themselves. He uses the term 'value extractors', as opposed to 'value enhancers' to denote those corporate-level decision-makers whose interests are sometimes personal, financial and short term in nature. For instance ROI ratios for the firm may appear to be strong, whereas in reality little or no plant investment has been made. The net result to this lack of investment in the plant is that the company is incapable of competing in the long term as a world-class player in markets.

2.3.4 The problem of the manufacturing image within organizations

The decline in the US fortunes in manufacturing is clearly linked to corporate attitudes toward manufacturing. Skinner (1985) relates how manufacturing had become 'a necessary evil in the corporation' (p.5). Indeed, manufacturing was seen as a 'problem' that had been 'solved'. Not only was production/operations largely viewed as a function without strategic importance, but also a function which was almost an 'irritant' to the organization; production/operations was associated with costs, whilst other areas, especially marketing, were associated with generating income.

Wickens (1987) best summarizes past attitudes when he says:

> Until the last few years companies themselves have constantly downgraded the role of production management. (p.163)

2.3.5 The contrast of images between marketing and production/operations

There has been an unjustified association with production/operations' role within firms, in contrast to that of marketing, which nonetheless accounts for an attitude along the lines of Figure 2.8.

Marketing's role is of course very important for the success of the firm and it is too simple to refer to marketing's role only in terms of the 4 Ps – Price, Place, Product and Promotion. However, these do act as a useful framework for marketing's role and such frameworks are used in marketing texts. The point must be made though that Price, Place and Product clearly fall under the capability of production/operations to meet the customer requirements for these competitive factors. As well as noting how competitors are pricing their products – and knowing how price-sensitive a particular market is – a key concern in pricing decisions will be cost. Much of the cost of a product will be centred around the cost of manufacture and if production/operations can drive down these costs, the firm will benefit. Moreover, this capability will satisfy customers and out-perform the competitors.

Similarly, 'place' or distribution has to do with the management of the supply chain, a major feature of which is the supplier relationships in which production/operations managers will be involved. Thirdly, the 'product' element refers to all those features which production/operations managers must meet in order to satisfy customers. It would seem obvious, therefore, that the liaison between marketing and production/operations must be close if the firm is to succeed in meeting customer requirements.

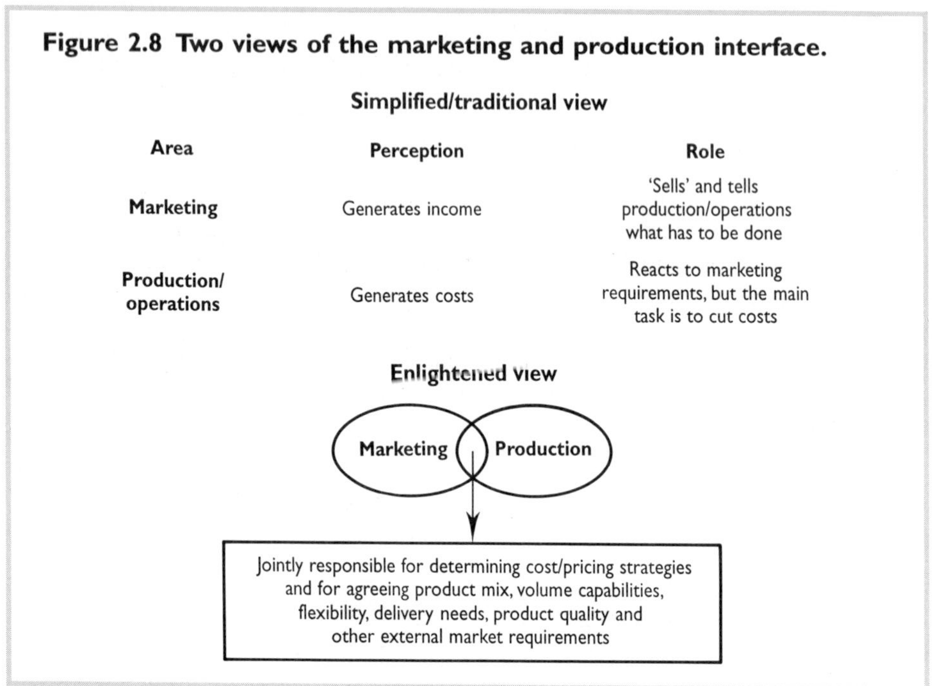

2.4 Reasons for the continued image problem of production/operations

In many companies today it would appear that the image problem still pervades. Hill (1990) suggests that there are several reasons for the lack of status of production/operations:

1. Production/operations managers' self-image.
2. The traditional view by the company of production/operations as a purely reactive role.
3. Little or no early input by production/operations in corporate debates on planning.
4. The lack of shared language between production/operations and other functions.

The fourth point is important here, because production/operations in some quarters has become linked to the concept of a technical function. This has tended to attract technical people, speaking technical jargon, becoming insular and excluded from corporate level debates. Production/operations staff in some companies have therefore centred on technical aspects and have lost sight of corporate objectives – in some organizations the production/operations group has therefore closed ranks. This is supported by Skinner (1985) when he writes about production/operations personnel:

> They are too detail orientated, too short-term orientated . . . too many production people . . . live in their own worlds. (p.214)

This is endorsed by Hill and Chambers (1989):

> Production, being traditionally placed in a reactive strategic role, is normally required to review change . . . primarily in terms of technical requirements and not in terms of the business. (p.24)

Lazonick (1991) states much the same thing when commenting how, in Britain

> highly trained technical specialists tended to be more closely integrated with shop-floor workers below than with general managers above. (p.49)

Hayes and Wheelwright (1984), in their assessment of the 'critical weaknesses' in the way that US managers manage their companies, conclude that there has been an ongoing relegation of production/operations from any involvement in the corporate strategic debate. The image problem stems to some extent from further and higher education and as a result production/operations seems to be unattractive to many graduates.

Wickens (1987) says how:

> The best graduates want to go into merchant banking, the professions, the Civil Service, the finance sector. If they think of industry or commerce it is in the areas of marketing, sales, finance or personnel that attract – rarely production. (p.162)

A possible reason for this view is the former portrayal of manufacturing in the media. In the United Kingdom, in films such as *I'm Alright, Jack* and *Kes*, the general portrayal of manufacturing (in Britain, anyway) was that the atmosphere in factories was grim, dirty, sweaty and generally distasteful and there was a continued battle going on between workers and management. The political dimension is often overlooked in texts on production/operations but, clearly, as far as the United Kingdom was concerned, industrial conflict which pervaded much of Britain's performance during the 1960s and 1970s, was a result of the ongoing worker/manager divide. The image of manufacturing was exacerbated by the association of the role of production/operations at the front-line being undertaken by the working class who were supervised/managed by the middle/upper class managers. This image is further compounded – in the United Kingdom at least – by the association of manufacturing, at the shop-floor level, being performed by staff who were relatively, non-academic and who therefore had to become apprentices. The unjustified and unfair association is that staff were taken as apprentices largely because they had failed academically, and that manufacturing was the best available alternative.

However, although times have moved on, the damage on manufacturing's image has been made and to some extent remains. The message is clear, though:

the dramatic improvements required in key industries in both the United States and United Kingdom will come about essentially through people. As Finniston, (in Bignell, 1985) observes, Britain's decline has been due to a large extent to:

> our failure to unlock the full contribution of those working in manufacturing industry – or to attract into manufacturing those with a contribution to make. (p.9)

The importance of human resources cannot be overestimated to world-class strategic manufacturing firms, and this is discussed in Chapter 7.

2.5 Present-day developments of production/operations' image

According to De Meyer and Ferdows (1991), manufacturing strategy has become central to the overall strategic planning process in many European companies: 10 action programmes were featured in the majority of their 224 'large European companies' in the report. In 1988–89 one of the programmes in the survey was to 'link manufacturing to business strategy'. In the 1991 survey, this programme featured as one of the top ten payoffs of benefit to the company.

In the United States, Hewlett Packard remain an excellent company at the forefront of new technology able to introduce new products at a rapid pace. Edmonson and Wheelwright (1989) link this success to their policy of uniting manufacturing and corporate strategies:

> the primary focus of corporate level manufacturing is as a catalyst, helping operating units to build the skills, knowledge, and behaviors required to accomplish their competitive objectives . . . The corporate group also has identified a handful of key aspects of HP's manufacturing capabilities that can be strengthened significantly through direction, co-ordination, and integration at a corporate level. (p.83)

In their analysis of companies in Europe, including DAF, Fiat, GEC, Olivetti, Philips and Thomson, Bolwijn and Kumpe (1991) found that a key ingredient was that:

> It was clear that all companies viewed manufacturing as a strength to be used in competition. As such there were overall, long-term manufacturing strategies as part of total strategies . . . Production within these companies is by no means an under-estimated function with line management having cost reductions as their sole responsibility. (p.24)

However, this approach still seems to be the exception rather than the norm, and it is clear that a change of attitude needs to take place not only at a corporate but also at a societal level. The basic image of production is still essentially that of people making things surrounded by lathes, oil, fumes and the like. With this in mind, it is hardly surprising that manufacturing is seen as this reactive, tactical role.

In general, therefore, the comments offered by Skinner (1985) seem to be pertinent:

> Manufacturing is generally perceived in the wrong way at the top, managed in the wrong way at plant level, and taught in the wrong way in the business schools. (p.55)

The way forward includes a new mind-set in terms of where production/operations is positioned within the hierarchy of the firm. Production/operations staff need to be more actively involved in business planning and to see their own role extending beyond the mere technical facets of the job. This view is supported by Samson and Sohal (1993) when they say that:

> manufacturing managers must become more than just implementers of engineering and marketing instructions on the shop floor. Raising the status of the manufacturing function involves getting the manufacturing manager involved in the business development/market competitiveness debate. Manufacturing managers need to be interfaced with and have an understanding of the firm's customers. (p.220)

2.6 Key reasons for having a manufacturing strategy

2.6.1 *The scale of managerial responsibility*

To Japanese companies, production/operations forms the basis of their competitive advantage. The competitive factor of production/operations is discussed in the next section. However, even if those within the manufacturing firm have difficulty accepting the competitive role that production/operations has, they should nonetheless be clear as to the weight of responsibility that production/operations managers have:

1. **Assets utilization** Production/operations will utilize something in the region of 80 to 85 per cent of company assets, both fixed (plant) and current assets, especially materials; it falls upon production/operations therefore to make the best use of the greatest amount of assets at its disposal.
2. **Costs of the firm** Production/operations activity will account for 80 per cent of company costs. Materials themselves can account for over 60 per cent of costs of sales in manufacturing; costs will always be a factor, even in less price-sensitive markets. Driving down costs will enable the firm to gain margins and, therefore, generate income to reinvest in the firm.
3. **Human resources** In manufacturing firms production/operations is clearly responsible for managing a high proportion of staff, particularly front-line personnel. Consequently, where total quality management (TQM) drives are taking place in manufacturing companies, much will centre around the

performance of production/operations personnel. Many of the quality initiatives through the likes of Deming and Juran centred on manufacturing, although, of course, TQM is central to service organizations as well.

2.6.2 *Production/operations as a competitive opportunity*

Over and above asset utilization, cost management and human resource factors, production/operations is crucial on a strategic, competitive level. As Slack (1991) observes:

> A sickly manufacturing function . . . will handicap a business's performance no matter how sharp is its business sense and competitive strategy cannot hope to be successful in the long term unless it expects Manufacturing's role to be both pivotal and direct. (p.1)

The inability of organizations to exploit opportunities is highlighted by Bessant (1991):

> Manufacturing history is littered with cases of firms or even whole industries which failed to recognize challenges and to adapt. (p.37)

Hayes and Wheelwright (1984) state that the problem often has to do with the market requirements in relation to manufacturing resources:

> Again and again we have found that the root cause of a 'manufacturing crisis' has been that a business's manufacturing policies and people . . . have become incompatible with its facilities and technology choices, or that both have become incompatible with its competitive needs. (p.35)

By contrast, in his research into successful US companies, Skinner (1985) found that:

> The outstanding features of these companies seemed to be that . . . they had forged manufacturing into a major and formidable competitive weapon . . . Manufacturing became a competitive resource because they had exceptionally short deliveries, or remarkable low costs, or could move fast in developing new products, or produced the same volume with lower investment than their competitors. (p.5)

Samson and Sohal (1993) note that:

> In the world's leading manufacturers, the production management function has become a high-status activity and is the powerhouse that energizes the competitive advantage that the marketing function can achieve in the marketplace. (p.217)

The operational capability is therefore a competitive weapon central to the corporate debate in such questions as:

> What business are we in and what business do we want to be in?

What volume increases in current products can be realized with existing capacity?
What *new products* can be introduced with our *existing processes* and technology?
What *new processes* do we need to ensure enhanced performance of *existing* products?
What *new processes* do we need to ensure rapid development of *new products*?

To ask these questions, which are corporate factors, without regard to production/operations capability and involvement is clearly short-sighted and tantamount to corporate suicide. Moreover, if the questions are asked with reference to production/operations capabilities, it will allow the firm to seek and exploit competitive opportunities in new and existing markets.

2.6.3 Key competitive variables

Porter (1980) argues that a firm must seek to be either a low-cost or differentiated player – a firm can do both but if it does, Porter suggests, it runs the risk of being out-performed by a more focused player. As we saw in Chapter 1 however, in the 1990s a firm might have to compete on both low cost and provide differentiation features (for which it cannot charge premium prices) at the same time. In the 1990s and beyond, other equally important competitive attributes are integral, as shown in Table 2.4.

These competitive factors would need to be weighted and assessed in terms of their particular requirements for specific markets. Companies need therefore to understand the core focus of their strategy and to determine how other, equally important competitive factors are needed to win in chosen markets, as seen in Figure 2.9.

In their survey of companies, De Meyer and Ferdows (1991) found the following competitive priorities to be of importance to their cited companies (224 total). We can list these and state the crucial role that production/operations has to play in achieving these objectives, as shown in Table 2.5.

Table 2.4 Competitive attributes

- Product quality
- Process quality
- Delivery speed
- Delivery reliability
- Flexibility – in terms of range, volumes and mix of outputs
- Rapid product innovation

Figure 2.9 Key competitive factors.

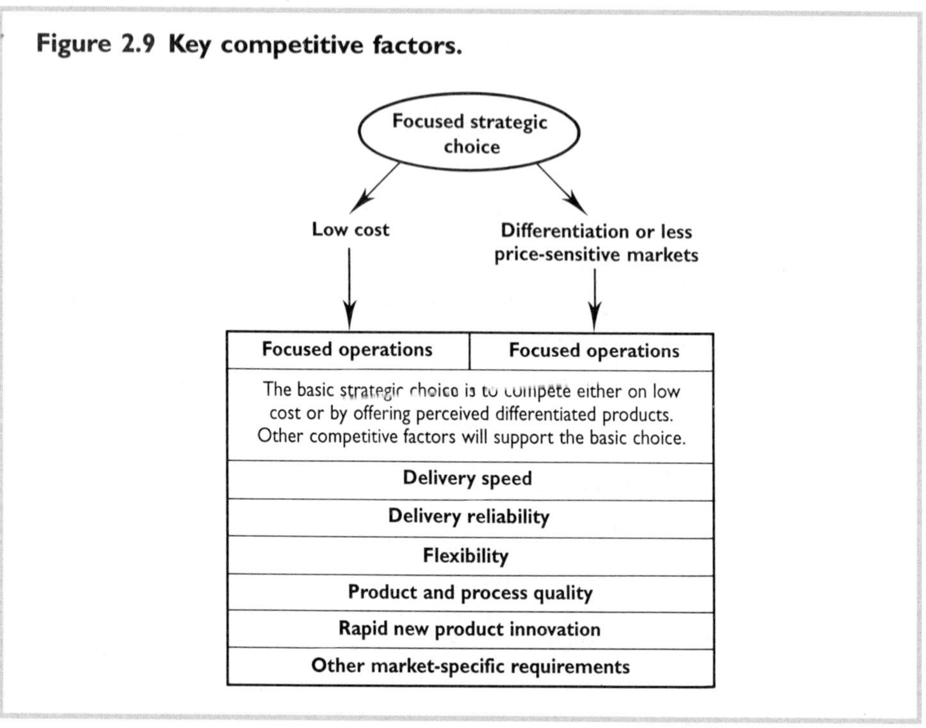

Table 2.5 The link between production and competitive factors

Competitive factors	*Production task*
Offer consistently low defect rates	Process quality
Offer dependable delivery products	Delivery reliability
Provide high-performance products or amenities	Product quality
Offer fast deliveries	Delivery speed
Customize products and services to customer needs	Flexibility
Profit in price competitive markets	Low-cost production
Introduce new products quickly	Rapid product innovation
Provide effective after-sales service	(non-manufacturing factor)
Offer a broad product line	Flexibility
Make rapid volume changes	Flexibility
Make rapid product mix changes	Customization, flexibility
Make product easily available	Delivery speed/reliability (distribution)
Make rapid changes in design	Flexibility

Since all of these are determined to a very large extent by the capability of production/operations to meet these requirements, it would seem logical to include this as part of the overall strategy-making process. The role of production/operations – and therefore the essential part of its strategic involvement – is ensuring that it supports the company; this goes way beyond simply providing capacity or concentrating solely on low-cost manufacture.

The test of this manufacturing strategy is the consistency with the overall corporate strategy and the contribution that it will make to the enterprise. Although production/operations' contribution will vary according to specific markets, there are general improvements that any manufacturing company can make in order to be competitive. Ferdows *et al.* (1986) attempt to unravel a step-by-step generic guide that any manufacturing change should follow:

1. First, high quality must be produced.
2. Then delivery reliability must be achieved.
3. Then production costs must be lowered.
4. Then production flexibility must increase.

Although this four-step process is most suited to high volume, relatively standard products, the need to improve quality, enhance delivery performance and reduce costs is important in any manufacturing firm. This certainly seems to have been the process model for Japanese success; quality became the first priority and other equally important factors then followed. This indicates that improvement in competitive areas will come over a period of time, rather than as a result of any quick-fix cost-cutting solutions. This is in stark contrast to much of Western manufacturing where, if cost cutting is to be made, it is done by firing or, as it is more euphemistically called, 'downsizing'. This approach is particularly ironic, in that direct labour costs will typically account for less than 10 per cent of costs of cars and high-technology products. The largest cost connected with key industries such as cars, telecommunications and computing manufacture is in materials management. Improvements in materials management must be made on a strategic basis, brought about by long-term commitment to improving materials handling and methodologies in the plant itself, coupled with strategic alliances formed with suppliers. Only with this strategic view can a manufacturing firm hope to improve and compete on a sustainable basis. The strategic view regarding the actual functional roles within production/operations must be in place, as shown in Figure 2.10.

2.6.4 Manufacturing and design

The importance of production/operations in relation to new product design and development is discussed in depth in Chapter 3. The role of design has sometimes appeared to be blurred and unfocused within some organizations. Thus, according to corporate whim, design will be placed under any of the following areas: marketing, production/operations, R&D or subcontracted in part, or whole. CAD/

Figure 2.10 The strategic view of production/operations activities.

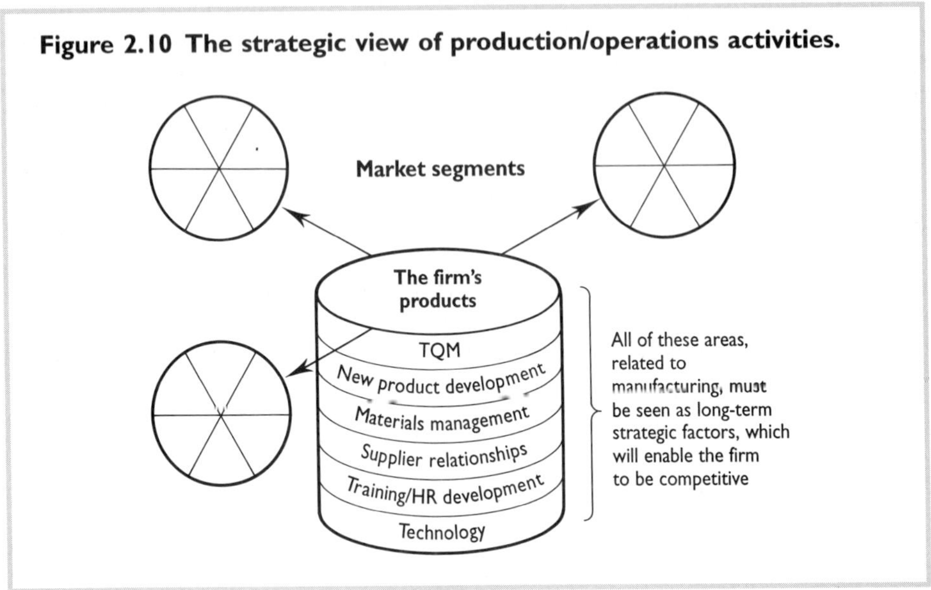

CAM developments have tended to link design with a purely technical tag. However, developing new products at such a rapid pace – and in such a variety that current and future markets are likely to demand – means that production/operations should be involved in the actual product design itself. If production/operations is not involved at early stages, then delays in product innovation may well occur. The shift from prototype to volume manufacture is critical and may well be difficult if the product is overdesigned, thus making process design and capability difficult. Overdesign will lead to excessive costs, delays in new product innovation and problems with delivery speed and reliability once a product has been launched.

2.7 Formulating a manufacturing strategy

2.7.1 Areas to consider in manufacturing strategy

The essential areas in manufacturing strategy include product technology, capacity, facilities and their location, process technology, human resources, operating decisions, the relationship with, and integration of, suppliers and process and product quality. Clearly, this is a massive task which demands much interface with other internal functions, together with other firms. Certainly key areas of a manufacturing strategy will include *at least* the following:

- **Capacity** This will directly influence long-term investment decisions regarding potential capacity and the size, timing and type will be important discussion points.
- **Facilities** This will include size, location, specialization and organization.
- **Technology** The need to spend wisely and appropriately on equipment and automation is vital here. Wrong decisions are costly and hard to transfer, the company is therefore stuck with an exit barrier. The downside to this is that the firm has to stay in an industry in order to finance the wrong technological investment.
- **Vertical integration** Although there has been a decline in activity regarding vertical integration in favour of enhanced buyer–supplier relationships, discussions will need to take place on the direction and extent, if any, of vertical integration for the company.
- **Workforce** The whole remuneration system is under major review by many companies – piecework and day rates are being replaced by a range of rewards linked to quality of output, pay for knowledge and other new approaches. Training for front-line personnel is now a requirement to compete at all in manufacturing, certainly in markets where quality is vital.
- **Quality** TQM is now a prominent feature in many companies and quality in terms of meeting customer satisfaction is a central competitive requirement in the 1990s and beyond. The internal customer is also relevant here, together with measurement in such areas as internal failure and defect prevention.
- **Production planning/materials control** This will include systems such as materials requirement planning (MRP), and just-in-time management (JIT) (discussed in Chapter 6). The planning, investment, and implementation of these systems has to be undertaken with a strategic viewpoint; the firm needs to ask how these systems might provide any competitive advantage for the company.
- **Organization** Organizations are becoming less hierarchical in structure; part of the reason for this is the empowerment of front-line production/operations personnel who, increasingly, are becoming their own managers, in such areas as quality, delivery and scheduling. Empowering front-line personnel is a requirement to competing. This reduces the involvement of supervisors and such empowerment can have dramatic results; Harley–Davidson reduced the number of their production schedulers from twenty-seven (when long delays in delivery and poor quality were evident) to just one. The result of this was that product quality requirements and delivery speed were subsequently met constantly. This change came from a change of policy from the most senior levels of Harley–Davidson which led to an obsession with quality, a rearrangement of the plant into focused areas and a commitment to empowering the workforce. This has allowed them to fight back against the Japanese domination in the motorcycle industry.

Table 2.6 The scope of production/operations in corporate strategy

No involvement	No involvement in shaping strategy
After the event	Production/operations' capabilities taken into account but only on a tactical level
Passive	Production/operations participates only in terms of expressing feasibility of a particular course of action
Active	Production/operations actively participates in defining the business strategy
Leader	Production/operations is actively involved in defining and shaping strategy

2.7.2 *Determining manufacturing's current contribution*

A useful starting point for companies is to see where manufacturing strategy is currently placed within the company's strategic-making process. Anderson *et al.* (1991) suggest that production/operations' role will be placed essentially in one of five positions in this process, as shown in Table 2.6.

This is similar to Hayes and Wheelwright (1984), who defined four stages in the evolution of manufacturing strategy's importance within the firm. Stage one is essentially reactive, in that it tries to ensure that production costs are in line with business objectives; stage two is to match the range of products offered by competitors; the third stage is when manufacturing tries to support the firm's competitive strategy; the fourth is more proactive, where manufacturing is seen as an essential means of gaining or sustaining competitive advantage. This is a useful snapshot, which serves to illustrate the current involvement – or otherwise – of manufacturing in corporate decision-making. What the firm must do is to analyze its current position. If the firm uses its senior manufacturing managers only as a means of driving down costs, it is depriving itself of a valuable input into corporate strategy. Good manufacturing managers – who have business acumen as well as technical know-how – have a central part in helping to determine the firm's competitive strategies.

2.7.3 *The process of manufacturing strategy*

Anderson *et al.* (1991) observe that there is very little available literature that addresses the actual process of implementing a manufacturing strategy. There are, however, a number of frameworks. Edmonson and Wheelwright (1989) believe that there are three modes of approach to formulating manufacturing strategy. The first two of these are largely reactive; the third is much more proactive:

> Its focus is on developing a set of distinctive competencies in manufacturing that provide a competitive edge in the market place: that is, developing

> capabilities that allow the organization to do things significantly better than their competitors, in areas that customers value highly. (p.68)

Hill (1989) states that distinctions have to be made between order-qualifying factors – which allow the company to compete in a particular market – and order-winning criteria – which are those features of the company's capability which will ensure that it can win in the marketplace. Once order-qualifying and order-winning criteria are determined, such factors as process choice and infrastructure must be put in place in order to best serve the company's aims in particular markets. This is a very useful guideline, although as we shall see in Chapter 4, order-qualifying and order-winning factors are not as easily mapped onto a particular choice of process as Hill (1989) implies. That aside, the distinction between order-winning and order-qualifying criteria is vital for the firm to understand.

In their study of 188 North American companies, Roth and Miller (1989) classified three types of manufacturing strategies which are shown in Table 2.7.

Where a company is, in terms of their heading under this model, depends on the markets that it serves and the requirements of the particular market, together with skills and abilities (acquired by learning and know-how) that the firm has gained. This builds on Hill's (1989) work and helps to link markets to process choice; for example, caretakers producing largely high volume, standard, products will be linked to a line process; the other two, marketeers and innovators will be arranged in batch, and areas such as focus, group technology and flexible manufacturing systems will come into play. The link between chosen markets and choice of manufacturing process is critical and is discussed in further depth in Chapter 4. The choice of manufacturing process (from project, job, batch, line and continuous process) provides one of the biggest clues as to what the company can and cannot do. A good understanding of production/operations capability will enable the firm to focus on the market segments that best match the capabilities of the firm, particularly in process choice.

The whole range of activities from planning to implementation is large and complex. However, a simple process outline can be formulated and Vonderembse

Table 2.7 Three classifications of manufacturing companies

Strategic type	*Order-winning criteria*	*Qualifying criteria*
Caretakers	Price	Delivery reliability Consistent quality
Marketeers	New products	Consistent quality Dependable delivery
Innovators	High quality products Design flexibility Speedy new product developments	Consistent quality

Table 2.8 A process model of manufacturing strategy

1. Analyzing the environment
2. Internal appraisal
3. Formulate corporate strategy
4. Determine the implications for operations
5. Examine the limitations that financial and technological factors place on operations
6. Design operations systems
7. Plan operations
8. Manage and control operations

Adapted from Vonderembse and White (1991)

and White (1991) offer an eightfold process plan when implementing manufacturing strategy, as shown in Table 2.8.

Production/operations must be involved from stage 2 onwards and this is certainly the case in world-class or Japanese approaches to formulating and implementing strategy. However, the typical Western approach to formulating strategy is that stage 4 would be the earliest stage and, more commonly, stage 6 is where production/operations come into the process, a role which is to react to plans and strategies already in place. By then the original corporate aim could be out of line with production/operations capability.

That is not to say, though, that strategy is purely resource-driven. What is being stated is that a firm must not enter markets in which it cannot compete – due to resource incapability. If a firm's resources are to be stretched (discussed in Chapter 1) then often another firm's contribution must come into play, either by acquiring that firm or by forming a strategic alliance. In essence, the process is a matter of matching the internal strengths and weaknesses of operations capabilities with the external opportunities and threats of the targeted markets, as shown in Figure 2.11.

There is no one fixed process of formulating strategy, but the following is offered as a workable method and the flow follows the process of chapters in this text, as shown in Figure 2.12.

However, the process is dynamic and flexible and must change as new information about competitors, customers, process developments and other pertinent data appears. It is suggested that manufacturing strategy is not so much a sequential check list as it is a series of interlinked factors which have to be viewed holistically and simultaneously, as shown in Figure 2.13.

These linkages can only be achieved if the following takes place. First, some of the previously perceived 'tactical' areas in manufacturing, such as materials management, for example, must be seen in a strategic context. Other areas of strategic importance are human resource development, quality, new product development and investment in appropriate technology.

Figure 2.11 Matching internal capabilities to external requirements.

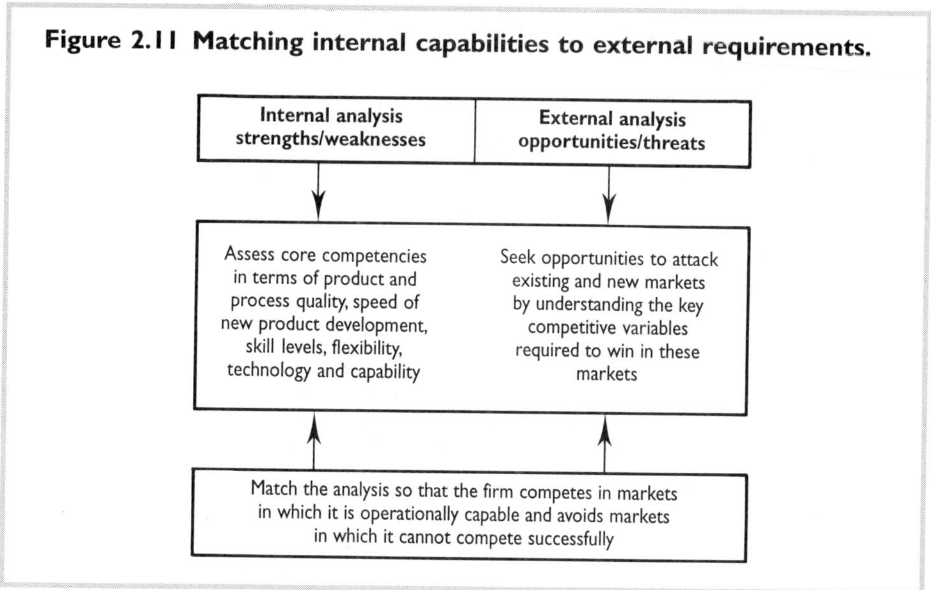

Second, there has to be constant dialogue and appreciation of each other's contribution to the corporate debate within the firm – in particular, marketing and production/operations must be closely linked and on the same side.

Third, other firms, particularly suppliers, must be seen in terms of strategic importance. Alliances and joint ventures with other partners must form part of the firm's strategy.

Fourth, there has to be a combined sense of urgency and timing, so that plans will be executed within specific time periods; these plans may well change, but the timing element will help to drive through the plans into specific implementation stages.

2.7.4 Competitive profiling in manufacturing strategy

Benchmarking has become a useful indicator for competitive analysis, where a firm's capabilities are evaluated against its competitors. For example, Xerox's turnaround in the 1980s owed much to an awareness of their initial failings against their competitors, whose performance was seen as the benchmark. Benchmarking is discussed further in Chapter 8 but it is also pertinent here. Slack (1991) proposes a grid of performance factors that need to be weighted according to a company's ability in relationship to its competitors. The X axis is the number ranking or 'score' in relation to competitors; the Y axis provides key competitive variables, such as cost, quality of product, quality of engineering, enquiry lead time, manufacturing lead time, delivery reliability, design flexibility, delivery

Figure 2.12 A model for formulating manufacturing strategy.

Corporate goals	These goals may be quite broad, e.g. to be the number 1 in an industry; to beat a competitor; to be world-class. They must not be purely financial in nature because this will limit possible opportunities for the firm and threaten investment in process and product technology
Market requirements	The needs of the firm's chosen markets must be clearly understood and regularly reviewed. All manufacturing decisions must be aimed at satisfying customers
New product development	New products must be developed in order to meet or create customer needs. The range, mix, and volumes of products must be known and production/operations should be involved from early stages of new product development (Chapter 3)
Manufacturing processes	The choice of manufacturing process, together with investment in technology, must be aimed at supporting the firm in the market and to provide competitive advantage (Chapter 4)
Quality	The world-class company is committed to quality as a way of life, rather than as a managerial fad. Quality means customer satisfaction and so all product and process efforts should aim to increase this satisfaction (Chapter 5)
Materials management	The firm must move away from quick-fix ideas of 'buying materials' to strategic partnership with suppliers. This is of corporate concern rather than a functional area; such alliances will provide competitive advantage, particularly in just-in-time management (Chapter 6)
Human resources	The world-class firm recognizes the vital input of human resources for ideas and innovations. The firm must create a dedicated, highly skilled workforce and must view training as an investment and not a cost (Chapter 7)
Strategic alliances	Strategic alliances can play a vital role in providing added value for the firm. Alliances can be for both product and process development. Learning can be enhanced by such strategic partnerships (Chapter 7)

Figure 2.13 The interlinking factors in manufacturing strategy.

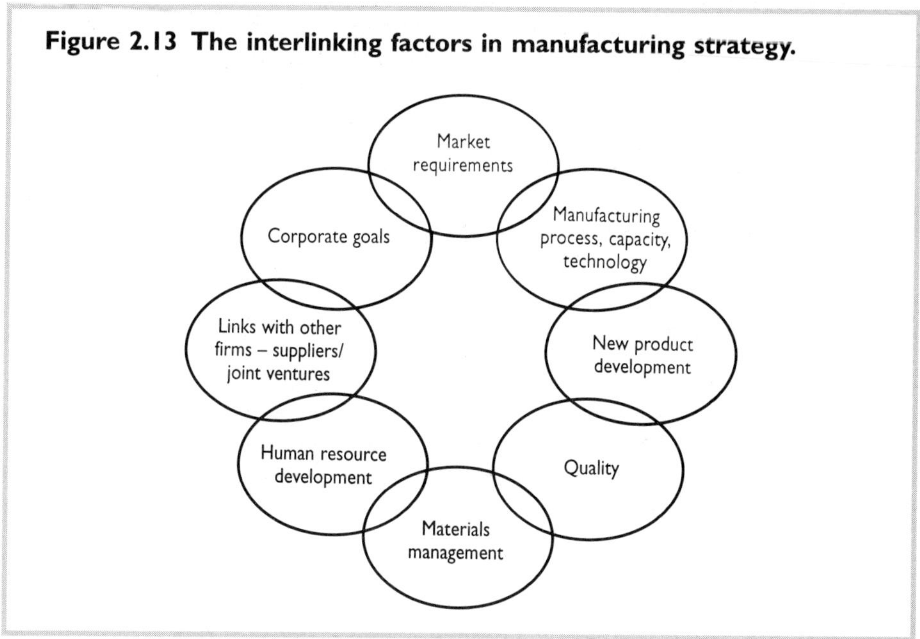

flexibility and volume flexibility. An example of the competitive grid is shown in Figure 2.14.

Whilst it is clear that manufacturing strategy cannot be formulated simply by following a check list, the grid does provide a useful list of competitive variables. Which of these variables are order winners, as compared to order qualifiers, will depend on the particular market that the company is serving. Obviously, successful completion of the grid (in other words for the grid to be of any use) demands that the company is aware of where it stands competitively and therefore the details have to be accurate, relevant and up to date. However, this can provide a useful starting point from the idea of generic market requirements and develops into competitive profiling.

2.8 Market forces and manufacturing: from craft to strategic manufacturing

As markets fragment with increasing regularity and new entrants come into the competitive framework from all areas of the globe, the need for companies is to move away from static processes and strategies to dynamic, quick-response, market-driven structures which allow the company to satisfy the customers which the company seeks to serve. Thus mass production will continue to give way to more focused approaches to manufacturing, such as flexible manufacturing and group technology (discussed in Chapter 4), which will better serve markets which demand frequent change of volumes, variety of products, variability and rapid new product development and introduction.

The problem with mass-production is that it does not address the requirement for quick response in terms of new product introduction or variability. This is summarized by Piore and Sabel (1984):

> Mass production required large investments in highly specialized equipment and narrowly trained workers. In the language of manufacturing, these resources were 'dedicated'; suited to the manufacture of a particular product – often, in fact, to make just one model. (p.28)

Skinner (1985) similarly identifies the characteristics of mass-production which included long production runs, stabilized designs in engineering, repetitive operations by workers, and many identical machines throughout the factory. Skinner further explains that the rapid change and product development and innovation are ongoing.

Figure 2.14 A competitive grid for manufacturing strategy.

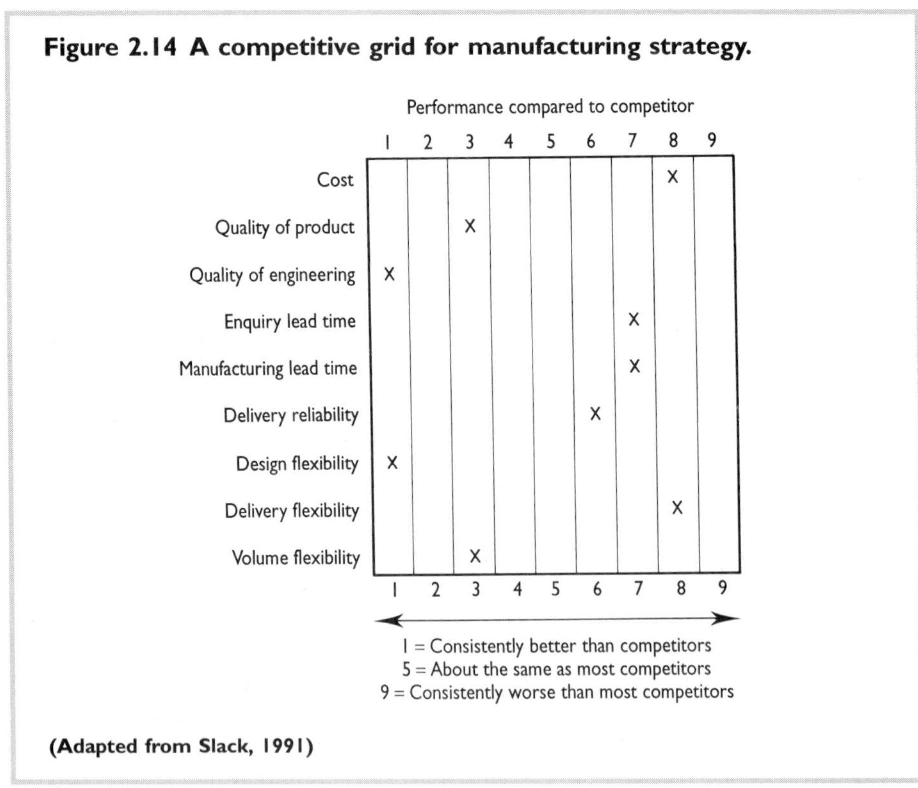

(Adapted from Slack, 1991)

We need only to review markets to see the rapid changes which have taken place from the 1980s:

- US car producers now offer more than twice the number of models offered in 1985.
- Siemens declares that by the year 2000, 50 per cent of its sales will be in products unknown today (Bolwijn and Kumpe, 1991).
- The PC market, once dominated by IBM, now has 60 per cent taken by 'IBM' 'no-name' clones.
- General Motors saw a decline from around 60 per cent of the US domestic market in 1979 to just over 30 per cent in 1995 due in part to improved performance of its domestic competitors, but caused mainly by the manufacturing capabilities of Japanese companies.

It is because of these changes that production/operations' contribution has become more central to the corporate planning process. This is described by Hayes and Pisano (1994):

> In a stable environment, competitive strategy is about staking out a position, and manufacturing strategy focuses on getting better at the things necessary to defend that position. In turbulent environments, however, the goal of strategy becomes strategic flexibility. Being world-class is not enough; a company also has to have the capability to switch gears – from, for example, rapid product development to low cost . . . The job of manufacturing is to provide that capability. (p.78)

This capability comes from having production/operations people involved in the agenda of the business itself, clearly understanding the needs and requirement of customers whose needs will change, sometimes fast and often, as greater choice becomes available to them from global competition. Clearly, there have been major developments in manufacturing practice over many years from craft to strategic manufacture. Other phrases have been used to describe the current era, including flexible manufacturing, mass customization, and lean production. However, as we shall see in Chapter 8, the phrase 'strategic manufacturing' is preferred here. The development of manufacturing practice from craft to strategic is described in Figure 2.15

2.9 The need for holistic management

Production/operations has a number of links to other areas in the organization. The main links are shown in Table 2.9.

Harmony between these departments and a shared vision are vital. Each department needs to be aware of targeted markets and the requirement to win in the marketplace. In short, the company needs to be holistic. The benefits of this approach are clear.

Hayes and Wheelwright (1979) state in their article that:

The experience of the late 1960s and early 1970s suggests that major competitive advantage can accrue to companies that are able to integrate

Figure 2.15 From craft to strategic manufacturing.

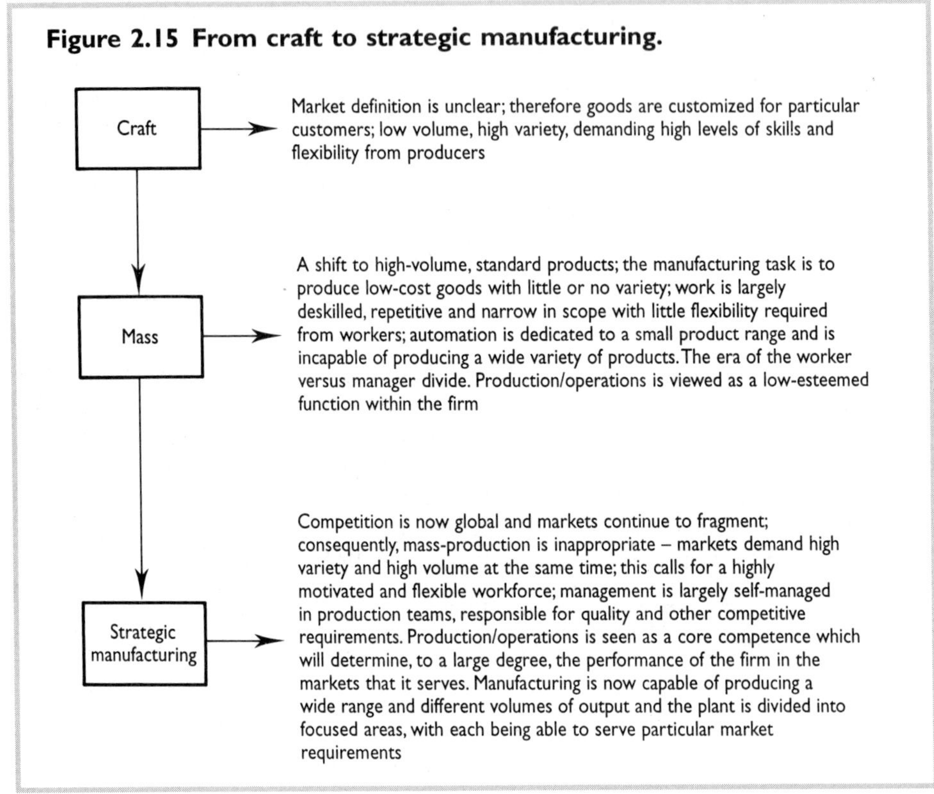

Table 2.9 Production/operations link to other functions

Human resources	staffing requirements, performance appraisal, recruiting, skills requirements, training, remuneration
Finance/accounting	Production costing, job estimates, all material and labour costs
Marketing	Product design including options and customization, delivery requirements, warranties, competitive costing
Engineering	Durability of products, scheduling, technological innovation

> their manufacturing and marketing organization with a common strategy. (p.3)

However, interdepartment conflict continues in some companies. As Garvin (1992) points out:

> Unfortunately, the three core groups – R&D, marketing, and manufacturing – normally respond to different goals and incentives. (p.7)

A key issue for corporate managers, then, is to harness ideas for a strategic vision from these different, and sometimes conflicting, areas and then to agree the shared vision which is now understood and owned by these different departments.

2.10 Evaluating the success of manufacturing strategies

Measuring the success of manufacturing is a major issue in itself. If manufacturing strategy is achieved by satisfying the strategic plan, then logically success has been achieved. If, however, the strategic aim has been realized, but the original plan was damaging to the company in the first place, then surely strategy has not been successful. It is also clear that financial criteria are not sufficient themselves. We have to think in terms of wider criteria for measuring success. To this end, Son and Young (1990) suggest that there should be no trade-off between productivity, quality and flexibility in manufacturing and that improvements in these three areas should increase simultaneously. Developing this, we can say that any assessment of manufacturing performance should be made in the light of response to market requirements, such as delivery speed, delivery flexibility, speed of new product development and product and process quality. Many of the above performance criteria must be measured. Failing to meet market requirements will result in the loss of business and ultimately exiting the market.

Conclusion

The national consequence of manufacturing is evident; Japan's success in many industries has much to do with their approach to manufacturing which is to take a long-term, strategic view of markets and manufacturing infrastructure in order to win in targeted markets. By contrast, the huge financial debt in the United States has accrued to trillions of dollars and their approach (in common with much of Western manufacturing) has been to place manufacturing in a tactical role, subservient to policies and strategies which are largely short term and financial in nature.

There seems to be a link between the perceived importance of production/operations in a company and that company's success. In their discussion on Japan's success – including the NUMMI project in the United States – Evans *et al.* (1990) state that:

> The Japanese experience – both in Japan and the United States – suggests that operations management is the key to success. (p.5)

However, the need to elevate production/operations and to link it to corporate strategy remains a difficult hurdle for companies who still see production/operations as a reactive function rather than a proactive competitive weapon. As Skinner (1985) states:

> a strategic point of view is frequently lacking. What is needed is a manufacturing strategy that links manufacturing to the corporate strategy. (p.21)

Skinner (1985) rightly observes, though, that:

> Few companies – in spite of Abernathy, Clark, Hayes, Leonard, Sasser, Skinner and Wheelwright and their pleas and formulae for developing a manufacturing strategy – do have a manufacturing strategy. (p.200)

To that list we might add the likes of Hill (1989), Samson (1991) and many others who similarly, reinforce the need for manufacturing companies to have an *explicit* manufacturing strategy. It would appear that, for the majority of companies, production/operations is still seen as a function, responsible for large assets utilization, the management of large amounts of people within the organization, and typically responsible for 80 per cent of costs, but a function, nonetheless, with short time horizons, rather than a strategic factor for the company. A manufacturing strategy can serve to clarify resources and the link to how a company might compete. Moreover, if senior production personnel can take an holistic view of the business, this may guide the business away from supposedly attractive markets the entry of which might damage the overall business.

This is supported by Hill and Chambers (1989):

> 'Markets seen as attractive by marketing may be rejected as unsuitable in the overall business context.' Although, conversely they argue, 'New markets that have proved difficult to penetrate can now be signalled as critical to the future.' (p.105)

A problem with companies is the divided attitude (marketing versus production/operations being a typical example) where in-house, managerial conflict is pursued to the cost of creating a focused and holistic company-wide strategy.

As early as 1979 Hayes and Wheelwright were urging companies to take an holistic view:

> Companies must make a series of interrelated marketing and manufacturing decisions. These choices must be continually reviewed and sometimes changed as the company's products and competitors evolve and mature. (p.63)

That is not to say, of course, that corporate strategy should be entirely led by manufacturing capability; it is to say, though, that production/operations has a key part in guiding the company into linking future markets with current and potential capability. The hierarchical nature of the corporate decision-making process (corporate to business to functional levels) has been well documented (Pearce and Robinson, 1982; Chakravarthy and Lorange, 1991). It is clear that manufacturing strategy as an explicit strategy from mainstream literature on strategy is absent.

That there are strategic issues in manufacturing cannot be in question if we consider that typical strategic questions will depend on at least the following factors:

1. The portfolio of products and the mix of volumes for each – manufacturing efforts must be focused in order to satisfy these requirements.
2. Product lifecycles – too often seen as the domain of the marketing department, but of direct influence upon manufacturing.
3. The timing of market entry and exit.
4. Make/buy decisions which help to shape the answer to the question, What business are we in?
5. Economies or diseconomies of scale.
6. Capacity decisions and their effect upon exit barriers from an industry.

Where manufacturing strategy is positioned appears still to be a matter of opinion. Academic literature seems to be divided and as confused as companies themselves. The notion of manufacturing as a competitive weapon is not new, but as Hayes and Wheelwright (1984) observe its practice is not widespread. Markets dictate operations' response and markets demand flexibility in terms of volume, process, product and volume.

A common theme throughout this book is that manufacturing strategy should feed into corporate strategy. This in turn means that there should be senior production/operations presence at corporate level. Manufacturing functions, entire corporations and, to a large degree, society itself need to shift away from past beliefs into enlightened views which will allow companies to be successful and nations to prosper. A new framework must be in place as a precursor to forming manufacturing strategy in the firm, as shown in Table 2.10.

Only when manufacturing companies have a vision which includes *at least* the above as part of their overall approach will they succeed in winning back markets and industries which have been given over to the Japanese and other world-class players. All markets now fragment at an alarming pace, with new entrants coming into them from all over the globe. For example, the biggest portion of market share in PC manufacture now comes from 'no-name' IBM clones from all areas, and major player companies like Compaq and Dell were not even in existence fifteen years ago. What is clear is that the recent fortunes of companies like General Motors and IBM have shown that old paradigms do not work and that a massive rethink has to take place in production/operations companies.

In a business world now full of uncertainty, where new entrants come into markets from all over the world, and where the rate of change is nothing short of

Table 2.10 Traditional and enlightened views of manufacturing

Key areas	*Traditional beliefs*	*Enlightened views*
Manufacturing's Importance *per se*	Local economic concern only	Of national importance
Production/operations' role within corporate strategy	Fringe – after all the corporate debate has taken place	Central to the corporate debate
Production/operations' involvement and image	Tactical and reactive	Strategic and proactive
Production/operations' role in the company	Essentially cost-cutting	Competitive weapon in factors such as delivery, flexibility, quality, design and capability
Market requirements	Static and known and, therefore, manufacturing's role is easy to determine	Volatile and changing, therefore needing high-level business skills from production/operations and not just their technical input
Product development	Driven by the marketing department	Involves a holistic effort including production at early stages of development
Process technology	A means of reducing labour	To be used alongside labour
Front-line production personnel's role	Repetitive, narrow tasks; low-level skill with little or no training	Multiskilled, a variety of roles, highly skilled, trained personnel to support the company in the market
Remuneration for front-line production personnel	Wages based on piece-work and day-rate schemes	Salary 'reward' according to skill, output quality, pay for knowledge with profit sharing and stock ownership possibilities
Alliances with other companies	R&D developments to share costs, often with hidden, secret agendas on both sides	Long-term alliances developing joint product and process improvements, including technology and improving other competitive factors such as delivery, costs, product quality, design and flexibility
Buyer–supplier relationships	Often distant and cost factors still dominate (e.g. in 1992 GM's abolition of all supplier contracts insisting that suppliers should once again 'bid' where low cost will be the dominant factor)	Long-term and committed from both sides so that both parties win as part of the overall strategy in gaining market presence. Joint ventures are mutually beneficial and go beyond just costs to other factors such as delivery speed and reliability, product quality and new designs

phenomenal, it would be simplistic and almost naive to create a static model which purports to be a panacea for successful competitive approaches. Each market segment within whole industries will have its own set of requirements and the means of winning in each of these segments will be subject to constant change and new demands. It is even too simple to speak of best practice, because this implies a target which, when reached, will ensure constant success for the firm. It is far wiser to speak in terms of a continuum, along the lines of continuous improvement in all areas of the business.

However, what becomes clear is that many organizations are almost designed *not* to be able to respond to these ever changing market demands – a major cause of this is that the hierarchical approach to strategy formulation and implementation (from corporate to marketing to production/operations in process) is too static. The ability to satisfy market requirements will, largely, depend on the operational capabilities of the firm. This demands that the production/operations' presence is felt at senior level in order to help shape the mission, strategy and policies of the firm. Once the broad strategies have been determined, there are two vital, interlinking factors that must be considered. First, the range and volumes of products, including new product development. Second, the manufacturing processes which will enable the range of products to be produced. Chapter 3 looks at production/operations' role in new product development.

Summary

- **In order to compete in markets which are now volatile, erratic and more dynamic than ever before, manufacturing firms need to be strategic, focused, and holistic in their approach.**
- **The role that production/operations plays is vital due to the weight of managerial responsibility in terms of assets utilization, costs and human resource management.**
- **Over and above this huge managerial responsibility, production/operations' contribution is vital because of the competitive advantages that can be realized if their capabilities are tied to market requirements.**
- **Generic competitive choices are essentially between low cost and differentiated products. In some markets, though, the manufacturing firm may have to do both simultaneously. In addition, other equally vital factors include delivery speed, delivery reliability, flexibility, product quality and the ability to introduce new products more quickly than competitors are able to do. All of these factors are directly related to production/operations capability to achieve them. No amount of marketing efforts can compensate for weak production/operations performance.**
- **There exists an image problem where production/operations'**

contribution will sometimes be relegated to an involvement after corporate-level decisions have already been made.

- **In Japanese and other world-class companies, production/operations' contribution to corporate planning is central. This involvement helps to guide the firm by matching the firm's core capabilities in manufacturing with market requirements. This will also enable the firm to stay out of market segments in which it cannot compete.**
- **The corporate planning process where production/operations links with marketing and R&D in an holistic approach is often sacrificed for short-term strategies based on financial criteria.**
- **For many Western companies a complete rethink In terms of how production/operations is viewed needs to take place in order to stand any chance of competing in highly competitive and very customer-driven markets.**

CASE Manufacturing strategy at Compaq

The computer industry is particularly competitive, especially in the PC segment. This was once totally dominated by IBM, but by the end of the 1980s a number of aggressive competitors had severely challenged IBM's domination. The three major competitors to attack IBM were Apple, Dell and Compaq. Apple had provided an alternative system to the IBM standard and had successfully attacked in the home-user and education areas of the PC market by producing a very user-friendly software application.

By 1992, many IBM clone-makers had entered the market. They were able to do so because barriers to entry were low, technology was easily accessible, mainly in terms of purchasing processor units from Intel and software from Microsoft and assembling the units into particular customer requirements. A breakdown of the world market share for PC units in 1992 is shown in Table 2.11.

As the *Financial Times* stated at the time:

> No-name manufacturers, mostly based in the Far East, make IBM clones. Their systems are based on powerful components easily available from a broad range of suppliers but they are produced in some cases, in garages and bedrooms. (29 October 1992, p.9)

Table 2.11 Percentage of PC units of shipments in 1992

Company	*% Units sold*
IBM	12.4
Apple	11.9
Compaq	6.6
NEC	5.1
Dell	3.5
Other	60.5

Source: Dataquest in *The Economist*, 30 January 1993, p. 58

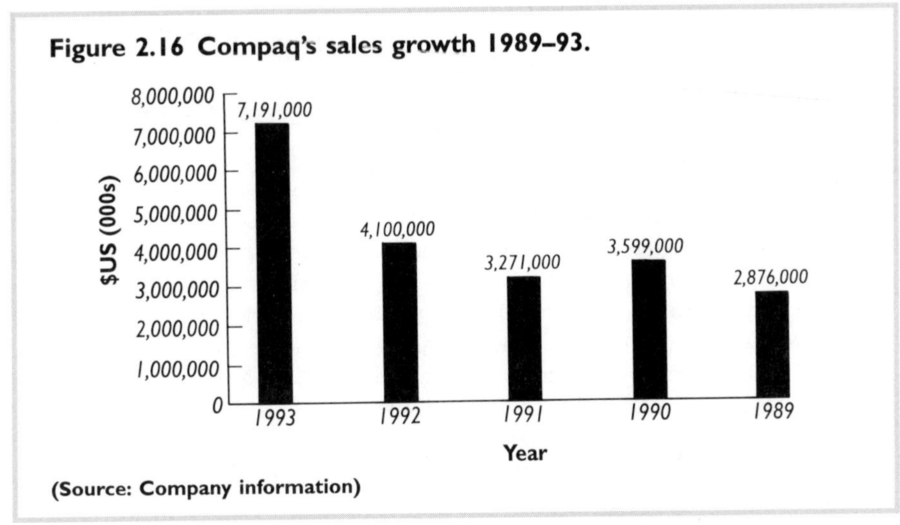

Figure 2.16 Compaq's sales growth 1989–93.

(Source: Company information)

Compaq managed to enjoy sales growth in both units and dollar value between 1989 and 1993, as shown in Figure 2.16. Its dollar sales growth rate was 25.7 per cent.

However, competition during this period continued to be severe, particularly from Dell. In addition, Compaq's profitability came under pressure.

Date	Net income ($000)
1993	462,000
1992	213,000
1991	131,000
1990	455,000
1989	333,000

(*Source*: Company Reports)

In fact, the decline in profitability in 1991 from 1990 was too much for Compaq's board and this resulted in the resignation of its founder and CEO, Rod Canion. The new CEO Eckhard Pfeiffer was appointed.

In 1992, massive price wars began to take place in the PC industry. Margins for the products became razor thin and the onus was on the manufacturers to produce low-cost PCs with added value factors such as particular customer configurations and after-sales service. In addition, rapid new product innovation was taking place with the developments of laptops, notepads and other small, but powerful units being introduced. By mid-1992, Compaq announced the introduction of forty-five new models and slashed prices by up to 32 per cent across all models. In-house production costs were reduced by 50 per cent. Equally impressive, though, was the integrated company-wide approach introduced by the new CEO.

As *Fortune* noted:

> Pfeiffer ... called weekly meetings of the company's top 125 managers to brief them on changes. Executives outside Houston listened in by phone. (14 December 1992, p.80)

Prior to the new approach, the three Compaq factories – in Houston, Singapore and Erskine in Scotland – had been underutilized. By 1994, however, the factories were working 24 hours per day. An integrated approach involving marketing, suppliers, design and production/operations helped to reduce costs on design, assembly and materials usage. Organizational complacency had been a factor; like other giant corporations, Compaq had begun to believe its own good business press. Now, however, Compaq has a culture of being totally customer-driven. Production/operations has been central to these dramatic improvements: product and process quality remains high; prices were reduced by an annual rate of 30 per cent between 1992 and 1994. In 1994 it introduced yet another product – the Aero subnotebook. This was launched to compete against IBM's Thinkpad 500, and did so by being priced $500 under the IBM model. Plants run just-in-time methods (described further in Chapter 6) to meet delivery speed, quality and cost requirements. Manufacturing has been rearranged into cells of manufacture rather than long production lines. Also, new plants were being constructed in China and Brazil. Between November 1991 and November 1993, Compaq quadrupled its manufacturing output with its existing facilities in the three manufacturing plants. Compaq had set their sights on beating IBM in PC manufacture. In 1994 they did just that and did so by having a manufacturing strategy which was clear, focused and customer-driven. In doing so they became the world's largest PC producers in 1994 (see Table 2.12).

Table 2.12 Percentage of PC units of shipments in 1992

Company	*1994 units (000s)*	*% share*	*% growth 1993/94*
Compaq	4830	10	56
IBM	4227	8.7	0
Apple	4125	8.5	12
Packard Bell	2285	4.7	103
NEC	1706	3.5	12
AST	1285	2.6	18
Dell	1233	2.5	7
Toshiba	1231	2.5	65
Hewlett Packard	1221	2.5	84
Acer	1190	2.5	63
Others	25167	51.9	25

Source: *Financial Times*, 5 April 1995

3 Issues in new product development

3.1 Introduction

This chapter looks at the role and importance of production/operations in new product development, as opposed to process development, which is discussed in Chapter 4. In reality, process and product developments are dependent upon each other and have to complement each other in order for the company to succeed. Technology links the two because *successfully* applied R&D will manifest itself either in process or product developments or indeed in both, as shown in Figure 3.1

In short, process developments are changes that enhance the methods of producing a product or service; product innovations are changes in the actual outputs. Managing the interface between process and product technology represents one of the biggest challenges to manufacturing firms. Technology processes (discussed in Chapter 4) must be in place to support the product. Successful management of this product/process link can come about by the firm's in-house

Figure 3.1 Linking process and product innovation.

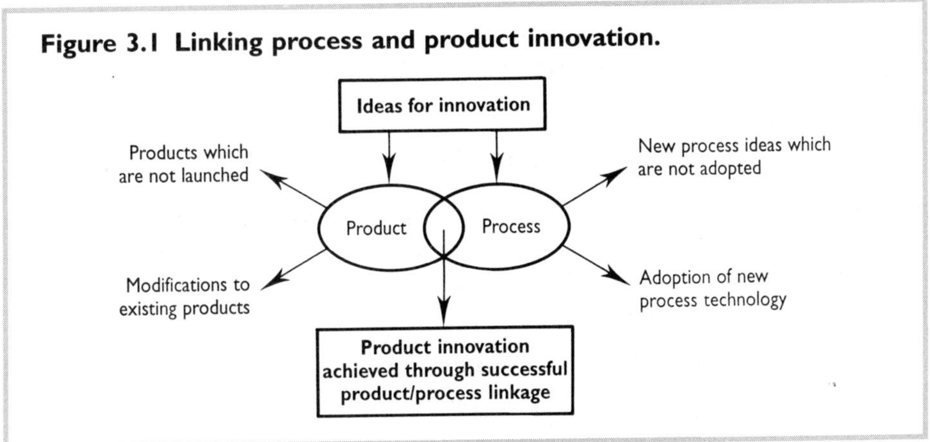

experience and by learning which might be gained from alliances with other firms.

It is important to note that once a product is launched, it is largely under the responsibility of production/operations to ensure that the range, volume and mix of products can be met on an ongoing basis. The link with marketing is vital here; feedback on product performance for customers has to be known by the firm so that it can improve its performance. This becomes increasingly important and indeed critical, when new products are launched; the mix of existing and new products has to be managed to ensure that customer requirements are met in terms of volumes, delivery speed, delivery reliability and any other pertinent market requirement.

New product developments on an ongoing basis and the speed of new development are very important for many industries but critical for two: telecommunications and computing, due to the short lifecycle of their products. For example, when Dell lapsed in terms of speed required for developing a new product – the Notebook – it paid the ultimate penalty by having to withdraw temporarily from this segment. In addition, because of the reduced product lifecycles of the PC products, Dell was left with a stock of obsolete components. Similarly, when IBM was late with the ThinkPad laptops, it immediately lost out to competitors, particularly Compaq and Hewlett Packard. IBM was also left with something like $100 million of components which it *had* to design into future products. Also, the delay of the PS/2 models meant that IBM had not launched a new product between early 1993 and mid-1994, which was way behind the other competitors who recognized the speed of ongoing development and product innovation as a requirement to compete.

3.1.1 New product development and organizational learning

New product development becomes a key element of organizational learning; this vital factor (learning) is discussed in depth in Chapter 7. Opportunities for learning come in a number of ways including:

1. Assessing the current development process that the firm uses and improving this in order to increase the speed and successful implementation of development.
2. Forming partnerships with other firms which are specifically aimed at product development, rather than process developments (the latter being exemplified at NUMMI and the Rover–Honda alliance).
3. Learning from past failures.

In terms of new products, it is clear that firms learn by benchmarking against other firms: Renault dismantled BMW, Mercedes and other cars in order to learn how to improve product technology; General Motors (GM) does the same with Japanese cars sold in the United States and Ford used technological learning to provide benchmarking characteristics which was at the core of the design to the Taurus and Mercury Sable models.

New product development provides an excellent means of learning from competitors and failure to learn can be disastrous. Carroll (1993) points to IBM's failure to learn from Compaq:

> Even once Compaq brought out its portable, IBM was so sure it understood the technology that it didn't buy a single Compaq system to see whether there was anything to be learned from it. When IBM brought its system out more than a year after Compaq . . . the system was too heavy and the screen was fuzzy. It died quickly . . . IBM relegated itself to a tiny slice of what became a $6-billion-a-year market by the early 1990's. (p.71)

The fate of IBM reveals the biggest insight into competing in the 1990s; the sheer power of IBM's marketing had caused it to become the standard for the industry. For a while, IBM depended very much on its own brand name and saw this as almost sufficient. However, from the 1980s a whole new group of competitors entered the market. At the core of their strategy was manufacturing capability, which included the ability to rapidly introduce new products on an ongoing basis. Outdated views based on high-volume scale (centred around existing products) quickly became replaced by enlightened approaches based upon rapid new product development, product reliability and low cost. All of these owe much to production/operations to provide these capabilities, admittedly as part of a company-wide, holistic approach, discussed later in the chapter. Once customers were able to have greater choice (provided by the introduction of alternative products from new entrants), computer customers could discern that IBM's PCs were not superior in design or technology and costs were higher.

Predicting the intensity of competition is difficult; entry barriers into certain segments of the computer industry are now low and, hence, the biggest constituent of the market for personal computers is with 'no-name' IBM clones which accounted for something in the region of 60 per cent of this market segment between 1989 and 1994.

Competition for both the computer and telecommunications industries is intense and the demand for new products is immense. However, it can be just as problematic in terms of *underestimation* of market requirements; in 1983 AT&T had predicted that cellular phones would not have more than one million users by the year 2000; there were, in fact, sixteen million users in 1993. Clearly, the ability to respond quickly to such changes in market demands – especially increased volume requirements – will largely depend upon production/operations. The role of forecasting is discussed with some humour by Starbuck (1993) in his article which questions the value of formal planning. He quotes IBM's former CEO, Thomas Watson who, in 1948, had stated:

> I think there is a world market for about five computers. (p.79)

Starbuck also humorously uses the statement from Bohr:

prediction is very difficult, especially about the future. (p.81)

As stated earlier it is, largely, production/operations who will manage this unpredictability in manufacturing products. More than ever before, products must be made in various volumes and configurations. In addition, product lifecycles are diminishing as new products come into the market, replacing products which in some high-tech industries might have been launched only a short while before.

3.2 A brief overview of reasons for new product launches

Generic reasons for launching new products might include:

- Meeting or even creating consumer demands – The latter being very common in telecommunications and computing where demand is created by technology 'push', which is discussed later in the chapter.
- Maintaining current levels of sales which might not be possible with current products at the end of their product lifecycle. As products reach the saturation and declining stages, volumes decrease. This means that existing capacity is often available which can become an opportunity, provided the company can exploit this. If not, capacity becomes an overhead and, therefore, a cost.
- Improving profitability – This is a factor where markets are saturated and no price increases can be realized without loss of sales. As margins become squeezed and volume increases are not possible, this means that profitability is threatened. Introducing new products therefore becomes a requirement in terms of generating income for the company.
- The firm might enjoy a 'first-to-market' reputation which it wants to continue; alternatively, the firm might be a rapidly responsive, 'me-too' player which could bring about competitive advantage over the first-to-market firm.
- Competitive requirements – The intense competition within high-tech industries means that there is no option but to continuously generate new products. For example, as part of the research undertaken by the author, twenty firms within the computing and telecommunications industries were asked two questions:

1. 'How much of the present sales turnover has been derived from products launched within the last five years?' To which all replied 'Between 60 and 80 per cent.'
2. 'In five years time, what proportion of turnover do you envisage from products yet to be launched?' Again, all stated 'Over 80 per cent.'

Products will either be proactive, first-to-market or me-too and reactive in nature – a simple matrix of the car and computing industries illustrates this division (Table 3.1).

However, as we will see later, being innovative is not by itself sufficient. The

Table 3.1 Examples of proactive versus reactive innovations

	Computing	*Cars*
Proactive	Apple, Commodore 'PET' and Tandy TRS microcomputers	Ford Sierra's aerodynamic shape
Reactive	ICL and IBM PC's	Vauxhall Astra's similar shape

is then faced with competing against substitute/alternative products from competitors whose cost structure might be lower or whose ability to compete in other ways such as delivery may be better than the innovating company. Kenney and Florida (1993) observe how, initially, Japanese firms out-performed others by copying, rather than creating new products:

> Japanese companies began to rebuild their R&D capacity by the early to mid-1950s. Initially, much of this was directed at imitation, reverse engineering and process development. For example, Sony secured access to the transistor developed at AT&T's Bell Laboratories and developed a transistor radio that proved an enormous commercial success. (p.55)

It is argued throughout this book that this success is largely dependent upon production/operations capability to out-perform competitors. It is also argued that much of the failure of product development has to do with production/operations being brought in too late into the development process. The winners of the future will be those manufacturing firms which, amongst other factors, recognize this and use this as part of their organizational learning and development. Being a reactive firm (see Table 3.1) is not necessarily a problem, provided that the manufacturing firm quickly emulates the proactive firm's technology and out-competes the innovator in other competitive areas – range of products, delivery speed and/or reliability, flexibility and cost. These competitive factors will largely be realized by the capability of production/operations and are things that a firm does via its operations' capability.

3.3 The strategic importance of new product development

In Chapter 1, it was stated that strategic decisions are those where:

1. Top management within the firm are involved and where they tend to have the ultimate decision-making responsibility.
2. There is a relatively long-term time horizon in terms of commitment from and implications for the firm.
3. The decisions are essentially seen as a means of creating competitive advantage for the firm.

These three criteria are central to successful new product development.

As Allen (1993) states:

> today the initial product planning conceptual framework and the decision surrounding it should be seen as a company-wide activity. This means it should be carried out on behalf of top management or the board, not performed separately from the main line, strategic thrust of the company. Perhaps it is a lack of understanding of this key principle that has led to the fall of many product planning dynasties in British, American and European companies. (p.27)

Without new products being offered on an ongoing basis, other factors such as low cost and delivery reliability are largely of secondary importance. This is not a new concept, nor is it confined to high-tech industries – Ford lost market share and leadership to GM in the 1920s because of its inability (and unwillingness) to introduce new models. Ford concentrated on scale economies rather than creating a range of models which GM managed to do. New products are therefore of strategic importance for the company, because without them the company's revenues will decline and the firm will cease to be competitive. Moreover, the company's image will be tarnished, market share will be lost and all other indicators of performance will be under threat. This is particularly true of IBM which has lost two-thirds of its market value, around $70 billion, since 1987 (*Fortune*, 14 June, 1993, p.58)

The vital competitive importance of new product development versus other competitive factors is highlighted by Allen (1993):

> In the Nineties, almost for the first time, we are seeing a greater concentration on product development as one of the key areas of company operations. (p.2)

and the reasons for the gulf between Western and Japanese firms is clear:

> it was not just labour efficiency, harder work . . . or lower design cost products that gave Japan the edge, but rather, their whole way of conceiving, designing and producing. (p.3)

The threefold approach advocated in Chapter 2, is pertinent here; Japanese firms (and in fact any world-class player) are holistic, focused and strategic in their decision-making approach when it comes to developing and launching new products. For all of Japan's superiority in process technology, it is their product offerings which have determined success in the market, in terms of product quality and reliability, together with product range and low cost.

3.3.1 New products as a competitive factor

New products are essential for the firm. It is the products themselves which make the company's presence felt in markets – production/operations and marketing efforts are there to ensure the success of the products. Before products are launched, therefore, they must be seen as a strategic factor under the heading of opportunities for the company. The urgency for rapid and constant product innovations is discussed by Lancaster and Massingham (1993):

> Today, most organizations must either innovate or go out of business. Clearly, then, innovation and the new product development which such innovation gives rise to is not just desirable but is essential to long-term market and competitive success. (p.128)

Davidson (1987) puts this more bluntly:

> The most important principle of product development, beside which all others pale, is that no other corporate activity matters more. Consumers buy product benefits, not advertising and promotions and the surest, and sometimes the easiest, route to corporate growth is through product superiority. (p.185)

The message is clear: new product development is an absolute requirement to competing successfully:

> Firms that get to market faster and more efficiently with products that are well matched to the needs and expectations of target customers create significant competitive leverage. Firms (that do not) . . . are destined to see their market position erode and financial performance falter. (Hayes and Wheelwright, 1992, p.1)

Rapid new product developments can also act as a means of fighting off aggressive competitors. For example, Honda's motorcycles fought off Yamaha's challenge by introducing or replacing 113 models compared to Yamaha's 37 in the same 18-month period. Honda's strategy caused sales to soar, while the effect upon Yamaha was devastating. It was also a strong signal to the likes of Suzuki and Kawasaki not to challenge Honda's supremacy. The fruits borne by being first to market with a new product are not confined to high-tech industries; Chrysler's innovative minivan was a 'crown jewel' (Chrysler's terminology) for the firm. Since the launch in 1983, Chrysler has practically owned the market segment – Ford and GM have been late to respond to this segment – and sales of the Voyager, Town and Country and Dodge Caravans have outsold many competitors' passenger cars in the United States. The minivan stands as a triumph for innovation brought about by a product champion (Iacocca) and a company-wide vision and effort. Sales of the Chrysler minivan since 1983 amounted to 3.7 million units by 1995, compared to 1.42 million for GM models and 1.44 million for Ford's units.

3.3.2 Targeting new products

By targeting products in focused market segments, the firm can gain advantage in the following ways:

1. **Going geographically where existing competitors have little or no presence** The opening of opportunities in markets such as the former Soviet Union is such a case.
2. **Attacking segments where marketing efforts are weak or neglected** This is true of the PC market segment, when Apple attacked where IBM had not paid sufficient attention: the education and home-user segments.
3. **Attacking by offering perceived added quality features** In this way, the firm can seek to differentiate its products from other firms in, for example, a low-cost segment where value added is perceived by the buyers. This has been the area in which the 'big three' car makers in America have enjoyed success models such as Chrysler's Cirrus, Dodge Stratus and Ford's Contour and Mercury Mystiques all have enhanced quality features which, a few years ago, might have been seen as (temporary) differentiated features. The reason for their renewed launches is to attack where Japanese quality has been most esteemed – the midsized, midpriced cars – in particular, the Honda Accord and Toyota Camry.
4. **Attacking where there is little brand loyalty** In the PC market segment, price is a major order-winning factor; little or no brand loyalty exists. Similarly, GM's decline has shown the somewhat fragile nature of brand loyalty within the car industry. GM's response has been largely a call for Americans to 'buy American'; even if this call to patriotism is successful, this may not result in more sales for GM; Ford and Chrysler may benefit instead.
5. **Attacking where there are gaps in the product line** Peters (1986) narrates how GM had been 'nibbled to death' since the 1970s by competitors who were offering models which GM neglected in its own product range. This includes important products such as four-wheel drives, turbos, minivans and subcompact cars.

In terms of competing on products Thompson and Strickland (1992) advise:

> As a rule, attacks on competitor weaknesses have a better chance of succeeding than attacks on competitor strengths, provided the weaknesses represent important vulnerabilities and the rival is caught by surprise with no ready defence. (p.115)

Clearly, this was the case in both GM's loss of market share, losing out to domestic and Japanese competitors which attacked where GM's presence was weak. This is ironic in view of GM's success against Ford in the 1920s, cited earlier. It would appear that learning both by failure or success (as in GM's success against Ford in the 1920s) can be *unlearned*. This is not surprising here, given that seventy years had elapsed. However, GM's success could have formed part of the story culture – a success story known and understood by its employees. If it had done so then, perhaps, the same mistake could have been avoided and it could, instead, have sought out areas of product innovation.

Failure to learn can come about by complacency, made worse by the size of the company and the arrogance that this can sometimes bring. The unlearning has been noticeable in the computing industry. Success stories of the 1980s – IBM, DEC and Wang, in particular – have shown that size of company and successful innovation are not one and the same thing.

Speed of product innovation is central to telecommunications equipment, and Motorola clearly showed this as a competitive advantage when it produced its pocket-sized cellular phone in 1989. By the time other competitors had entered – in 1991 – Motorola had sold over $1 billion worth of phones. Speed of development – aside of the required, ongoing, frequency – for products is a vital factor which provides competitive advantage. Speed is relative, of course; in telecommunications/computing speed is measured in terms of weeks or months; in the car industry, speed is measured in terms of years.

Car firms line up products to compete directly against each other in the same segment. For example, in Europe, the revamped 1994 Volkswagen Polo was launched to compete against the Ford Fiesta, Vauxhall Corsa and Fiat Punto. In order to compete *at all* within this segment, Volkswagen had to increase the level of its standard features to include five doors, automatic transmission, anti-lock braking, power-assisted steering, driver and passenger airbags, air conditioning, electric windows and central locking. Only a short time before, these features would have been seen as differentiated; in the 1990s and beyond the product quality requirements are always increasing and must be seen as the minimum requirement. What might have been order-winning factors can become mere order-qualifying criteria, as competitors copy the innovating firm over a period of time.

New products become a means of reasserting a presence in the market. For GM, new or redesigned products became the focus for Chevrolet, whose 16 per cent of market share in 1994 showed a decline since 1990. The response from Chevrolet was aggressive, launching three cars:

1. **Midsize Lumina** To compete against the Ford Taurus, Chrysler's LH Sedans, Honda Accord and Toyota Camry.
2. **Compact Cavalier** Positioned in the segment including Ford Escort, Chrysler's Neon, Toyota Corolla, Nissan Sentra and Honda Civic.
3. **Sub-compact sport Blazer** Pitched against the Ford Explorer and Jeep Grand Cherokee.

The role of manufacturing in all three was vital, most noticeably in the Lumina segment:

> Chevy can make a profit at such aggressive prices because the new models cost less to manufacture. The 1995 Lumina has 900 fewer parts than its predecessor and takes 30% less labor to assemble. (*Business Week*, 25 July 1994, p.71)

It must be said, however, that the role of production/operations as an early input into the development process is still untapped by many firms. We shall see that the 'big three' US car makers have learned, gradually, that production/operations involvement is central and crucial, rather than reactive and peripheral. This shift represents one of the greatest developments in Western manufacturing – learning to think laterally and holistically, rather than the traditional, sequential, function-to-function approach. Clearly, new product development is a strategic factor. To have production/operations involvement kept at bay is at worst suicidal and will at best serve only to launch products which are late to market, sometimes overdesigned, and often with oncosts added in order to pay for the cost of long development.

3.3.3 New products as a facet in quality enhancement

New product development within the car industry emerged as a feature of the firm's required quality offering in the 1990s. The added quality concept is *miryokuteki hinshitsu* which in Japanese means providing customer fascination and delight, not simply ensuring required features such as safety and reliability. This goes beyond Taguchi (1986) who talks of 'designing in quality', because the Taguchi approach was mainly concerned with features such as reliability and consistency. This development – customer delight – means that the absence of defects becomes *assumed* (through process technology) and the main thrust comes by adding significant technological advances (product technology). Examples of this enhancement of product delight, which is an enhanced quality factor in the car industry are given in Table 3.2.

However, it is a massive statement on how far behind GM continued to lag in product and process development when the GM Saturn model, which had supposedly been a major challenge to Japanese quality, had to be recalled in August 1993 because of potential major fire hazard problems in the ignition system. The cost of this complete recall was estimated at over $8 million in repair costs alone. It remains to be seen how much damage has been caused to future sales, together with the blemished image of GM's products. The assumption of

Table 3.2 Examples of customer delight features in the car industry

- Nissan's Infiniti Q45 produced the first 'active' suspension, whereby the hydraulics levelled out the car when cornering
- Honda's Accord liquid-filled engine mount dissipates engine vibration while idling
- Honda's door locks, stereo buttons, indicators and other equipment are designed to require the exact pressure to move them, giving the car a more comfortable feel and enjoyable experience
- Suzuki's LS 400 instrument panel has won over many customers with its neon pointers and other lights that seem to 'float in space'
- The Mercedes 500 SL has a filter which sifts out pollen to 5 microns and a residual engine warmth to maintain the interior heat in short journeys

Source: 'A New Era for Auto Quality', *Business Week:*, 22 October 1990

process quality as an assumed feature in products is still not the case for a number of major companies in the West.

Customer expectations have risen enormously since the 1980s due in part to greater performance levels from production/operations in firms. Hayes and Wheelwright (1992) identify this in the computer industry when they state:

> In addition to the explosion of variety, firms in the hard disk drive industry have to meet demands for dramatic increases in reliability (tenfold in five years) and decreases in cost (5 percent to 8 percent quarterly). (p4)

3.4 The role of R&D in new product development

3.4.1 *Technology push and market pull*

Developing new products arises both from technology push from the provider (manufacturer) and market pull, where the firm responds to customer needs and desires. These two factors are not mutually exclusive as might be implied by the terms push and pull but rather flow into each other, as shown in Figure 3.2

Products provide income for and represent the companies in the market. Their role, therefore, is fundamental to the growth and success of a company. A problem – and opportunity – for high-tech firms is that they are researching products for which, possibly, no market currently exists. Rosenbloom and Cusamano (1987) state that Sony's approach with the VCR was clearly along push lines, aside of any market research: 'You can't research a market for a product that doesn't exist' (p.16) – and Johansson and Nonaka (1987) discuss how the push approach comes from Japan's distrust of Western types of marketing research:

> (the CEO at Sony's), disdain for large-scale consumer surveys and other scientific research tools isn't unique in Japan. Matsushita, Toyota and other well-known consumer goods companies are just as sceptical about the Western style of market research. (p.16)

Honda, for example, does not have a marketing department. Part of this approach owes much to Japan's view of manufacturing as part of the competitive

Figure 3.2 The 'push-pull' cycle in innovation.

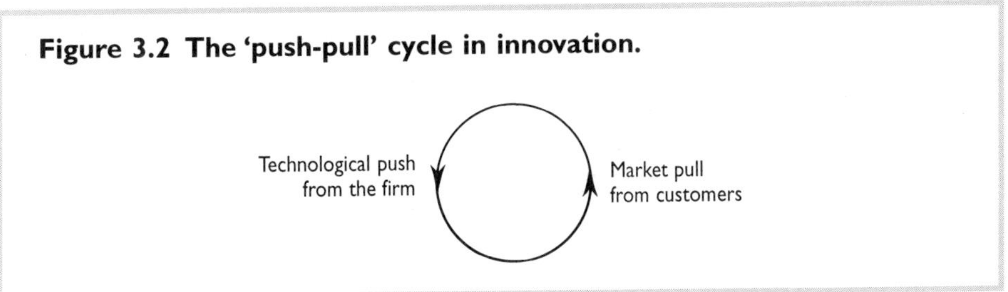

offering – Twiss (1992) observes how Canon's 'view of the transfer process starts with the need to master key areas technology' (p.9). The mastering of technology centres on the interface of technology innovation with manufacturing capability.

3.4.2 *The role of patents*

The source for new product ideas is wide and will include suppliers, competitors, sales/marketing personnel, government needs, customers and the firm's R&D activity. From this can come enhancement to existing products or ideas for entirely new products. Another area is the creation of patents, which the firm will own and then license. Patents can act as a means of advantage, because other firms will be dependent upon the firm who owns the patent; exclusive ownership rights are up to seventeen years in the United States and can act as a barrier to entry, provided that the patent is not mimicked in another form. The role of patents can also serve as part of any firm's technological scanning where the firm scans global technological trends on an ongoing basis. However, the success of the patent is down to the firm's ability to establish the patent product as a standard; Matsushita did so with the VHS standard, which allowed them to create vast numbers of licensing agreements.

Twiss (1992) concludes:

> both technology push and market pull have an important part to play in successful innovation . . . this can only be achieved by a close relationship between . . . the technologist and the marketer. (p.9)

The technologist must also link closely with production/operations on whom the firm will largely depend in terms of transferring ideas and prototypes into volume manufacturing. Only if this transition becomes successful will the firm gain or hold existing market share and fight off competitors in market segments in which new products are targeted.

3.4.3 *R&D and new product development*

Success in technology push comes from linking R&D with manufacturing capability. The inability to do so will result in failure. Applied technology becomes a reality only when turned into volume products; Ohmae (1990) suggests that the failure rate of company R&D is as much as 90 per cent.

It is hardly surprising that expenditure on R&D in industries such as car, computing and telecommunications is enormous. For example, IBM's research expenditure is shown in Table 3.3.

Sustained R&D seems to be very dependent upon volume in the computing and telecommunications industries. For example, Intel produced 40 million 486 chips in 1992, together with a relatively small number of the Pentium chips-volume (and profit margins) enables Intel to invest $2.5 billion annually in R&D

Table 3.3 IBM's R&D Expenditure: 1990–1994

Year	*Amount ($ millions)*
1990	620
1991	620
1992	600
1993	550
1994	500

Source: Author's interviews with IBM

and new plant capacity. To compete at all R&D investment is central and, as *Fortune* observes:

> For almost everyone else (other than Intel) the economics of chipmaking seems daunting. It costs nearly $1 billion to build a state-of-the-art microprocessor plant, and with each new generation of technology, the cost doubles. (14 June, 1993, p.74)

It falls to the role of R&D technology, linking with manufacturing capability, to ensure that products do reach markets and are sustainable. Technology is the application of scientific knowledge to a new product, process or service.

Total spending of R&D in selected companies shows the vast amounts incurred (Table 3.4). R&D expenditure is a requirement to compete; breakthroughs in process and product development will only come as a result of this or by forming alliances with other firms. What is clear, however, is that – unfortunately for the firms – there is little or no evidence to suggest that a linear relationship exists between amounts of expenditure and company performance. For example, GM has steadily lost US market share in spite of massive expenditure on R&D.

3M invests 6.5 per cent of its annual sales in R&D – twice the percentage of the average company (Kotler, 1994) and Hewlett-Packard spends 10 per cent of sales

Table 3.4 R&D expenditure of selected companies for 1993

Company	*1993 R&D expenditure ($ millions)*
General Motors	6,030
Ford	5,021
AT&T	3,428
DEC	1,530
Motorola	1,521

Source: Standard & Poor's Compustat 1994

on R&D as a matter of policy (source: Author's interviews). Technology becomes a means by which firms compete, and have to compete on a global basis:

> automobiles, and semiconductors are examples of industries where advances in technology are so costly that global sales are necessary in order to remain competitive. (Dussauge *et al.*, 1992, p.31)

Applied R&D does not have to centre on the development of one product only. Volume centred on the basis of one product is not the aim of technological development. As Dussauge *et al.* add:

> technological innovations often bring costs down – sometimes significantly – thus making the cost reduction solely attributable to economies of scale seem comparatively minor. (p.47)

3.4.4 Basic technology strategies

Over 80 per cent of R&D is still undertaken by large firms employing more than 5000 persons (Krajewski and Ritzman, 1992). In simplistic terms, a company is either a technological leader or technological follower. Porter (1985) provides a matrix which plots basic technology strategy against generic strategies, as shown in Table 3.5.

We have to be a little careful with the matrix, though. The idea that cost and differentiation are mutually exclusive is not as appropriate for the 1990s as it might have been for the 1980s and before. World-class competitors do both. Some firms have been able to achieve both at the same time and have gained market share and profitability in doing so; the Japanese success in a number of industries demonstrates that low cost and differentiation are compatible. However, the matrix does indicate the importance of learning; the follower enters the market or introduces a substitute product by learning from the innovator.

One factor that should be kept in mind with IBM is that, perhaps surprisingly given its R&D expenditure, it has often been a me-too company, following what

Table 3.5 Technology and competitive advantage

	Technological leadership	*Technological followership*
Cost advantage	Pioneer the lowest cost product design	Lower the cost of the product or value activities by learning from the leader's experience
	Create low-cost ways of performing value activities	Avoid R&D costs through imitation
Differentiation	Pioneer a unique product that increases buyer value. Innovate in other activities to increase buyer value	Adapt the product or delivery system more closely to buyer needs by learning from the leader's experience

Table 3.6 Examples of IBM's reactions to technological innovation

Product	*Pioneering company*	*Date*	*IBM's product*	*Date*	*Gap (years)*
Mini computer	Digital PDP-8	1965	IBM series I	1976	11
Personal Computer	Apple	1977	IBM PC	1981	4
Engineering workstation	Apollo DN100	1981	IBM RT PC	1986	5
PC Laptop	Toshiba T-100	1986	IBM L40	1991	5
RISC workstation	Sun Microsystems	1987	IBM RS/6000	1990	3

other companies have pioneered. Admittedly, by virtue of its size and power (in the past at least), its launch of products in certain areas would mean that an IBM standard had been created. However, its past has been one of reaction to product innovation, rather than pioneering, despite $25 billion spent on R&D between 1982 and 1992. Table 3.6 shows the me-too approach which served IBM in the past. It did not need to be first to market because of the brand loyalty that it once enjoyed. However, the PC segment in the 1990s had little brand loyalty and IBM has been forced to react far more quickly than before.

In the past the strategy was possible; in the 1990s IBM has struggled in a way best summarized by *Fortune*:

> In a mature industry, it has had a hard time keeping up with innovative competitors that have made some of its products look like dinosaurs. (27 July 1992, p.49)

3.4.5 *R&D development strategies*

A major decision for the firm is in its R&D strategy. Not every company is in a position to go it alone and others simply do not wish to do so. Costs for R&D are huge and therefore companies face a range of possibilities in developing new products, shown in Table 3.7. These options can be both stand alone and complementary in the firm's R&D strategy.

Table 3.7 Types of technology development strategies

Internal development
Purchasing or 'buying' decisions in technology
Contracted development
Licensing
Technology trading
Joint ventures/collaboration

- **Internal development** This will be exclusively for the organization and no sharing of technology or new products will be forthcoming; patents can be an integral part of the organization's strategy here.
- **Acquisitions in technology** This is where a company simply acquires the technology that it needs either as a process or product which might form part of another product within the organization's product portfolio. GM's purchase of the computer company, EDS as a means of modernizing its own information technology is such a case.
- **Contracted development** Where a company lacks the in-house skills or does not have the time or resources to devote to development, this can be contracted out to independent laboratories, universities or other government agencies. In this way, the firm stays with its core business. The firm can if necessary then abandon research with relatively low costs.
- **Licensing** This is where a company allows other companies to use the process or products for which the licensing organization owns the patent; Matsushita's VHS dominated over Beta technology through this approach, which then allowed other producers easy access to this technology via licensing.
- **Technology trading** This is common in the US steel industry, where know-how is swapped in terms of cross-training among the companies. This is not welcome in some industries, but has become more commonplace due to the high costs of developing technology independently.
- **Joint ventures/collaboration** This is where two or more companies pursue specific new technology development. Ideally each party comes with different skills and the two then complement each other; this is common in the car industry, with Rover–Honda and the GM/Toyota NUMMI project being examples. Joint ventures are increasing and are common in many industries.

Harrigan (1986) states how:

> In today's global business environment of scarce resources, rapid rates of technological change, and rising capital requirements, the important question is no longer, 'shall we form a joint venture?'. Now the question is, 'Which joint ventures and cooperative arrangements are most appropriate for our needs and expectations' . . . followed by 'How do we manage these ventures most effectively?' (p.10)

Mowery (1988) made an interesting distinction in terms of developments of collaboration; telecommunications' alliances were largely based around joint *product* development and innovation; alliances in the car industry tended to be in terms of *process* developments. However, in both industries, another explicit gain has to be mentioned – notably access to geographical markets. Toyota's link with GM (NUMMI) was largely motivated by this. This was in addition to GM's motive: process learning. Rover's link with Honda was essentially motivated by the need to learn from Honda's process capabilities. Other reasons for collaborating will

Table 3.8 Examples of joint ventures in the car industry

- Ford's Festiva, which was designed in the United States, was engineered by Mazda in Japan. However, it is actually being built by Kai in Korea for the US market
- Ford owns 25% of Mazda; Mazda owns 8% of Kai; Ford, in turn, owns 10% of Kai; Ford and Volkswagen have a jointly managed holding company, Autoina, which involves over 15 plants in South America
- The Mercury Capri was designed by Ghia and Italdesign in Italy; it is assembled in Australia, essentially from Japanese components, for the US market
- Ford's Probe car was designed in the United States, engineered by Mazda and is assembled in Mazda's US plant
- GM's Pontiac LeMans is very similar to the German-designed Opel Kadett. However, the LeMans is fabricated by Daewoo in Korea
- Chrysler has part-ownership in Mitsubishi; GM owns part of both Suzuki and Isuzu

Source: Author's interviews

include any cost, speed, creating technical standards, technological learning and technological diversification.

However, Mowery's (1988) distinction between product developments in telecommunications and process developments in the car industry is not strictly true. In the car industry, the role of joint ventures in terms of new *product* development is clear from the following examples shown in Table 3.8.

Joint ventures – including, in some cases cited above, part ownership – are common in the car industry. The joint ventures in the telecommunications and computing industries tend to be joint funding of R&D expenditure in particular projects, rather than ownership of shares in each other's companies. In fact, ownership of another company in order to 'buy into' a new market segment seems to be less successful than joint ventures or internal developments. Ford's purchase of Jaguar, and GM's purchase of Saab seem to be less successful than Nissan's development of Infiniti, or Toyota with their Lexus, or Honda with their Accura. Cordero (1991) suggests that purchasing another company, rather than development, is a last option, to be used only where companies are so far behind competitors that they cannot innovate or develop new products competitively.

Table 3.9 gives examples of alliances in the computer industry.

The last example, ICL/Fujitsu, is more of a purchase than an alliance, because Fujitsu owns 80 per cent of ICL. However, the purchase is not one of total ownership and, in that sense, the link is more of a partnership than acquisition.

In telecommunications, a number of alliances have been formed as a means of entering, developing or remaining, in key segments. A good example of this is MCI, as Table 3.10 shows.

The MCI example shows the desire to compete in a number of segments coupled with an unwillingness to do so alone.

Table 3.9 Examples of alliances in the computer industry

Companies	*Focus of Alliance*
Sun/ICL	RISC technology via Sun's 'Sparc' system
IBM/Motorola/Apple	Power PC chips to compete against Intel
IBM/Toshiba	$200 billion plant in Japan to manufacture high-resolution colour flat screens for laptops
IBM/Siemens	Joint production of 16 megabit DRAM memory chip in IBM France
IBM/Mitsubishi	Mitsubishi sells IBM mainframes under its own name by an arrangement which augments IBM's own sales
IBM	Intel: joint development of new generations of microprocessors
IBM/Apple	Joint ventures especially in multimedia technology that merges data, graphics and video
Fujitsu's/ICL	ICL provides Fujitsu with workstations and PC's for sale in both Japan and worldwide markets. ICL has also become involved in improving Fujitsu's mainframe systems – already regarded as 'the world's best mainframe designer' (*FT*, 17 March, 1992 (Survey p.v)

Much merger and acquisition activity took place in the telecommunications industry in the 1990s, as shown in Table 3.11.

3.5 New product developments and related industries

Computing and telecommunications products tend to be launched from a technological push approach, rather than simply responding to customer feedback to products already launched (*Forbes Industry Survey*, 29 March 1993). New products are not launched in isolation, but are often related to associated industries. For example, both the computing and telecommunications industries are dependent upon developments in microprocessor technology. Any breakthroughs in this, especially from major microprocessor suppliers like Intel, will have great impact upon the two industries. The role of suppliers is discussed in depth in Chapter 6. However, a discussion of the importance of the buyer–supplier relationship in new product development is pertinent here.

Table 3.10 A sample of MCI's alliances in 1994

Type of market/development	*Alliance*
Wireless: mobile radio services	17% stake in Nextel Communications
High-speed digital network	Stentor, Canada
Global network services	BT owns 20%; $4.3 billion in MCI

Source: Author's interview with MCI Communications Corporation

Saxenian (1991) argues that alliances with 'innovative suppliers' are hard for other players to emulate. This depends to what extent the supplier is locked in to the buyer. Intel's chips have become the key ingredient for IBM clone manufacturers, all of whom are locked into the supplier relationship with Intel. However, Intel's involvement has been central at key points in product innovation in the computer industry. For example, in 1986, Compaq had formed a strong link with Intel, whose 80386 chip was faster and performed better in every competitive variable against IBM's AT machine. From then on, IBM's marketing efforts alone would no longer be able to convince customers that there was

Table 3.11 Examples of mergers and acquisitions in the telecommunications industry

- Northern Telecom established a strong presence in Europe as a result of acquiring STC
- Bell Canada (BCE) acquired a 20% holding in Mercury Communications and, as part of the deal, Cable & Wireless, Mercury's parent, became a partner in BCE's UK cable TV business
- Thomson's exit from the industry, which was a French Government ruling, meant that much of the activity was taken over by Alcatel, the subsidiary of Compagnie Générale d'Electricité. Alacatel then purchased the European business of ITT and the French group thus took the leading position in Europe
- Ericsson took over Compagnie Générale des Constructions Telephoniques after fighting off potential bids from AT&T and Siemens
- AT&T entered the European market from which it had been formerly excluded through American anti-trust legislation. AT&T bought a 50% stake in APT a jointly held company with Philips. AT&T has invested heavily in the manufacture of multiplex equipment in western Europe as part of this deal
- AT&T also developed a partnership agreement with Italtel, designed to develop digital switching technology in Italy
- The merger of GEC with Plessey has produced a massive collaboration
- Northern Telecom of Canada has emerged as a strong competitor in America. AT&T's reaction to this has been the deal under which it will absorb the switch manufacturing activities of GTE, the leading independent US public exchange producer
- Alcatel established a position in US ancillary products through the purchase of ITT
- In Japan, NTT's monopoly ended due to deregulation and the supplier companies, NEC, Fujitsu and Hitachi have lost some of their close relationships with both NTT and each other
- Motorola established a strong position in Europe and also bought into the Scandinavian market with the purchase of Storno in Denmark

something unique about IBM's hardware *per se*. The critical importance lay in Intel's chips themselves. 'Intel Inside' was the crucial factor and every PC manufacturer was faced with the choice either of forming strategic partnerships with Intel or to compete against Intel by providing alternative technology. Apple's alliance with Motorola is an example of competing against Intel.

The importance of microprocessor technology push upon the computer industry was highlighted by *Fortune*:

> Twenty years after its invention, the microprocessor . . . has suddenly brought forth PC's as powerful as mainframe computers. In the process it has destroyed thousands of jobs, unseated CEO's at world-renowned companies, reshuffled tens of billions of dollars of shareholder value, and set off convulsions that will wrack the 50,000 companies in computing – and all their customers – through the end of this century. (14 June 1993, p.56)

The reduced instruction set computer (RISC) system is a major challenge to Intel's dominance of microprocessor technology and is produced by IBM, Motorola and Digital without Intel's supply. However, Intel has, in turn, pushed even greater microprocessor technology with its Pentium processor, which is rated at a new high of 100 million instructions per second (MIPS). Intel's importance can be traced back to 1969. Since then each breakthrough in their R&D, in terms of low costs, extra memory capabilities or computing speed, has directly influenced new product launches by major manufacturers/assemblers in the computer industry. Examples of such breakthroughs are given in Table 3.12.

3.6 Types of new product development

There are several types of new product developments, summarized by Booz, Allen & Hamilton (1982) and given in Table 3.13.

The above categorizations are helpful but we need to bear in mind that products do not necessarily sit in a single category; for instance, product developments in the telecommunications industry are serving to change the shape of the industry itself. Merging technologies will produce products which will make the distinction between telecommunications and computing difficult if not impossible. For example, *Business Week* quotes the President of Bell Atlantic:

> five years from now, we will not be able to remember which companies were telephone companies and which were long-distance or wireless . . . The telecommunications world as we know it is gone – shattered. (24 January 1994, p.88)

For instance, AT&T have focused developments in the information highway on the telephone, rather than the PC which is being pursued by other players: digitized films, games and data are being geared to advanced telephone equipment:

it's going to be increasingly difficult to figure out what's a game machine, what's a computer, and what's a telephone. (AT&T Consumer Products Division President in *Business Week* 24 January 1994, p.37)

Table 3.12 Microprocessor development between 1969 and 1992

Year	*Product development*
1969	First microprocessor: 4004, which had a 4 bit internal register power
1974	8080 microprocessor which doubled the power of the 4 bit: this revolutionized the computer industry, providing 64K of memory
1978	8086 microprocessor launched which had 10 times the power of the 8080 and had 1MB of memory
1979	8088 microprocessor which was used in the first IBM PC. This had the same power as the 8086 but was cheaper and allowed IBM to produce a competitively priced PC
1982	80286 microprocessor which replaced the 8088, creating far greater speed in calculations; also memory was expanded to 16MB
1985	80386 microprocessor doubled data size to 32 bits and cutting processing time in half. This was also linked to DOS systems for the first time
1989	80486 microprocessor includes a floating-point mathematics co-processor; also processing power has been increased fourfold on its predecessor, and allowed further cost reductions to be made in PC manufacture
1991	Pentium: this expands to 100 MIPS, which is the typical power of a mainframe. However, this chip sells at less than $1000 which is a major, additional threat to mainframe producers, particularly IBM

Adapted from Rosch (1989), Boling (1990), Schlender (1991)

Table 3.13 Categories of new product developments

New to the world products	New products which create an entirely new market
New product lines	New products which enter an existing market
Additions to existing lines	Products which supplement the firm's current portfolio
Improvements to existing products	Replacing current products by offering perceived enhancements
Repositionings	Products which are tailored and targeted to new market segments
Cost reductions	Products that compete on lower costs

With these developments have come problems over legislation in the United States; legislation at the beginning of 1994 was designed to ensure even greater competition within the telecommunications industry, a trend that has continued since the break-up of the AT&T monopoly in 1984. Deregulation means that new entrants have provided new technologies resulting in the combination of product groupings.

3.7 The failure factor in product innovation

There are many reasons why product innovations fail. Kay (1993) suggests that there are three main problems in innovation:

1. The process itself is costly and uncertain – A technically successful innovation might not be profitable.
2. The process is hard to manage – Innovating firms require special skills.
3. Rewards of success are hard to appropriate – Innovations can be copied and improved by competitors.

The fact that R&D activity is not by itself sufficient was mentioned earlier. The success of applied research to actual products has much to do with production/operations. Kay (1993) mentions how EMI has declined in televisions, computers and radiology scanner technology. This was in spite of the fact that:

> EMI was one of the most effectively innovative companies there has ever been. It was a pioneer in television, a leader in computers, its music business was at the centre of a revolution in popular culture, and its scanner technology transformed radiology. Today only its music business survives. (p.101)

The major reason here was the inability to translate innovation *per se* into a sustainable advantage through its manufacturing capability. Powers (1991) summarizes the problem with new product development:

> New product development is a major concern of business product development managers and represents one of the greatest risks to a firm's short-term financial success, not to mention its long-term viability. (p.195)

The failure rate of new products is enormous and varies according to the markets targeted. Reasons for failure include:

- Launching a new product which although innovative, is replaced by another entrant's product which then becomes the standard. VHS became the standard over RCA's play-only videodisc and the Beta format in video. Once the standard had been established, this allowed Matsushita (responsible for establishing the VHS standard) to fend off the threat of another type of video format, the 8 mm alternative. An important point to note here is made by Kay (1993):

> Technical quality plays little part in the choice. VHS is certainly no better than Sony's Betamax format. IBM's PC became the dominant standard although . . . it offered little in the way of advanced or original design. (p.109)

- Failure to develop from the laboratory to manufacture – Ampex's attempts at the video recorder, where the manufacture of the tapehead made product quality difficult to control, is such a case. This factor is discussed later in the chapter, but we can say here that this is a major concern for manufacturing firms; the transfer from one-off laboratory conditions to volume manufacture is a massive challenge and without it successful innovation will not take place. Failing to make this transfer from prototype to volume manufacture has cost some companies dearly:

> The expensive and complex recording machinery developed by Ampex and other American manufacturers had to be converted into a practical consumer product . . . The Japanese efforts were characterised by close coordination of design and manufacturing and an intense and sustained effort to develop simplified designs for both the product and the process. In contrast, the three U.S. efforts to develop a consumer VCR ran into serious manufacturing problems, which were never overcome. (Dertouzos *et al.* 1989, p.73)

The involvement of manufacturing from early design stages to actual volume manufacture is fundamental. The inability to manufacture because of overdesign is a central area of concern and is discussed later in this chapter.

Johnson *et al.* (1974) and Booz, Allen and Hamilton (1982) plotted the failure rate of new products on a decay curve along the lines of Figure 3.3.

Figure 3.3 The failure of product innovation.

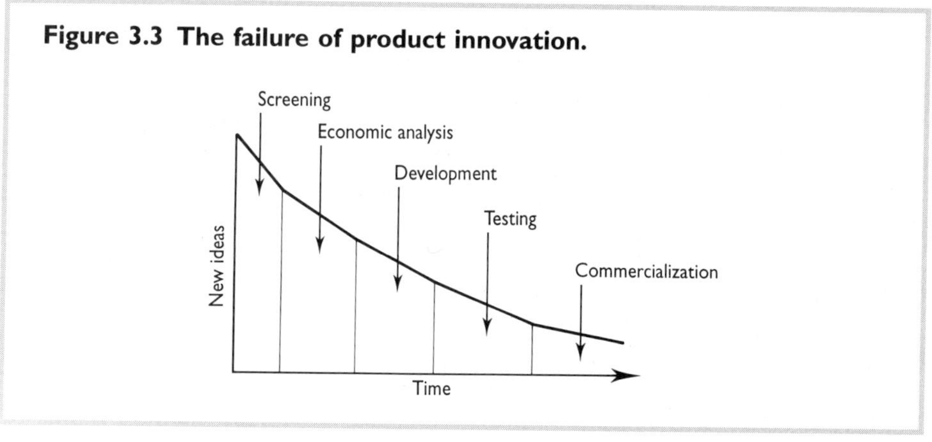

The study by Booz, Allen and Hamilton (1982) suggested that it took seven ideas to generate one successful product. From Booz, Allen and Hamilton (1982) and Rothwell *et al.* (1974), a number of major factors can be seen as integral to successful innovation:

1. The product met market needs and the firm had a good understanding of these needs.
2. The product fitted the internal strengths of the organization, much of which are directly linked to production/operations' capability.
3. Successful innovating firms develop more *efficiently*, though not necessarily more *quickly* than firms which fail in product innovation.
4. The responsible individuals in successful innovations are usually more senior in the organization than their competitors who fail. This is an important point and is indeed a message throughout the text; production/operations' presence is often lacking at senior levels of the firm. While this presence is not sufficient to the success of new products, it is necessary. Much of the success of the innovating firm will depend on the firm's ability to translate ideas into volume manufacturing. Clearly, much of this responsibility rests with production/operation.

3.8 Basic considerations in new product development

As new product ideas are generated and developed, they will become questioned in terms of economic feasibility, market potential and so on. Decisions will depend upon a combination of hard and soft factors. The hard factors include risk analysis, financial criteria, such as ROI, decision trees and matrices. The soft considerations include how the firm's image and reputation might be enhanced by producing a new product. The soft factors should not be underestimated; the firm will sometimes make 'unreasonable commitment, based on inadequate evidence' (Peters 1986) and still be successful. This soft factor may well override all of the number-crunching conclusions. Both hard and soft considerations will come into play, but the fact of the matter is that success of a product is known only *after* the product is launched. There are, of course, no guarantees of success. In a sense therefore, product innovation is an act of faith; massive expenditure will often have been incurred and the success and duration of a product's life is unclear, even with the best of information, research and other customer-driven approaches.

Garvin (1992) argues that new products progress through three stages:

1. **Product research** Where basic R&D takes place, creating new knowledge and allowing a concept to be developed.
2. **Product development** Which includes market research, prototypes, field testing and creation of specifications.
3. **Final design** The development and approval of design, including bills of materials of the final product.

All of this includes risk and Garvin (1992) divides this risk into the following areas:

- **Market risks** Demand is uncertain until the product is completed. The actual volume of purchase is uncertain.
- **Competitive risks** Because of the uncertainty in predicting competitive responses. One of the planning requirements for a firm is in trying to establish likely competitive response to a particular strategy, especially in new product development (Porter, 1985)
- **Technological risk** Due to the unknowns of newly developed methods and materials; this can be reduced by production/operations' early involvement in the process.
- **Organizational risks** Structures, staffing and the culture of an organization might alter because of a new product; in particular, training and new skills may be needed.
- **Production risk** Volume manufacture of a product will reveal possible problems of producing a product on large scale that might not be revealed at the prototype stage
- **Financial risk** Large amounts of money have been incurred through R&D, marketing efforts and production and the payoff is uncertain. Each of these are distinct yet complementary to the overall concern and each imposes particular demands on managers. However, failure is as much due to lack of company commitment as it is to market responses after a product has been launched.

Before the product reaches volume manufacturing, a number of questions will be asked along the lines offered by Whitney (1988):

Will it work?

Will it sell?

Will it make a profit?

Can it be manufactured?

These questions need to be addressed by all key areas in the firm and, with the possible exception of 'Will it sell?' all other questions directly involve production/operations in providing solutions to the questions. Surrounding any product innovations are two tenets which organizations must be aware of and these are described by Garvin (1992):

1. Most innovations fail
2. Firms that do not innovate die. There is something unsettling and paradoxical about these observations. Faced with the first rule, risk-averse managers might well conclude that new products and processes are to be avoided . . . But faced with the second rule, most managers would reach a far different conclusion. New products and processes are essential because,

without them, their organizations are likely to have no future at all. (p.322)

This is a dichotomy facing all managers involved in product innovation. However, firms can learn from failure. Provided that they learn quickly and do not emulate mistakes, initial failure does not have to be a catastrophe for the firm. The pitfalls facing innovation include the following:

1. There is no real market for the product.
2. A need exists but the product does not match the need.
3. The product, *per se*, is capable of meeting the market requirements but the perception is not clear to the market and, is, therefore, replaced by a better marketing effort from a competitor. (Adapted from Kotler, 1994)

Two disasters exemplify the massive costs of failure to two industries. Texas Instruments lost $660 million in its failure to be a player in the home computer business. In the 1950s, Ford lost $350 million on the infamous Ford Edsel. More recently, DEC targeted IBM's mainframe with the VAX 9000: the sales were envisaged to reach $3 billion but never exceeded $500 million per annum in sales; in 1990 DEC introduced the MIPS architecture which, by 1994, had not proven popular; DEC's $483.5 million purchase of minicomputer operations from Mannesmann and Philips resulted in an annual loss of $617 million in 1991. DEC's case is not unique, but does prove the extent of expenditure; success brings rewards, failure to anticipate market needs reaps disaster; DEC suffered a $2.8 billion loss in 1992. DEC's performance illustrates the massive uncertainty involved in technological innovation.

3.9 The process of new product developments

Kotler (1994) suggests that there are distinguishing phases in new product development, as shown in Table 3.14.

However, we must not think of these as mutually exclusive steps. We must also bear in mind that, even if the process is accurate in terms of the steps themselves, there will be – or at least should be – representatives from all functions at most stages, certainly from idea screening onward; a good idea, from a purely marketing point may not necessarily be good for the firm. In addition,

Table 3.14 Phases of New Product Development

Idea generation → Idea screening → Concept development and testing → Marketing strategy development → Business analysis → Product development → Market testing → Commercialization

Adapted from Kotler (1994)

there may be leaps forward or back depending upon the response, as Crawford (1991) states:

> the process is fluid, changing. If a concept fails its screening test with intended consumers, it heads back to the ideation stage or even further back to the opportunity identification stage. And if a competitor makes a surprise entry, the project may take a risky skip of several stages right into production. (p.37)

This latter leap is certainly the case in the computer and telecommunications industries; new product speed is vital and there is not the luxury of completing vast amounts of marketing tests before launching new products, simply because other competitors are launching their products.

IBM launched their original PC without any market test. However, Crawford (1991) suggests that one of the reasons for failure behind the IBM Junior was lack of market research. Although there is not one single, fixed process of new product development, it is clear that product launches typically occur after the following type of process is undertaken:

- **Idea generation** (from any number of sources) Innovative companies tend to encourage new product ideas from anywhere within the organization. 3M, it is reported, never rejects new ideas immediately. Ideas may also come from outside of the company, in particular, those other organizations involved in the supply chain of the company, including suppliers and distributors.
- **Initial screening and analysis** Market research still precedes the majority of new product innovations and in one survey 56 per cent of CEOs stated that inappropriate market research was a major obstacle to innovation (Knight, 1987). Objections and questions will be raised in terms of the feasibility and the economic sense of the proposal. This is a vital stage of assessment; issues of how a new proposal fits with existing products will be discussed and possible cannibalization of existing products must be avoided. However, even the most scientific of marketing research is not without its critics; the original marketing research undertaken by Xerox for its photocopier process was not encouraging, but it is now central to everyday business. GM suffered in the 1980s by producing a range of cars which looked very similar. This was confusing for customers; moreover, it presented an opportunity for GM's competitors. Ford did so in a successful TV campaign which contrasted the similarity of GM's range to Ford's distinctive car appearance.

  In essence, the following questions will be probed: potential demand (volume) of the product; the probable lifecycle; the threat of emulation from competitors providing copy or substitute products; overall development time for the proposed new product, and the resource capabilities and demands of the new product. Another major consideration is in how existing process technology that the firm owns can support the proposed product. Process choice, capacity and skills levels are all important considerations. The following are particularly important for production/operations managers.

- **Initial product design and development** Detailed engineering will take place to make the idea capable of being produced, although computer aided design (CAD) will enable the design process to be undertaken more efficiently and with greater speed, the initial design may well be revised a number of times, although overdesign must be avoided.
- **Prototype testing** At this stage the product may perform poorly, in which case it might well be abandoned. Restricting the prototype testing to one unit is not the best way to proceed because, although debugging of one unit will be achieved, there will be no opportunity to see the difficulties in manufacturing a number of units.

  The caveat on this approach is that the role of production/operations can be ignored until the transfer from the lab prototyping to volume manufacture. By this time there may well be a mismatch between product assembly requirements and process capability. Also the sheer transition from one-off manufacture to volume is an entirely different manufacturing process, (as discussed in Chapter 4). This approach is, rightly, attacked by Hayes and Wheelwright (1992):

  > First, it reinforces and legitimizes the separation of design engineering and manufacturing process engineering and limits the overlap between these two functions . . . it is not until late in the product development effort . . . where the entire organization's contributions are brought together and tested as a system. (p.272)

- **Final design** This essentially precedes volume manufacturing but when a new product is released, customer feedback may require modifications. Even though the aim would be to get it right first time, some – preferably minor – changes, may need to be made, reflecting customer feedback; mechanisms need to be in place to allow this to happen.
- **Volume manufacturing** This will highlight problems of shifting from one-off or small batch manufacture to larger volumes. By this stage, it is vital that manufacturing infrastructure in terms of process choice, control systems and people skills requirements are known and in place.

As a model, then, Kotler's (1994) approach can be useful *only* if it involves an holistic effort from the beginning, rather than allocating stages of the development process to particular functions. This is particularly true if production/operations' involvement is left until volume manufacturing. By then, problems may be ingrained and delays will be inevitable. Since speed of development is vital, delays must be avoided. These stages are not necessarily mutually exclusive and the sequential approach does not mean that each stage is allocated to a particular group. Instead, multidisciplinary groups should be involved, particularly in the actual design of the product. It becomes clear that design is of strategic importance and is not just a functional/operational area. The move away from function-to-function approaches to new product development is clear and the importance of the holistic approach is discussed below.

3.10 Organizational considerations in new product development

3.10.1 The manufacturing/marketing interface in new product developments

All products can be plotted on an overall lifecycle; for example, in the computing industry, the hardware associated with producing hard copies can be traced along the following generic lifecycle, which in the early 1990s would have looked like Figure 3.4.

It is because of shortening lifecycles and the fact that new entrants are continually introducing new products, that companies have to be clear where their products are on the lifecycle. This will then determine such areas as allocation of funds on existing products, R&D expenditure for future products and expenditure on marketing efforts. Production/operations should be involved in the early stages of new product design. This involvement is central to Hewlett Packard's approach:

> (there has been) earlier involvement of manufacturing . . . We were as bad as anybody else. We'd invent the product and kind of heave it over the wall and say, 'hope you guys can make this; good luck'. We don't do that anymore. We have manufacturing people and marketing people involved from really the definition stage. (Address given by Lew Platt – Hewlett Packard Executive Conference, July 19 1993)

At the feasibility stage of a new product launch, areas will be probed that clearly impinge on production/operations' role including: creating alternative designs and concepts for the product; clarifying operational requirements in terms of capacity, envisaged volume, process choice and skills requirement; and logistic requirements for distribution. With this in mind, the holistic approach – includ-

Figure 3.4 Lifecycle positionings for printers (in 1994).

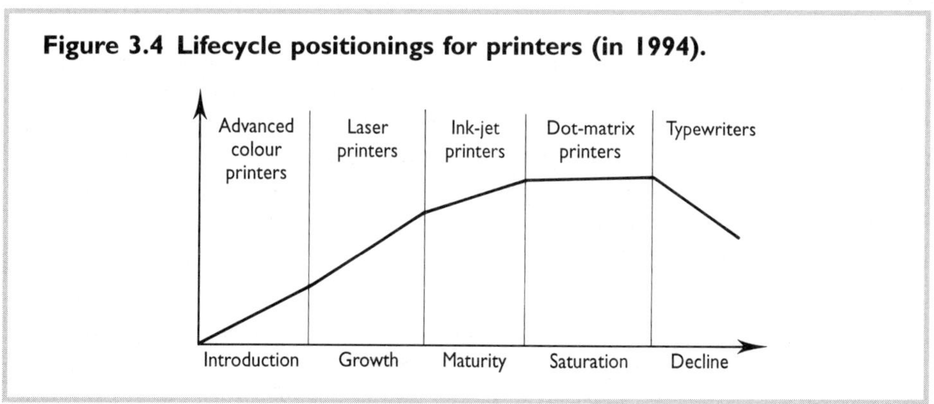

Table 3.15 The marketing/operations interface in new product development

Marketing				*Operations*
Market assessment volume	⇐	**Initial screening**	⇒	Ability of current operations to meet volume and cost requirements
		⇓		
Developing marketing strategy; product concept	⇐	**Initial design**	⇒	Basic design – ideally with suppliers' involvement
		⇓		
Refining market strategy in terms of buyers, pricing and promotion decisions	⇐	**Development**	⇒	Design development; prototype testing
		⇓		
Executing marketing strategy	⇐	**Product launch**	⇒	Full-scale production capability. Continuing product and process improvements

ing both marketing and production/operations – is vital at all stages of the product launch. The important link between operations and marketing is evident from Table 3.15.

The interface between manufacturing and marketing is evident when product strategy is developed in terms of when a product should both enter and exit a market. This can be discussed in the context of the product lifecycle and Hayes and Wheelwright (1979) have summarized the marketing/operations link shown in Table 3.16.

Although the product lifecycle's effect upon operations is discussed in more detail in Chapter 4, in terms of the link with manufacturing processes, Table 3.16 serves to highlight the need for production/operations and marketing to work closely from the beginning of a product launch and to devise strategy together. This will allow for high volumes to be reached when required and will also allow for the appropriate process choice to be employed to support the product strategy in relation to the lifecycle of the product.

3.10.2 The need for the holistic approach in new product development

The sequential approach to product launches was, largely, along the lines of Figure 3.5.

Table 3.16 Operations involvement in the product lifecycle

Strategy	*Stage to enter*	*Stage to exit*	*Implications for operations*
Enter early and exit late	Introduction	Decline	Transition from low-volume flexible producer to high-volume low-cost producer
Enter early and exit early	Introduction	Maturity	Low-volume flexible producer
Enter late and exit late	Growth	Decline	High-volume, low-cost producer

Adapted from Hayes and Wheelwright (1979)

This sequential approach is hardly holistic in nature, although several functional areas are involved. The problem with this approach is that much of the work is after the event – in other words much of the cost of launching the product comes with inquests after the product has been launched, in terms of failure in the marketplace. Japanese manufacturing firms have tended to spend far greater amounts and place greater resources in early stages of product development and production/operations' involvement is central. This difference is graphically shown in Figure 3.6

This has become one of the key learning aspects that the West has slowly gained from the Japanese approach. For example, GM creates simultaneous engineering groups when new models are being devised, Chrysler has process-

Figure 3.5 The sequential (traditional) approach to new product launches.

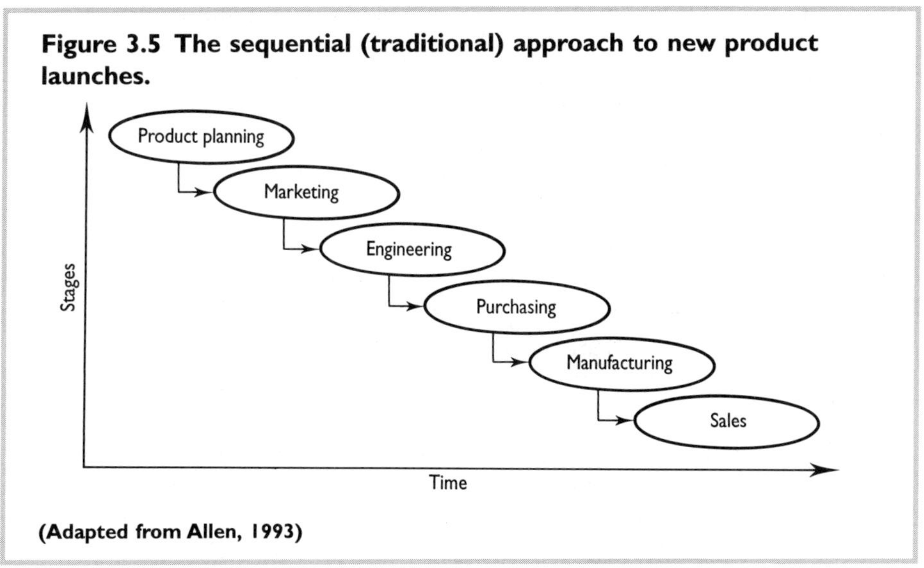

(Adapted from Allen, 1993)

Figure 3.6 The contrast between Japanese and USA's traditional approaches to new product development.

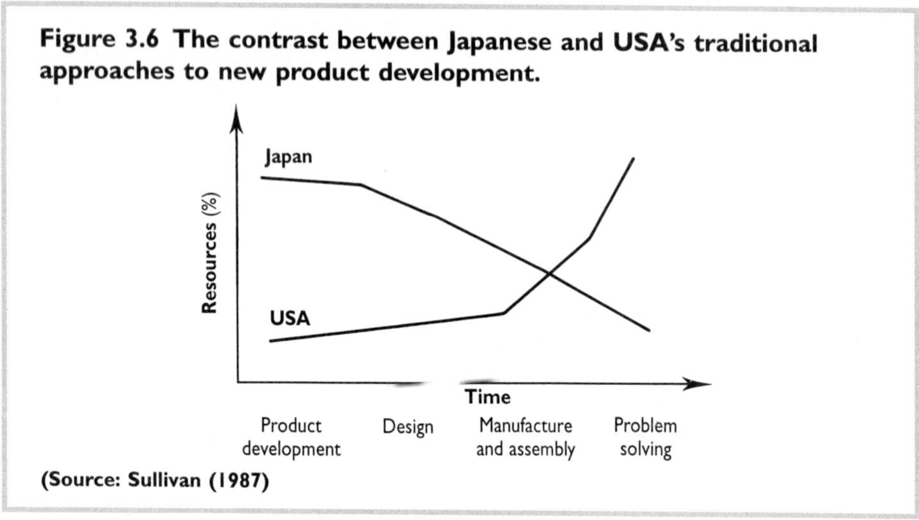

(Source: Sullivan (1987)

driven design groups for their new models and Ford call their approach The Team Concept; in short , all of the 'big three' seem to be learning – admittedly slowly and painfully – that new products are best launched by a combined holistic effort, rather than a mutually exclusive, function-to-function approach. Dertouzos *et al.* (1989) note that it was Ford who first adopted the holistic approach:

> Ford was the first American automobile company to experiment with the use of cross-functional teams to speed the development and introduction of a new model. The product-development team for the Taurus included representatives from planning, design, engineering, manufacturing, and marketing. The specialists worked simultaneously rather than serially, and the success of the Team Taurus project convinced Ford of the problem-solving potential of this approach. (p.123)

The launch of new products is not the sole prerogative of the marketing department. As Powers (1991) states in his marketing text:

> One of the most difficult aspects of developing and launching a new business product is that virtually every part of the organization must be involved. This involvement includes not just participation in the process but also an almost synergistic support for the success of the development and launch. (p.213)

Several interdepartmental conflicts may arise during product innovation; marketing and production/operations could be one source of conflict; production/operations and engineering/design could be another. The following can be typical areas of conflict: engineering may be later than scheduled with design but the onus will fall upon production/operations to deliver to the market when first required; engineering may exceed their budget while production/operations are restricted to their original allocation; design might be excessive, making it needlessly difficult to assemble, test and manufacture; there may be frequent changes to engineering designs, parts or methods. As Schmenner (1990) states:

> Engineers seem to have a penchant for specifying items that are hard to purchase and/or require a long lead time, although a little ingenuity could have made use of off-the-shelf items that are easily obtained. (p.679)

Dealing with these conflicts and providing a culture by which they are diffused or preferably do not arise in the first place, is a key managerial task. If they are not dealt with, then the company will suffer in the marketplace in terms of speed of delivery, product image and typically cost.

Clark, as reported in Womack *et al.* (1990) indicates that Japanese car manufacturers design and introduce cars at twice the rate of American manufacturers. Womack *et al.* (1990, p.118) clearly show the contrast between Japanese and other manufacturers in bringing new cars to market:

	Japanese	**European**	**American**
Average development time per new car (months)	46.2	57.3	60.4

However, since the publication of Womack *et al.* (1990), the position has changed somewhat; Chrysler, for example, can now launch a new car at the same pace as Honda; Ford, together with some divisions within GM, can do the same. For many industries, new product development is a central requirement and the *speed* of new product introduction is fundamental. There are a number of suggestions for accelerating the speed of new product development and these are summarized in Table 3.17.

3.10.3 The role of cross-functional design teams

A number of writers have drawn attention to the distinction between the Western and Japanese approaches to the design process. For example, Adam and Ebert (1992) observe how in many firms in the West the development process:

> subdivides the overall development effort into subtasks for technical specialists in diverse departments . . . Consequently, the development process is executed sequentially in isolated stages. The result is slow, nonintegrated, and expensive development. (The Japanese) get new products into the marketplace twice as fast. (p.127)

Bessant (1991) elaborates upon this fact when, discussing the Japanese approach to new design, he states:

> Central to their success was the concept of what could be called integrated design. Very close links were formed between product designers, marketing, and manufacturing representatives such that the final product was the

Table 3.17 Methods to speed the new product development process

1. Overlapping development phases – Instead of the sequential process that has caused many Western companies to be late to market, it is clear that some of the developments can be made concurrently. Not all phases are linear, and some phases are not dependent on what has preceded. Concurrent development therefore compresses the real-time development, making it quicker
2. Fewer development phases can be implemented – This is made possible through CAD/CAE which allows parts and subassemblies to have been tested without prototyping
3. Incremental development, along the lines of *Kaizen*, sees progress evolving from a core product. Constant, small developments, particularly in cross-functional teams results in seemingly large developments over a period of time
4. Better use of prototyping – Not just as a one-off unit – will show how easily or otherwise it will be to manufacture. The normal approach to prototyping is to use one unit only as a means of debugging and then to go from this to volume manufacture. Small batches will allow problems of producing to be highlighted, which is important when manufacturing in large volumes

> result of continuous dialogue throughout the design and development process rather than the traditional Western approach which is essentially sequential in nature. (p.197)

Bessant (1991) records how Honda cut its 5 year new-car development cycle in half, and how Hewlett Packard reduced its time for developing printers from 4.5 years to 22 months. The innovative desk-jet printer was launched by Hewlett Packard just 26 months after the company first explored the concept and the product has been a major success, achieved through multidisciplinary teamwork within the company. Cross-functional teams, centred around a particular product is the norm at Motorola in all new product developments. Motorola uses the term contract driven teams.

Cross-functional teams, rather than merely technical specialists, have to be part of any organization's strategy to ensure that the market requirement is met. A success story of this approach was in the development of the Ford Taurus which replaced the Honda Accord as the biggest selling car in the United States in 1992: Ford used Team Taurus to bring together representatives from design, engineering, manufacturing, sales, marketing and service and suppliers in the earliest stages of the car's design to bring about this success.

AT&T used the design team approach when designing the cordless phone and in doing so reduced development time by 50 per cent, while lowering cost and increasing quality.

This design team approach, including suppliers and distributors, is an important development for many firms and, as Quinn *et al.* (1990) state:

> the key to strategic success for many companies has been a carefully

> developed coalition with one or more of the world's best suppliers, product designers . . . distributors . . . Apple is one company that profits from such an approach. Honda Motor Company is another. (p.64)

General Motors' Oldsmobile division is an example of where learning from the Japanese, in terms of product development, has been fruitful; the Aurora, replacement for the Tornado Coupe, was developed through an holistic approach:

> Aurora illustrates GM's progress toward fixing its product-development efforts . . . all departments from engineering to marketing worked simultaneously on Aurora, cooperating in the early stages. (Kerwin, 1994, p.90)

What distinguished this development from most other General Motors efforts was the attention to customer input; 20 customer groups were targeted and 4200 interviews were held prior to design of the Aurora.

Although there is not one fixed approach to design teams, Cordero (1991) offers useful advice:

> Multifunctional teams are physically close and share information about market needs, technical feasibility, product costs, manufacturing capabilities, etc. to ensure that product development simultaneously considers all interfunctional requirements. Moreover, these teams work closely with customers, watch customers, and involve suppliers early in product development. (p.287)

This holistic approach is evident from Hewlett Packard:

> We have spent a lot more time working on defining the product before we start the project . . . (before) we'd get half way in, and marketing would say, 'gee, I can't sell that; it's missing this and this' . . . and somebody from manufacturing would say, 'gee, how do you expect me to make that? I don't have the technology in place'. (Hewlett Packard Executive Conference, 19 July 1993)

The static function-to-function approach, shown in Figure 3.6, is now being replaced by a dynamic, holistic approach, the result of which is that delays are reduced and the product quality is greatly enhanced from the beginning (Figure 3.7).

In the early 1990s, the contrast between IBM's and Compaq's approach to new product development was striking. Basically, Compaq shunned the IBM approach:

> under which a final list of customer requirements was sent to development, which did a prototype and sent that to manufacturing, which then figured out how to make products in volume . . . Compaq turned everybody loose on the problem at once. The process was as messy as a dog fight, but it cut months out of the time it took to get a product on the market. (Carroll, 1993, p.147)

Figure 3.7 The holistic approach to new product launches.

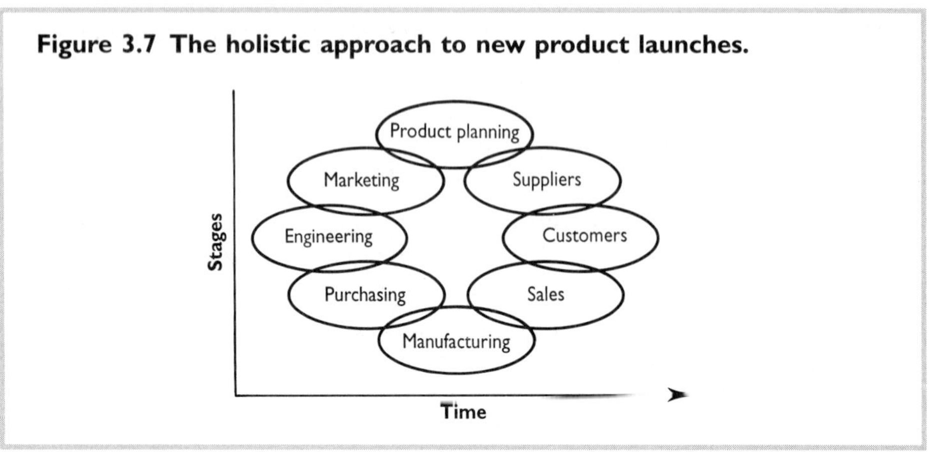

In view of the speed required in many markets, Compaq's approach is a *minimum* requirement for firms in terms of process, for many firms, particularly large, multinationals, it will fly in the face of the perceived wisdom of the past.

3.10.4 Key organizational roles in new product development

Some debate continues in terms of the value of formal planning in relation to new product development. In his TV programme, *The Business of Excellence*, Peters (1986) tells how Quinn (1980) had placed a bet with anybody who could come up with a substantial innovation which had come about via a formal planning committee. Apparently, there have been no takers. Mintzberg (1994), however, continues, after debating the role of formal planning, to say that there is some value in having formal planning groups and Oakley (1992) suggests that, in high-tech industries, there is a link between successful new product launches and the planning which precedes the launch. The problem in the 1990s and beyond is that speed of new product launches is critical and can be slowed by the bureaucracy of a planning committee within a firm. It has been argued by Rothwell *et al.* (1974) that there are three key players within the organization whose roles facilitate new product development and these are shown in Figure 3.8.

1. **The technical innovator** Essentially, the technically knowledgeable person who has the understanding of the technology itself, but who might lack the managerial skills for a new product to be accepted within the organization.
2. **The product champion** Who promotes the product within the organization and who is often identified with the product. This person has to gain the funds or sponsorship to enable the product to be launched; their own careers are to some extent dependent upon the success or failure of the product.

Figure 3.8 Key organizational roles in new product development.

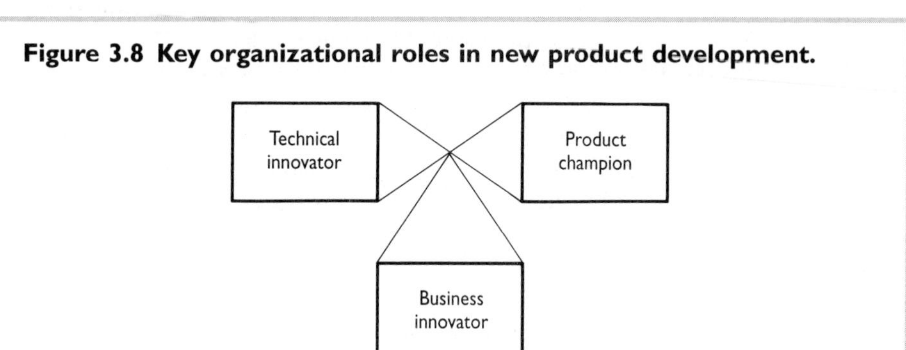

3. **The business innovator** This person has the status, authority and financial resources to both support and protect the product champion; without this support the new product would not be launched.

In reality, there are other stakeholders both inside (e.g. marketing, R&D, finance and production) and outside of the organization (suppliers, distributors and shareholders), whose interests are at stake and who clearly have input into whether a new product will be launched. What the above threefold distinction – technological, product and business innovator – offers though is to clarify the fact that new products are very rarely launched by one person or only one particular group. In addition, the technical champion is not necessarily the best person to manage the company; for example, Steve Jobs was the technical champion in the early days at Apple, but he recognized the need for a professional manager and recruited John Scully to manage the company.

3.10.5 New product innovation as a function of organizational type

Product innovation will depend on the culture of the organization itself. Organizational culture is discussed in Chapter 7, but Rogers (1983) suggests that there are five types of organizations involved in new product introductions:

1. **Innovators** These are companies determined to be first to market, even if their product does not become the subsequent standard for the market. Such companies are adventurous but might be considered 'headstrong or even extreme' (Bateman and Zeithaml, 1993, p.599). Often the organization is dominated by one person, sometimes the founder (Sinclair at Sinclair Research, or Foster at Apricot) or a subsequent CEO. Innovation is therefore thrust upon the organization, sometimes with disastrous results; the C5 from

Sinclair and the massive automation investment by GM (in the name of process innovation) in the 1980s being prime examples.

2. **Early adopters** This group is vital to the success of new technology and includes organizations which are industry leaders. The organizations tend to be relatively large, more profitable and more specialized. Their response to new product developments from others is rapid and they quickly learn to emulate, sometimes with added features of their own.
3. **Early majority** This group is more deliberate and take longer to decide. Such organizations are 'important members . . . of an industry, but typically not the leaders' (Bateman and Zeithaml, 1993, p.600). Their strategy is largely one of reaction and they enter at the growth or maturity stages of the life-cycle.
4. **Late majority** This group is even more cautious and tends to adopt only out of necessity or market pressures after players are already in place within the industry.
5. **Laggards** This group is extremely suspicious of change and are late entrants to market, coming at the decline or possibly saturation stages of the lifecycle. Their response is usually based only on cost and little differentiation is offered.

Late majority players would now include the no-name IBM clones who, by 1994, made up over 60 per cent of the PC market producers. Late majority and laggards do not typically compete by offering something differentiated within the existing market segment; instead they compete essentially on price. This is clearly the case within the PC market segment. The five categories offered above therefore provide insight into the actual corporate strategy adopted by organizations. Industry leaders such as Xerox, 3M, Hewlett Packard and Merck use product innovation to build and maintain their competitive position. However, innovation and early adoption demands large investment, and being a risk-seeker is not the appropriate strategy for every organization.

There are many reasons for wanting to be innovators or first to market and they include at least the following:

- The enhancement of corporate image and status within the industry.
- The ability to charge premium prices (if the market is willing) in order to recover major costs of R&D and promotion.
- The inability of competitors to copy will allow the company to enjoy sustained profitability: this will mean capital growth for the company. The longer the delay of other entrants, the longer the first-to-market firm has to gain profits for yet further R&D and product innovation.
- Patents can be used as a barrier to entry: for example Polaroid has successfully kept out Kodak from the instant photography market. In 1991 Kodak paid $925 million to Polaroid for patent infringements.

- High switching costs may be established: for example, Apple's domination of education markets has seen off IBM's (and others') attempts to attack this niche. By the time other competitors tried to enter this segment, considerable investment had been made by institutions (Apple's customers). The customers were largely tied – and committed – to Apple.

Whichever of these five categories the firm falls into, the strategy can be realized only if production/operations capability is in place. For example, speed of innovation is vital for innovators and early adopters. Other factors such as delivery reliability, flexibility and cost, all of which are linked to the capability of production/operations, will feature in the other categories.

3.10.6 New product development and company culture

Major innovators have a culture which facilitates ideas for both process and product development. Kanter (1991) offers six rules to inhibit such developments shown in Table 3.18.

While this is deliberately sarcastic on Kanter's part, it does contrast with 3M's culture regarding innovation given in Table 3.19.

While the majority of new ideas will fail, it is clear that the innovative companies are those which are committed to idea generation, knowing that from these a few will be successful which in turn will sustain the company, particularly in telecommunications and computing, where constant product innovation is a requirement to compete at all. In terms of organizational culture, it is clear that rigid hierarchies tend to kill new ideas and as Bateman and Zeithaml (1993) state:

> Flat structures reduce bureaucracy and allow flexibility and innovation . . . the organization should create a horizontal orientation in which communications flow across functions. The best way to do this is to establish cross-functional product teams. The aim should be to destroy the tradi-

Table 3.18 Organizational factors in preventing innovation

1. Be suspicious of any new idea from below. After all, top management thinks of all the good ideas
2. Make people go through several organizational levels before getting your approval
3. Give criticism at every opportunity
4. Keep people in the dark about what's going on in the firm
5. Manage tightly; control everything to the *n*th degree
6. Have the attitude that you (top management) already know everything there is to know

Source: Kanter (1991)

Table 3.19 3M's approach to innovation

1. Set goals for innovation
2. Commit to research and development
3. Inspire intrapreneurship
4. Facilitate, do not obstruct
5. Focus on the customer
6. Tolerate failure

Adapted from Mitchel (1989)

> tional boundaries between design, engineering, manufacturing/operations, marketing, and other functions. (p.610)

Northern Telecom were clearly behind others in terms of speed of product innovation and as part of their reform reduced twenty-five job categories to five. Faster innovation is not just about reducing the number of levels in the company hierarchy. For innovation to be a central part of the company's culture, there needs to be incentives to encourage suggestions and proposals. Training is also central; Motorola spends over $40 million on training per annum and sees this as an investment which will encourage new ideas to come forward for both process and new product developments.

New product development may actually be a major catalyst for cultural change within a firm. Such a cultural change has taken place in Chrysler since the 1980s, and it would be oversimplistic to credit this entirely with its former CEO, Iacocca, important as he was to the company. Ford has changed dramatically since the early 1980s when poor performance threatened the company. The concept to customer – 'C to C' – approach adopted by Ford has been the focal point of new product development and has found enormous success, particularly in the Taurus and Explorer product developments.

However, entrenched culture is difficult to change and remains a massive challenge to large companies. Carroll (1993) provides this insight at IBM:

> But it's hard at IBM to do anything that hasn't been done before. New things tend to get shot down, or at least debated to death as IBM's marketing forces and related product groups raise objections . . . Anyone at IBM wanting to do something with any kind of speed finds himself using old ideas. (p.133)

However, this largely reflects the past at IBM. The massive restructuring that has taken place internationally – but most strikingly in the United States since 1992 – shows that IBM have had to rethink their whole business structure. What had been appropriate for IBM in 1960s and 1970s was not so for the 1990s. IBM divisions are now based around focused product groups, largely autonomous, and speed of product innovation could be a central factor to IBM's future.

3.11 Computer-aided design

Firms must not lose sight of the strategic importance of design. The success of the product itself owes much to the design and the success of many successfully designed products over a period of time will help to ensure the success of the firm itself. As Whitney (1988) states:

> In short, design is a strategic activity . . . it influences flexibility of sales strategies, speed of repair, and efficiency of manufacturing. It may well be responsible for the company's future viability. (p.83)

Computer-aided design (CAD) can enhance the capability of the firm both in terms of the quality of the design and the speed of new product introduction. It can also help in terms of response to existing products. Cost and delivery factors have been reduced at Motorola with the help of CAD. Motorola's Fusion production site, which concentrates on pagers, uses CAD to turn customer-specific requirements into virtual manufacturing before assembly takes place. Once the assembly is seen to be viable, instructions go to the manufacturing facility, thus avoiding waste, downtime and delays to customer. A typical CAD system will consist of one or more design workstations, a processor, secondary storage, a plotter and/or other output devices. The stages of CAD tend to be as shown in Table 3.20.

CAD has profoundly effected the design process and has impacted on areas such as flexibility, the speed of new product development and cost, all of which in turn are competitive, and therefore strategic factors. In particular major benefits would include:

1. **Product quality** CAD allows designers to develop alternatives and to be aware of possible problems at early stages of design.
2. **Shorter design time** This clearly influences both cost and actual development times to market.

Table 3.20 A process flow of computer-aided design

1. Geometric modelling (synthesis) – either two- or three-dimensional modelling; wire-frame or solid modelling
⇓
2. Analysis (engineering analysis which amongst other factors will seek optimization of assembly)
⇓
3. Evaluation and design review – where dimensions are provided and kinematics linkages are seen
⇓
4. Final presentation through automated draughting

3. **Manufacturing cost reductions** Design changes are easily facilitated; group technology further helps this by grouping together families of components for manufacture.
4. **Database management** A common database means that information will be accurate and current. In addition, speed of transfer and document revision are made much easier.
5. **Enhanced capabilities** The ability to rotate a design in apparent three-dimensional mode gives rise to real-life application of the design in terms of clearance and other important engineering considerations. Also, the linkage and combination between designs are made possible where needed.

CAD also allows the designer to be free from the more mundane areas of design; standard or commonly used parts can be called up and transferred to a new design without having to redraught them each time. Parts can be exploded and engineering requirements in terms of material type, weight, stress capabilities and other key areas can be easily identified.

Cost of design is a major feature in the car industry; for example, 70 per cent of the cost of manufacturing truck transmissions is determined in the design stage (Whitney, 1988). It is vital therefore that design is seen as a competitive factor and that tools such as CAD are in place. The need to be holistic is clear with CAD, even though CAD is typically seen as a specialist or technical prerogative. Common technology between key areas is vital:

> There are many different CAD systems available, and transmitting data from one to another and into manufacturing systems is not as easy as it should be . . . as many as 25% of designs transmitted to small tool and die shops as CAD files have to be printed out as blue prints and re-entered into the computer because translations between programs are so poor. (Manufacturing Technology Survey, *The Economist*, 5 March 1994, p.10)

CAD enables three-dimensional modelling to take place and reduces the need for the number of prototypes. It is vital that manufacturing and design systems integrate. As Bradshaw (1989) points out:

> The gap between design and manufacturing is enormous in many companies and the source of many problems. They often have different computer systems, and frequently the data produced in the design department has to be re-inputted into the manufacturing computer. (p.3)

This is endorsed by Hutchins (1988):

> the design function is central to the achievement of all of the company's goals, and must take account of manufacturing feasibility. It is not good enough to suggest that design is responsible only for design, and production for production . . . a flaw not detected until manufacture will involve modifications to tooling, jigs, fixtures and process set-ups. (p.98)

Again, the role of production/operations is important to technological developments with CAD. If not, CAD will only be a technological indulgence, rather than part of the firm's weaponry.

3.12 Indications of design effectiveness

An indication of design will rest in 'non-failure' of the product in terms of how it performs. Hutchins (1988) describes design failures including:

1. Incorrect materials.
2. Vague/ambiguous specifications for materials treatments, etc.
3. Inadequate allowance for fatigue/strength loss over the specified life of the product.
4. Not allowing for environmental factors, including dirt, fumes, etc.
5. Poor design for manufacture, including ease of manufacture and cost.
6. Inadequate user and installation instructions.

Much of the success of the design of the product is only known once it is being used and therefore this becomes very much part of the quality issue. A failed design means a failed product and dissatisfied customers.

As a general guide, Table 3.21 can be used as good criteria for design.

The last point is exemplified at AT&T, where an integrated circuit had been designed to amplify voice signals; in the initial design the ease of manufacture was largely ignored, making the product extremely hard to manufacture because of unnecessarily stringent requirements. AT&T's engineers made a minor change – with little cost – and as a result, massive improvements were made in being able to manufacture the switch.

To merely design to satisfy manufacturing requirements has to be put into context; designs should be a means of satisfying external customers, rather than internal processes. However, design for manufacturing can become a means of

Table 3.21 General criteria for design

1. Designing for function so that the product will perform as intended – this is central to quality (Crosby, 1979)
2. Designing for *reliability* so that the product will be seen as consistent – again a quality factor
3. Designing for *maintainability* so that the product can be economically maintained – this is vital in cars
4. Designing for *safety* to reduce any possibility of hazardous effect and environmental damage – in the computer/telecommunications industries concerns are raised in terms of long-term exposure to screens. However, in the car industry product failure is potentially fatal – hence GM's recall of all Saturn models in August 1993
5. Designing for *ease of manufacture* so that the product can be easily made, allowing high volume to be achieved, if needed, and at less cost

Table 3.22 Specific indicators of design effectiveness

1. Minimizing the number of parts used (thus avoiding overdesign)
2. Percentage of standard parts should be large
3. Using *existing* manufacturing resources
4. Reducing the cost of the first production run will indicate if the design is realistic
5. Monitoring the first six-month cost of design changes
6. The total product cost will show targeted cost and reveal overdesign factors

Adapted from Schonberger (1986)

providing customer satisfaction including reduced costs and increased speed of response to customers. Hayes and Wheelwright (1992) described how NCR's design for manufacturing approach resulted in a 75 per cent reduction in assembly time, 85 per cent fewer parts, 65 per cent fewer suppliers and 75 per cent less direct labour time.

Clearly, most of the above are related to factors of quality and in design there is the meeting point of *process* and *product* technology. Basic criteria for design effectiveness are shown in Table 3.22.

1. **Minimizing the numbers of parts used** This can be facilitated by using components that have been used in similar or former models. New Japanese car models make great use of components that have been used in other models. In computing and telecommunications, the microprocessor technology can be used across a range of models; of course when new technological breakthroughs in microprocessor technology take place, this places a range of models, and components, as outdated.
2. **Percentage of standard parts** Using standard materials and parts whose quality is already known enables consistency to be achieved, which ties in with quality. Although the need is to be customer-specific, manufacturers have been notorious for overdesign and there are indications that increasing the number of standard parts (or reducing the range of components and materials) is vital. Volkswagen, for example, plan to reduce the number of basic chassis platforms from sixteen in early 1994 to four by the year 2000. This is part of Volkswagen's global strategy:

> According to (the) VW research and development director, the new Polo shares about 40 per cent of its components, by value, with its half-sister, the Seat Ibiza . . . (they) share dashboards, as well as rear axle and suspension, and some engines and gearboxes. (*Financial Times*, 29 August 1994, p.4)

The launch of the Nissan Maxima in 1994 was noted for the aggressive pricing – $2,500 less than the previous year's model; a key reason for this was a 10 per cent parts reduction. This seems to be a long-term strategy for Nissan:

> Nissan is slashing costs by reducing the number of models, sharing more components in different cars. (Armstrong, 1994, p.27)

That learning can be undertaken on a division-specific basis is evident from IBM with the Proprinter; the key to the success was a multidisciplinary approach which was designed for manufacturability. The number of components was reduced from 160 to 63 and the assembly of 20 parts was replaced by one plastic moulded frame. As Dertouzos *et al.* (1989) comment:

> Though hardly a startling organizational breakthrough, this was nonetheless a departure from standard practice among American manufacturers. (p.69)

3. **Using existing manufacturing resources** This gels with the idea of *kaizen*, improving incrementally (including the design process) rather than incurring massive expenditure on new manufacturing technology.
4. **The cost of the first production run** This will show if the design is both realistic and able to be produced in larger volumes. At this stage modifications can and should be made as required. It will also highlight the link between process choice and volume.
5. **First six-month cost of design changes** Design changes in the first six months will indicate the thoroughness of the original design.
6. **Total production costs** Total costs will show if design has met targets within the overall budget. If it has been exceeded, then either the company or customers will bear the cost; in a price-sensitive market the latter may not be possible, in which case the firm's profitability and opportunity for reinvestment will be jeopardized.

3.13 Modular design

Flexibility has become a key competitive variable. Ideas of scale, based around huge volumes of one particular product, have given way to a wide range of product offerings in far smaller quantities. To reduce costs and to provide flexibility, it is clear that design modularity is becoming increasingly common in a number of industries. Modular design allows economies of scale to be gained in materials usage by creating a range of modular systems which when combined make a large volume, from which customers can choose: a PC system may have five monitors, three keyboards, four computers and three printers. The combination from this would then be $5 \times 3 \times 4 \times 3 = 180$. The major benefit is the perceived choice for the customer. However, from the manufacturer's view, inventories now become a matter of subcomponents, rather than finished goods which, in turn, reduces inventory costs. In addition, such an approach lends itself to just-in-time – final products will be constructed by 'pulling' the modular requirements for assembly. Dell have used modularization as a key factor in their manufacturing strategy; speed of response, together with customer-specific requirements are what Dell's deserved reputation is based upon.

Modular design is now part of best practice in the car industry. For example, Nippondenso builds components which include generators, alternators, radiators and anti-skid braking systems. All design is made by cross-functional teams which aim to allow any combination of basic parts to be possible; all parts can fit together physically and functionally. Nippondenso's main customer is Toyota, who boast of being able to produce thousands of customer variations per model. In order to match Toyota's needs, therefore, Nippondenso is capable of producing a comparable range of modular assemblies.

The modularity extends into full products, rather than component similarities; the Toyota challenge in the 1991 UK advertising campaign boasted that the Toyota range (including 5, four-door saloon types, five-door versions, estate cars and coupé versions) provided a range for all types. Ford, in contrast, at this stage (1991) could offer only slight variations around their Fiesta.

Modular design allowed Honda to quickly tailor the Honda Accord for their own market. Although hugely successful in the United States, the Accord was not seen as sufficiently distinct for the Japanese market. As a result of modular designs, Honda was then able to provide a facelift for their own market while retaining the existing technology in the car.

In Michigan, Ford have invested over a billion US dollars around the concept of the modular engine, aimed at providing over twelve variations of a core engine concept. The approach was team-based with production/operations involved from the beginning. Not only has this allowed the modularization to take place – most engines will share 75 per cent of parts – it has also been achieved with a 25 per cent overall parts reduction. Modular design is not an engineering whim, but a strategic tool to satisfy fragmented markets, requiring wide product offerings.

Conclusion

It is clear that product innovation is of strategic importance. Without constant innovation a company cannot compete at all. As such, new ideas for innovation must be part of the organizational culture. For example, Toyota's *kaizen* includes ideas for new product improvements, as well as process developments and its continuous improvement approach means that Toyota 'can manage the product supply process much faster than firms emphasizing breakthrough innovation strategies' (Cordero, 1991, p.292).

In 1990, Womack *et al.* wrote:

> Toyota is offering consumers around the world as many products as General Motors – even though Toyota is still half GM's size ... Toyota needs half the time and effort required by a mass-producer such as GM to design a new car. (p.64)

Lean production is critiqued in Chapter 8, but what we can say here is that Western car manufacturers, including Chrysler and GM have improved in their rate and speed of new product introduction in the 1990s. Such innovation is, sometimes, divisional-specific rather than a company-wide, multidivisional occurrence. In any event, such process improvements in innovation, GM's Aurora and Chrysler's Neon and Viper for example, owe little to their becoming lean manufacturers. Instead it owes everything to a change of attitude, moving away from the past sequential, function-to-function method to a cross-functional team approach, with design for manufacture being a central feature.

Speed of product innovation is essential for computing and telecommunications and is becoming more important in the car industry than it has been in the past. Chrysler, for example, has reduced their design-to-market time from five years to three and this has been accomplished by issues discussed in this chapter: a culture which encourages new ideas from all levels of the organization, an emphasis on teamwork when developing designs to full manufacture and beyond and excellent design technology which enhances accuracy, speed and reduces overall costs.

It is argued by Peters (1992) that speed is at the core of business requirements today. Included in this is the demand to innovate products in a constant and speedy manner. However, successful innovation can only be made if companies take an holistic view of their business – including other companies in their supply chain – in order to create designs and products which will be successful in the market. The explicit requirement for firms is constant innovation, realized through the match between process and product technology, providing successful products to the market. The implicit task for this to happen is for the firm to be continuously learning via technological scanning, joint ventures/alliances and by constantly reviewing the development process (and learning from this) in order to achieve greater levels of innovation.

A brief overview of changes in product development is seen in Table 3.23.

Table 3.23 Summary of changes in new product development

	Past approach	*Enlightened approach*
Source Of ideas	Top–down and/or specialist	Company-wide
Development process	Function-to-function; sequential	Multifunctional groups
Characterized by	Fear of failure	Constant innovation
Production/ operations' involvement	Reactive – real involvement only when it was time to volume manufacture	Central; design for manufacture is a key issue
Organizational learning	Considered unimportant	New product development is a major opportunity for learning

Underpinning all this is the requirement to be customer-driven in all that the company does, in other words, to be obsessed with product and process quality, which is the area under discussion in Chapter 5. However, in order to meet customer needs, the manufacturing processes must be in place. Manufacturing processes are discussed in Chapter 4.

Summary

- **New product development is of strategic importance and is not just the prerogative of one department.**
- **Design has to be made in the context of an holistic approach – a company-wide effort whose collective contribution will help to ensure customer satisfaction.**
- **Failure rates are enormous and may be reduced by a company-wide, rather than a single-function drive in product innovation.**
- **The sequential, function-to-function approach is outdated and has to be replaced by simultaneous, cross-functional teams in order to reduce the real time of innovation.**
- **Speed of new product development is becoming increasingly important and is a critical factor for the computing and telecommunications industries.**
- **The link between production/operations, marketing and design areas is vital from the conception of a new product.**
- **R&D on an ongoing basis is central to new product development but is not in itself sufficient. Applied research is only successful when ideas are translated into volume manufacturing**
- **New product development is a key opportunity for organizational learning through the development of technology itself or by forming alliances with other companies to jointly develop new products.**
- **There are some good rules of design which are offered in the chapter and companies can use these rules as criteria for product design.**

CASE Ford

In 1992 the Ford Taurus became the best-selling car in the United States, replacing the Honda Accord. This was a success story for Ford which, like Chrysler and General Motors, had felt the pressure of Japanese competition since the 1980s. The Ford Taurus revolutionized US family car design and remained the best-selling car in the United States in 1994. Other successes during this period for Ford included the Explorer sports utility vehicle and the redesigned Mustang car. These models helped Ford increase its share of the US car and light truck market from about 23 per cent in 1987 to 25.4 per cent in 1994.

Figure 3.9 Ford's sales and income: 1989–93.

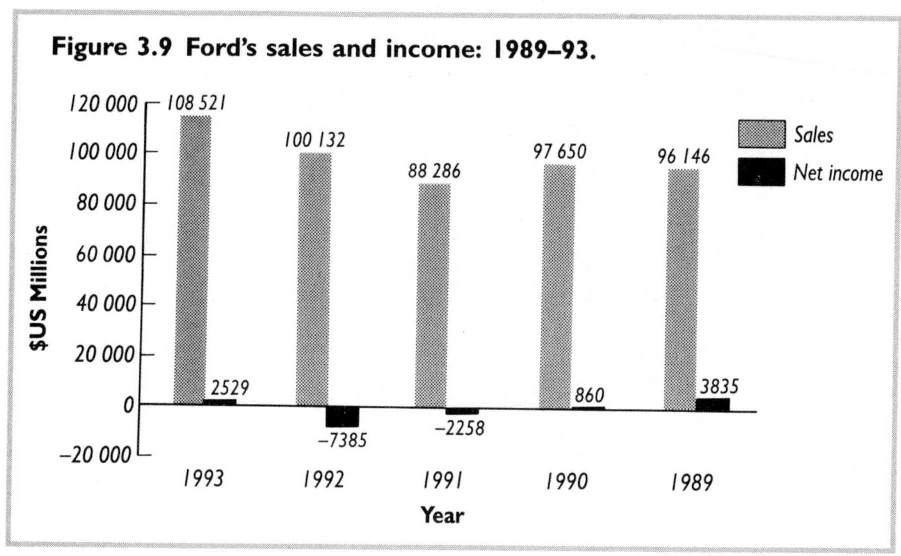

Despite this success, big losses had been made in 1991 and 1992 (Figure 3.9).

Ford had cut its workforce by over 30 per cent and closed fifteen plants during the 1980s. Ford improved productivity in its plants ahead of GM and Chrysler and had the most productive North American factories among the 'big three' in the early 1990s.

However, a big step change took place with the introduction of the Mondeo. First, the Mondeo illustrated Ford's development in terms of their supplier base; only 270 suppliers were used world-wide, a third of the usual total. In world-class fashion, Ford now wants to build world-wide relationships with an even smaller group of suppliers.

Second, the Mondeo became a powerful means of learning; Ford wanted to become more global in their approach to new product developments and the Mondeo was a major effort by Ford to produce an international car. The Mondeo in Europe is very similar to the Ford Contour and Mercury Mystique in the United States. The Mondeo took six years to develop, longer than recent new GM and Chrysler models and was the most expensive car launched, over $6 billion. The Mondeo was first launched in Europe, where it achieved leadership of the mid-sized segment of the European market. The Contour (and the similarly designed Mercury Mystique) were then launched in the United States in the hope that they would emulate the success of the Mondeo.

The process of new product development for the Mondeo included three engineering centres. The result of this was a car which had the same platform, suspension and power trains. However, the look of the US models is slightly different to the European one. The differences for each market meant that tooling for five different styles was required for the eight major plants in the United Kingdom, Germany, Mexico and the United States. The Mondeo was not quite a global car though. Such an idea was impossible when the company's

European and American operations were distinct, with separate model ranges, organizational structures, engineering teams and factory practices.

However, the Mondeo meant that Ford then began to reorganize in order to make global products a reality. The rationale behind Ford's global approach is simply scale; a number of products could be launched from a common design base. The CEO, Alex Trotman, is quoted as saying that the one Mondeo project resulted in three new models, two new engines, two new gearboxes and nine new or improved factories.

Ford announced plans to combine two units – North American Operations and Ford of Europe – into a single unit, Ford Automotive Operations. Until this point, Ford has had separate geographic divisions, developing cars of essentially the same type, but with different characteristics aimed at their particular local markets.

Alex Trotman said that the reorganization was to:

> combine the resources of a large and very successful company with the speed and responsiveness of a small company. (*The Economist*, 23 July 1994)

The reorganization involved Ford creating five vehicle programme centres (VPCs), four in North America and one in Europe. The European VPC, with research and engineering centres in both the United Kingdom and Germany, would be responsible for developing small and medium front-wheel drive cars for sale in Europe, America and Asia.

The other four VPCs, based in Detroit, would develop large front-wheel drive cars, such as the Ford Taurus, rear-wheel drive cars, personal trucks, sports utility vehicles and commercial trucks.

The global products themselves will all be focused on mid-range cars. This means that Ford has not lost sight of particular market tastes. In Europe, for example, cars like the Lincoln Town cars have none of the importance that they have in the United States. It would not make sense to have a global Lincoln Town car. It does make sense to combine design efforts into producing potentially global cars in a particular segment of the market.

The reorganization is a massive change and, possibly, a huge gamble. The vision seems to have come from Alex Trotman:

> I have envisaged Ford with a global organisation since the late 1960s. It's a natural evolution ... Now is the right time for such a change. The tools are there – computers and communications – and we have a strong balance sheet. If you make big changes when times are difficult, expediency often takes precedence. (*The Economist*, 23 July 1994)

If it takes too long to reorganize, or fails to exploit the common resources to produce new products more rapidly and less expensively than before, this development could well be a disaster for Ford. If the gamble pays off, Ford will have pioneered one of the most dramatic approaches to new product developments.

4 Manufacturing investment, process choice and strategy

4.1 Introduction

This chapter examines the importance of technology, plant layout and process choice as part of the strategic manufacturing planning process for the firm. The focus is therefore on *process* technology, rather than *product* technology, which was discussed in Chapter 3. The focal point in both chapters, however, is how technology enables a company to successfully compete in markets.

Process choice is a major strategic decision; no amount of reactive, tactical measures can hope to compensate for inappropriate investment in wrong processes which do not match the market requirements in which the firm is competing. Decisions have to be based on current and future market demands, and not technical or engineering indulgence by particular people within the firm. As Twiss and Goodridge (1989) state:

> All new technology inevitably changes an organisation to some extent . . . The contribution of technology is too important for corporate success to be left to the judgement of the technologist alone. The technological tail cannot be allowed to wag the corporate dog. (p.xvii)

However, part of the problem is that, in many Western manufacturing firms, there is no technological/manufacturing presence at senior levels within the firm whose input might help in guiding the extent and applicability of technological investment made at corporate level. The consequence of this is that sometimes there have been massive amounts of investments in technology that have gained no benefit for the firm. The actual sums invested in technology and process choice tend to be large, so purchasing fixed assets for manufacturing tends to have huge financial implications for the firm.

4.1.1 The link between layout, process choice and technology

The three major internal decisions facing a manufacturing company are:

1. The layout of a plant.
2. The basic choice of process.
3. The amount of investment in – and types of – technology.

The three decisions interlink but are not synonymous. Process choice should include layout as part of the planning process, and technology links into, but is not limited to, process choice or layout, as shown in Figure 4.1

4.1.2 *Inappropriate technological investment*

These decisions are critical and must be made with the aim of equipping the firm to be more competitive in the market. Wrong investment decisions in automation will result in wasted funds (often many millions of dollars) and wrong process choice decisions will cripple the company's capability to satisfy customer demands in particular markets. Process choice and technology are vital for many industries because key competitive factors for customers include cost, delivery speed and flexibility, all of which can be enhanced by appropriate technology. If appropriate investment in technology and the choice of process are made, this will become a central part of the firm's competitive weaponry. If wrong decisions are made, a huge liability and financial millstone is in place.

Keller (1993) tells how inappropriate investment was made at GM:

> While Smith provided the money for automation and supported it completely, he clearly didn't understand it – nor did his engineering staff who encouraged him. With its 260 gleaming new robots for welding, assembling, and painting cars; its fifty automated guided vehicles to deliver parts

Figure 4.1 The interrelationship between process choice, plant layout and technology.

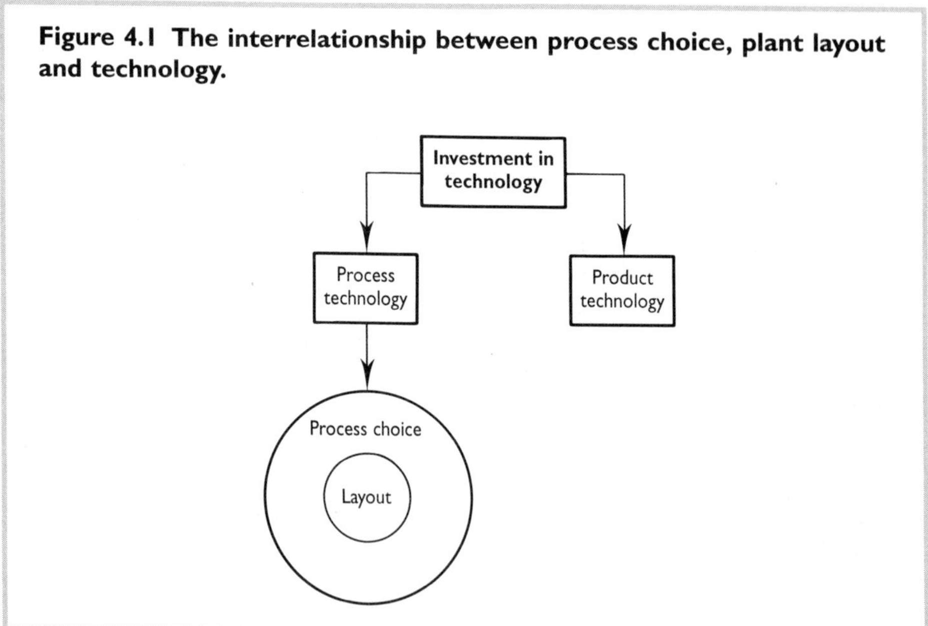

> to the assembly line; and a complement of cameras and computers to monitor, inspect, and control the process, the plant put stars in Smith's eyes. He believed it held the promise of a new era of efficiency and quality and would eventually become a model for all assembly plants. What it became was a nightmare of inefficiency, producing poor-quality vehicles despite the heroic efforts of workers to correct mistakes before they were shipped to dealers. (p.169)

4.1.3 Process technology and organizational learning

Another point that needs to be made is the importance of organizational learning in the firm's technological accumulation. The role of learning is discussed in depth in Chapter 7, but a note is relevant here. Technology by itself will not bring benefits to the firm; it is rather in the successful application of the technology brought about by know-how and experience which will provide advantage for the firm. This is emphasized by Grindley (1991):

> Learning . . . includes formal and informal training, but the most difficult knowledge to acquire is the 'know-how' built up by experience over long periods working with the technology. It is an accumulation of innumerable small details which becomes specific to the technology and to the firm. (p.39)

The firm-specific learning accumulated by the firm had been noted by Pavitt (1990). However, as discussed in Chapters 3 and 5 on quality and new product development, this can be focused even further; in some cases, learning is divisional-specific. Learning gained in a particular GM plant, for example, is not guaranteed to be transferred to another.

4.1.4 The strategic importance of process choice and layout

The layout of a plant and the investment in technology to facilitate manufacturing processes seem, very often, to be couched in tactical terms, rather than strategic importance in production/operations textbooks. This is not surprising, because this view is also held by many Western companies. Part of Japan's success in manufacturing has come from its recognition of plant capability as a strategic weapon, and not simply a tactical factor. We can contrast the tactical versus strategic view of layout in Table 4.1.

However, in some texts good layout is seen purely in terms of satisfying the following general criteria, albeit on a tactical level:

Minimizing factors	**Maximizing factors**
Cost	Product quality
Transport/movement time	Plant utilization
Inventories	Flexibility
Material waste	Customer satisfaction
Overheads	Labour utilization

Table 4.1 Two views of layout

Tactical	*Strategic*
The task is simply to make the best possible use of plant space	Layout links to process choice and is critical in supporting the company efforts in terms of cost, delivery, flexibility and other market requirements

The past solution to layout was seen in terms of maximizing the use of machinery. In managerial terms, the word 'maximize' is, largely, meaningless, but in any event this maximizing was supposedly achieved by using computing/managerial tools, including string diagrams and relationship charts. Such tools can be important, but do not address the strategic planning requirements for plant investments and the whole tone is one of detachment from the strategic vision of the company. Resource-driven ideas such as maximizing machinery usage has therefore given way to more customer-driven approaches to production/operations management, as shown in Table 4.2.

4.2 Basic layout types

The three basic layout types are:

1. Fixed position.
2. Process layout.
3. Product layout.

These types of layout in themselves do not provide much insight into their competitive, strategic importance until they become linked to and part of the basic choice of process, as discussed in section 4.3.7 on process choice. However, a brief discussion of the characteristics of types of layout is appropriate here.

Table 4.2 The changing task of manufacturing management

Period	*Product range*	*Production task*	*Volume level*	*Finished product made*
1950–1970s	Narrow	Achieve supposed economies of scale by large production runs	Very high	To stock
1980s on	Wide	Meet specific customer requirements in terms of cost, delivery, range and flexibility	As required – flexible	For customer order

Figure 4.2 Fixed position layout.

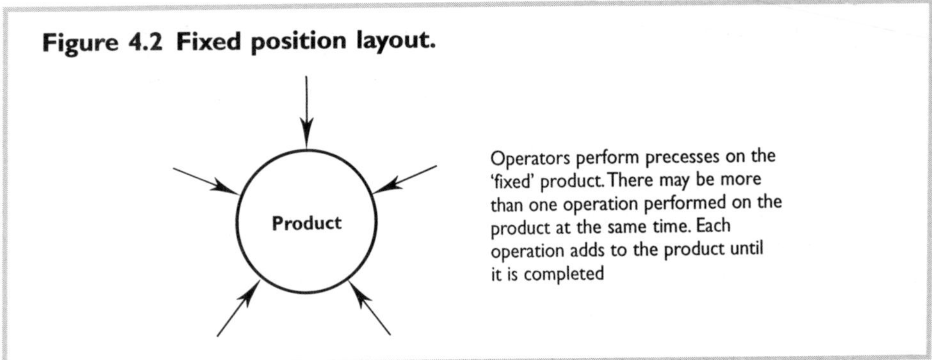

4.2.1 Fixed layout

A layout will be fixed if the product that is being manufactured is heavy, bulky or fragile and in this approach operators come to the product itself. The product is centred around a focused area: aircraft manufacture and shipbuilding are examples of this and such a layout is shown in Figure 4.2.

4.2.2 Process layout

In a process layout, similar groups of machines are located together and are available to potentially make a wide range of products. The machines are not laid out in a particular sequential process. They are grouped together according to their machine type or in order to allow manufacture of a particular family of products in a 'focused cell' to take place. In process layouts two approaches are commonly used:

1. Process layout by function, as shown in Figure 4.3.
2. Process layout in a focused group or family product cell, as shown in Figure 4.4.

With the functional approach process, the machines are not dedicated to a particular product family but are available for a range of products. The product does not move in sequence, but goes to a machine centre as and when required for the particular product. The big advantage of process-oriented layouts is the flexibility in both equipment and labour assignments that they bring. The breakdown of a particular machine will not halt an entire process and work can therefore be transferred to other machines in the department. This type of layout is ideal for manufacturing parts in small batches or job lots and for producing a wide range of parts in different sizes and forms.

Figure 4.3 Process layout in a functional approach.

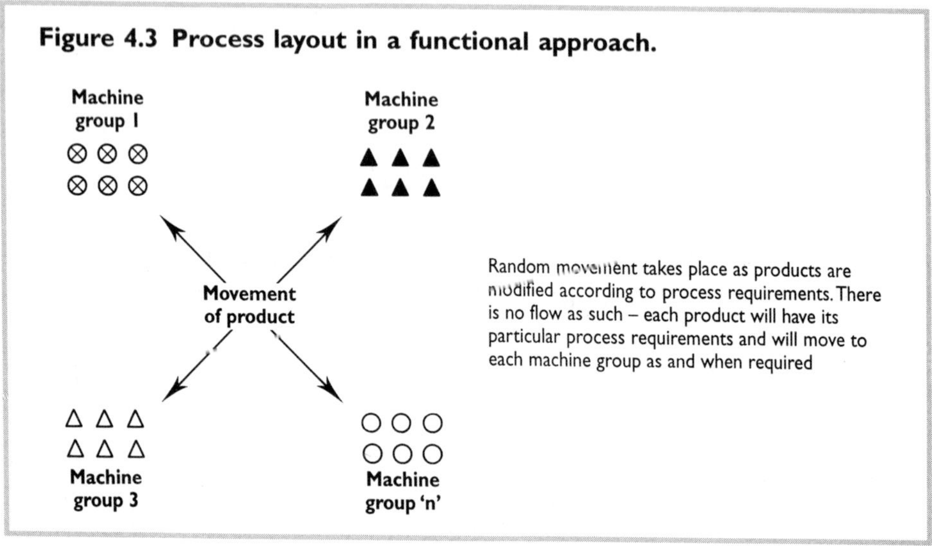

The second approach, shown in Figure 4.4, is to group machines together around a focused product family cell.

With this approach, areas of the plant are dedicated to particular product types in a focused cell of manufacture. Machines are grouped together in a way to best support the manufacture of a particular family of products. The variety of products around a particular group or cell may be quite large, but the essential nature of the product will remain and will therefore warrant a cell of its own, distinct from other product family cells.

4.2.3 *Product layout*

In a product layout, machines are dedicated to a particular product – or a very similar small range of products – and each stage of manufacture is distinct from the next, as shown in Figure 4.5.

Figure 4.4 Process layout in a product family cell.

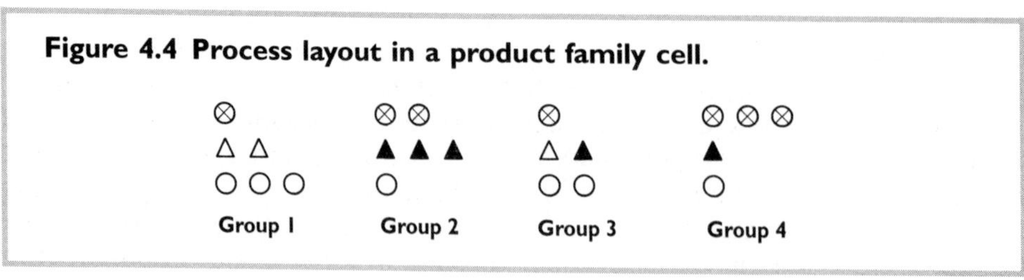

Figure 4.5 Product layout.

○ ○ ○ → ▲ ▲ ▲ → △ △ △ → ⊗ ⊗ ⊗ → Assembly/packing

Each of the above stations is laid out in an operational sequence specific to the manufacture of a particular product or a very small product range.

4.3 Overview of process choice

Investment in a particular choice of process is a crucial decision that a company has to make. What becomes clear is that each process choice carries an initial trade-off. This is in terms of what the process choice itself can offer to markets and, by contrast, how a particular process choice *limits* the capability of the company to enter certain markets and to produce other types of products. With this in mind, process choice has to be seen as a strategic decision, tied to the questions, What business are we in? and What choice of process best suits the market requirements in which the firm is competing? It is clear that in a business world where markets are constantly fragmenting and where rapid change is a requirement, investment in technology has to reflect this change. Investment in technology should not be made on a too narrow and limited process capability.

4.3.1 *Types of process choice*

There are five basic process types that a company has to choose from: project, job, batch, line and continuous process. The choice of manufacturing process that a company adopts has to reflect the needs and requirements of the markets that the company serves. This is an obvious point of course but it is nonetheless neglected in many plants in the West. The essential features of each process choice are as follows.

4.3.2 *Project*

The nature of these products is large-scale and typically complex. In manufacture, this includes such products as civil engineering, aerospace and some major high-tech projects; flight simulator manufacture would tend to fall into this category, for example. Projects tend to be one-offs, where repetition of exactly the same product is unlikely. The nature of the products undertaken in project manufacture is essentially unique by virtue of their not being repeated in exactly the same way. The distinguishing feature between project and job manufacture is that during the process of completion the product in project manufacture tends to be fixed; bridge manufacture, tunnel construction and shipbuilding are typical of this process choice type. This ties the process choice (project) with type of layout (fixed).

Scheduling of projects tends to be undertaken in *phased-completion*, where each phase of completion will be distinct and separate from the subsequent stage. At the simplest level, management tools like Gantt charts will be used. Alternatively, more complicated programmes like Project Network Planning will often be used.

4.3.3 *Job processing*

Job processes are used for one-off or very small order requirements, similar to project manufacture. However, the product can often be moved during manufacture; making special haute-couture clothing is a clear example. Perceived uniqueness is often a key factor for job manufacture. The volume is very small and, like project manufacture, the products tend to be a one-off in terms of design, very unlikely to be repeated in a short period of time and, therefore, investment in technology in order to create a particular product is unlikely. However, job processes are most applicable in the following:

1. Making prototypes of new products – even if the end volume is likely to be high for the product, it makes sense to produce a one-off or very low volume, which lend itself to job manufacture.
2. Making unique products such as machines, tools and fixtures to make other products.

Typical characteristics of job processes are set out in Table 4.3.

From this we can determine that the nature of the process choice (job) links it to the basic type of layout (process).

4.3.4 *Batch*

As volume begins to increase, either in terms of individual products increasing in volume or in the manufacture of similar types or families of products, the process will develop into batch manufacture. The difficulty in batch manufacture is that competitive focus can often become blurred. The batch process is therefore often

Table 4.3 Key characteristics of job processes

1. Investment in automation is for general purpose process technology rather than product specific investment
2. Many different products are run throughout the plant and materials handling has to be modified and adjusted to suit many different products and types
3. Detailed planning will evolve around sequencing requirements for each product, capacities for each work centre and order priorities; because of this, scheduling is relatively complicated in comparison to repetitive line manufacture

difficult to manage and the key to managing batch is to map the range of products either in terms of job or line characteristics. Batch has to be arranged either in terms of the similarity of finished products or by common process groupings.

As a starting point, then, each product has to be determined by its volume; focused cells of manufacture will then be arranged so that low and high volumes can be separated. Typical examples of this in manufacture will be in moulding products; these would be distinguished by determining those products which need much labour input (hand laminating in glass reinforced plastic, for example) and high-volume standard products, where considerable automation would be appropriate. Batch is the most common form of process in engineering and is the most difficult to manage in some ways. Only by determining the volumes of each product and dividing these into low- and high-volume sections can a company hope to be focused and in turn customer-driven. Table 4.4 illustrates the characteristics of batch manufacture.

In general, batch processes link to process layout, although high-volume batch will tend to have a type of line (product) layout, depending upon how often the product is reproduced.

4.3.5 Line

As standardization of a particular product increases, so a line process becomes more appropriate. High-volume standard products, like particular models of cars, TVs, hi-fi, VCRs and computers, lend themselves to line processes, often arranged in a U-shape. Each stage of manufacture will be distinct from the next and ideally value, not just cost is added at each stage of manufacture until the product is completed. The line would be dedicated to a particular product (with possible variations of models) and introducing new products that are very different from the former product is difficult or even impossible to realize on an existing line

Table 4.4 Key characteristics of batch processes

1. Automation, especially for lower volumes of batch manufacturing, tends to be general purpose, rather than dedicated to a particular product, whose volume does not demand product-specific investment in automation
2. Scheduling is complicated and has to be completely reviewed on a regular, ongoing basis – this applies to new products, one-offs that may be required, together with relatively high volume, standard products; all of these types will need to be scheduled
3. Operators have to be able to perform a number of functions – this is obviously true of job type processes. In batch, though, this flexibility is crucial, in that it will allow operators to move to various workstations as and when required
4. Where automation is being used, set-up time should be short. The ideal set-up time is quick enough to accommodate run lengths of just one unit, switching over to other models and volumes as and when required

Table 4.5 Key characteristics of line processes

1. Process times should be fast, which is critical in order to satisfy delivery speed requirements
2. There should be simplification in production planning and control and the tasks themselves should also be simplified for each workstation
3. There should be small amounts of work in process; in fact, work in process (which, in accounting terms, can be viewed as an asset) is a liability to the company which can ruin cash flow and stifle quick response to market requirements
4. Materials handling between stations should be placed as closely as possible to each other
5. Materials flow and control is critical. Just-in-time lends itself most noticeably to line or very high-volume batch production. Stock-outs have to be avoided although, at the same time, excess stock is a waste and a liability, rather than an asset (materials can be viewed as an asset on the balance sheet which is misleading and alien to world-class manufacturing

Source: Schonberger (1986)

manufacturing process. It is clear therefore that the process choice (line) ties it to the product type of layout. Key characteristics of line processes are shown in Table 4.5.

Since much of the discussion on automation, which appears later in the chapter, is based on developments around line processes, it makes sense to briefly discuss some of the disadvantages of line processes which include the following:

1. There can often be a lack of process flexibility and introducing new products on existing technology can be difficult. This is alleviated to some degree by similar subcomponents, which become included in the design for new products and which then allow the new product to be made on existing lines.
2. As standardization and volumes both increase relative to batch and job manufacturing processes, investment in technology also increases. Special product-specific technology is used and this often involves vast amounts of investments (for example, GM's $80 billion investment in automation in the 1980s).
3. Each workstation is dependent upon the next. Consequently the speed of the line is determined by the lowest capacity of a particular work centre; moreover, in standard lines, if one set of machines do not operate the whole line can come to a stop, thus preventing any production.

4.3.6 *Continuous process*

This is when a process can theoretically run all day for each day of the year on a continuous process. A chemical refining plant would be a good example of this type of process. Key characteristics are shown in Table 4.6.

Table 4.6 Key characteristics of continuous process

1. The volume of a product is very high and the process is dedicated to making, typically, only one product
2. Huge investment in dedicated plant is often required
3. Much automation tends to be evident and labour input is one of policing rather than being highly skilled as an integral input to the overall process

4.3.7 Linking process choice and layout

There are clear associations between the basic choice of process and type of layout. We can summarize this in Table 4.7.

Table 4.7 serves to focus the importance of layout in terms of its link to process choice. It is process choice, however, which provides the major clues in terms of how the firm should compete. We can also add a number of factors which tie together the more strategic factor (process choice) with plant layout (Figure 4.6).

Hill (1989) and Hayes and Wheelwright (1984) provide useful insight into production/operations tasks for each process, as shown in Table 4.8.

4.4 Process choice and strategy

The actual process choice enables a company to focus on what it does best. The problem for manufacturing companies is that it is easy to cause a mismatch between process choice and the market that is being served. The choice of process is initially linked to the factors of volume and variety, as shown in Figure 4.7.

As volume increases therefore, the basic process choice should change from project or job to line, or continuous process, depending on the nature of the

Table 4.7 The link between process choice and layout

Process choice	*Type of layout*
Project	Fixed
Job	Process
Batch	Process/product (see note 1 below)
Line	Product
Continuous process	Product (see note 2 below)

Notes:

1. The link between batch and type of layout would depend upon volume and variety – in low-volume/high-variety batch, process layouts would be used; in high-volume/low-variety batch, product layouts would be appropriate
2. Continuous process differs from line due to the fact that a line process can be stopped at a particular stage and the product will be at *that* stage of production; in continuous process, stopping the process is an exception and is very costly

Figure 4.6 Key headings linking process choice and layout.

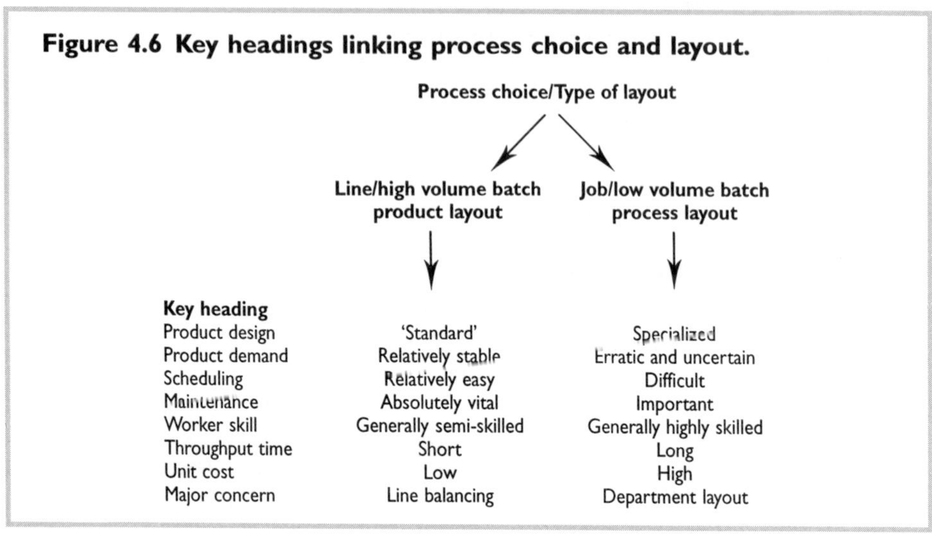

product. Batch manufacture will reflect either end of this continuum, depending on whether the volumes and variety of products are low or high. As volume increases, the amount of flexibility tends to be reduced and investment in product-specific technology tends to be greater.

On a strategic level then, the following should be clear before movement to the right of the continuum is made:

1. Cash flows to pay for the fixed costs have to be available – As movement to the right of the continuum in Figure 4.7 continues, so the increased investment in product-specific technology tends to increase.
2. The risk of lower demand for the product has to be insignificant – In other words, the particular product or at the very least very similar products have to be sustainable in terms of volume to justify investment. More important than the link to volume is the fact that process choice actually states what the

Table 4.8 Process choice and production/operations tasks

	Project	*Job*	*Batch*	*Line*	*Continuous process*
Dominant utilization	Essentially labour	Labour	⇔	Plant	Plant
Process technology	General purpose	Universal	⇔	Dedicated	Very dedicated
Process flexibility	High	High	⇔	Low	Inflexible

Figure 4.7 Basic process choice.

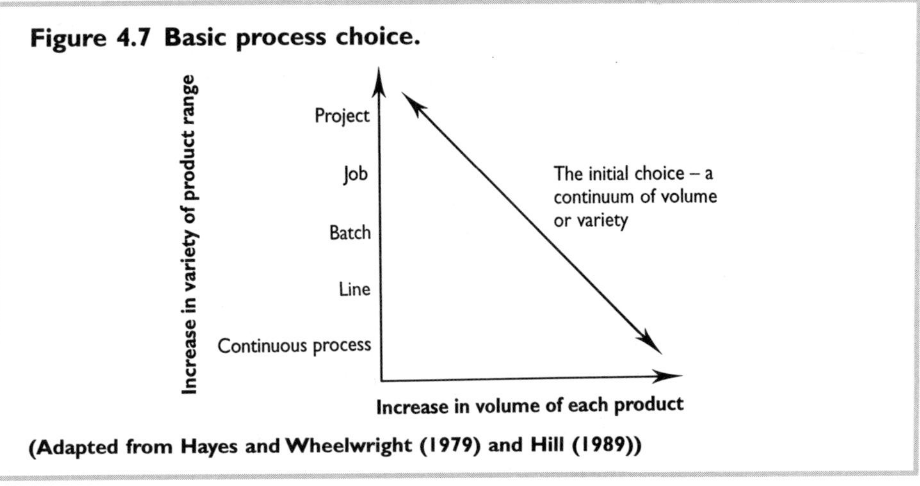

(Adapted from Hayes and Wheelwright (1979) and Hill (1989))

company sells in terms of its capabilities and how the company can compete. Although there may be more than one process type used within the same company, there will often be a core process which is best suited to support the company in the market. This link between process choice and corporate and marketing strategies is shown in Figure 4.8.

Figure 4.8 The link between process choice and marketing strategy.

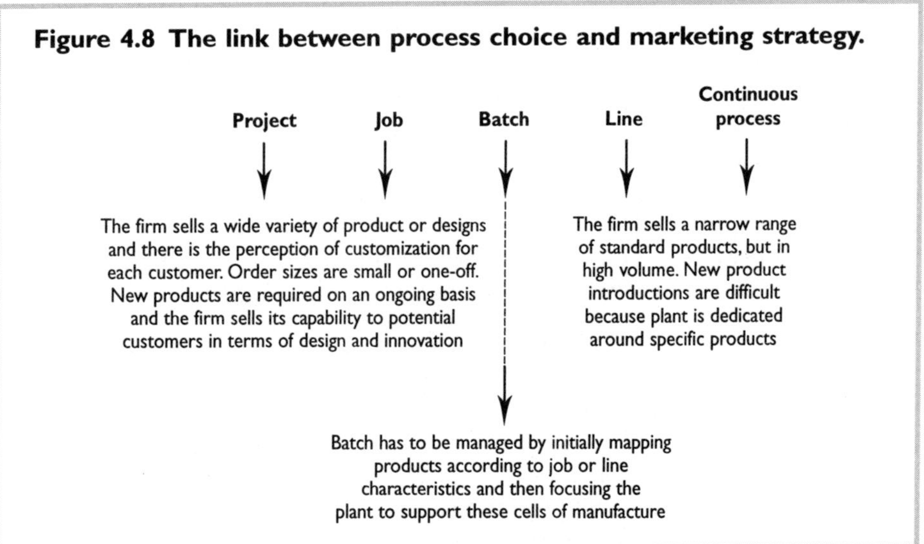

Table 4.9 Linking process choice and order-qualifying/order-winning criteria

Criteria	*Project*	*Job*	*Batch*	*Line*	*Continuous process*
Order-winning	Delivery quality-design capability	Delivery quality-design capability	⇔	Price	Price
Qualifying	Price	Price	⇔	Delivery quality-design capability	Delivery quality-design capability

Note: There is a greater number of order-winning and qualifying criteria than listed above – the above list is indicative only

Hill (1989) makes the very useful distinction between order-qualifying and order-winning criteria. Order-qualifying criteria are those factors that a company needs in order to compete at all and order-winning criteria are those factors which a company needs to achieve in order to win in the marketplace. These can be tied to process choice, as shown in Table 4.9.

This framework is important for the company in that it maps how the process choice ties in to competitive factors. However, we have to be a little careful by not being too rigid with the use of this framework for two reasons:

1. A firm may produce the same type of product for two markets under one process choice. The particular needs of each market will be different, even though the process choice is the same; a good example of this would be in the manufacture of flight simulator units. The two markets are commercial and military and the requirements for these two are entirely different in terms of cost, delivery reliability and added features which may be required for each. Although there would be different detailed processes used in building the simulators, in order to satisfy particular requirements of both markets, each simulator product would be made under a project process choice.
2. What were order-winning criteria may, over time, become order-qualifying, if other competitors copy the technology or the firm loses whatever the differentiated feature may originally have been.

The problem for many companies is that they become unfocused in their attempts to be all things to all markets, rather than focused on what the firm does best. This is particularly true of batch production, which is often difficult to manage. Since over 60 per cent of manufacturing in the West is based around batch manufacture (Groover, 1987), it is vital that the problems associated with batch manufacture are clearly understood and that these problems are avoided. In order to do this, a company has to be fully aware of the particular needs of each customer group for whom it is manufacturing under batch processes. The firm then needs to focus parts of the plant by particular product groups and often particular customer-specific areas.

4.5 Process choice and marketing strategy

Process choice must support market requirements. If markets fragment or customers change, then the link between in-house process capability and market requirements has to be re-examined and if necessary reconfigured. If the volume, range or varieties of existing products alter, a reassessment of the process/market link must be made. This may sound obvious but is sadly not addressed in many companies. For example, in the car and computing/telecommunications industries, there have been dramatic changes due mainly to rapid and constant new product introductions. To have outmoded processes when all this change is taking place will ruin the firm's ability to compete. Successful companies are those whose in-house manufacturing and assembly plants can accept change and constant flexibility to meet customer needs. A mistake which is often made is to confuse variety with overall volume, as shown in Figure 4.9.

Figure 4.9 is best described by the following case on which it is based.

CASE The Southern Cosmetics Company

This case is based on a firm making cosmetic products for several large retailers. In scenario 1, the firm used line processes (rightly so) in order to meet high-volume, standard product requirements for products A,B,C and D. However, the firm then lost part of its business (products C and D) to a competitor. This represented something in the region of 50 per cent of the firm's sales turnover and, coincidentally, 50 per cent of its manufacturing output. In a desperate attempt to replace this loss of business, the firm then won new orders which meant that they now had to produce a range of products: A,B,C,D,E,F and G.

A and B remained as before, namely, standard high-volume products; C–G were products with various ranges, variety and mixes of volume requirements placed on them. Unfortunately, the firm attempted to continue with its dedicated line processes, with disastrous results. The core business (products A and B) was not being satisfied due to the constant changes in set-ups for the other products. In addition, the line was unable to cope with the constant changes of variety, variability and volumes for products C–G.

This problem was resolved by focusing the cosmetic plant into two distinct areas: high-volume (line process) for products A and B and low-volume (batch process) for products C–G. The firm had to focus in this way and by doing so, it satisfied the market requirements. It is vital therefore that a firm monitors its process choice to make sure that it continues to satisfy customer needs.

Market demands in many industries mean that pressure of both variety and volume have to be addressed. The traditional line process, which mass-produced one product, fails to meet the requirement of variety. In car manufacture, variety around a particular model is a requirement in the 1990s. Toyota claims to be able to provide over 40,000 configurations around particular models and Bessant (1993, p.203) notes how 'Japanese producers have been introducing model changes and variants at the rate of 100 per year'. Similarly, in computing

Figure 4.9 Process choice and market requirements.

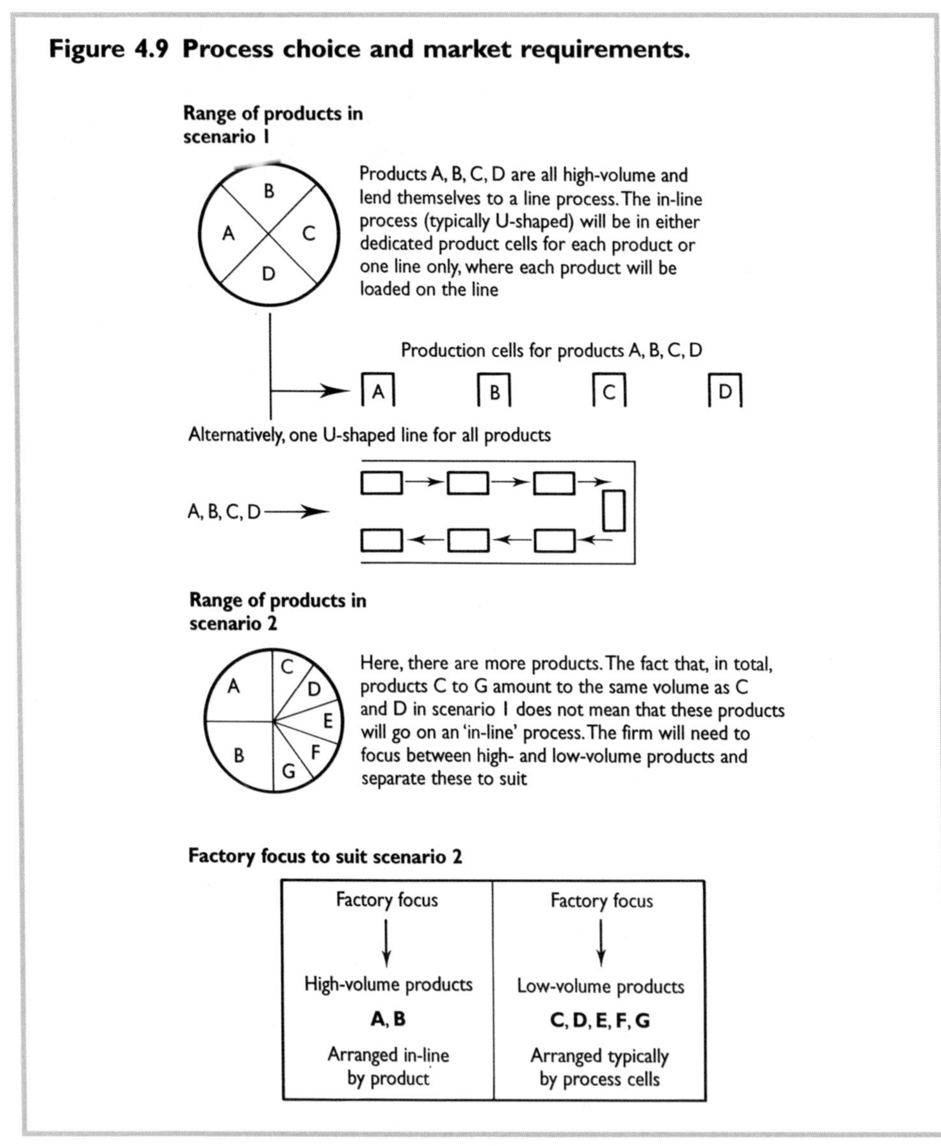

manufacture, variety pressures have meant that traditional line processes are not appropriate to meet the wider, more customer-specific requirements. For example, Dell computers now ensure that modular assembly is achieved to suit particular customer requirements. The requirements of high volume, coupled with high variety, means that these market needs have to be understood and met by manufacturing capability.

We can see how the increase in variability, forces manufacturing back up the continuum toward high variety/lower volume, rather than standard very high-volume processes. This movement in the continuum is shown in Figure 4.10.

Instead of mass-production through narrow dedicated lines, modifications around the middle area, batch, is the solution where flexible manufacturing systems (FMS) and group technology (discussed later in the chapter) are employed. However, both FMS and group technology are different approaches to manufacturing and not just a modification of batch manufacture, but hybrid solutions where both variety and volume may be achieved. This development, technology which is loosely centred under batch manufacture, is shown in Figure 4.11.

Production/operations managers need to be able to manage this middle area of high volume/high variety and there are two important issues that help here. These are:

1. Factory focus.
2. The importance of the product lifecycle for production/operations.

Figure 4.10 Process choice and market requirements.

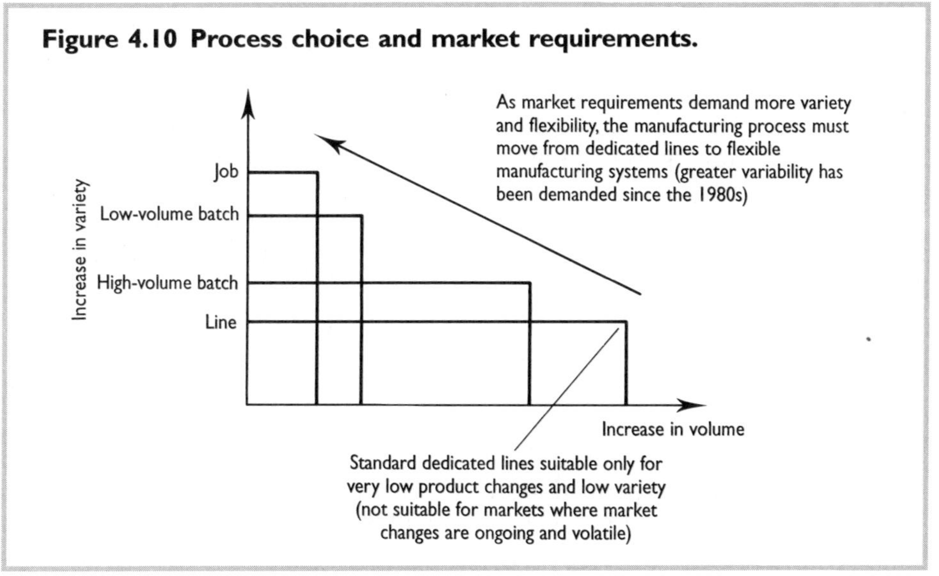

Figure 4.11 The application of FMS and group technology on process choice.

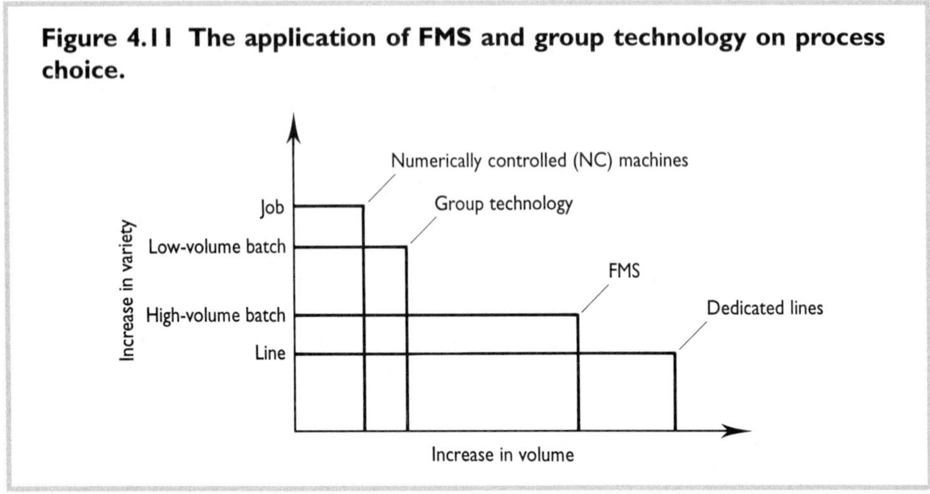

4.6 Factory focus

The idea of factory focus was first proposed by Skinner (1974):

> a factory that focuses on a narrow product mix for a particular market niche will outperform the conventional plant, which attempts a broader mission. (p.113)

That is not to say that a plant can only produce one product; rather, when an additional product is introduced, an analysis of the processes which best support the product has to be made and, if needed, another area (or cell) of the plant has to be dedicated to the manufacture of this product. Areas or cells of the overall plant will therefore be focused and arranged according to particular product requirements. Distinctions in terms of process requirements and volumes for each product will be made and the plant focused accordingly.

In a survey conducted by Ingersoll, cited in the *Financial Times* (14 May 1991), it suggested that over half of the UK's engineering companies have implemented cells in their plants:

> Well over 90 percent of manufacturers who have implemented cells have seen an improvement in performance and over 40 percent describe the improvement as significant. (Section III, p.1)

An approach which does not take into account these factors will undoubtedly result in failing to meet customer requirements, including delivery, flexibility and cost factors. Focus may be in terms of focused process cells or (where there is sufficient volume) focused product cells. In addition, it is vital to know where a product is in terms of its position in the product lifecycle. We need therefore to link focus with the product lifecycle.

4.7 Process choice and the product lifecycle

The choice of process and layout has clear links with the product lifecycle. The lifecycle diagram serves to show where a particular product is in its lifecycle and where it should be placed in terms of process choice. In the early stages of the product's life, the focused area of manufacture will be in a low-volume batch cell group; it may return to another low-volume focused area at the decline stage of its life. In the growth, maturity and saturation stages, the product is best manufactured in a group of high-volume batch cells and as volume increases, single line process is most appropriate, generally in U-shaped lines. The product lifecycle and the link to process choice are shown in Figure 4.12.

Two things must be understood about the product lifecycle:

1. Not all products will go through every stage of the lifecycle.
2. The length of time that the product may stay in a particular stage of the cycle will vary; the stages are not the same length of time for every product.

The product lifecycle is not a predictive tool and only serves to point out that a product can be plotted, in terms of volume, at a particular point in time. The product lifecycle reveals that as a result of volume, particular focused cells of manufacture will serve products in the growth-to-maturity stages. Other low-volume cells may be used at the introduction and decline stages.

A firm must link manufacturing processes with product requirements, so movement from one process choice to another has to take place when any of the following factors is present:

- A new or substantially modified product is being introduced.
- Competitive factors and priorities have changed.

Figure 4.12 The product lifecycle and the link to process choice.

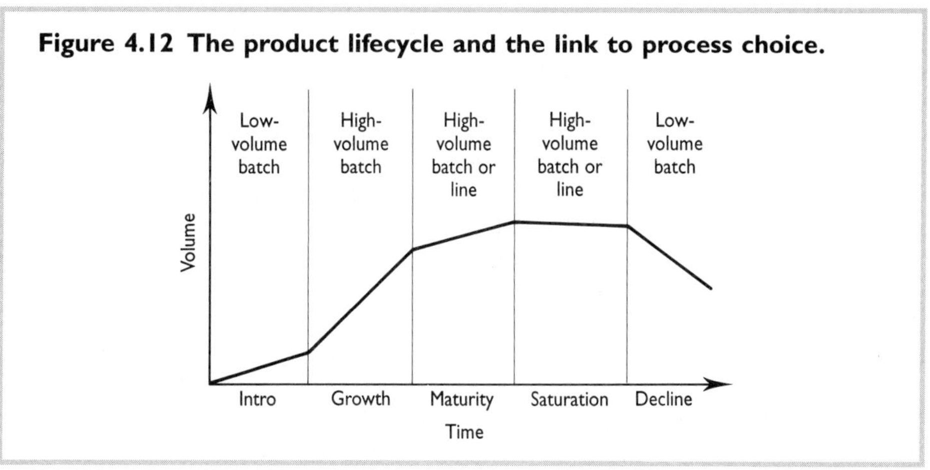

- Volume changes occur.
- The current performance of a product is inadequate.
- Competitors are gaining advantage by a better process approach or new technology.

The point of the product lifecycle in relation to manufacturing is that it reveals that volume changes demand that one fixed process is not sufficient or indeed applicable for a product over its life. As a result, flexible systems have to be in place to facilitate this change over a period of time. Investment in these processes, although expensive, is increasingly viewed as a competitive requirement. It is clear therefore that a standard line cannot hope to satisfy the market requirements of variety, flexibility and so on which will impact on products over a period of time. Instead, flexible manufacturing systems cater for such variety and FMS is now discussed.

4.8 Flexible manufacturing systems (FMS)

4.8.1 Definition of FMS

Some debate continues as to the exact nature of FMS. Bignell (1985) suggests that:

> To dispute whether a system is FMS or not FMS is not so worthwhile. FMS is something that marketing and academic people sell, and to concentrate the discussion on FMS (rather than on flexibility) is to move away from the heart of the matter. (p.100)

FMS is a computer-controlled system with several workstations, each focusing on different operations. Hundreds of tool options are available and once a batch has been completed under one setting the machine is retooled for the next setting, awaiting the next batch. Luggen (1991) refers to various definitions proposed by other authors on FMS and concludes that:

> Regardless of how broadly or narrowly FMS is defined, several key items emerge as critical to a general definition of FMS and repeat themselves . . . Words like NC machine tools, automatic handling systems, central computer controlled, randomly loaded, linked together and flexible all serve to help define a very general description and definition of FMS. (p.7)

Standard FMS includes the following:

1. A number of workstations, such as computer numerically controlled machines that perform a wide range of operations.
2. A transport system which will move material from one machine to another; loading and unloading stations where completed or partially completed components will be housed and worked upon.

3. A comprehensive computer control system which will co-ordinate all the activities. The activities will include:

    - The control of each workstation.
    - Distribution of control instructions to workstations.
    - Production control.
    - Traffic control.
    - Tool control.
    - System performance monitoring.

4.8.2 The emergence of FMS

FMS forms part of the overall advancements in computer-integrated manufacture (CIM) although it is a distinct area in its own right. FMS is a means of managing the manufacture of products which have been forced to the middle of the continuum between variety and volume. FMS offers speed and flexibility in terms of change of tooling, together with precision and consistency of reliability. FMS cells are arranged around a group of products where perceived variety of the product plays a role and where volume lends itself to a high-volume batch process choice. If the volume were very high and the product variability minimal, then a line process would be most applicable. FMS allows a product to be made in a number of variations and in different volumes over a period of time. FMS is central to world-class plants which can make a number of variations around a particular model. This contrasts with the very rigid and narrowly defined product specification approach where little variation was allowed, standardization was central, and where high volumes of one particular product were the norm.

FMS grew out of the fact that varieties of batches of finished goods were expensive to make under systems which saw volume and attendant truths of economies of scale being the dominant feature in manufacturing. Since over 50 per cent of manufacturing in the United States uses batch technology in units of 100, 50 or fewer (Groover, 1987), it became clear that an alternative approach to mass-production had to be developed, and FMS offered this.

FMS is best suited when the variations that occur are nonetheless around a basic stable design; all products use the same family of components; the number of components is moderate (10–50); the volume of each component is also moderate (1,000–30,000 annually), but lot sizes can be as small as one.

4.8.3 Benefits of FMS

Flexibility comes from satisfying a number of different customer needs; this demand pull was well summarized in 1982 by Naisbitt:

> There are 752 different models of cars and trucks sold in the United States – and that's not counting the choice of colors they come in. If you want a subcompact, you can choose from 126 different types. (p.12)

The range has increased dramatically since 1982 and continues to grow. This means that fixed automation which can only offer a very limited range is now clearly outmoded and out-performed by flexibility which is customer-driven. Bolwijn and Kumpe (1990) observe how competition has been the driving force of flexibility which has to be reflected in automation to support this variety:

> Product offerings from the Far East have made customers much more quality-conscious and accustomed them to frequent model changes. And traditional batch-manufacturing techniques lack the flexibility required to bring out high-quality new products at yearly intervals or less. To meet the fast-changing demands of today's fashion-conscious markets without maintaining huge stocks of finished products, companies need greater flexibility, smaller batch sizes and continuous flow – in short, precisely the benefits promised by FMS. (p.294)

This flexibility will manifest itself in a number of ways, including both flexibility in manufacturing and flexibility in market requirements. Browne *et al.* in Bignell (1985) state that manufacturing flexibility will include the following: machines, process, products, routing, volumes, expansion, operations and production. They see this flexibility linking together as in Figure 4.13.

We can also add that market requirements in the 1990s and beyond will include *at least* the flexibility set out in Table 4.10.

Luggen (1991) suggests that there should be benefits along the following lines with successful FMS installations:

1. Inventory reduction of 60–80 per cent.
2. Direct labour savings of 30–50 per cent.
3. Increased asset usage approaching 80–90 per cent.
4. Floor-space reduction of 40–50 per cent.

Figure 4.13 Manufacturing flexibility.

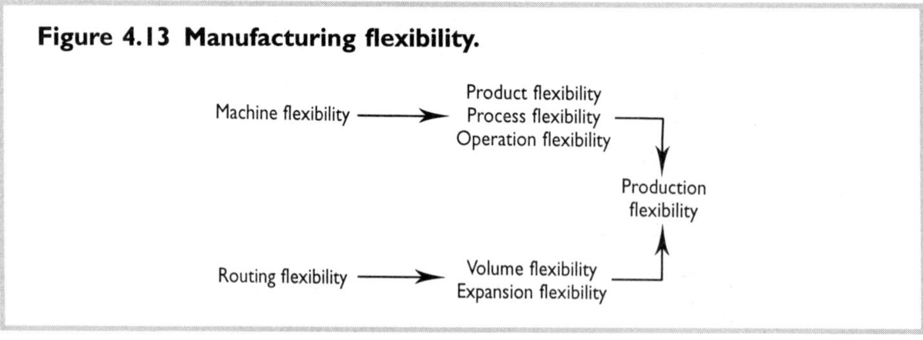

Table 4.10 Market requirements in terms of flexibility

Product variety	More different models, styles, colours, etc.
Product customization	Increasingly tailoring products to suit a particular customer's requirements
Product innovation	Frequent changes of model and introduction of new products to the marketplace
Delivery flexibility	Delivering on short lead times and in quantities to suit customer needs, not manufacturing efficiency
Demand flexibility	Coping with seasonality, fashion and other types of demand variation – matching capacity to demand

Adapted from Bessant (1991)

However, these would be dependent on the suitability of the FMS in terms of capacity, layout of workstations, processing flexibility and avoidance of other factors such as machine breakdown and downtime. FMS is not in itself the panacea and along the lines suggested by Schonberger (1986), it is vital to correct bad practice first *then* automate. What is also clear is that 'throwing money at automation is stupid' (Peters, 1990) and that careful investment along incremental lines is most appropriate. Bateman and Zeithaml (1993) provide useful insight into the strategic, competitive importance of FMS in car manufacturing.

They speak of Japanese manufacturing where FMS is used and state:

> (FMS) allows them (Japanese manufacturers) to build up to eight different models on a single assembly line. In the United States most assembly lines and some entire plants are dedicated to a single model. If the model isn't selling, the line shuts down . . . US auto executives must plan only models that can sell at least 200,000 units. In contrast the Mazda Miata can sell 20,000 units in the United States without taking a financial bath. (p.579)

This has clear benefits for both manufacturer and customer:

> Mazda's production plans for a Monday are final on Friday afternoon, compared to the three weeks' lag time at General Motors . . . Dies can be changed in minutes, whereas in US plants changing dies took hours or even a full workday . . . Mazda can deliver a tailor-made car in one week, compared to three weeks for US manufacturers. With the advantages of speed, quality and customized products, flexible manufacturing appears to be a mode of operations that auto makers must adopt for long-term survival. (p.580)

Kaplan (1986) describes the success of FMS at Yamazaki Machinery Company in Japan. As a result of the $18 million investment in FMS, the following occurred: the total number of machines was reduced from 68 to 18; number of employees from 215 to 12; floor space from 103,000 to 30,000 sq. ft; processing time of parts from 35 to 1.5 days. All of this is impressive and, in Japanese eyes, shows clear justification for investment. However, the company reported a total savings of $6.9 million after 2 years. Including a saving of $1.5 million per year for the next 20 years, the projected total return is under 10 per cent per year. In most US companies, the 'hurdle rate' to justify investment is generally 15 per cent or higher (Heizer and Render, 1993) and therefore this investment would be viewed poorly, in spite of the many other competitive factors which it provides. The justification for investment in FMS and other automation is discussed later in the chapter.

Impressive results gained from investment in FMS and other automation are clearly evident when looked upon from the viewpoint of competitive advantage gained from the investment; Bolwijn and Kumpe (1990) cite the manufacturers of pump cylinder blocks who invested $15 million in FMS rather than $1.3 million to replace just its worn-out boring equipment. As a result of this investment, overall manufacturing costs were reduced by 30 per cent and inventory by 85 per cent, while achieving massive improvements in product quality. As Bolwijn and Kumpe (1990) state:

> Since it (the firm) can now make 99 percent of customer requirements directly to order, it has gained an important competitive advantage. (p.293)

In his analysis, Bessant (1989) found that the following benefits had been attained by implementing FMS:

	Average	**Range**
Cost of FMS (£m)	2.4	0.8–>10
No. of employees	2100	50–16 000
Batch size	120	1–2000
Part family	240	2–4000
Lead time	–74%	40–90
WIP	–68%	25–90
Stock turnover	+350%	50–500
Machine utilization	+63%	15–100

Besides being more customer-driven in approach, FMS also serves to enhance manufacturing performance. Bessant (1991) cites a report of FMS successes in Germany, where sixty firms were surveyed in depth. In each case, improvements were achieved in the following areas: reduced lead times, improved quality, labour savings, increased product variety, reduction of downtime and parallel set-ups, enabling greater efficiency and productivity.

Bessant (1991) summarizes the benefits of FMS:

> a point which emerges from a number of studies is that the benefits of FMS investment often come more from the organizational changes which it catalyses than from a narrow set of physical equipment which is installed. It forces a new way of thinking on the firm and it is this change in approach which is critical in obtaining the full benefits. (p.121)

Table 4.11 Key characteristics of successful FMS

1. Machine utilization – short set-up and changeover times are critical to avoid downtime and other non-productive factors
2. Avoidance of queues around areas of limited capacity. One of the traditional problems associated with batch manufacture is that products are pushed through the manufacturing system, regardless of whether the next stage of operation is ready
3. Proper built-in quality systems as part of the overall manufacturing process have to be in place. In traditional batch – push systems – quality becomes disguised (Schonberger, 1986) and FMS does not in itself attempt to address this. FMS has to be alongside quality systems already in place to ensure that product and process quality standards are met

However, the above successes noted by Bessant are not automatic; requirements have to be met for this to take place.

4.8.4 Requirements for successful FMS

A number of key characteristics need to be established for successful FMS and these are set down in Table 4.11.

Part of the requirement with FMS is that front-line operators are trained and highly skilled. As we shall see in Chapter 7, training continues to be an issue and clearly becomes the first casualty in a recession or when a particular firm wishes to cut costs. For some firms, training becomes seen as a cost factor rather than an investment.

In FMS, the interface between technology and human involvement (Table 4.12) is central.

Human skill and judgement are vital to successful FMS. As Fogarty *et al.* (1989) write:

> just as the efficiency of a traditional job shop depends on the art and craft of the setup operator, the efficiency of an FMS depends on the skill of the

Table 4.12 The FMS/human interface

Main areas of computer control	*Main areas of operator's control*	*Either/both*
Machine tools	Preventive maintenance	Load materials
Materials handling	Data entry – especially part numbers	Unload finished parts
Integration of the activities between materials and machine tools	Entering new or revised programmes	Remove/add tools

> programmer. System design and programming of the direction, monitoring, and control of the integrated materials handling and machining processes are also key factors in the efficiency of the FMS. (p.711)

and

> A common fallacy is to assume that problems with people can be avoided by automation. In fact, to realize the full benefits of computer integrated manufacturing, people and automation must be integrated. (p.711)

Although the last quote referred to CIM, it is especially significant to FMS which is a component of CIM.

4.8.5 Types of FMS layout

Layouts of FMS are of interest. They reflect the variety and variability required of market requirements in relation to layouts. Clearly, this is a major advance upon the more traditional narrow, mass-production lines. FMS layouts will typically fall into a number of types, as shown in Figure 4.14.

Figure 4.14 Types of layout in flexible manufacturing systems.

1. In-line (typically in a U-shape): where work is transferred from one station to the next in a defined sequence

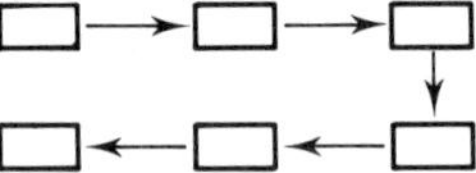

2. Loop: where parts move around the loop but can be off-loaded at any point

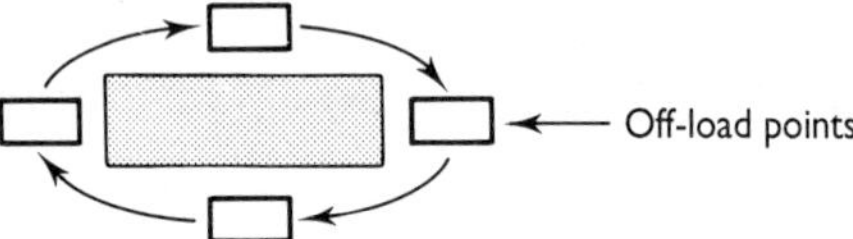

3. A ladder: where the loop approach is modified to have cells within cells, where components can move into a particular cell from the overall flow of the overall loop

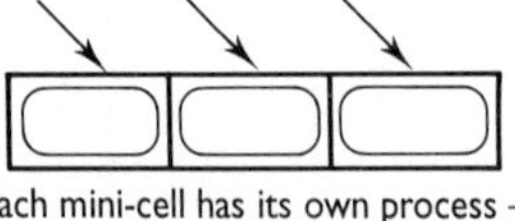

Each mini-cell has its own process – components/materials move into each cell as required

4.9 Group technology and factory focus

As we saw earlier, the idea of focus goes back to Skinner (1974). He talked of 'plants within plants', the idea being that each area of the plant would be dedicated to focused cells of manufacture. In essence, cells will be arranged either by product or process and technology will be housed in each cell to suit. FMS lends itself to product focus; group technology lends itself to process focus, where a group of machines forms a cell in order to build a range of components. The manufacturing process for these components is similar, although the components will then go into a range of finished final products rather than one particular product group.

As Schmenner (1990) states:

> In essence, group technology is the conversion of a job shop layout into a line flow layout. Instead of grouping similar machines together, group technology may call for grouping dissimilar machines together into a line flow process all its own. In the new arrangement, a part can travel from one machine to another without waiting between operations, as would be customary in the job shop. (p.289)

Regardless of the actual end product, many components are manufactured together according to their similarities. This approach is summarized by Groover (1987):

> a plant producing 10,000 different part numbers may be able to group the vast majority of these parts into 50 or 60 distinct families . . . the processing of each member of a given family would be similar, and this results in manufacturing efficiencies. (p.433)

We can make a useful distinction between *part design* attributes and *part manufacturing* ones, which are two approaches to grouping technology together, as shown in Table 4.13.

Table 4.13 Part design/part manufacturing characteristics in group technology

	Part design attributes		
Basic external shape	Major dimensions	Basic internal shape	Tolerances
Length/diameter ratio	Minor dimensions	Material type	Surface finish
	Part manufacturing attributes		
Major processes	Operation sequence	Production time	Batch size
Annual production	Fixtures needed	Machine tool	Cutting tool

Adapted from Groover (1987)

4.9.1 Benefits of group technology

The major benefits of a parts numbering system, which forms an essential part of group technology, include the following:

1. It facilitates the formation of part families and machine cells.
2. It lends itself to quick retrieval of designs, drawings and process plans.
3. It reduces design duplication.
4. It provides reliable workplace statistics.
5. It facilitates accurate estimation of machine-tool requirements and logical machine loading.
6. It rationalizes tooling set-ups, reduces set-up times, and reduces throughput time.
7. It allows rationalizing and improvement in tool design.
8. It aids production planning and scheduling procedures.
9. It improves cost estimation and facilitates cost-accounting procedures.
10. It provides for better machine-tool utilization and better use of tools, fixtures and manpower.
11. It facilitates NC part programming.

Successful implementation of group technology will result in areas such as improved design, reduced raw materials and purchases, simplified production planning and control, improved routing and machine loading and reduced set-up times and manufacturing process times. We can see how the process of how group technology results in greater manufacturing performance from Figure 4.15.

4.9.2 Problems of implementing group technology

Despite these benefits, some resistance to group technology exists, essentially because of the following factors:

1. The problem of identifying part families from a massive range of finished products.
2. The expense of parts coding and classification.
3. Rearranging the plant into a new layout on group technology lines.

Like any advancements brought about by change, the human resource factor in manufacturing is important. Production/operations staff need to understand any change and be part of it. By doing so the three problem areas cited above can be alleviated.

4.10 Overview of automation

The tactical, rather than strategic, view of layout discussed earlier also spills over to technology as seen in Table 4.14.

Clearly, large sums of money can be spent on automation. One option for the firm, therefore, includes *not* spending on process technology. By not investing, though, the firm faces great likelihood of not being able to compete against world-class firms. The basic possibilities of technology decisions are shown in Figure 4.16.

Figure 4.15 Improvements achieved through group technology.

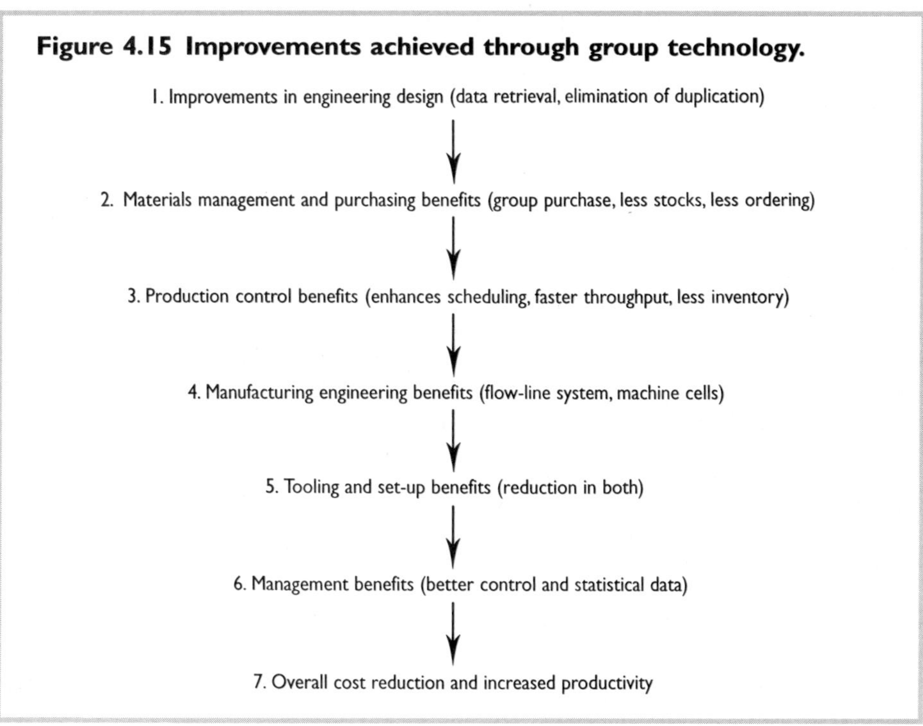

Table 4.14 Contrasting strategic and tactical views of technology

The narrow tactical view of technology	*The broad strategic view*
The responsibility of a technical specialist	Seen as a total system which supports the firm's competitive position in the market
Seen as a separate entity	An integrated system for the whole firm
Only for specific products	Providing capability – current and future
Justification made only by accounting criteria	Justification made by long-term, competitive factors, such as cost, delivery and flexibility
Massive investment for complete change	Incremental spending – part of *Kaizen*

Figure 4.16 Technology investment decisions.

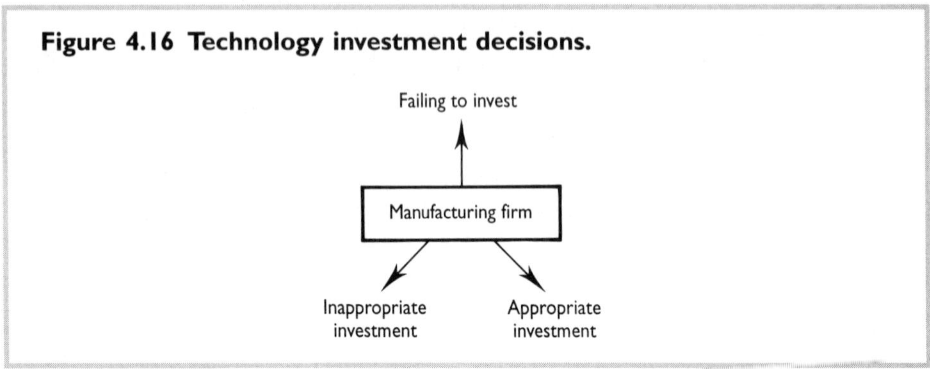

As well as the obsession that can arise with overautomation, there is the problem of not investing at all. The reality, of course, is that the plant is then unable to compete on a world-class basis but, in terms of accounting measures – particularly return on assets – the firm will appear to be financially strong. This accounting emphasis is rightly attacked by Hamel and Prahalad (1994):

> Even before the current wave of downsizing, U.S. and British companies had, on average, the highest asset productivity ratios of any companies in the world. Denominator management is an accountant's shortcut to asset productivity. (p.9)

The point here is that, in accounting terms, if the denominator is small, and the numerator (the return or amount produced from the asset) large, the equation looks favourable, whilst in reality masking the reduced capability that the firm has.

Vast investment in process technology does not in itself guarantee competitiveness. For example, GM's most automated plant in Hamtramck, Michigan has lower productivity and poorer quality performance than GM's labour-intensive plant at Fremont, California, which houses the NUMMI project.

Keller (1993) provides insight into the problems of technology at General Motors:

> The legends of the maniac robots of Hamtramck were many. There was the robot whose task it was to install windshields, but instead was misdirected by the computer command to drop them; the unsupervised paint robots that sprayed everything in sight except the cars; and the robot which systematically installed body parts on the wrong cars. (p. 170)

Technology is not simply confined to operational investment, related to plant layout; technology also refers to a number of key activities that help to enhance the performance of a company in all of its areas. For example, in their survey of over 500 North American plants, Giffi and Roth (1991) found the following areas of automation to be common in their cited firms:

Area of automation	**Number of plants with at least moderate experience (%)**
Personal computers	91
CAD	72
Industrial computers	62
CNC machines	54
E-mail	54
Bar-coding (shipping)	40
EDI	40
Bar-coding (shopfloor)	32
Robotics	28
Automated materials handling	24
Automated storage/retrieval	20

The activities listed above are not only related to the transformation process *per se*, but relate to other production/operations management activities centred around planning, controlling and organizing. The extent to which a company automates will be determined by external factors including market requirements and competitive benchmarking as well as internal considerations, including actual funds available and the company's attitude toward risk. The benefits of appropriate automation are widespread and not just in labour cost savings. As Gaither (1992) observes:

> Today, automation projects are initiated not just for labor cost savings, but also for improved product quality, fast production and delivery of products, and, if flexible automation is used, increased product flexibility. (p.188)

Unfortunately, investment in technology in many firms in the West has been noticeable either for its lack of investment or alternatively in inappropriate overspending which fails to produce any advantages.

As the *Financial Times* (14 May 1991) states:

> The West's struggle to compete with Japan's growing manufacturing superiority has been marked by false starts and expensive excursions up blind alleys. Western companies failed initially to understand the nature of the difference in manufacturing philosophies, believing that low labour costs and heavy use of technology were the answer. (Section III, p.1)

General Motors invested sums greater than the gross national products of many countries in automation but finally conceded that its market share was shrinking and it was losing out to lesser automated, but world-class manufacturers. The decline in GM's market share coincided with the massive technology investment undertaken by the company.

4.11 Computer-integrated manufacturing (CIM)

The use of technology in manufacturing processes falls under the overall umbrella of computer-integrated manufacture (CIM) which will increasingly be central to much of manufacturing. As Groover (1987) states:

> The CIM concept is that all of the firm's operations related to the production function are incorporated in an integrated computer system to assist, augment and/or automate the operations. The computer system is pervasive throughout the firm, touching all activities that support manufacturing. (p.721)

Initially, investment in CIM was aimed at satisfying the following:

1. Increasing product reliability.
2. Decreasing production costs.
3. Reducing the number and types of hazardous human tasks.

However, the environment for this was essentially mass-production on fixed production lines whose characteristics included:

1. Long production runs.
2. Stabilized engineering designs.
3. Very repetitive operations.
4. The use of many identical machines in the production plant.

The days of utilizing machinery and technology just for these purposes have long gone – simply because market requirements have changed and manufacturing efforts have to be focused on meeting these changes. What the production/operations manager needs to do, therefore, is to see CIM beyond the purely technical aspects. All CIM decisions have to focus on the following:

1. *High product quality.* Market pressures for high product quality will ensure that this is a standard requirement.
2. *High flexibility.* A range of models around a particular product is now very much a requirement. Small batches of many products will be the norm, rather than very high volume of one product. FMS facilitates such requirements.
3. *Fast delivery.* Because of reduced process times, customer orders will be satisfied much more speedily.
4. *Computer-driven, integrated systems.* CAD/CAM will be standard and will enable much quicker design changes and new product delivery.

To summarize, Gaither (1992) rightly points out that:

> Manufacturing flexibility has become the cornerstone of operations strategy in the 1990s and production processes being designed today are increasingly anchored to this cornerstone. (p.208)

4.12 The scope of investment in manufacturing technology

Investment in automation can include the following areas:

- Machine tools for parts processing.
- Assembly machines.
- Industrial robots.
- Materials handling and storage systems.
- Inspection and quality control systems.
- Computer systems for data and management control.

In some cases these will be interlinked and interdependent as a complete production/operations management system; others will be independent of each other. A materials requirement planning (MRP) system (discussed in Chapter 6) for example, although clearly dependent upon technology for materials control, does not rely upon investment in process technology such as robotics or FMS.

There are two basic types of automation: fixed and flexible (or programmable). Fixed automation consists of investments in lines to produce a very narrow product range in a fixed sequence. Many Western car manufacturers' plants are dominated by fixed automation. Fixed automation in car manufacture would include integration of machine engine blocks, transmission housings and similar high-volume standardized parts. Ford's Aerostar (minivan model) plant has 40 robots and 24 gantry units and, 97 per cent of the 4000 spot welding and much of the paint application are provided by robots. (source: Author's interviews)

In essence though, it is fair to say that initial investment in fixed automation tends to be heavy and the inflexibility that the single or narrow range of product line produces is theoretically compensated for by the large volumes envisaged coming through the line process. If large volumes are not achieved, then investment is not justified. However, before this investment is made, serious questions have to be addressed in terms of the variety (and not just volume) required by markets to ensure that technological investment is not too narrow, which would fail to satisfy the variety requirements of a market segment.

Flexible automation in contrast, is achieved through programmable applications which allow a mix of mid- and low volume with mid- to high variety. A machine that makes a variety of products in relatively small batches will have a programme for each particular product and/or process and the task will be to ensure that the appropriate programme is entered.

4.13 Types of automation

4.13.1 Numerically controlled machines

Numerically controlled (NC) machines are large machine tools which are typically programmed to manufacture small-to-medium sized batches. NC machines are particularly common in metalworking functions such as turning, milling and grinding operations. Intricacy is an integral part of the NC capability and machines will drill, bore, mill or grind many different parts into a wide range of shapes and sizes. NC machines have been updated to computer numerically controlled (CNC) units. CNC machines are suited to high volume products where variety pressures mean that quick changeovers and set-ups are vital. Often the machines are stand-alone, each controlled by its own computer, normally linked to the overall CAD/CAM system. More than 40 per cent of NC machines are in Japan (Krajewski and Ritzman, 1992). In fact, since the early 1980s Japan has spent twice as much as either American or European industries on automation and half of this investment has centred around NC machines.

NC machines were developed in the United States during the Second World War, for use with machine tools in the military. Developments took place with the use of microprocessor technology and NC gave way to CNC machines. In NC machines, a code of instructions is supplied and operations are performed on a particular stage of a product. The advantage of such machines was the increased precision and accuracy over manual systems. In addition, some flexibility was offered because general purpose machinery could be altered in terms of its application by changing the coded instructions. In machining centres, tool changes are controlled by computer and a wide variety of tools become available from the machine centre's carousel.

Any CNC system will consist of three basic features:

1. *A programme of instructions*. This will be a detailed process list for the equipment in terms of positions of tools, speeds and other functions.
2. *A machine control unit*. This will read the programme and convert it into applications.
3. *Processing equipment*. This is the actual performance of the NC machine. The co-ordinates, positioning, speed and tools are now applied to a component in a particular operation.

The contribution of CNC to successful FMS is considerable:

> The most significant reduction in production lead times, however, has been achievable through the integration of CNC machine tools into Flexible Manufacturing Systems and the consequent reduction in transport and queuing times at each machining centre. (Hill, M., in Storey, 1993, p.143)

4.13.2 Industrial robots

The first industrial robot was installed in General Motors in 1961. Since then there has been a gradual increase in their usage. Their applications can usually be under three distinct categories:

1. Materials handling.

2. Processing operations.
3. Assembly and inspection.

The innovation of robotics gave rise to fears that mass unemployment would result and that workerless factories would be the norm. In fact this has not been the case and it is important to understand the link between robots and humans:

> robots have not displaced men and women . . . despite the fact that their advent gave rise to yet another wave of speculation about the workerless factory. They have a role in manufacturing and have been used well in Japan . . . The Japanese have understood that, if work is designed properly for robots, they will do it well – but they are not able to replace people at jobs that have evolved to need a human's innate ability to fit the world and ideas and intentions to that of deeds and objects. (*Economist Manufacturing Technology Survey,* 5 March 1994, pp.8–9)

Reactions to industrial robots have not always been positive, although research into current practice in 1986 revealed the following:

Characteristic	**Actual experience**
Investment cost	From $20,000 to $100,000 depending on sophistication
Payback period	Typically less than three years
Return on investment	Typically from 12% to 18% with some as high as 40%
Operating life	From 15,000 to 25,000 hours
Annual maintenance cost	10% of initial investment cost; major work after 10,000 hours
Best volume levels	Between 50,000 and 500,000 units per year
Installation time	1–5 days, depending on complexity

In general, robots are versatile, computer-controlled machines programmed to perform specific tasks. Most are stationary and floor mounted and the arm is able to reach difficult areas.

These movements will all be controlled by NC (numerical control), but two distinct applications will be *position* control which ensures correct positioning and *contour* control which controls the actual path of the application.

All of these are movements of position before application takes place, but it is the hand or end effector which performs the actual work. This includes materials handling, spot welding, spray painting, assembly and on more intelligent machines, the actual inspection and testing of products. The main benefits of robotics include consistent process quality and the ability to perform tiresome and repetitive/monotonous tasks without declining in either output or quality. By the beginning of the 1990s, there were around 338,000 robots in existence in the following areas:

USA: 37,000 Europe: 56,000 Japan: 220,000 and 75,000 elsewhere (*Financial Times*, 14 May 1991, Section III, p.1)

The number of robots in the United States is likely to increase dramatically by the end of the 1990s and much of this increase will be in both automobile and telecommunications/computing industries. The former will use robots for painting, soldering, welding and materials movements, whereas in the electronics industry robots will be used to assemble circuit boards and electronic components. The precision that robots can offer is most noticeable; robots can move their arms in vertical, radial and horizontal axes and apply spot-welding guns, arc-welding, paint spray, rotate spindles for metal-cutting operations, and apply heat and water-jet tools to extremely high specifications.

The most applicable settings for robot applications would be where:

1. There is a hazardous work environment for humans – Unsafe, unhealthy or uncomfortable, hence the investment in spray applications and continuous welding applications.
2. The work is repetitive – There has clearly been a move away from the Taylor/scientific management approach which, in part, caused workers to be deskilled, performing repetitive and monotonous tasks. A robot is capable of performing this work with greater consistency and repeatability than a human.
3. The work is very difficult for humans – This is aside from the hazardous factor and may include parts or tools which are too intricate for humans to apply. It may also include heavy handling requirements.

4.14 The debate on investment in process technology

4.14.1 The financial problem

Put simply, investment in technology is not a question of choice as to whether or not to invest. The only choice – if a firm is to remain in the business – is in the *type* and *extent* of process technological investment.

One of the major debates on investment is the measurement of success in investment. One of the problems associated with this is the justification (or otherwise) of the investment using financial cost accounting as the criterion. As far back as 1974, Dean stated that:

> because of our obsessive concentration in short-term gains and profits, US technology is stalemated. (p.13)

Such sentiments have been echoed by many others. By contrast, both Germany and Japan take a much longer term view of investment:

> When they invest, they are often prepared to sacrifice the short-term for longer-term profits, which accrue from market share and increased volumes. (Hill, 1989, p.198)

This is supported by Ohmae (1982) who, describing the investment by two Japanese companies, stated:

> in neither case . . . is any attention given to return on investment (ROI) or payback period, let alone to discounted cash flow. In both, the dominant investment criterion is whether the new business is good for the company as a whole. (p.20)

Drucker (1987) adds to this when he questions the validity of traditional accounting methods as the means of justifying investment:

> The conventions are very inadequate, inappropriate . . . It gives (companies) the wrong information. They don't know what the real savings are . . . Cost accounting gives you information on the cost of doing, but not on the cost of not doing – which is increasingly the bigger cost. (p.59)

The problem with accounting measures is that there is a static approach; Net present value (NPV) assumes that factors such as market share, price, labour costs and the company's competitive position in the market will remain constant. However, the fact is that all of these factors will change and, more importantly, they will degenerate if the company retains outdated production methods which will not allow it to compete in key factors such as cost, delivery speed, reliability and product innovation.

Hill (1989) urges the need to understand order-winning criteria in the discussion for the firm when deciding to invest:

> With these (order winning criteria) established and reflected in the evaluation of the manufacturing performance, then their importance can be assessed and taken into account in judging appropriate investments . . . (the company) must ensure that these critical decisions reflect the business and not accounting decisions. (p.197)

Gaither (1992) states that ROI will continue to be part of the investment decision, but other factors have to be considered in addition:

> Although returns on investment will continue to be an important criterion . . . the term returns will take on new and expanded meaning. Improved product quality, faster delivery of customer orders, increased product and volume flexibility, reduced production costs, increased market share, and other advantages will have to be factored into these future capital-budget decisions. (p.209)

Justification for investment has to go beyond replacing labour to the idea of competitive advantage in other areas such as product quality, delivery speed and delivery reliability. In volume manufacturing, labour would typically only account for 10 per cent of total costs and therefore fixed costs and materials would be the biggest cost factors.

At Allen-Bradley's $15 million assembly plant, which includes 50 machines making 125 configurations of starter motors, it was the closeness of corporate and production/operations strategy which helped with the decision to invest:

> After deciding to compete anywhere on price (corporate strategy), the company justified the facility investment decision (operations strategy) on the basis of quality, cost, market share, competition, and profitability. 'If there is a time to ignore conventional return-on-investment calculation, it's when your long-term goals are at stake' said . . . the CEO. (*Industry Week*, 26 May 1986, p.16)

4.14.2 The justification for investment in process technology

Typical reasons for investment in process technology would include the following:

1. Cost reductions per unit – Fiat reduced its number of employees from 138,000 to 72,000 over a decade due to its investment in robotics.
2. Quality improvements – The precision that robotics can offer on areas that might be influenced by safety considerations; the repetitive nature of jobs, where human error might be evident, is reduced by the use of robotics.
3. Reduced process times – The effect of this is upon delivery speed and reliability, two competitive areas of increasing importance to manufacturing. Motorola invested in automation and, as a result:

   > The Florida plant makes pagers at the same cost as does Motorola's Singapore plant, which uses cheaper labor but is not integrated. And the domestic plant delivers, overnight, custom-built pagers that used to take nearly six weeks to supply. (*Wall Street Journal*, 4 June 1990, 'US Contractors Trail Japan in R&D', p.9)

4. Greater capacity – This, in turn will effect productivity and will result in greater volumes being attained in the same plant.

Although the equipment that will be purchased will be high-tech, complex and scientific, the purchase of equipment has to be made after asking simple questions along the following lines:

- How does it support the firm in the market?
- What will it cost?
- What will it do?
- What will it require?
- How certain are the costs, potentials and requirements of the new technology?

The investment on automation can be huge. Each decision has to be made with a view to best supporting the company in the market rather than an investment for its own sake. Market requirements in terms of product quality, cost, delivery speed and reliability, flexibility and volume have to be known and, to some degree, anticipated, for the investment to be justified. If the above questions on competitive factors are answered, the company is then in a position to make appropriate investments; if the questions are ignored or unanswered, then investment largely becomes a function of the whim of particular power-holding individuals or groups within the company. Such seems to have been the case with GM's decision-making process in investment in technology during the 1980s. This decision-making process at GM contrasts sharply with that of Japanese companies.

As Itami, in Urabe *et al.* (1988), states:

> 1) a fundamental reason for the rapid growth of the post-war Japanese economy was the rapid progress of technology accumulation
> 2) this was made possible by corporate efforts to develop and amass technology
> 3) one factor in the quickness and effectiveness of corporate technology accumulation was the Japanese corporate system developed in the post-war era (p.27)

Innovation in Japan tends to be in incremental approaches, which is clearly part of the overall philosophy of *Kaizen* discussed in Chapter 5, rather than complete change at one point in time.

When appropriate investment is made, a necessary ingredient to world-class manufacturing capability is in place. The key to all of manufacturing success is focus – having 'plants within plants' which are separate from other focused areas by the nature of the product.

4.15 Failures with automation

Unfortunately, there is much evidence to suggest that many failures exist in firms which have tried to introduce technology into manufacturing processes. Bessant (1993) suggests that the main reasons for this include:

1. *Widespread 'technophilia'*. A love of technology, or novelty attraction, for its own sake rather than an understanding of the contribution that it might bring to the manufacturing firm.
2. *An application gap*. Lack of awareness of particular needs to which a specific technology might be applied.
3. *Lack of support skills in using the new technology*. In other words, the technology itself was fine, but the basic skills required to exploit this in firms were inadequate; flexible manufacturing systems tend to require flexible, multi-skilled human resources to suit. If this human resource capability is not in place, FMS will fail.
4. *Supplier problems*. Some suppliers lacked experience with the increasing amounts of new technology being offered by them. The motive of the

suppliers of technology was to sell without necessarily being expert in its application.

5. *Looking for quick-fix solutions*. In other words, looking to technology as the cure-all, instant solution to the problems that the firm might have.
6. *A lack of strategic framework or rationale for the investments in technology*. Not surprisingly, perhaps, a narrow, technical view was taken in some firms, rather than a wider strategic view of technological capability.

The main theme to all of this is the failure of the firm to see technology as a supporting factor to capabilities already in place rather than as a substitute for poor skills and lack of know-how. This is best summarized by Grindley (1991):

> To exploit technology the firm must have a range of business capabilities as well as technical skills. Coordinating these to produce competitive products is the essence of technology management. (p. 38)

Conclusion

This mass-production system has had to change to suit a volatile, ever-changing environment with new competitors coming in from all over the globe. Mass-production's process strategy emphasized efficiency in production; world-class strategic manufacturing firms, on the other hand, emphasize product quality, differentiation and any other offering perceived to be important for their customers. Since the inception of automation, the following stages have appeared:

Phase	**Main role**
CNC machines	Increase precision and sustain process quality
Group technology	Gain process synergy; reduce tooling and set-up times
FMS	Improve flexibility and reliability; reduce costs, set-up times

We can take this one stage further and link process innovation with developments in markets, as shown in Table 4.15.

Only with an understanding of the basic process choices available, together with a conviction for appropriate investment in process automation, can a company hope to compete in markets. Without these key areas of understanding in place, a company will be tied in with the wrong basic process choice and spend vast amounts of money on automation which does little to enhance the company in the competitive environment.

A clear understanding of process choice has to be in place before massive expenditure is made on automation. Once this understanding is in place, a number of principles can then help in the use of new process technology:

1. Design the product for automation – This will often require a significant

Table 4.15 The link between process innovation and market developments

Decade	*Market requirements*	*Product strategy*	*Process strategy*	*Manufacturing's role*	*CIM role*
1960 stable	Price	Few varieties	Efficiency	Long runs	Did not exist
1970 New competition	Price, quality	Quality	Efficiency, quality	Quality	CAD CAM MRP
1980s Increased competition	Price, quality	Differentiation quality, wide range	Efficiency, quality, flexibility	Short runs	CAD/ CAM FMS CAPP
1990s Volatile, dynamic	Price, quality, uniqueness, niches	Constant flow of new products, differentiation	Efficiency, quality, flexibility, innovation	Strategic, ability to adapt and quickly	Fully linked CIM

Adapted from Bolwijn and Kumpe (1990)

rethink in key areas such as materials, product design and assembly; modular designs are increasingly used for this purpose.
2. Ensure proper interface between operator and equipment.
3. Implementation should occur in stages – This ties into the Japanese view of *Kaizen*, improving by increments but on a continuous basis.
4. On the human side, each workstation should enjoy as much autonomy as possible – while interaction between operators is encouraged and desirable as part of best practice, there should not be dependency across workstations.

Successful implementation of CIM in all forms will be dependent on the firm's clear and correct understanding of present and, to some extent, future market needs and investing in the appropriate automation to support these needs. Investment should be in stages as part of the firm's continual incremental improvement. It should be made as a holistic decision, rather than as a result of the force of one particular group within the company and justification has to go beyond mere accounting criteria to a long-term, company-wide commitment to satisfying customers in what are now erratic, volatile, dynamic and ever-changing markets. Piore and Sabel (1984) speak of 'flexible specialisation'. This goes some way to coining the phrase which summarizes the task facing production/operations. More appropriate may be the phrase, 'flexible and focused manufacturing'. A firm needs to be flexible in terms of volumes and varieties, focused in the sense of configuring and reconfiguring technology and all plant efforts into customer-specific areas. Such an approach is far superior to the undifferentiated mass-production lines which dominated much of Western manufacturing in the past.

In this book we have seen that the firm must:

1. Develop strategic plans, determining how and where the firm will compete in markets.
2. Provide products that at least match and ideally exceed customer expectations.
3. Have manufacturing processes and technology which support the firm in the market.

Underpinning all of this is the quest for quality, to provide goods and services which provide customer satisfaction and which will in turn allow the firm to prosper. Quality is the focus of Chapter 5.

Summary

- **There are five basic types of process choice. These are project, job, batch, line, and continuous process. Each of these links to a particular type of layout: fixed, process or product.**
- **It is vital that the production/operations managers understand what each process choice can and cannot do. In particular, process choice states what the company sells and what it is able to offer.**
- **Increasingly, because of the volatile nature of markets, production technology is centred around the middle of the continuum between volume and variety. The production/operations manager has to have flexibility as a key point in scheduling production and managing the plant.**
- **Flexible manufacturing systems and group technology have emerged as important developments in managing production. These have come into play because manufacturing today is not about long production runs with little variety. Instead, there may well be numerous changeovers and set-ups required to produce varying numbers and different types of products in the same plant.**
- **The major feature of layout of plants in the West – particularly the United States – has been one of high worker and machine usage; in Japan, by contrast, layout and investment in facilities has been made for flexibility and the ability to quickly shift to different product models or to different outputs of production.**
- **Process technology is not a quick-fix solution and investment must be made alongside skills and capabilities. Investment has to be made to support the company in its chosen market and should not be at the whim of a particular technical specialist, but should be a holistic decision for the company.**
- **Vast amounts of investment have been made in some plants with little**

competitive advantage being gained as a result. However, when appropriate investment is made it, will allow the firm to manufacture to world-class standards, provided that it is used to meet the needs of the markets in which the firm is competing.

- **Process technology is a requirement to meet the demands of the needs of markets. In order to meet these needs, technology can be used for rapid changeover and set-up times, volume and variety mixes, delivery speed and reliability requirements and for ensuring process quality. However, technology must not be seen as a replacement for human resource capability.**
- **Investment in technology is a strategic decision. Investment must be made to enable the firm to support the markets in which the firm is competing.**

CASE IBM's manufacturing plant in Scotland

IBM undoubtedly suffered many aggressive attacks by a number of smaller, leaner manufacturers from 1985 onwards. Once called an 'excellent' company (Peters and Waterman, 1982), IBM has been one of many American giants which have had to rethink their entire strategy and to reconfigure their organization. This is most noticeable in their PC business. In one year alone (1987/88) IBM lost one-third of its PC market share to Apple and Compaq, neither of which had been serious threats to IBM back in the early 1980s when IBM's dominance seemed to be assured. IBM's sales and profit performance between 1989 and 1993 is highlighted in Figure 4.17.

Figure 4.17 IBM sales and profits: 1989–93.

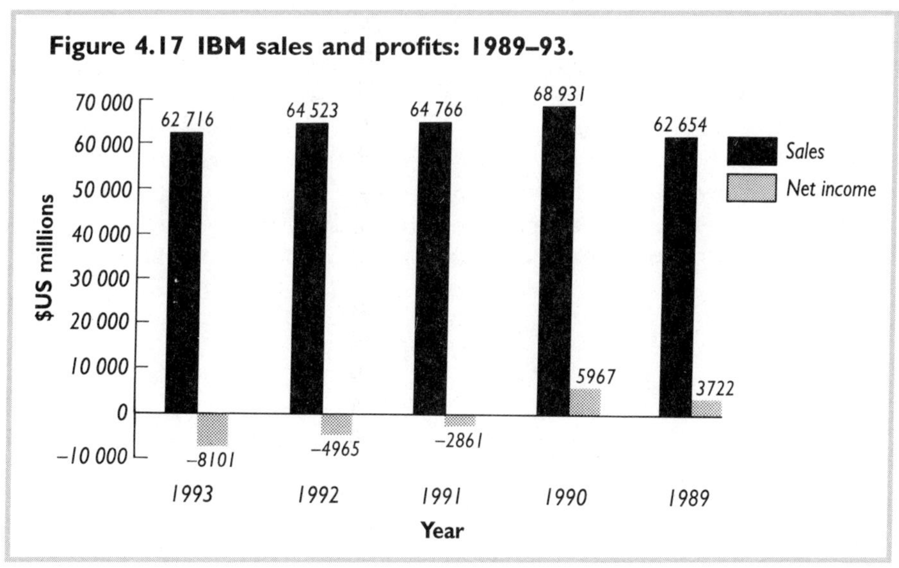

However, by the mid-1990s, advances in manufacturing performance were being made in some IBM plants, notably at Greenock in Scotland. By 1994, the Greenock site was IBM's biggest manufacturing site for PCs.

The PC market in the 1990s is volatile and has margins which may be best described as razor-thin. The manufacturing plant has to meet intense cost requirements together with other pertinent market needs. IBM's share of the European PC market, which had reached 15 per cent in 1990, declined to about 12 per cent by 1992. Intense rivalry from other manufacturers was manifested in competitors undercutting IBM on price for similar products, and responding more speedily to customer orders. One such major threat to IBM came from Dell Computers which by 1992 was able to produce particular customer configurations within 48 hours and to price less than IBM products.

IBM PC was set up to respond to these types of competitive pressure. IBM at Greenock took over the distribution of PCs in Europe, the Middle East and Africa, and fourteen distribution operations in different countries were closed down between 1992 and 1994. Prior to this, a particular IBM subsidiary would contact Greenock and provide a forecast of its needs, then stockpile computers when they arrived from the plant. In 1993, the major shift in emphasis was that IBM in Greenock would manufacture to customer orders, rather than make to stock in the hope of selling the finished inventory. IBM focused areas of the plant into cells of product families, rather than producing on one line for all products.

Greenock began the process with its Valuepoint range of low-priced computers, then moved on during 1993 to the PS/1, PS/2 and Thinkpad notebook ranges. The change saw gradual but marked improvements in terms of speed to customer orders; by the end of 1993, IBM Greenock was able to complete the shipment of any product configuration within a maximum of ten days of receiving an order.

Between 1992 and 1994, IBM's facility at Greenock greatly reduced its unit manufacturing costs, and at the same time, increased its volume of output by 50 per cent. Since the plant switched to manufacturing to order, it has cut its inventory by 25 per cent in absolute terms, whilst output has risen by between 15 and 20 per cent a year. The cost of processing of orders and the delivery of the product to the customer has been reduced by two-thirds. While IBM's fortunes may not have improved throughout the entire company, IBM's plant in Scotland has shown that improvements can be made on a divisional level. The plant is focused, customer-driven and able to compete against other PC manufacturing plants. Using focused cells has allowed the plant to respond rapidly to customer needs; the cells have resulted in reduced costs and greater flexibility.

5 Quality as a strategic factor

5.1 Introduction

The strategic importance of quality is highlighted by the fact that quality was the major distinguishing feature in manufacturing performance between the West (except Germany) and Japan between 1970 and 1990.

In the 1950s the term 'made in Japan' had tended to mean cheap and poorly made; by the 1990s, 'Japanese' served as a term for world-class quality in some industries. It has taken the decimation of a number of Western firms, often in 'secure' territories, either geographical (particularly the United States) or in markets (such as cars and semiconductors), to realize that quality is a central strategic issue. Quality performance has separated, and will continue to separate, winners from losers in markets.

A number of studies in the 1980s alerted the West to the differing performances in quality between Japanese and US firms. For example, Garvin's (1983) investigation of American and Japanese air conditioners showed that the worst produced units (all American) had between 50 and 1000 times the failure rate of best produced units (all Japanese). The irony of this of course is that Japan's development in quality owed much to American gurus – in particular Deming and Juran – who were largely ignored in the United States until many years later. However, by contrast, the Deming Award in Japan has been seen nationwide on Japanese TV for many years and is revered as a great achievement for the recipient.

What becomes clear is that, although quality is now seen as a company-wide activity, much will still rest on the performance of production/operations' capability. Quality in the 1990s and beyond is seen in terms of speed, cost (especially in reducing waste), delivery capability, flexibility, service and other customer requirements. These requirements will be satisfied – or not satisfied – by production/operations' ability to meet requirements.

5.1.1 The problem with quality

A survey undertaken by *Fortune* (18 October 1993) found that up to two-thirds of managers thought that total quality management (TQM) had 'failed' in their companies. The problem of quality often lies with the impatience of organizations which remain focused on short-term horizons, based essentially on financial criteria. The fruits of successful quality drives are, often, not immediate – the Japanese learned quality over many years before becoming world-class manufacturers. Also, although the quality factor is central and necessary, it is not by itself sufficient to ensure success. GM, for example, has been given the Baldridge Award (discussed later in this chapter) for its Cadillac division. GM has also achieved a number of high ratings from the JD Powers' surveys (an industry 'bible') and the Saturn car received outstanding ratings in customer satisfaction surveys. In spite of all this, GM has seen downturns in market share and profitability since 1979. The problem was that, by the time GM became committed to company-wide quality, a great deal of damage had already been done:

> In contrast to the success of TQM pioneers is General Motors' decade of decline (the 1980s) GM did not mount a strong TQM effort until the decade was nearly over. By that time . . . other companies' efforts – notably Ford's – were paying off . . . in 1990 a new training program addressed the missing ingredients: customers, statistical process control, cross-functional teams, work cells, quick response and so on. One GM executive, attending one of the 1990 sessions, said: 'This is the training we should have had in 1987'. (Schonberger, 1994, p.113)

One of the problems for GM is that it still seems to be centred on short-term results, as exemplified in its hard-line approach of cost-cutting from its suppliers in 1992; this undoubtedly brought quick-fix results in terms of profitability by the first quarter of 1994, but the long-term repercussions will not be known for some time. GM's attitude to quality may be tainted by this short-term view, whereas quality is a lifetime commitment with continuous learning and ongoing improvements being a requirement.

In 1992, GM's corporate strategy was expressed as a move from 'market share with profitability' to 'profit first' (GM Company Information). This may well be a return to a quick-fix mentality, on GM's part, based on profitability rather than continuous improvement.

There is some evidence, discussed later in this chapter, to show that the gap in quality performance had lessened between Japan and the West by the early 1990s, particularly in the car industry. Womack's *et al* (1990) description of the car industry was largely a reflection of the 1980s and, as will be shown later, performance in Western car manufacturing had improved in the early 1990s. However, in both the Womack book *The Machine That Changed the World* and other more recent data shown later in this chapter, the findings are largely centred around production/operations performance in terms of defects, speed of innovation, process times and other key competitive variables.

5.2 Quality as part of the mission statement

The theme of quality is mentioned in the mission statements of many firms. For example, 'Quality is Job number 1 for Ford' and 'Quality is our most important product' (General Electric). Ford further develops their mission statement by adding that:

> The operating philosophy of Ford Motor Company is to meet customer needs and expectations by establishing and maintaining an environment which encourages all employees to pursue never-ending improvement in the quality and productivity of products and services throughout the corporation, its supply base, and its dealer organizations. (Ford Company information)

Clearly, for Ford, process quality is an holistic approach which involves all stages from suppliers to end customers. This approach is also central to Toyota:

> Satisfied customers assure our future. Our number 1 target is CS (Customer Satisfaction). We are always open to customers' voices. They enable us to better our ways of operation. (Toyota Company information)

This serves not merely as a message to customers, but as a catalyst for company-wide purpose and commitment to quality. This is particularly important to production/operations, who will be charged with the responsibility of constantly measuring process quality.

5.3 Defining quality

5.3.1 A definition for the 1990s and beyond

Much debate continues on definitions of quality and, as Garvin (1992) states:

> Quality is an unusually slippery concept, easy to visualize and yet exasperatingly difficult to define. (p.126)

Various definitions of quality are offered in Table 5.1.

The BS 4778 definition is meaningless unless it is seen in the context of customers whose 'given needs' must be satisfied in order for quality to take place. From this point of view, a better definition, certainly in terms of how markets perceive quality, is offered by Feigenbaum (1983). Quality is:

> the total composite product and service characteristics . . . through which the product or service in use will meet the expectations of the customer. (p.7)

Feigenbaum (1983) adds further insight to our understanding of the definition of quality when he ties it to quality control:

Table 5.1 Definitions of quality

Juran (1974, p. 2)	'Quality is fitness for use'
Adam and Ebert (1992, p. 596)	'Quality is doing it right first time, every time'
Adam and Ebert (1992)	'You pay for what you get (quality is the most expensive product or service')
American Society for Quality Control (ASQC) and British Standards BS 4778 (1987)	'The totality of features and characteristics of a product or service that bears on its ability to satisfy given needs'

> control must start with identification of customer quality requirements and end only when the product has been placed in the hands of a customer who remains satisfied. (p.11)

However, whether or not quality is 'conformance to specification', 'fitness for purpose' or any other definition, we can say that quality products and services in the 1990s are those that are aimed at satisfying customers. In short, this moves the emphasis from the deliverer – offering products or services to the market – to the receiver of these products or services, that is, the customer. To argue whether quality exists other than in terms of the customer is to put the question on to a philosophical level; quality then ceases to be a strategic competitive weapon, central to any organization serious about total quality. However, only by looking critically at the existing internal operations can an organization begin to satisfy both internal and external customers. The importance of the role of the internal customer is discussed in Section 5.9.3.

More important than definitions offered by standards, gurus or whatever, are the definitions offered by companies themselves. The focus for the firm is described by Ciampa (1992):

> 'A company with a firmly established Total Quality mindset is totally dedicated to the customer's satisfaction in every way possible . . . all activities of all functions are designed and carried out so that all requirements of the ultimate customer are met and expectations exceeded. (p.6)

For example, Hewlett Packard define quality as:

> a set of product or process attributes that provide a value to customers that meets or exceeds their expectations. The Company recognizes two kinds of customers: external and internal. External customers are companies and individuals who purchase HP goods and services; internal customers are people and departments inside Hewlett Packard whose performance is directly affected by the performance of co-workers. (*Hewlett Packard Quality Manual 1990*, p.1)

This has set the whole tone for quality for Hewlett Packard. Customer satisfaction, via approaches to quality in their production/operations' capability, is central to Hewlett Packard. In interviews conducted by the author in the USA and UK plants of Hewlett Packard, the common link was that operational efforts were measured in terms of process and product quality and that operators knew the importance of their efforts in terms of satisfying customers.

Although a successful quality drive will result in simultaneous improvements in a number of key competitive areas, the firm can achieve these improvements only by being committed to a strategic view of quality, rather than a quick-fix means of reducing costs.

5.3.2 Further factors in defining quality

Three further factors emerge in trying to determine the nature and extent of quality:

1. **The changing tastes in customers** Quality has both subjective and objective elements; in some consumer markets, the subjective factor will be dominant. Tastes will tend to change over a period of time and with these changes, the definitions of a quality product will alter over time. In high-tech firms, this will have importance in that the firm will attempt to push technology. As we shall see technology push may fail because, although the product will be superior, it will not be seen by customers as satisfying their needs. However, at the same time, because of the phenomenal rate of change, the high-tech firm has little choice but to push technology.
2. **Measuring quality** Process quality can also be measured objectively. This has essentially to do with the in-house statistical approaches (statistical process charts) and other tools which attempt to show that a process is under control and, by implication, quality has occurred (with the caveat that external customers ultimately determine quality). The focus of quality lies in customer satisfaction. A company can undertake quality drives and be successful at enhancing process quality but fail to produce products that customers want. However, the objective measurement of quality is important: Hewlett Packard and Yokogawa achieved remarkable improvements in their joint approaches:

   Assembly defects reduced from 0.4 per cent to 0.04 per cent
   Soldering defects reduced from 0.4 per cent to 0.003 per cent
   Manufacturing lead-times reduced from 2 months to 2 weeks
   Productivity increased by 91 per cent
   Profits rose 177 per cent
   Market share increased 214 per cent
   Manufacturing costs reduced 42 per cent

Inventory reduction 64 per cent
(Adapted from Young, 1985)

Although the initial aim of process quality is not simply to reduce costs, cost reductions will undoubtedly occur in successful quality drives because waste, excess and other non-added value activities will reduce, often dramatically. For example, Motorola saved $700 million in manufacturing costs between 1987 and 1992 (*Economist*, 1992, January 4, p.61). The financial measurement of quality performance is not the only means of measuring quality; in Exeter, New Hampshire, for example, savings of over $12 million were gained by Hewlett Packard in quality improvements. However, of equal importance to Hewlett Packard was the fact that speed of delivery was also enhanced, as was the rate of successful product innovation. (source: Author's interviews)

Other objective quality performance measurements can be cited: for example, Peugeot in Coventry used to be able to produce only 600 cars per week; now, as a result of quality initiatives, it can produce nearly 3000 Peugeot 405s per week. (source: Author's interviews)

3. **The debate on high and low quality** In a sense the distinction between high and low quality is largely meaningless; quality is no longer a term, associated with high-end market tastes but is rather measured by each particular customer segment within an overall market. Each of these may have different needs and requirements; the onus is on the firm to identify these particular market segment requirements and then to provide customer satisfaction. In the car industry, a Lincoln Town Car might, traditionally, be seen as higher quality than a Ford Escort, for example. However, if both cars provide satisfaction to their respective customer segments and perform without recall or other quality problems, then both products are quality products. In that sense, therefore, it is questionable that improved quality will typically mean the ability to charge higher prices.

In the 1990s, quality means meeting customer requirements; this may mean competing on cost if the market so demands and any other competitive variable. Customer satisfaction is the minimum requirement and, ideally, the firm should seek to provide customer delight, providing those features and characteristics which provide delight and not simply matching the customer requirements. We saw examples of customer delight in Chapter 3; minimum requirements of safety, reliability and basic specification had been met and, in addition, features which heightened the customer's enjoyment were then added.

In the PC segment of the computer market, price was the order-winning factor in the early 1990s and any company unable to compete on this basis would have been threatened or would have had to exit the industry because customer requirements (low cost, with the assumption of reliability and ever-increasing capability) would not have been met.

Apricot Computers, for example, had the technological capability to match or even exceed competitors; however, what it was not able to do was to compete on low cost in the PC segment and, subsequently, the manufacturing division of Apricot was sold to Mitsubishi, leaving Apricot to concentrate on software and services.

Customer expectations will rise in each segment as firms jockey for position. This then results in the continuing raising of minimum conditions that firms have to meet in order to compete *at all* in certain segments. This is particularly true in the car industry: in 1987, Mercedes, BMW, Porche and Volvo led the way with airbags and other formerly luxury features. However, airbags, anti-lock brakes, stiff side-impact protection and electronic transmissions are now common to other manufacturers' products such as Chrysler's Neon and Dodge models. Similarly, GM and Ford have these formerly luxury features on many of their non-luxury models.

To summarize, we can say that there has been a change in emphasis when defining quality and Table 5.2 illustrates this.

5.3.3 Attributes of quality

A useful framework which shows how eight attributes contribute to our understanding of quality is shown in Table 5.3.

Not all of these will necessarily apply in each case. A useful approach for the firm is to use the list, then to rank the attributes in terms of importance for its customers. In addition, the list can be used as a point of comparison between the firm's offerings and its competitors.

5.3.4 Process and product quality

Quality is a comprehensive term and it is vital to distinguish between *process* and *product* quality; they are dependent upon each other in terms of the overall quality offering, but each has a specific focus. A product can be a 'quality' product which, if it is not supported by process enhancements (delivery speed, cost, various ranges and any other customer requirement) will fail as a total quality offering. Conversely, a quality assurance system may well be in place, where

Table 5.2 Modern definitions of quality

Past definitions	*Enlightened definition*
Ideas related to 'high end' 'exclusivity', 'prestige' items	Knowing customer requirements for every segment in which the firm is competing. Providing customer satisfaction (as a minimum criterion); providing customer delight (as an ideal) by combining product and process quality for customers, then adding special features which heighten the customer's enjoyment

sophisticated process charts and other tools are being used to ensure process quality, but the product itself may not be perceived as providing satisfaction to the customer; if this is the case then there is a failure in product quality. This plagued DEC in the early 1990s; they concentrated on minis, rather than PCs and even at the end of 1994 were banking on the Alpha chip as being the way forward for the firm. The problem is that, at this time, such technological advances were not perceived as vital, or even as a requirement by the customer. DEC concentrated on fine-tuning the technology and failed to recognize the overall needs of the customer. DEC's senior vice president, Pesatori, stated this much in the *Financial Times* interview:

> Somehow our engineering resources have become disconnected from the real needs of the market. (9 September 1994, p.6)

This is an example where technology push (discussed in Chapter 3) will fail if it is not tied to customer requirements. The fact that DEC's Alpha is the 'fastest chip on the planet' is not the issue.

As discussed in Chapter 4, it is clear that a firm needs to be holistic (with customer requirements being central) in developing new products and technology. Hill (1990) and Levitt (1960) speak of marketing myopia, but it is also clear that engineering or technical myopia can also get in the way of providing

Table 5.3 Eight attributes of quality

Performance: the primary operating capabilities of a product

Features: These are 'bells and whistles' attributes which are aimed at adding value over and above the basic performance variable listed above

Reliability: this is to do with failure, a facet important in all quality assessments but vital (literally life and death) in cars

Serviceability: the speed and competence of repair; ideally this is an attribute that might not be required often. However, ease of serviceability is important and is linked to design quality

Durability: this will depend on a particular market; for example, it is less of an issue in high-tech markets where products are viewed as *consumer*, rather than *durable* products because product lifecycles are shorter than before

Conformance: this is the extent to which a product meets its specifications – weight, width and size are features here

Aesthetics: this is a development of the features element and will not apply to every market – the subjective element is prominent here

Perceived quality: this is the overall perception that a person has; for example, durability cannot be realized except over a period of time; perceived quality is the prior belief before purchase is made

Adapted from Garvin (1987)

customer satisfaction. Basically, *product* quality depends on those features of the end product which serve to satisfy the customer; *process* quality is required to ensure that the product has been made under quality assurance systems. This will then underpin the product quality in terms of cost, delivery, flexibility and the mix/range requirements of the customer segment. Clearly, these process requirements will largely fall under the role of production/operations and the ability to meet requirements is vital. However, it is markets themselves which determine a quality product. The failure of the Sinclair C5 vehicle in the United Kingdom, for example, was not due to a failure of process quality but because the product itself failed to attract customers. In short, it was a product, not process, quality failure.

Linking process and product quality is the key to successful overall quality improvements. Between 1985 and 1991, Hewlett Packard's Terminals Operation made a series of aggressive changes in order to regain its competitive position. It reduced product cost by redesigning the entire product line for improved manufacturability and flexibility. It also improved product availability by introducing a new distribution requirements planning system to create a process by which the distribution centre pulled product from the factory. As a result, HP was able to announce that it offered the industry's lowest priced, highest quality terminals with off-the-shelf availability.

5.4 The strategic importance of quality

Lee and Schniederjans (1994) summarize the strategic importance of quality when they state:

> The only basic weapon for economic superiority today and in the twenty-first century is product or service quality. World-class quality provides an organization with the only insurance that it can compete successfully – whether it is American, European, or Japanese. (p.50)

and

> Competition is fierce in today's business environment and product quality is becoming increasingly recognised as the prime consideration in many purchasing decisions . . . There are numerous well publicised cases . . . in which intense competition has been the change agent compelling companies to adopt more advanced quality systems and total quality management to improve product quality. (p.12)

Quality has emerged in terms of strategic importance because of two interrelated factors:

1. **The number and capabilities of new entrants into markets** This has raised competition between new and existing players, all of whom have to compete to world-class standards.

2. **The greater amount of choice that customers have** Largely as a result of the number and abilities of new entrants.

These two factors have been particularly noticeable by the intense learning by the Japanese who, ironically, have become the teachers to the West in terms of quality practices.

Another major factor behind the emergence of quality as a strategic factor is that technology is now more accessible to customers, which means that companies have to compete in other customer-specific areas. In the computing industry, the days when customers were locked in to a proprietary system, often at great expense and with little possibility of switching to another supplier, have long since gone. Open, easy to use systems, without dependence on the installation science of a particular supplier, means that customers have far greater choice. This has had enormous benefits for customers, but placed high standards on manufacturing capabilities. Production/operations have to be able to respond to changes with great speed to meet the mix, range and volume of customer requirements. One of the success stories in the United Kingdom has been ICL, which was the first to be awarded ISO 9000 (discussed later in this chapter) in the computer industry, and its Manchester factory regularly achieved recognition as one of the five best factories in the United Kingdom and was the only manufacturer in Europe to be profitable in the early 1990s.

The ability to learn quickly and to commit to quality has been evident by the Korean car makers. Korea's 'big three', Hyundai, Kia and Daewoo, made impressive advances in the 1980s. However, it was clear that quality would play an ongoing part with Hyundai which despite sales of $9 billion in 1993, suffered because of product quality problems. Its response in 1994 was to re-educate employees involved in making and delivering cars, and it sent personnel to the United States to see the intense competition there and insisted that every finished car would be test-driven at least three times: in Korea, in the US port of entry and finally by the US dealers themselves.

The importance of quality as a strategic factor was highlighted in *Business Week*:

> Detroit, for instance, finally caught the quality wave in the 1980s and it's hard not to shudder at the thought of how the Big Three would be faring today if they were still turning out Chevy Citations instead of Saturns. And much of the rest of U.S. industry would be locked out of the game in today's global economy without the quality strides of the past few years. (8 August 1994, p.54)

The problem is that, by the time the US big three, particularly General Motors, had taken notice, a great deal of market share had been lost to other competitors, most noticeably to the Japanese. The 'big three' had been locked into old paradigms of manufacturing, based on ideas of scale, vast amounts of investment in technical processes and aiming to reduce labour content, rather than harnessing workforce capabilities through investment in training and process quality.

The need to see quality in terms of strategic importance is clearly expressed by Hamel and Prahalad (1994):

> The quality deficit, which cost U.S. automakers so much market share in the 1970s and 1980s, was more than just 'poor execution' . . . Japanese auto companies realized decades ago that new and formidable competitive weapons would be needed to beat U.S. car companies . . . The new weapons . . .were quality, cycle time, and flexibility. Twenty years later, Toyota's foresight has become GM's implementation nightmare. (p.76)

What also becomes clear from that statement is the ability of the Japanese to think long-term in order to win in markets. Quality is therefore a strategic factor as part of this long-term mission and not a cost-saving device for the short term.

5.4.1 The firm's strategic response to quality

The tools and techniques of quality (discussed later in this chapter) are not, by themselves, sufficient; a strategic view, often involving cultural change within the firm, must take place. Kanter, in Romano (1994), suggests that TQM fails in some firms because it is launched as a programme, unconnected to business strategy, rigidly and narrowly defined and expected to bring about instant and miraculous transformations. However, a strategic view of quality is one which sees quality as a long-term competitive requirement, an ongoing, unending means of out-performing competitors. A major theme throughout this book is that in order to compete at all in markets which are highly fragmented and volatile, a manufacturing firm has to be *strategic*, *focused* and *holistic* in approach. These three factors will not by themselves guarantee success, but they are necessary to compete at all in the 1990s and beyond. Nowhere is the threefold approach for production/operations management more appropriate than in the area of quality and TQM, as shown in Figure 5.1.

At Hewlett Packard, the holistic approach is a central theme in their quality manual and, more to the point, is evident in their practice; design and quality teams work closely, design for reliability and design for manufacturability are seen as vital in all hardware development, and contact between R&D, manufacturing and marketing is constant and close.

5.4.2 Quality as the central focus in manufacturing

In the past, the production mix was seen as satisfying the following criteria: 'The right quantity, at the right time, at the right place, at the right quality'. This terminology is old-fashioned and, largely redundant – moreover, quality is seen as one of four attributes, rather than the core around which all production/operations efforts must be focused. Instead we have to see quality being the ability to create the right numbers, at the right time, at the right cost, together with satisfying any other customer requirement, as shown in Figure 5.2.

Figure 5.1 The holistic, strategic and focused approach to quality.

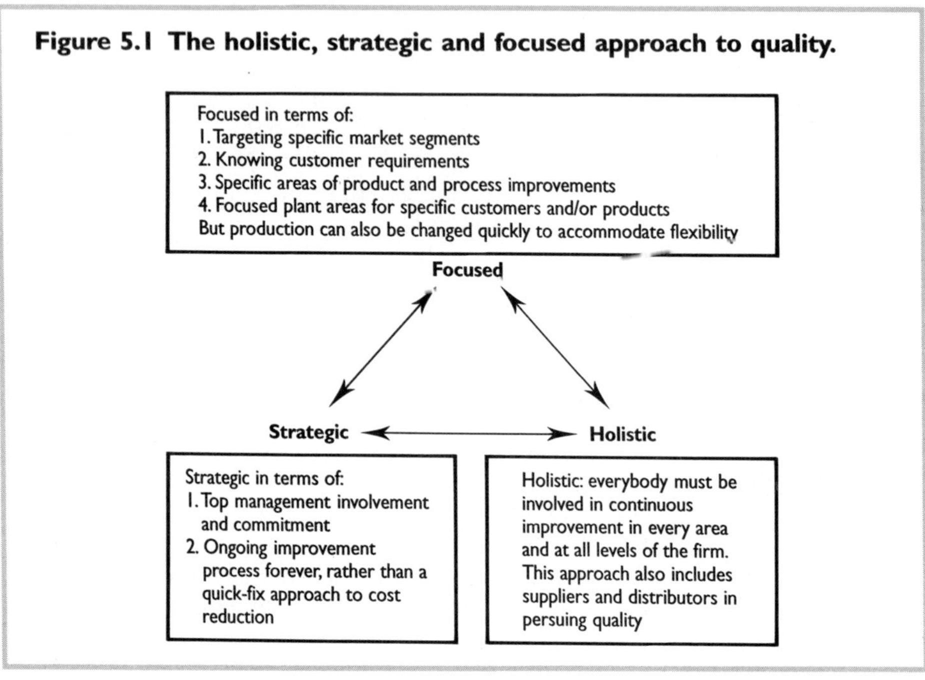

Figure 5.2 Quality as the central focus of manufacturing.

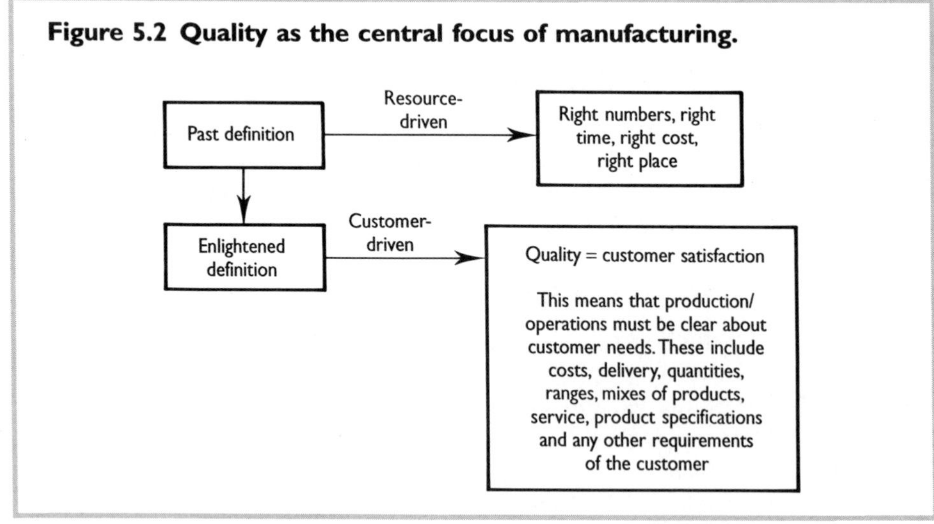

5.5 The evolution from inspection to TQM

TQM has evolved from a number of other areas of quality. This development can be traced from the inspection/quality control era, especially in Deming and Juran's involvement in Japan. It should be noted, though, that both believed in quality at all levels and areas within the firm. Deming (1986) suggests that the vast majority of quality problems are caused by management, in particular with not having quality systems in place and by management failure to train front-line personnel. Deming's fourteen points (1986) although they have changed slightly in content over time, make it clear that quality must be at all levels and all functions within the firm.

Ishikawa is associated with company-wide quality control, although some of the ideas behind this are paralleled in Deming, Juran, Crosby and Feigenbaum. By this approach, quality is seen not only in terms of product or process but also in terms of after-sales service, the style of the firm itself and human involvement and commitment in every facet of quality throughout the firm.

The company-wide approach was exemplified in Ferry (1993) when he quotes a British operator who observed:

> when I went to Japan I saw that they actually owned every problem belonging to their job. If a machine broke down, the operators, the members of that team owned that problem . . . if a major problem did arise during production, the entire team would stop, tackle the problem and solve it. (p.19)

The development from inspection to TQM reveals the increasing strategic importance of quality since the 1950s: quality in the 1950s and 1960s tended to mean conformance to specification; the nature of this was conforming to process quality in-house criteria. This was, incidentally, major progress from the typical production which was largely dependent upon mass-production with quality being checked at the end of the process. By the 1980s and 1990s, however, quality became seen in terms of a total commitment from all areas of the supply chain. The scope of each stage of developments in quality is shown in Table 5.4. The evolution of quality from the tactical and functional approach found in inspection to the strategic setting of TQM is shown in Figure 5.3.

5.6 Total quality management (TQM)

TQM has been a major 'buzz-word' of management since the 1980s. However, quality is not a flavour of the month term. Quality has been the key factor distinguishing the winners and losers in many industries. The element of 'total' is crucial here, because quality must pervade every area of the firm if the quality drive is to be successful. For the customer a successful drive will result in better products and services, often produced at lower cost, with few or no product quality failures. Delivery speed and reliability will often be improved, due to

Table 5.4 Stages of development in quality and related activities

Stage of development	*Activities*
Inspection	Salvaging, sorting, grading and corrective actions
Quality Control	Quality manuals, product testing, basic quality planning, including statistics
Quality Assurance	Third party approvals, advanced planning, systems audits, SPC
Company-wide QC	Quality measured in all areas of the firm
TQM	Continuous improvement, involvement of suppliers and customers, employee involvement and teamwork

better in-house process quality capabilities. For the firm, benefits of successful TQM may include enhanced reputation, increased market share, lower cost production and, consequently better profit performance. However, it must be stressed that TQM is not simply about improved financial performance. This improvement in profitability and other financial criteria is brought about as a result of strategic thinking toward quality, rather than simple, quick-fix, cost-cutting approaches. Whatever the industry, what becomes clear is that TQM embraces the following points:

1. **Top management commitment** Both in terms of setting an example and their willingness to invest in training and other important features of TQM.

Figure 5.3 The evolution of quality management.

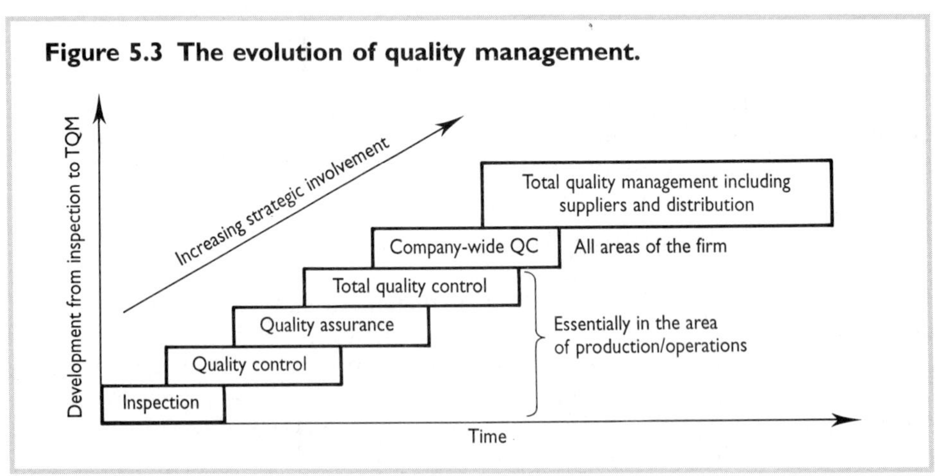

Interestingly, Deming would only agree to work with Ford if the invitation to do so came from the CEO (the invitation had been given by a less senior director). This was more than an anecdote – it helped to establish commitment from the most senior position at Ford, without which the improvements may not have occurred.

2. **Continuous improvement** Deming, Juran, Crosby and other quality gurus may have slight differences in their actual approaches to quality. What becomes a common denominator though, both for them and firms involved in quality, is that quality is a moving target and, therefore, a firm must have a strategic commitment to always improve performance. Signposts, in terms of amounts of rejects and scrap act as guidelines rather than as a completed goal. A firm must continuously improve and go, for example, from percentage defects to parts per thousand, then parts per hundred-thousand and so on, committed to reducing defects as a way of life.
3. **All aspects of the business** The quality drive relates to all personnel within the firm and also outside – all aspects of the supply chain. For example, in their plant in Derby, Toyota worked for over eighteen months in terms of sourcing and training their suppliers in the United Kingdom. (Source: author's interviews). Other, similar, examples are evident in Europe and the United States; whenever a Japanese transplant has been targeted, great amounts of effort have been made to ensure that the supply chain is involved in TQM and that specifications are clear and attainable before the first cars are produced.
4. **Long-term commitment** TQM is not quick-fix but ideally an everlasting approach to managing quality. From inspection to TQM, as each stage developed, the preceding stage was included as part of the next stage; TQM therefore, *includes* company-wide quality control, rather than ignoring it. An essential part of TQM is a company-wide quality policy. Oakland (1994) suggests that this should be owned at all levels, but devised by senior management, whose job it is to ensure TQM, as shown in Table 5.5.

   This approach is clearly evident at Toyota who state:

   All Toyota employees in their respective functions pledge to:

Table 5.5 Senior management responsibility in TQM

1. Establish an organization for quality
2. Identify the customer's needs and perception of needs
3. Assess the ability of the organization to meet these needs economically
4. Ensure that bought-in materials and services meet the required standards of performance and efficiency
5. Concentrate on the prevention rather than detection philosophy
6. Educate and train for quality improvement
7. Review the quality management systems to maintain progress

Adapted from Oakland (1994)

1. Consider customers first.
2. Master basic ideas of QC; adhere to the cycle of management: plan, do, check and act; judge and act on the basis of concrete facts and data; provide standards to be observed by all concerned; all personnel should contribute to kaizen.
3. Put them (QC ideas) into practice.

The reason for doing so is:

> to improve corporate robustness so that Toyota will be able to flexibly meet challenges. (Adapted from Toyota Company information)

The same sort of mentality is practised within Rover which, in language echoing a number of gurus, offer the following as a quality process:

1. Get to know the customer
2. Measure the Cost of Quality
3. Prevention not Detection
4. Right First Time
5. Continuous Improvement
6. Everyone responsible

(Rover Purchasing Group)

This development means that an ongoing discipline has to be in place in order for quality to be a strategic weapon for the organization. Such an approach has been undertaken by Rover in the United Kingdom, partially as a result of the link with Honda.

Rover's documentation and training emphasizes several quality factors at Rover, shown in Table 5.6.

5.7 The cost of quality

The costs of quality are those factors, essentially under the heading of process quality, in which performance has failed. These failures bring costs which can be measured in monetary values including, in the worst scenario, loss of business

Table 5.6 The extent of quality involvement at Rover UK

1. (Philosophy) prevention, not detection
2. (Approach) management led
3. (Scale) everyone is responsible for quality
4. (Standard) right first time
5. (Scope) company wide
6. (Theme) continuous improvement

Source: Rover Group

and poor company image. There are four main areas of costs of quality. These are prevention, appraisal, internal failure and external failure, and these are shown in Figure 5.4, where the difference between traditional and enlightened approaches to quality are shown. While quality is not just about reducing costs, these will reduce because of improved process capabilities, which will drastically reduce all forms of waste (Figure 5.4).

1. **Prevention** These are the factors which must be in place to prevent defects occurring; such measures include explicit, company-wide training, planning and procedures. In Garvin's (1983) study of Japanese versus American manufacturing, he found that the added cost of prevention – which resulted in better quality Japanese goods – was half the cost of rectifying defective goods made by American manufacturers. This was endorsed by the corporate director of quality assurance at Firestone, who is quoted in Gaither (1990) as saying:

   > For every dollar you spend on preventing defects, you save two dollars or more in reduced scrap, product failures and other costs. (p.687)

   The approach of prevention is a great challenge to manufacturing firms. The approach has to be supported by a view of training as an investment, rather than a cost, together with a move away from the manufacturing mindset of 'producing as much as we can and inspecting batches at the end of the process'

Figure 5.4 Differences in approaches: changes to absolute and relative costs in quality.

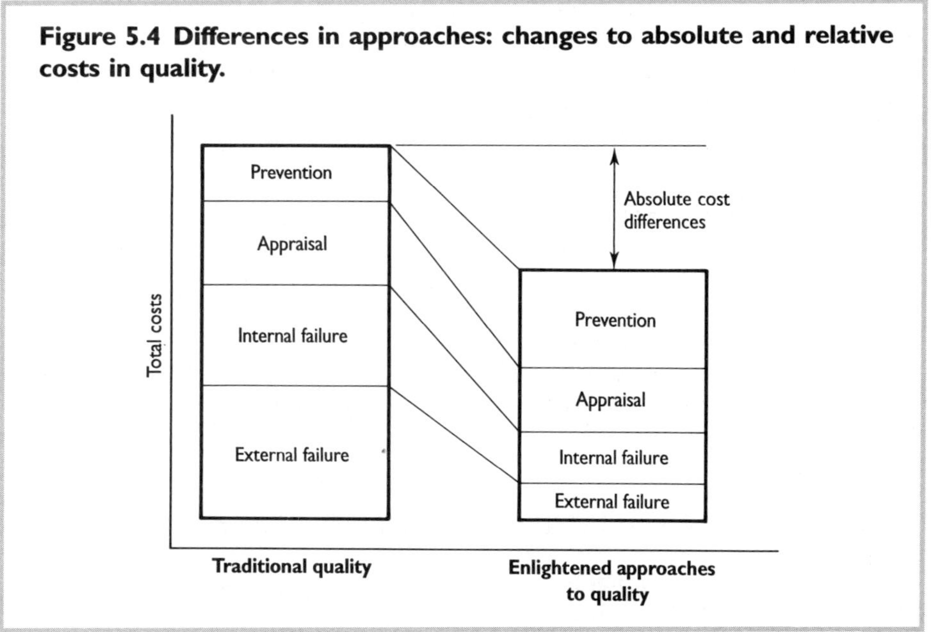

to, if necessary, slowing down the process, initially, in order to get it right first time throughout the entire process.

2. **Appraisal** This is the continuing inspection and auditing which take place to ensure that process quality is in place. Quality laboratories may also be part of the appraisal process, where a product or component is analyzed outside of the immediate production area. Inspection, in addition to built-in statistical processes, will often take place in the early stages of a quality drive in critical areas of production, for example:
   (a) In operations that have historically caused problems.
   (b) Before costly operations take place – reworking on a costly area is particularly expensive.
   (c) Before an assembly operation which would make disassembly difficult
   (d) Finished goods – the extent of inspection of finished goods will diminish over a period of time, as the disciplines of quality management become integral to the operational process.

   It must be emphasized that the aim is to build quality into the process and that to a large extent the process will pre-empt problems.
3. **Internal failure** This includes scrap, rework, downtime, disposal and waste. Waste is anything which does not add value. The cost of this will appear as an overhead, which will impact on pricing strategy. A firm with high overheads will be out-performed by lean or world-class, strategic manufacturers, whose costs will be lower and who can typically respond to customer requirements much more competitively. Even the most customer-oriented companies can have quality problems; chassis problems occurred on Dell's 4386/33 midsize systems but were corrected prior to customers receiving them.
4. **External failures** This is the most costly of all quality failures. Reputation might be lost, the firm's image will be tarnished and the firm will have to pay in terms of warranties, liabilities, product recalls, loss of goodwill and complaints. Hutchins (1988) makes an important point which is relevant here:

   > It is most unusual to find any computations which take into account the consequential losses. For example, there is the time spent in placating an irate customer; the loss of machine time; the effect on scheduling; the costs associated with the purchase of replacement materials . . . the cost of stockholding associated products which must be held in temporary storage awaiting the arrival of satisfactory replacement parts is never included in the figures. Neither are any estimates relating to the loss of sales revenue. (p.39)

5.8 The evidence and real cost of quality failure

The damage inflicted by failure in quality can be enormous. In the 1980s a number of reports in the car industry compared Japanese and Western quality; for example, a *Business Week* report showed the following:

	Number of problems per 100 cars (60–90 days ownership)
Japan	129
USA	180

(*Business Week*, 8 June 1987, p.131)

Womack *et al.* (1990) revealed a number of poor performance indicators of Western car manufacturers and in 1991 the USA's 'big three' recalled 6.2 million cars for safety reasons, while Japan's 'big three' (Toyota, Honda and Nissan) recalled only 297,500 vehicles (*Wall Street Journal*, 24 March 1992, Sec. B, p.1).

However, the amount of safety recalls, although a very good indicator, is not the only criterion; a model with high quality ratings (e.g. Lexus) may be recalled, whilst another model with poor paint application or loose trim fittings may not be. However, recalls are a good indicator, particularly because the need for recall centres upon the essential quality feature in cars: safety. In 1994, Chrysler recalled 15,000 Neon cars, together with LH and LHS sedans to repair faulty electrical wires. Ford had to suspend production of the Mustang sports car temporarily, because of bad welding on the wiring harness, which provides electrical power. In 1992, when 1100 Saturn cars causing possible damage to the cooling system, had been shipped to customers, GM provided the customers with brand new cars. In 1993, the Saturn plant had to recall over 350,000 cars because of faulty generator problems (34 fires were reported due to this quality failure) and the cost of this was around $8 million.

Also, in 1993 GM had to repair half a million leaky gaskets on their Quad 4 engines – the cost for this recall was estimated at $22 million (*Wall Street Journal*, 16 February 1993, Sec. B, p.9) and in 1993 US car makers recalled 11 million vehicles to fix a range of defects on cars. However, this figure included Japanese transplants in the United States – Honda, for example recalled 900,000 vehicles in 1992 to repair petrol leaks. A summary of recalls is shown in Table 5.7.

We should bear in mind that many of the recalled models cited above were manufactured in a period where quality did not have such great and explicit importance for some firms. GM, for example, only began a company-wide approach to TQM in 1987. Its quality performance has improved since then (see Section 5.8.1, below).

Computers have also been prone to recall, although the recalls of cars are more vital because lives are at stake. In 1993, Dell had to recall 17,000 320/325 SLi notebook computers because the machines were prone to overheating. In the same year, Dell abandoned a new line in notebooks because the product quality did not match that of competitors; the 320 and 325 models had been discontinued by the time of the recalls.

5.8.1 Evidence of quality improvement and learning

It would be inaccurate to present the above information without balancing it with the fact that there have been dramatic increases in quality performances in US and European manufacturing. A good indication of this improvement comes from the JD Power & Associates quality surveys on US cars. The 1994 survey of initial quality counted the average number of defects found on each 1993 model during the first 90 days of ownership. Although Toyota once again dominated the JD Power & Associates quality survey for 1993 cars, General Motors and Ford both received overall quality scores higher than all but the three largest Japanese car makers. In 1993, GM averaged 1.08 defects a car, which was down 21 per cent from the 1992 Power survey, the biggest improvement of any manufacturer. Power's American cars averaged 1.13 defects a car, a big improvement from the defect rate of 1.36 defects in the 1992 survey, and a massive improvement on the average of 6 to 8 defects recorded by the US 'big three' during the mid-1980s.

However, the Americans trailed Asian manufacturers (including Korean), which averaged 0.94 defects a car, down from 1.05 defects the previous year. The gap between US and Japanese defects would have been somewhat wider had the Japanese been given a separate average. European car makers averaged 1.28 defects a car in the survey, down from a 1.58 average in 1992.

One of the most telling statistics was that the Toyota Camry, produced in Georgetown, USA, had a lower defect rate than the same model built in Japan. The problem of complacency can creep in, though. It would be foolish to believe

Table 5.7 Recalled cars in the United States in 1994

Number recalled	*Models*	*Reason*
1.8 million	1988–1993 big Chevrolet and GMC pickup trucks and sport-utility vehicles	Hose could leak transmission fluid and cause a fire
1.6 million	1986–1993 Ford sedans Ford Taurus, Mercury Sable and Lincoln Continental sedans	In northern states where salt is used on roads, the vehicle subframe may corrode, drop onto frame and cause steering loss
1.1 million	1990–1993 Ford pickup trucks with dual gas tanks	Faulty valve could lead to spillage and fires
967,000	1986–1987 Honda Accords, 1983–1987 Honda sedans and Honda Preludes	Possible gasoline fires fuelled by gas from rusted out gas filler tubes
678,000	1985–1991 GM vans Chevrolet Astro and GMC Safari minivans, 1989–1990 Chevrolet and GMC Suburbans	Bolt failure can cause seat backs to collapse with front bucket seats

Source: *The Wall Street Journal*, 24 February 1994

that quality has been achieved once and for all, although Chrysler's president was quoted as saying:

> In the old days the Big Three were four times as bad as the Japanese. It was eight American defects to one Japanese defect per car. But now that everyone is around one it just doesn't matter. (*Wall Street Journal*, 27 January1994, B, p.1)

Interestingly, although there does not appear to be a great deal of difference in quality defects, Chrysler, for all its improvements, remained in third place in terms of quality ratings in the early 1990s. Chrysler had 1.48 defects per car in 1994, twice that of Toyota's 0.74 defects rate.

5.9 Human factors in quality management

5.9.1 *Employee empowerment*

In 1988, in an address to a group of US executives, Konosuke Matsushita stated the following:

> We will win, and you will lose . . . Your companies are based on Taylor's principles . . . You firmly believe that good management means executives on one side and workers on the other; on one side men who think, and on the other side men who can only work. For you, management is the art of smoothly transferring the executive's ideas to the workers' hands . . . For us, management is the entire workforce's intellectual commitment at the service of the company. (Shores, 1990, p.270)

The scathing attack by Matsushita offers the biggest challenge to many traditional approaches in Western manufacturing: the transformation from the 'us and them' syndrome to the company-wide holistic approach. Resistance to this might include the cost of doing so (training), together with the reluctance to relinquish management power. Basically, a change of culture often has to take place as part of the quality drive. Success in quality will depend to a very large degree on employee empowerment. A quality system will include the following:

1. The message that quality is everybody's concern.
2. Quality tools and techniques, including statistics, that are available to everyone and not just management.
3. Much greater authority to the front-line employees, including the empowerment to stop a process rather than wait for management involvement.

The lack of employee development owes much to the way that manufacturing has evolved. We can categorize three distinct phases:

1. **Craft** Craft manufacture preceded the era of mass-production which largely developed from the 1920s. Craft manufacture tended to have the following

traits: relatively low volume, high variety and highly skilled workers making essentially to custom design for customers. We can take this a stage further and say that the choice of process in this approach would essentially be in a 'job-shop/low-volume batch' manufacturing process. Process quality was an integral part of craft manufacturing.

2. **Mass** Mass-production was based on ideas of large-volume, low-variety, essentially around a line-manufacturing process. Over a period of time labour became, largely, deskilled. The operator's role became very routine and standard, almost mechanical in nature, and process quality and manufacture became separate entities. Quality control now came under the role of 'quality expert', rather than as part of the manufacturing process at each stage of the operation. Not surprisingly, these were the underlying conditions which gave rise to industrial unrest, particularly in the United Kingdom and United States in the 1960s and 1970s.
3. **Japanese/world-class, strategic manufacturing** Under this approach, human involvement is central to provide for market needs which increasingly demand flexibility in terms of volume and variety, rather than standard products produced in high volumes. The manufacturing firm now has to produce any volume, in greater variety with rapid speed and constant product innovation. It has taken painful learning for many Western companies to move away from standardization (with little human involvement and input) to quality being a central feature of the firm's offering, which in turn demands human commitment and involvement. The development from craft to strategic manufacturing and its link to quality is illustrated in Figure 5.5.

   A number of initiatives have been undertaken by Western firms, committed to quality. One of these initiatives has come from the Japanese approach of quality circles.

5.9.2 *Quality circles*

Quality circles (QCs) play an integral part in achieving and maintaining process and product quality. The circles were initially developed in Japan in the 1960s and have proved to be one of many ideas transferable to the West. It must be kept in mind though that quality circles will be successful only if senior managers are prepared to be committed to implementing ideas for change that might come from them.

Toyota refer to quality circles as 'small group improvement activities' (SGIAs). Although quality circles will differ according to the nature of the industry in which they operate, common features tend to include the following:

1. Identifying a particular problem that a group needs to investigate.
2. Forming a group, from a range of levels and across a number of functions within the firm.
3. Freedom to suggest improvements from every member within the group.

4. Decisions on implementation are left, largely, to the group.
5. Disbanding the particular group and the creation of further ad hoc groups for other quality investigations.

This not only serves as a means of improving process quality. QCs also greatly enhance employee involvement and feelings of responsibility and morale are heightened. This is spelt out by Toyota:

> At Toyota we recognize the following three primary aims (for QC Circles):
>
> 1) To raise morale and create a pleasant working environment that encourages employee involvement;
> 2) To raise the levels of leadership, problem-solving and other abilities; and,
> 3) To raise the level of quality, efficiency and other worksite performance. (Toyota Motor Corporation Human Resource Division – 'QC Circles')

Japanese transplants make extensive use of quality circles. For example, in the Marysville, Ohio plant Honda's QCs are part of everyday life and an integral part of their approach to manufacturing.

Figure 5.5 Quality in craft, mass and world-class strategic manufacturing.

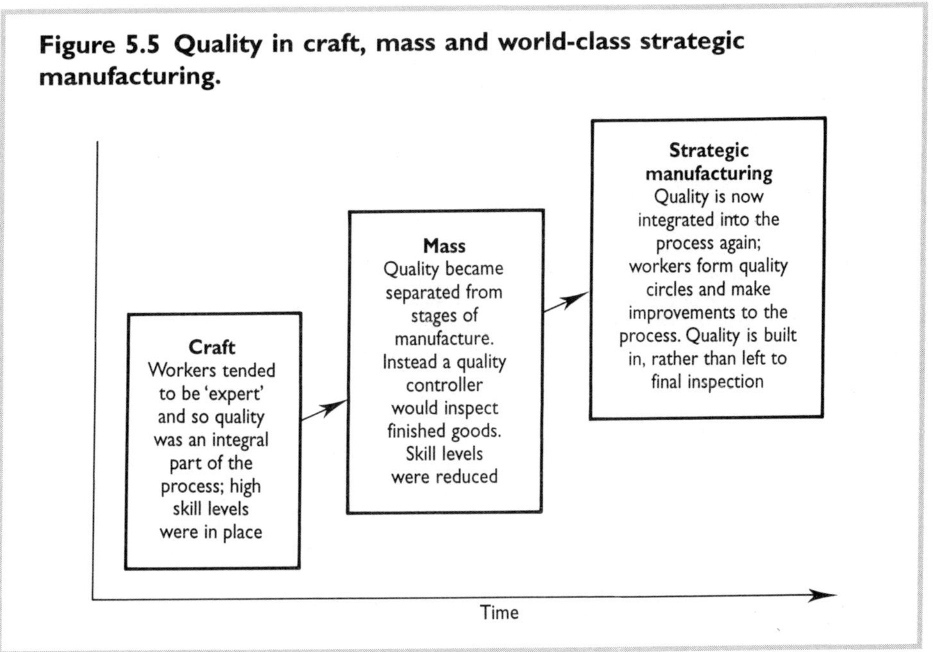

5.9.3 *The internal customer concept*

For a number of companies the idea of the internal customer is vital to achieving quality; Hewlett Packard, for example, use the term constantly in their quality documentation. In doing so, there is the commitment to see the next person in the process as a customer, rather than as an unidentified part of a wider system; this brings a human, psychological link to the manufacturing process and, in the words of Ishikawa (1985), 'The customer is the next process' (p.107). This approach is shown in Figure 5.6.

This approach can only be undertaken when massive changes are undertaken in the basic way that work is arranged. This often means a substantial cultural change in the firm; quality becomes everyone's concern, good teamwork is a requirement and worker–manager conflict must disappear. Schonberger (1994) offers the following as minimum change factors:

> *Jobs*: Process improvement is part of everybody's job – not left to managers and specialists
> *Teams*: Multifunctional work-flow teams, high potential; single-function teams, low potential
> *Titles*: Associates, not workers
> *Managers*: Everyone – not just supervisory people. The former manager class becomes facilitators
> *Leadership*: Inspirational leaders are rare; teamship, shaped by the demands of TQM, fills the void. (p.110)

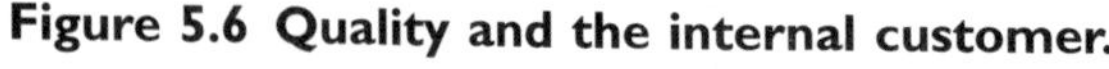

Figure 5.6 Quality and the internal customer.

1. The traditional approach to quality management

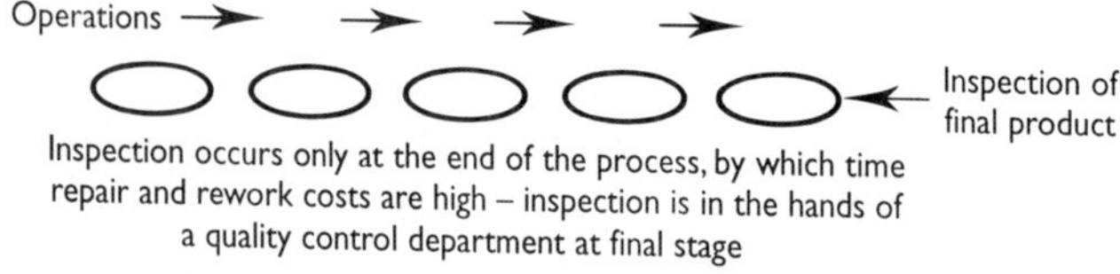

2. The enlightened internal customer approach

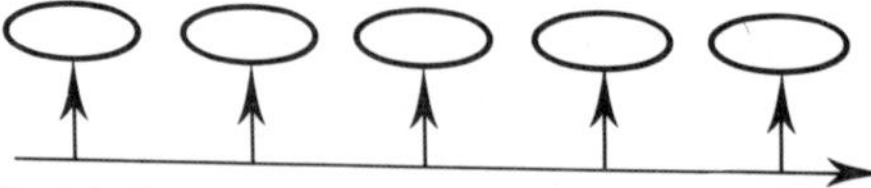

Quality is built into the process; each workstation is responsible for quality and the internal customer approach is in place. Each workstation has empowered employees, responsible for each stage of the process

This change has emerged in some Western plants; in Chrysler's Neon plant there are boards with charts detailing quality audits performed on the car every 20 yards or so, or where there is another internal operation to be performed. Similarly, in the joint venture between Ford and Mazda, which produces the Ford Probe, Mazda MX-6 and 626 cars, a quality information management system (QIMS) ensures that quality information is compiled every 6 minutes, as opposed to the former 30 hours which it used to take in order to compile data on quality.

5.10 *Kaizen*

Kaizen focuses on small, continuous improvements over the long-term.

> The essence of kaizen is simple and straightforward: kaizen means improvement. Moreover, kaizen means ongoing improvement involving everyone, including both managers and workers. The kaizen philosophy assumes that our way of life – be it our working life, our social life, or our home life – deserves to be constantly improved. (Imai, 1986, p.3)

Although *Kaizen* is not, in itself, a 'tool', it is an approach which has been transferred from Japan to the West with some success. In the West, change was typically seen in terms of large-scale innovation as opposed to incremental change, which has been the Japanese approach. The Western approach was also seen in terms of large investment, particularly in plant technology. While Japanese manufacturing firms have invested in technology, they have, in addition, improved performance by a long-term approach to process quality. *Kaizen* involves everybody (a holistic approach), is focused in application, and is seen as strategic in terms of a means of out-performing other players over a long period of time. This is in direct contrast to many Western approaches, which have been too short-term, concentrating only on the bottom line and always seeking the quick-fix solution. The contrast to Toyota is striking:

> The benefits for the Company include having a highly motivated workforce which increases competitiveness, in addition to the more obvious direct benefits in quality and efficiency that come from QC Circle KAIZEN or worksite improvement. (Toyota Motor Corporation)

Notice that profitability and other financial measures are not cited as reasons for quality improvements; these short-term, financial measures are seen as realizable only after the strategic vision of quality is in place. Toyota has over 6000 manufacturing QCs alone (besides non-manufacturing divisions) and each circle handles an 'average of four topics each year'. (Source: Author's Toyota interview.)

One of the major reasons behind Japan's phenomenal success has been the obsession with quality, the ongoing and never-ending pursuit of producing at lower cost, at faster speeds and meeting customer needs through continuous improvement. A number of writers have documented Japan's ongoing obsession with continuous improvement, aiming for zero defects. Imai (1986) describes how *Kaizen*, continuous improvement, should be part of the everyday life of an organization.

5.11 Quality awards

In the United States, the Malcolm Baldridge National Quality Award is given to firms who can demonstrate quality achievements. The Baldridge Award breaks up into the categories shown in Table 5.8.

The problem of awards or standards was highlighted by Ciampa (1992):

> The Malcolm C. Baldridge Quality Award has become something of a brass ring for American business. Many executives want to go after it for the right reasons- to use it as a means of becoming a better company – but many more, it seems, may be pursuing it for the wrong reasons – bragging rights or something that will 'play real well in the marketplace'. (p.4)

AT&T became the first company to win the award twice. The Transmission Systems Business Unit of AT&T's Network Systems Group was awarded the 1992 Malcolm Baldrige National Quality Award in the category of manufacturing companies. Transmissions Systems is one of six strategic business units within AT&T Network Systems, which is one of the largest of AT&T's manufacturing groups and a world-wide supplier of network telecommunications equipment for public and private telephone networks. AT&T used the seven Baldrige categories as a blueprint, and put in place a TQM approach that earned the unit a Baldrige Award two years ahead of their overall goal. However, if we ever needed reminding that it is customers and not awards that determine quality, it is in the fact that, soon after winning the award, AT&T announced it would cut 1000 out of

Table 5.8 Baldrige Award categories

Area	*Point value*
Leadership	90
Information and analysis	80
Strategic quality planning	60
Human resource development and management	150
Management of process quality	140
Quality and operational results	180
Customer focus and satisfaction	300
	1000

Source: 1992 Award Criteria, The Malcolm Baldridge National Quality Award, US Dept of Commerce

6000 jobs at its Merrimack Valley Works, North Andover, Massachusetts, due to a slowdown in orders for communications transmission gear made by the plant.

5.11.1 Quality standards

There are national levels of quality, including Japan's Industrial Standard, the British Standard BS 5750 and ISO 9000 which is used in Europe. The ISO 9000 standard, published in 1987, aims at ensuring demonstrative uniform quality levels for products and services. This standard has, not surprisingly, been both applauded and criticized: Motorola, one of the companies most committed to quality, are outspoken critics of the standard. Compaq, by contrast, saw its ISO 9000 award in its production facility in Erskine, Scotland, as part of an ongoing global certification plan. (source: Author's interviews.)

In the United States, a number of American standards, originally linked to military specifications, have been used with varying degrees of applicability to other industries. Again, these standards, like the Baldridge Award, must be put into context. If a firm believes that it has achieved quality as a result of being certified to a quality standard, it is wrong and misguided. All the firm can demonstrate is evidence of quality systems in place. The irony, of course is that firms go out of business, probably still proud of their certification to a quality standard, because they have not met customer needs as well as their competitors. Firms must not pay so much attention to in-house processes that they fail to anticipate and respond to changing needs of customers. Customers ultimately decide the quality of the firm's products and services, not some awarding body.

5.12 Tools and techniques

The aim of process quality is to continuously improve towards zero defects and no waste in operations. This has to be constantly measured in a never-ending pursuit, where costs of quality diminish and where customer satisfaction increases:

> Quality is free. It is not a gift, but it is free. What costs money are the unquality things – all the actions that involve not doing jobs right the first time. (Crosby, 1979, p.2)

The discipline of quality is what drives continuous improvement. In order to measure current and future progress, a number of tools are typically used, including Pareto charts, cause and effect diagrams, stratification, check sheets, histograms, scatter diagrams and SPC charts. The following are offered only as brief snapshots rather than as an in-depth discussion. The focus throughout this book has been on *strategic* rather than *tactical* areas where these tools would be used. However, the successful use of these tools will impact on the strategic capability of the firm and for that reason they are discussed in the following sections.

5.12.1 Quality function deployment (QFD)

In his work on quality function deployment (QFD), Akao (1990) states:

> we can define quality function deployment as converting consumers' demands into 'quality characteristics' and developing a design quality for the finished product. (p.5)

and, speaking of the effect of QFD Akao (1990) observes how:

> the use of quality function deployment has cut in half the problems previously encountered at the beginning stages of product development and has reduced development time by one-half to one-third, while helping to ensure user satisfaction. (p.3)

QFD is important because it links together three vital areas:

1. **Customer requirements** A list of customer requirements is made and each requirement is ranked in terms of importance to the customer.
2. **Company capability** This is done by means of a 'how-to' list; the firm has to be aware of how it will meet the customer requirements.
3. **Competitive analysis** The firm will score its abilities to meet customer needs against other competitors.

QFD, amongst other things, attempts to go beyond meeting customer expectations to providing customer delight: a house of quality chart is constructed to link the list of customer wants (which are ranked in order of importance) with company 'how-to' provide priorities, as shown in Figure 5.7.

Toyota use QFD for all new product launches as a means of detecting and solving design changes. Burn (1990) states how by using QFD Toyota were able to avoid quality problems at later stages in product development:

> Over 90 per cent (of problems) occurred well over 12 months before production was scheduled to commence, enabling production to be undertaken with greater confidence, far less anxiety and more cheaply. (p.81)

This is clearly part of the right first time approach that Japanese and other world-class players undertake in all aspects of the business, including design. The 'big three' car manufacturers in the United States have learned the importance of QFD from Toyota, especially in terms of how Toyota encourage their suppliers to use QFD, and now use QFD as part of their approach to quality. The importance of the QFD approach is that it encourages a holistic/integrated approach. As can be seen from Figure 5.7, the following are features in the house of quality:

- Customer requirements.
- Competitor analysis.

- A relationship chart linking customer requirements and the 'how-to' list

5.12.2 Pareto diagrams

The Pareto analysis (the 20:80 rule) has many applications, an important one of which is in analyzing quality defects. Class A items will be those where the 80 per cent number of occurring defects will be centred round the same 20 per cent grouping of causes. This is shown in Figure 5.8.

The strategic importance here is that, unless all items are identified and dealt with, particularly the Class A causes, competitive factors such as cost and delivery may be threatened. Pareto analysis is best undertaken in quality circles; groups can identify major causes themselves and then take responsibility for changing processes in order to make improvements.

Figure 5.7 QFD: house of quality.

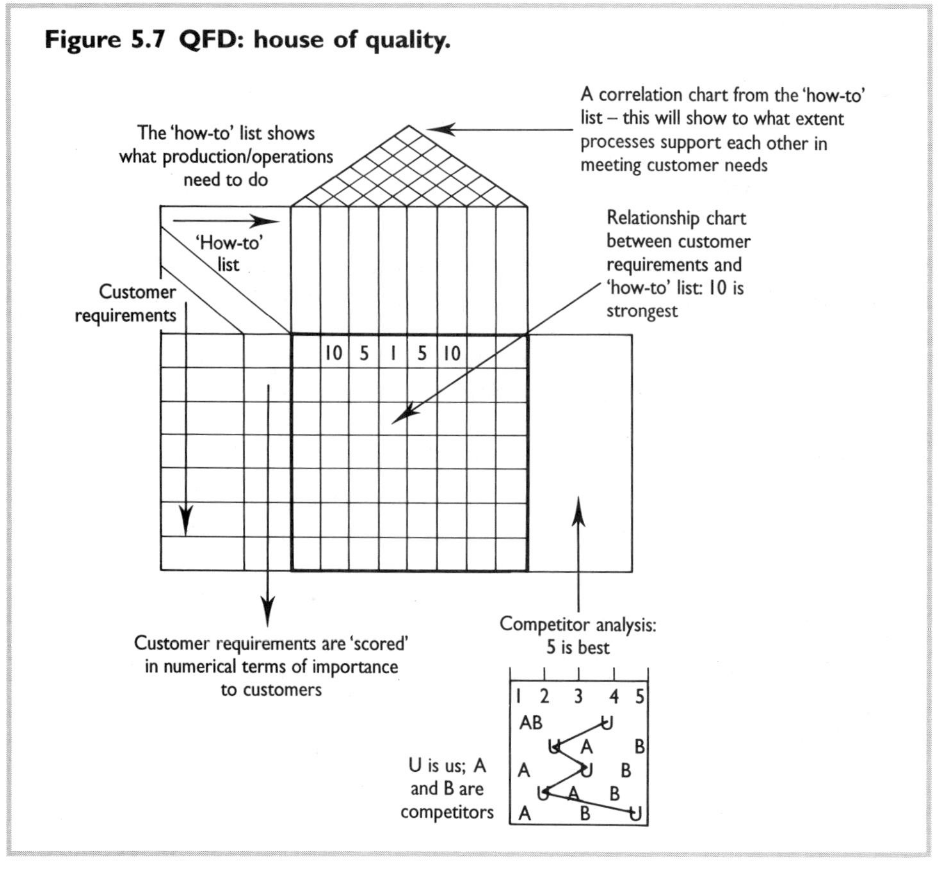

Figure 5.8 Pareto diagrams in quality management.

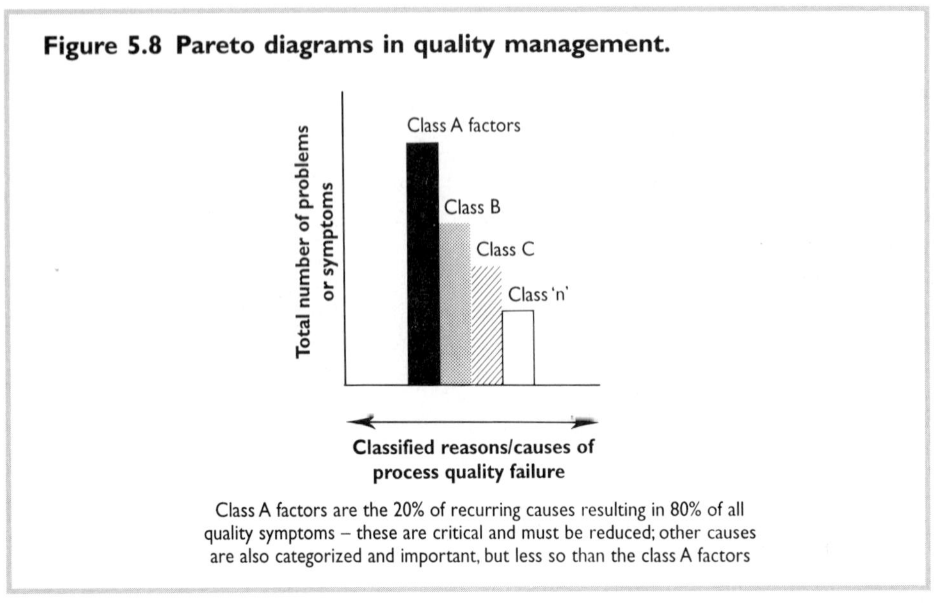

Class A factors are the 20% of recurring causes resulting in 80% of all quality symptoms – these are critical and must be reduced; other causes are also categorized and important, but less so than the class A factors

5.12.3 Ishikawa diagrams

Ishikawa is chiefly remembered as the founder of quality circles. Although this is quite commonplace now, the formation of these circles was innovative. The Ishikawa (or cause and effect) diagram is one of a number of tools and techniques that can be used within these groups and can be a valid discipline in the pursuit of ongoing process quality improvements. Toyota divide problem awareness into four basic categories: manpower, machine, methods and materials, and use this as the basis for Ishikawa diagrams, as in Figure 5.9.

The key to the success of the Ishikawa diagrams is clear in Toyota:

> In preparing this diagram it is important that all members of the QC Circle work together to collect all the necessary data and to discuss every detail. (Toyota Motor Corporation)

This holistic approach, which encourages active involvement from all levels and across all functions, is clearly apparent at Toyota. It results in high motivation and involvement for operators and also serves to focus attention on reducing problems in the manufacturing process – a snapshot of all problems is visible, brought about by brainstorming from a focused quality circle. In this way,

Figure 5.9 The Ishikawa diagram.

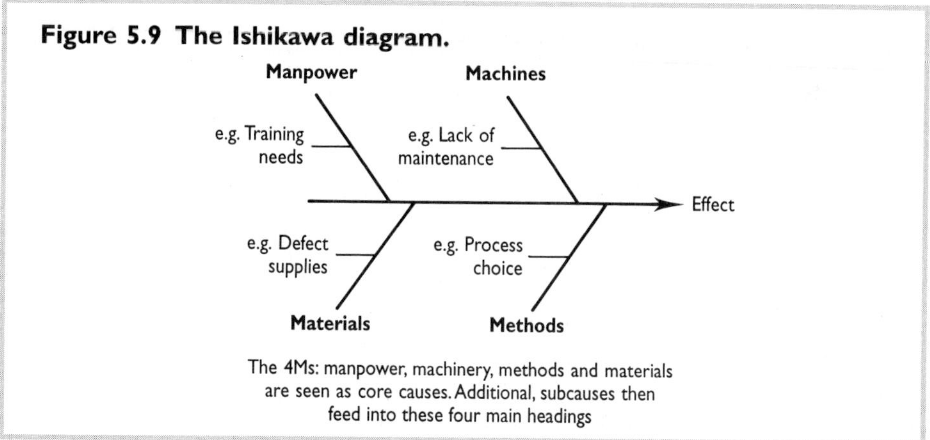

The 4Ms: manpower, machinery, methods and materials are seen as core causes. Additional, subcauses then feed into these four main headings

problems are owned and responsibility for dealing with problems is made much more urgent and accountable by the group.

5.12.4 Statistical process control (SPC) charts

In using statistical process control (SPC), the operator is charged with the responsibility of ensuring that a process is under control. Deming (1986) showed that SPC charts are more reliable than 100 per cent inspection; he argued that even if every item is inspected, there is no guarantee that faults will be detected. In addition, the cost of 100 per cent inspection is prohibitive and such an approach will affect delivery speed and delivery reliability, both of which are important competitive factors. The operator takes regular samples of a product coming to a particular workstation. These are then measured and charted on the SPC chart. The measurements could be in terms of weight, height, width and so on. By doing so, the process is being proactively managed; if there is a trend in the reading showing that the samples are beginning to move toward either end of the upper or lower control limits, the process can be stopped before rework and scrap problems occur. In this way the quality process is one of prevention, rather than failure and so the threat of producing goods for customers which are faulty (the ultimate cost of poor quality) is diminished. The importance of SPC is highlighted by Schmenner (1990):

> Control charts are used to separate random causes of variation in product quality from non-random, 'assignable' causes of poor quality (operator error, faulty setup, poor materials). Assignable causes often demands a lot of work to remedy, but remedied they can be. Typically, such remedies may involve better training, more precise directions, improved fixtures, different materials, improved tooling and the like. (p.565)

A number of charts can be used, the most typical being:
X charts: Where there will be a central location (mean) and distribution around the mean.
R charts: Where the range is used as a measure of the dispersion.
***p* charts**: Where the number of defective (non-conforming) items are plotted.

Charts are created along the following lines:

1. An operator will take samples of the existing operational performance – For example, 20–25 sample readings would be used. Each sample would contain 4 or 5 readings.
2. From the 20–25 samples, with *n* readings equal to 4 or 5 for each sample, results can be plotted, in terms of *actual readings* and the *frequencies* for each reading.
3. Upper and lower limits can then be established – A minimum of three standard deviations around the mean can be computed; this sets a control limit at 99.7 per cent level.
4. The operator then continues to sample further readings regularly – These are then charted on the SPC to see if the process is under control.
5. Patterns of behaviour are observed – Where readings are heading toward either upper or lower control limits.
6. Causes for problems in readings must be determined and rectified. Quality circles would be used for this purpose.
7. Ideally, the control limits need to be moved nearer to the mean to improve uniformity and three standard deviation readings should be increased.

An example of the X chart is shown in Figures 5.10 and 5.11.

We can use this information to set upper and lower control limits, as shown in Figure 5.11.

Process quality has to be tied to product quality for a complete quality offering to be offered to customers. A process control chart may well ensure that a product is under set process guidelines but by itself provides no clues as to whether the product is meeting customer requirements.

The interesting factor about this is that much of the remedy has to do with management attitudes: large amounts of money will often have to be spent in order to avoid future problems. Training, although central to this remedy, is still too often viewed as a cost, rather than an investment and is all too often waived in favour of other short-term priorities. The use of SPC is not for technical complexity, it is rather a means of monitoring quality in order to continually improve performance. Motorola have used SPC to such effect in their plants that they have gone from three standard deviations to six in monitoring quality. This means that for every one million operations there will be no more than four defects.

This has enabled Motorola to be a world-class manufacturer, able to compete on cost and delivery requirements. In addition, their product innovations are

Figure 5.10 Statistical process control charts – setting the distribution around three standard deviations.

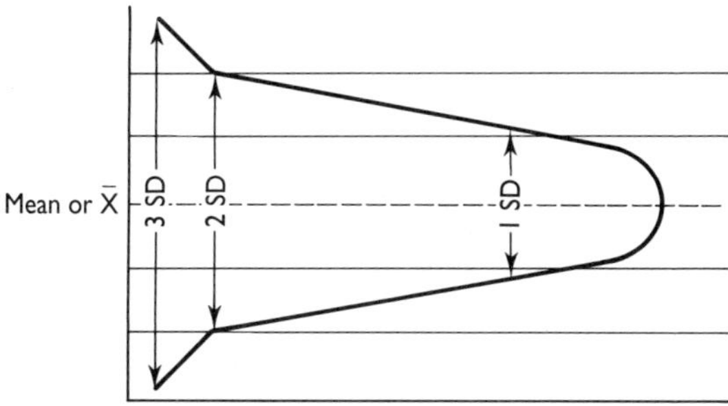

Under a normal distribution the following will occur:

1. 68.3% will fall within one standard deviation of the mean
2. 95.4% will fall within two standard deviations of the mean
3. 99.7% (or 997 out of 1000) will fall within three standard deviations of the mean

Figure 5.11 Statistical process control charts – applying upper and lower control limits.

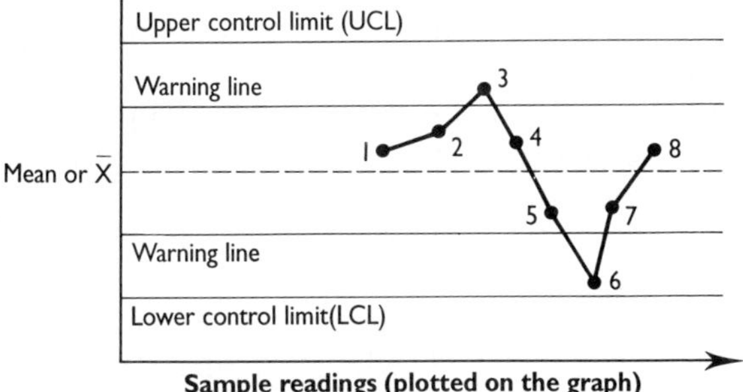

In the above example, all eight readings are within acceptable limits. However, three factors emerge:

1. Reading no. 6 is very close to the lower control limit and, if this is a common occurrence, the causes for this must be investigated
2. The operator must be trained to ensure that the process does not go out of control
3. Three standard deviations (or building in 99.7% certainty) of process control should always be improved and is the minimum requirement; Motorola, for example, has six sigma (six standard deviations either side of the mean) process control charts. They can speak in terms of defects per million! This has massive competitive advantages in terms of delivery and lower cost brought about by lack of rework, scrap and other wasteful problems

rapid and ongoing due, at least in part to the elimination of waste in all forms, which in turn releases capacity and improves efficiency.

5.13 TQM and work study

The focus of this chapter is on the strategic importance of quality. It may be surprising, therefore, that work study is included. The reason for doing so is that the strategic importance of quality is lost on some companies who abandon quality efforts, frustrated by the seeming lack of improvement in their business performance. It will become clear that work study can play a vital part in this measurement and the result of this will have strategic consequences for the firm.

To some, quality and work study would be seen as separate issues. However, many quality drives fail because process quality is not measured and work study provides appropriate tools and techniques, often ignored in quality drives, for measuring process quality. The major writers on quality, who initially focused on manufacturing environments, particularly Deming and Juran, have offered a number of areas of improvement for each organization to adopt. Thus Deming (1982) has fourteen points of quality management, Juran (1988) has ten and Crosby (1979) has fourteen tools for quality improvement. Curiously, the explicit approaches and offerings from work study have largely been ignored by these writers. Many firms will fail in their quality efforts, which are abandoned after short periods of time. One factor behind companies abandoning TQM is that they are not measuring quality sufficiently.

Work study can provide the discipline needed to adopt the internal customer approach as an organizational way of life when undertaken as an ongoing process. Brown (1994) observed how work study methods were being used in quality drives in a number of plants in the United States and United Kingdom and Adler (1993) reported how NUMMI used work study as a central feature of manufacturing performance. Work study is not in itself an absolute assurance of quality. Rather, some of the tools and techniques offered by work study methods, in particular method study, can serve the organization in measuring progress in terms of reduced lead times, lower cost and faster responses to delivery, all of which are important competitive factors in providing customer satisfaction and, therefore, quality.

5.13.1 The image problem of work study

The role of work study has been underplayed in recent years. Too often, work study has been seen as a technique representing the 'bad old days' of the worker/manager divide when industrial relationships in companies were poor. Clearly, the worker/manager divide – the 'us and them' syndrome – is alien and destructive to TQM. However, work study in itself is not responsible for creating the atmosphere in which this is likely to occur and some of the basic tools and techniques, together with the mentality behind modern work study methods can serve as part of the quality drive.

We would be foolish to attribute Japan's success to their supposed rejection of Taylorism. As Schonberger and Knod (1991) rightly state:

> Some writers have said that the rejection of Taylorism is one reason for Japan's industrial success. That is nonsense . . . The Japanese are the most fervent believers in industrial engineering in the world . . . In the Just-in-Time approach problems surface and then people apply methods study (and quality improvement) concepts to solve the problems. Time standards are widely used in Japanese industry . . . to plan how long to expect a job to take, assign the right amount of labor, and compare methods. (p.701)

In Adler's (1993) observation on the NUMMI project, he states that:

> NUMMI's intensely Taylorist procedures appear to encourage rather than discourage organizational learning and, therefore, continuous improvement. (p.101)

and concludes that:

> time-and-motion discipline . . . need not lead to rigidity and alienation. NUMMI points the way beyond Taylor-as-villain to the design of a truly learning-orientated bureaucracy. (p.102)

Taylor has, in fact, been misrepresented; we saw earlier, for example, how Matsushita, quoted in Shores (1990), scathingly spoke of Western manufacturing being under 'Taylor's principles . . . (where) you firmly believe that good management means executives on one side and workers on the other' (p.270).

However, this is both unfair and misleading; Taylor (1947) saw best practice being the result of *combined* efforts between management and workers. He spoke of 'prosperity' for both employer and employee:

> Scientific Management . . . has for its very foundation the firm conviction that the true interests of the two are one and the same. (p.10) and that intimate cooperation with the management and the help . . . from the management . . . (p.14) was vital.

Indeed, Taylor states that 'This close, intimate, personal cooperation between the management and the men is of the essence of modern scientific . . . management' (p.26) and that 'In place of the suspicious watchfulness and the more or less open warfare which characterizes the ordinary types of management, there is universally friendly cooperation between the management and the men' (p.28). Also, far from seeing the worker as deskilled (as is sometimes associated with him), Taylor emphasized the importance of training:

> it follows that the most important object of both workmen and the management should be the training and development of each individual. (p.12)

Clearly, therefore, the association with, and labelling of 'Taylorism' as some sort of device against the workforce is unfounded. Unfortunately, this association seems to continue and has carried over to the bad image of work study.

5.13.2 *Total quality and work study*

The British Standard definition defines work study as:

> The systematic examination of activities in order to improve the effective use of human and other material resources. (BS 3138, 1979)

The definition ties in with and should be linked to the philosophy of continuous improvement in all aspects of the business. Undoubtedly, TQM will focus the company on being customer driven. With this often comes a change of organizational culture from product-offered to customer-driven in style. This cultural change and other soft systems issues are vital. However, what often becomes neglected is the need to monitor improvements and to quantify work on a continuous basis. Every organization involved in TQM should actively seek out areas of improvement on an ongoing basis. One of the major benefits of TQM should be increased productivity, measured in terms of:

$$\frac{\text{Output}}{\text{Input}} \quad \textit{(measured in individual variables, e.g. labour, machine hours)}$$

Individual inputs need to be recorded and measured against their output. Methods need to be employed to determine particular inputs so that their contribution to the business can be quantified, analyzed and hopefully, improved. Productivity measures are vital since and as Drucker (1986) states,

> Without productivity objectives a business does not have direction. Without productivity measurements it does not have control. (p.27)

Work study divides into two complementary areas: method study and work measurement.

5.13.3 *Method study*

Method study is in essence, looking critically at processes in order to improve performance, which is exactly the requirement for any organization intent on total quality management. The method study approach of SREDIM can be a very practical approach to total quality. The acronym acts as a reminder of a systematic approach to improving performance in the workplace:

- **Select** A specific area of work or process in order to improve it.
- **Record** All relevant facts of the particular area or process.
- **Examine** All factors in the present process.

- **Develop** A better approach or process.
- **Install** The new method as a standard of excellence.
- **Maintain** This new standard as the minimum, whilst actively seeking for further improvements on a continuous basis.

The SREDIM approach acts as a closed-loop management system and has much to offer. In the select stage, a problem-solving focus group (or quality circle) will home in on a specific area; the next stage is to record – all facts will be recorded in order to measure process performance *as it is* – this recorded information has to be exhaustive, relevant and applicable; the examine and develop stages tie closely together and provide front-line personnel the opportunity to brainstorm for areas of improvement and in this way ownership of change is gained and created by the group; in the install stage, new methods are used as the new process standard. Lastly, the maintain factor allows the change to be continuously monitored and controlled. This provides a disciplined and focused approach to the continuous management of quality.

As far back as 1955, Mundel had provided a list of activities to be examined, techniques to be used and, most importantly, the 'results desired from the study' which would be of use and applicable in TQM today. Typical result categories are given as:

> Eliminate avoidable delays, reduce the processing times, eliminate delays, reduce fatigue, reduce idle time ... by eliminating or combining tasks and simplifying methods, reduce travel time and distance. (p.27)

These are exactly the sort of results that would be sought after in a TQM programme; the tools and techniques were already in place to a large degree through method study but these tools have often been ignored in many quality drives. These tools would include flow diagrams, process charts, operation charts and multi-activity charts. In Mundel (1955), we can find approaches which would clearly benefit a TQM programme; by adding a fourth column, the TQM variable becomes clear, as shown in Table 5.9).

The SREDIM approach can also be a central feature of problem solving for quality circle groups. If it is conducted properly, SREDIM becomes a systematic problem-solving approach, drawing upon established method study techniques but applying them to total quality issues; cost, speed of delivery, reliability of delivery, conformance to specification and customer satisfaction, as shown in Figure 5.12.

The five symbols used in method study can serve as a simple yet powerful approach to measuring current processes, in terms of time and other factors in order to make improvements. The five symbols are:

O:	Operation	**∇**:	Controlled storage
D:	Delay	⇒:	Transport
□:	Inspection		

Table 5.9: Linking work study and TQM

Mundel (1955)			*Brown (1994)*
Characteristics of operation being analyzed	*Recommended technique*	*Results desired from study*	*TQM measurement*
Several operations being performed in sequence	Flow diagram Process chart	Eliminate delays Reduce process time	Delivery speed and reliability
Worker moving from place to place	Flow diagram Process chart	Eliminate delays Improve process time	Reduce transport and process time, reduce cost
Two or more workers working together	Multiactivity	Reduce idle time and process time, reduce travel time and distance	Reduce cost; improve morale, delivery speed and reliability

The symbols are used to track process flow by plotting the current process on a sheet with all five symbols shown at the top, as shown in Figure 5.13.

Obviously, the aim is to have as much pure operation activity as possible; this is the only activity which adds value, the others are essentially non-productive cost factors. The aim is to eliminate these waste factors in order to reduce costs and throughput times and to increase productivity and improve the overall process flow, both in manufacturing and service settings. Waste is best described as *anything* that does not add value to the process; using work study techniques, specifically the five symbols above, we can plot the process and we know that the only activity which truly provides value is the O (operation); none of the others adds value. Method study can be a powerful and focused approach to continuous improvement in all aspects of the business and can benefit key areas such as:

Figure 5.12 The SREDIM/ total quality control interface.

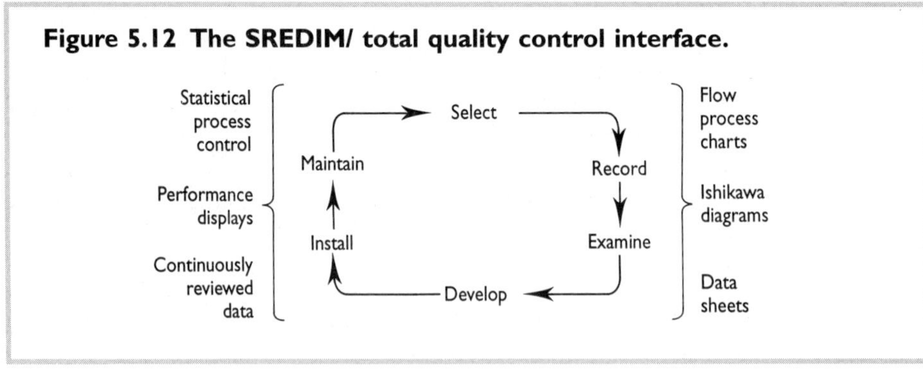

Figure 5.13 Work study symbols.

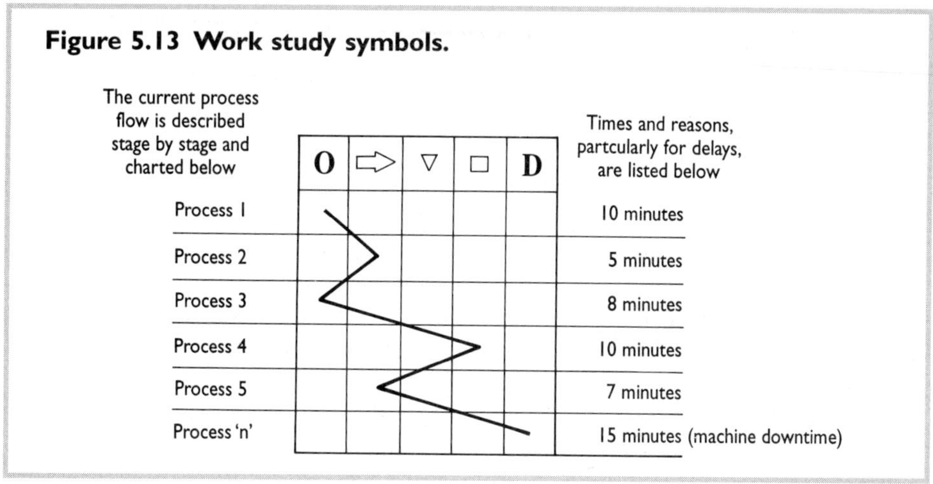

- Department layout
- Tools design
- Process design
- Workplace layout
- Product design
- Materials handling
- Quality standards

5.13.4 Work measurement

In addition to method study the other ingredient to work study is work measurement. The British Standards definition of work measurement is:

> the application of techniques designed to establish the time for a qualified worker to carry out a task at a defined level of performance. (BS 3138, 1979)

The defined level has at the centre to have conformance to product quality specification and not be simply a matter of output regardless of product quality. However, as well as being vital for key competitive areas such as cost and delivery, the timing of tasks, and the knowledge that times taken are realistic and competitive can have direct impact on the following areas:

- Costing systems
- Machine utilization
- Incentive schemes
- Production scheduling
- Manpower planning
- Capacity planning

The implication of this is that throughput times can be reduced, costs driven down and the company can become leaner and more competitive. A past problem with work measurement was that it was sometimes used as a device to exacerbate management/union relations: if standards were set that were too low, management would object, whereas if the standards were too high, union pressure was felt. It must be emphasized, though, that work measurement does not in itself create these tensions and as Krajewski (1987) points out:

> 'The nature of controversies such as these point to the need for effective work-force management and the structure of appropriate incentives. (p.212)

The total quality approach must have zero defects as its aim and therefore any compensation must have this at the forefront. The appropriate incentives go far beyond any piece-rate or similar old-fashioned approaches; factors such as company-wide profit sharing, stock ownership and performance-related pay (in terms of product quality measurements) can be realized directly as a result of work study methods. For example, Lincoln Electric, a leading maker of arc-welding equipment, uses work study methods as a means of determining compensation; workers are responsible for their own quality and this approach has caused the exit of several major companies from the industry.

Ford uses its own 'modular arrangement of predetermined time standards' (MODAPTS) as part of their commitment to improved quality and productivity. The success at the Norfolk, Virginia plant means that this will now be used in all American plants. TQM and work study are clearly linked at Ford.

If we combine the benefits of work measurement and method study the list will include at least the following:

- Improved design/specifications of the product or service
- Better use of materials
- Improved use of equipment
- Improved working conditions
- Less absenteeism
- Better use of people
- Improved layout of premises
- Reduction in fatigue
- Improved morale
- Less labour turnover

It is clear, therefore, that the tools and techniques offered by modern work study greatly enhance the capability of organizations both to compete externally and perform more efficiently internally. Too often, however, work study is ignored as part of TQM.

5.13.5 *Quantifying quality: a role for work study*

Far from being mutually exclusive areas, quality and quantity sit together in total quality. Changes and results must be quantified on a regular basis. Quantifying data are central to the SREDIM approach because the before and after scenarios have to be both measured and compared. Quantifiable data are obviously central to work measurement. Quantifying results is vital in order to measure and monitor improvements within the organization. Work study methods demand that progress is quantified on a regular and ongoing basis. Companies seriously involved in total quality should actively seek out areas of improvement in all aspects of the business. Statistical processes do not need to be complex; they do need, however, to be monitored by front-line personnel in all departments of every organization purporting to be involved in total quality. Typical areas of concern in quality in which work study methods can be of direct benefit are in the following quality areas:

1. Prevention costs

These will include:

- Design, including tooling specifications. Whilst Taguchi methods are central, method study would also help to improve process and product design.
- Preventative maintenance (a Japanese obsession).
- Analyzing quality levels, problem solving and introducing new methods (SREDIM).

2. Appraisal costs

The SREDIM approach would apply to:

- Inspection and testing of internal processes.
- Testing new product prototypes and ensuring their cost and product viability.

3. Internal failure costs

These will include:

- Scrap – parts and materials.
- All rework.
- Product failure and redesign.
- Analysis of process downtime.
- Analysis of process set-up time (vital for just-in-time processes).

In the best of companies statistical methods such as control charts (R charts, X-bar charts) are used alongside work study charts in order to track the process and aim for zero defects and continuous improvement in all areas of the business. When these three factors are analyzed on a continuous basis, then the likelihood of the fourth cost of quality, external failure, with the likely loss of image and possible damage to external customer relations, is reduced dramatically.

5.14 Total productive maintenance (TPM)

The Japanese have always seen prevention, rather than cure, as a central theme and they have a '4S' approach to housekeeping:

- *Seri* Sorting (simplifying tasks, labelling items, waste disposal).
- *Seiton* Orderliness (allocating items, label locations).
- *Seiso* Cleaning (maintain tools, clean workplaces and desks).
- *Seiketsu* Cleanliness (safety, minimizing waste).

Table 5.10 Measurements of utilization for TPM

Machine effectiveness	=	Machine availability	×	Performance efficiency	×	Rate of quality
	=	$\frac{\text{Planned time less downtime}}{\text{Planned time}}$	×	$\frac{\text{Planned cycle time}}{\text{Actual time}}$	×	$\frac{\text{Total output less defects}}{\text{Total output}}$

This forms a discipline to ensure regularly that breakdowns of equipment do not occur. Each operator is charged with maintenance responsibility and 'owns' the machine under his/her responsibility. Lubrication and simple repairs are undertaken; spare parts availability must be known and all problems with the machine have to be recorded. Measurements of machine use can be used along the lines of Table 5.10.

Preventive maintenance will enhance the process and will ensure a 'right first time' approach. A number of companies are using total productive maintenance (TPM) as a vital part of their quality drive; Pirelli Tyres in their UK plant in Carlisle have used TPM as one of the core areas of their successful quality drive. The competitive importance of TPM lies in the overall reduced costs of machine maintenance, greater operational efficiency and reduced downtime, enhancing delivery speed and reliability.

5.15 Implementing the process of quality management

There is no single fixed approach to implementing quality. However, quality is a driving force which has to be central to the firm's efforts and from this all activities within the firm must be harnessed in order to satisfy customers. A few clues can be offered, from a corporate view of the firm, although the following is not offered as a rigid, step-by-step approach. A firm should at least:

1. Target customers whose requirements match the core competencies of the firm, much of this has to do with production/operations capability.
2. Determine the exact requirements of the targeted customers.
3. Create products which meet or (where appropriate) exceed customer requirements.
4. If the firm does not have capability on its own, it must create alliances with other firms in order to meet customer requirements.
5. Ensure that process quality is in place and in doing so meet (and exceed where appropriate) customer requirements of low cost, delivery speed, delivery reliability, range of products and flexibility.

In manufacturing terms, explicit guidelines can be offered for implementing quality. Interestingly, there are parallels between implementing quality and just-in-time approaches (discussed in Chapter 6) and these include:

1. **Reducing lot sizes** The traditional push system of manufacturing (discussed in Chapter 6) has tended to manufacture in batches which has often meant that quality problems have become hidden. Under small lot sizes, these quality problems become readily visible and must be rectified.
2. **Reducing buffer stocks** This is a central feature of just-in-time (discussed in Chapter 6) and in terms of quality, reducing safety stocks means that operations have to be performed right first time because there are no buffer stocks, just-in-case operations go wrong.
3. **Reducing production rates** A successful quality drive will undoubtedly improve productivity. However, as part of the learning process, it is important that production rates are, initially, reduced so that quality problems are revealed and consequently eliminated.
4. **Using automation where possible to ensure consistency** This does not in any way down play the empowerment requirement of human resources; rather it allows proper empowerment to take place, leaving the more mundane aspects of inspection to automation, where possible. This then frees operators to be more managerial in their approach to operations.
5. **Working continuously with suppliers on improving quality** The strategic role of suppliers is discussed in Chapter 6, but we can say here that the role of suppliers is important to all firms intent on providing quality products. Rover embarked on their quality drive in 1987 and saw suppliers as vital to this; admittedly the learning gained from their alliance with Honda played a part, but Rover has its own quality manuals, including requirements from their suppliers.

   Rover is clear about its dependence on suppliers:

   > Best Practice is not a 'one-off' exercise to reduce Rover Group prices . . . it is our intention to work together on a continuous basis to further the viability of both of our businesses . . . there is no end point to Best Practice (Rover Purchasing Group UK, 1993, p.5)

Since the introduction of Rover's 1991 quality initiative – RG2000 – Rover has paid even greater attention to their relationship with suppliers. What has emerged over recent years has been a number of company awards given by firms to suppliers; Chrysler and Ford, in particular, award their suppliers with achievements for meeting company requirements.

Conclusions

Although a number of studies of Western manufacturing showed that much of the West lagged behind the Japanese, in process quality improvements, it must be noted that some manufacturing learning, admittedly from the Japanese, was taking place even in the most criticized Western companies. For example, progress in quality at General Motors has been taking place, particularly in the Saturn plant. The plant was noted for its process technology although, for GM, the major advance was in its management of people; at Saturn, over 160 work teams were created in largely autonomous roles. Each team would be responsible for hiring, process control (including licence to stop the production line) and payment consisted of base salary plus bonuses related to quality performance.

Similarly in the Buick Division, the amount of defects of the LeSabres was 180 in 1987 which was reduced to 80 defects per 100 cars in 1991, which matched Honda's quality levels (*Power & Associates Survey*, 1992). Honda's transplants produce cars of equal quality to those in Japanese cars, in terms of defects (Honda company information). This points to the transferability that is possible from Japan to the West. There is no great mystery to achieving quality; the Japanese achieved their quality capability as a result of help from the Western gurus, but Japan followed these teachings and the West did not. The West, with few exceptions, has paid the price for this and at long last quality is now being seen, in some firms at least, in terms of the strategic importance that it merits. However, there needs to be a change of approaches for such a transformation to be in place, as shown in Table 5.11.

The biggest challenge for many firms is to see quality as a strategic issue, rather than as a quick-fix, cost-cutting solution. Time horizons need to be long term, combined with a sense of urgency to improve in all areas of the business every day. This includes improving on those areas in which the firm *already* excels, as well as those areas in which improvement might seem more obvious. Cultural change is often a requirement for TQM to be a reality, first by seeing external customers as the most important focus, then by introducing the concept of the internal customer. In this way, the slogan, 'get it right, first time, every time', changes mere words to a way of life. By seeing quality in strategic terms, firms may have a chance of competing; without this view, firms are likely to decline and go out of business.

Table 5.11 Comparing old and strategic views of quality

Old views	*Strategic (competitive) quality*
Quality is defined in-house	Quality is defined by the customer
React to quality problems	Prevent quality problems occurring
Inspect	Build in quality process to avoid inspection
Acceptable quality levels	No defects is the criterion
Try to improve performance	Continuous improvement
Output versus quality	Output *because* of quality
Quality is technical	Quality is managerial
Quality is measured by one area	Quality is measured in every area

Summary

- **Quality is defined in terms of providing customer satisfaction. This means that the firm needs to be fully aware of customer needs and to satisfy them.**
- **Quality is of strategic importance; it is a long-term, competitive weapon which must form the core of the firm's approach to business.**
- **Quality is a requirement to compete in any market; by providing quality goods and services the firm can compete; without quality the performance of the firm is likely to diminish.**
- **Quality can be divided into** *process* **and** *product* **quality;** *product* **quality includes those features which appear in the final product. They can include basic specifications, together with added features which provide value for the customer;** *process* **quality includes the ability to produce at relatively low cost, with assured delivery and flexibility. Product and process quality must combine in order for a complete quality offering to take place.**
- **Minimum standards of quality are increasing, due to the number of competitors in most markets who all provide added features in order to improve their competitive position. Once this takes place, other competitors will, typically, copy this and the advantage then becomes common throughout the industry until a new feature emerges.**
- **There is a hard side to quality – statistical process control and other 'tools' discussed in the chapter; there is also a soft side – the cultural, organizational change, including the idea of the 'internal' customer. Both hard and soft factors need to be in place if quality is to take place.**
- **Improvements in quality must be continuously measured. This becomes a means of encouraging employees when improvements have been made and also alerts staff to improvements that have yet to be made.**
- **Quality includes all aspects of the business and is, therefore, everyone's concern – all employees, suppliers, distributors and customers.**
- **The tools and techniques of work study can play a vital part in measuring quality.**
- **Quality is a way of life and demands lifetime commitment. It is not a managerial fad and is certainly not something which is accomplished once and for all. The firm must have continuous improvements (***Kaizen***) taking place.**

CASE TQM at Motorola

Motorola is the world's largest supplier of equipment for wireless applications. It began as a manufacturer of car radios, but has diversified into the overall business of mobile communications. Their products include cellular phones, two-way radios, pagers, semiconductors for the car industry and microchips for use in other equipment. In the early 1990s, it formed a partnership with Apple and IBM to produce a processor to compete directly against Intel. Before this partnership, Motorola was already the number two US maker of chips. The result of this alliance was the Power PC, which was produced more cheaply than the competitive product, the Intel Pentium chip.

Motorola is a technology leader; it spends 10 per cent of sales on R&D. It began the ambitious Iridium project in 1992, which was designed to launch over sixty low-earth orbit satellites. Each of these would be capable of handling data, voice, paging and fax messages. Product quality is therefore a key issue for Motorola. It wants to be first to market and to remain a technology leader.

At the same time, Motorola is firmly committed to process quality. The combination of technological leadership and quality has paid off in a number of competitive ways, including rising sales and healthy profits, as shown in Figure 5.14.

As can be seen from the graph in Figure 5.14, Motorola has enjoyed a growth rate of 15.2 per cent in sales and 19.6 per cent in profits during this five-year period. This profitability has not come about by any downsizing; in fact Motorola's number of employees increased from 89,000 in 1983 to 120,000 in 1993. Instead, this profitability owed everything to a strategic commitment to quality.

Figure 5.14 Motorola's sales and profits: 1989–93.

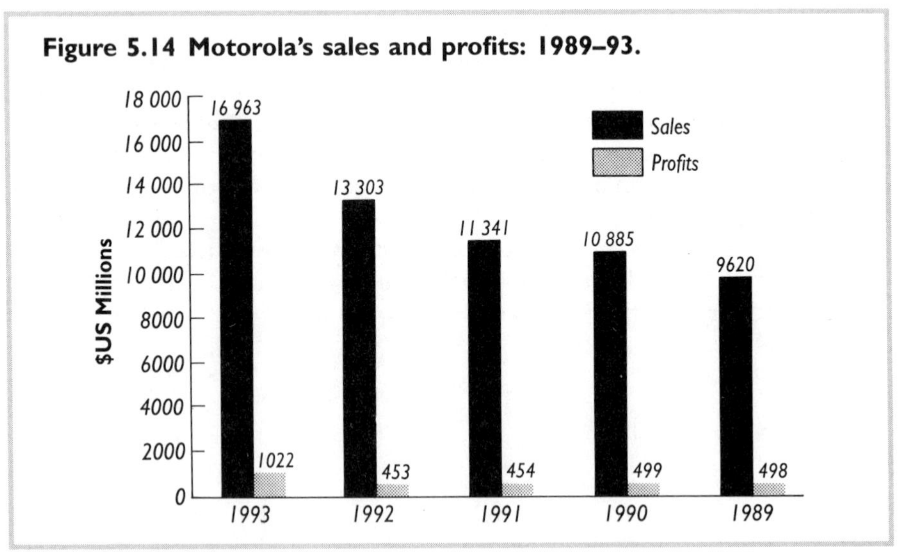

The evolution of quality performance at Motorola is an interesting example of commitment to continuous improvement. Motorola is in an intensely competitive industry; cost is a vital competitive factor and therefore waste must be avoided. Quite simply, the organization cannot afford to be spending operational time and capability on rework, scrap, overtime, downtime and so on. In addition to the actual cost factors, the industry is noted for the requirement for rapid product innovation on an ongoing basis. Motorola cannot afford to be using operations' time in terms of rectifying mistakes; this will bite into available capacity and slow down response and manufacturing speed. With this in mind, Motorola is firmly committed to continuous improvement. Their former CEO, Robert Galvin, described the progress of the quality drive at Motorola:

> We set an initial goal to reduce defects, paperwork, delivery etc ... to one tenth ... For example our ... yield on a transistor was 5,000 defects per 1,000,000 devices, not bad when translated into 99.5 per cent good, but too bad for the user. (from Statement on *Motorola Quality Experience*, Motorola, Schaumberg, Illinois, November, 1988)

The changes at Motorola included identifying quality champions for each area of improvement. In addition, massive reorganization took place, including integrating functions. Regular quality system reviews became a way of life at Motorola whereby improvements were sought in all areas of the business. The results of all of these changes were dramatic:

1. By 1989 Motorola had managed to reduce defects to 200 parts per million.
2. By 1991 they had 370 per cent reduction in defects per million parts
3. 5.1 sigma capability had been achieved.
4. Manufacturing flow time had been reduced by 40 per cent.
5. Production increased by 60 per cent, with no additional input from labour man-hours.
6. Between 1987 and 1991 Motorola reduced its defect rate for all manufactured products from 6000 to 40 parts per million.
7. The value of sales per employee doubled in the same period.

By 1993, Motorola could speak in terms of 6 sigma, or four defects per million operations.

For Motorola, the quest for quality continues; clearly for them competitive advantage is based around its operational capability and the firm continues to spend vast sums on training, ensuring that the commitment continues into the next century.

6 The strategic importance of inventory management

6.1 Introduction

6.1.1 The contrast between Japanese and Western practice

Nowhere has the contrast between Western and Japanese manufacturing been more evident than in materials or inventory management. This area has also been one of the great areas of organizational learning by the West in terms of how it has tried to emulate some of the practices which have underpinned Japan's success in key industries. In short, many Western manufacturing firms have tended to view materials management as a tactical activity; this same tactical attitude has also applied to manufacturing in general. Consequently, purchasing/materials management has been performed in the main at lower levels of the organization and has been relegated to a reactive function, again much like production/operations. In the West, this has meant that purchasing has been seen as a buying function responding to production requirements, after they have been, in turn, determined by marketing. In Japan, by contrast, materials management has been seen in terms of strategic importance, as part of the manufacturing arsenal which will serve to out-compete other players in markets. There is evidence that the former approach is changing and this is discussed later in this chapter. In some firms, though, there is a suspicion of Japanese practices in materials management and learning in some organizations has been painfully slow and erratic.

6.1.2 The holistic, focused and strategic approach to inventory

Throughout this book it has been argued that manufacturing firms in the 1990s and beyond must be holistic, focused and strategic in approach; this is particularly applicable in the manufacturing firm's management of inventory:

1. **Holistic**. The value chain model, discussed in Chapter 1, is useful in mapping the manufacturing firm's activities. The manufacturing firm must look at the whole supply chain and see where the firm itself adds value through its own production/operational capabilities. The firm can then form alliances via added-value partnerships in the supply chain.
2. **Focused**. As a result of the holistic view that a firm must have, it can then

focus on what it does best, its core competence, rather than being involved in all aspects of and activities within the supply chain. The firm must also be focused in terms of targeting particular suppliers with whom it will form its partnerships. This is in direct contrast to the former unfocused approach of many manufacturing firms in the West, in having a very wide supplier base, with little or no collaboration between manufacturer and supplier.

3. **Strategic**. Once the firm is clear in terms of its focus it will then, if it is to remain in the market, form strategic, long-term partnerships with other players in the supply chain. As we shall see later, this means that a manufacturing firm will view itself as part of an extended enterprise, in which strategic partnerships are formed for each other's competitive advantage against other such partnerships within a particular industry. A strategic view is also important for the internal production/operations performance of the firm. Rather like TQM, which greatly impacts upon materials management, there has to be a long-term view of continuous improvement in materials management, rather than a short-term tendency to cut costs.

6.1.3 The shift from asset to liability

The major shift in thinking is to move away from the idea of materials as an asset (which can be shown on a balance sheet as part of the firm's 'worth') to the idea of materials as company liability, the bad management of which (especially in production/operations areas) will weaken competitive capability in terms of delays, increased costs, reduced output and poor responsiveness to market requirements. The sheer cost of bought-in materials from suppliers reveals how important it is to the buying company.

6.1.4 Examples of expenditure

General Motors spends over $35 billion in the United States alone and data in *Purchasing Magazine* in 1993 showed that Ford was the largest US corporate spender on supplies; Ford's purchasing department spent $58 billion in 1992, compared to $52.4 billion for General Motors. General Motors, the second largest spender, sells more cars than Ford, but purchases a fair share of parts from its own components group, making its outside spending lower. The same report showed that Chrysler had become the third largest spender, moving ahead of IBM, General Electric and Du Pont. Chrysler spent nearly $24 billion with outside suppliers in 1992, up 38 per cent over 1991. The 'big three' US car manufacturers alone account for over 28 per cent of the total amount of spending by the top 100 corporate buyers. A survey by *Business Week* (22 June 1992) showed that sales of car parts in the United States amounted to more than $100 billion and that the number of people employed in parts for car companies exceeded 600,000, a similar number to that of employees of the 'big three'.

6.2 The scope of materials management

Materials management embraces all those activities which are involved in the supply chain from raw materials to end customer. The manufacturing firm is not necessarily involved in all areas of the supply chain. The most exhaustive system would be as shown in Figure 6.1.

The essential feature here is that cost will definitely be added at every stage but the world-class firm ensures that value is added as well. The biggest shift for many firms is in moving away from ownership of suppliers (vertical integration) to forming alliances with suppliers. This buyer–supplier relationship is discussed later in this chapter. We can say here, though, that the buyer–supplier relationship presents one of the biggest opportunities and challenges for many firms. The

Figure 6.1 The complete materials flow process.

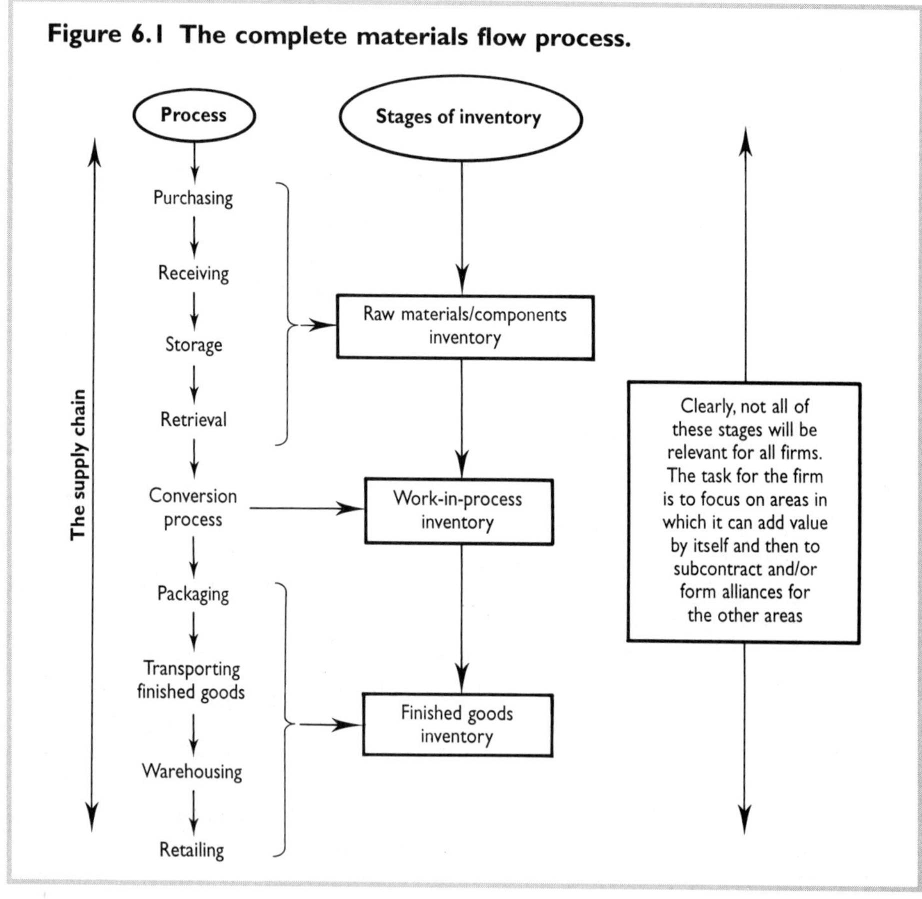

linkages are delicate and intricate and need careful management. Certain stages in the supply chain show that in the car, computer and telecommunications industries, suppliers are particularly important in terms of:

1. *The absolute volume* (both units and monetary value) that suppliers produce (e.g. Intel, AT&T, Bosch).
2. *The concentration of suppliers' output in particular geographic areas*. For example, an average PC will have at least the following links in the supply chain, some linkages of which are dependent on specific plants:
   (a) A PC uses an Intel microprocessor; by 1994 over 50 per cent of Intel's most popular microprocessor, the 486 chip, came from a single factory in New Mexico.
   (b) The PC's microprocessor and a handful of other chips are encased in ceramic packages made in Japan's Kyocera Corporation, which had 70 per cent of the world market in the mid-1990s. Over 50 per cent of its packages are made at a single plant in Kokubu, Japan.
   (c) The computer's hard disk drive has a data-reading head supplied by TDK Corporation, which accounts for an estimated 45 per cent global market share, in 1994, from a single factory in Kofu, Japan.
   (d) The dicing saws used to cut the PC's chips from silicon wafers are built by Japan's Disco Corporation, which builds 70 per cent of the saws at only two factories in Japan.
   (e) The circuits on every chip in the computer were printed by precision tools called 'steppers', 50–70 per cent of which are made by Nikon Corporation at a single factory in Japan.
   (f) Circuit designs on every chip were engraved on a quartz plate called a photomask, 40 per cent of which Dai Nippon Printing Company makes at two factories in Japan.
   (g) The steppers that built the circuits all use special ultraviolet light bulbs, 70 per cent of which are made by Ushio Incorporated at a plant in Japan.
   (h) Over 60 per cent of the world's blank quartz plates for photomasks are made by Hoya Corporation at two locations in Japan.

The above example seems to be typical of linkages within suppliers in the electronics industry (Hamilton, 1993; Author's data from Intel).

A telling quote comes from the *Wall Street Journal*:

> Even a superficial scan suggests there are multiple situations . . . where things converge to a single supplier two to three tiers back from the main supplier. (27 August 1993, Sec. A, p.1)

The above example exemplifies how the scope of materials management is often immense. It requires the very best of managerial skills in ensuring that linkages which on the surface look volatile and often wholly dependent on activities outside of the firm are brought together in perfect synchronization.

6.3 Tactical/functional roles in materials management

There are a number of activities in materials management which are essentially tactical in nature: allocating part numbers, providing codes for grouping parts and associated clerical duties such as packing and receiving (unless parts go direct to the workstation from the supplier). However, too often this has been seen as the sum total of materials management, when in reality it becomes clear that materials management becomes a powerful strategic weapon, a means of outperforming other competitors in areas such as costs and delivery. Unfortunately, the former tactical association with materials management has brought with it quick-fix solutions and techniques, the most noticeable of which is the economic order quantity, discussed later in this chapter.

6.4 The competitive importance of materials management

Inventory management is a critical factor in the success of manufacturing firms. Inventories impact upon the competitive capability of the firm in a number of ways, including cost, delivery speed, delivery reliability and flexibility. Such competitive importance in the car industry is outlined by Carlisle and Parker (1991):

> With purchased components and materials representing 60-80% of the manufactured cost of automobiles.. any excessive inefficiencies between US car makers and their suppliers will only serve to reduce margins all along the manufacturing chain, as they can no longer be passed along so easily to the marketplace. (p.23)

Quality is a central consideration in choosing suppliers and other major competitive factors for manufacturers in relationship to suppliers are cost, delivery capability, supplier involvement in product innovation through joint designs and flexibility – the ability to respond rapidly to fluctuations of customer demand. Failure to respond can have massive consequences; IBM had enormous troubles in 1994 trying to fulfil requirements for the ThinkPad PC and the Personal System/2 desktop. The problem here was backlog of orders which suppliers were unable to satisfy. Apple, by contrast, at the end of 1993, had $1.5 billion in inventory due to over-purchase from suppliers. A pertinent statement from an Apple vice-president was, 'Backlog is bad, but inventory is worse' (*Wall Street Journal*, 21 October 1993, Sec. B, p.1). In contrast, Dell was able to avoid backlogs and huge inventory costs, a principal factor in this being its production/operations capability, tied to strong supplier links; supply and demand were matched because of manufacturing capability being able to custom-build computers. Inventory management has a massive impact upon the firm's performance in terms of response to customer requirements of delivery speed and reliability.

6.4.1 *The factor of costs in materials management*

In terms of costs alone, materials can play a major part, and the importance of reducing materials costs to improve the firm's profitability is evident from Figure 6.2. However, it is important to realize that in the West many firms will seek to reduce costs by downsizing the number of personnel rather than attacking materials costs. This is interesting for a number of reasons:

1. Getting rid of people takes little or no managerial skill.
2. In many industries where downsizing of personnel occurs, the labour costs represent a small percentage of total costs – for example, less than 10 per cent in computing hardware manufacture, and no more than 15 per cent in high-volume car manufacture, whereas materials will often account for over 60 per cent of costs. Managers have therefore reduced only a small portion of costs.

Figure 6.2 An example of the importance of materials on the firm's costs and profitability.

Firm's current position:	£ millions	
Sales	100	
Materials	60	(60% of costs)
Labour	15	(15% of costs)
Overheads	15	(15% of costs)
Gross profit	10	

If the firm's cost structure remains the same yet it wishes to increase profits to £11 million, it will have to win 10% more business in extra sales – not easy in times of recession

Sales	110	(10% increase)
Materials	66	(60% of costs)
Labour	16.5	(15% of costs)
Overheads	16.5	(15% of costs)
Gross profit	11	

Alternatively, a reduction of £1 million on materials costs will bring the same profit figure; in addition a reduction in materials will often enhance production/operations performance

Sales	100	
Materials	59	(59% of costs)
Labour	15	(15% of costs)
Overheads	15	(15% of costs)
Gross profit	11	

3. Getting rid of labour is a quick-fix solution. However, morale in the workplace will be damaged; recruiting suitable personnel when there is an upturn in the firm's fortunes may also prove difficult. The Japanese have tended to have no downsizing in their firms.
4. Concentrating on shedding labour in order to reduce costs fails to address the area of largest costs – materials – which has to be undertaken in a strategic way by improving in-house production/operations performance in avoiding all forms of waste and externally by forming strategic partnerships with suppliers.

Both the internal and external strategic factors of materials management are discussed in the section on just-in-time.

6.5 Stock-holding

Stock-holding will take place to some degree in all manufacturing firms. The problem lies in the actual amounts stored at each stage of production, the essential three being:

1. Raw materials.
2. Work-in-process.
3. Finished goods.

Raw materials and finished goods are both critical, because of the effect upon outside suppliers and customers at either end of the supply chain. The work-in-process phase is, in itself, vital for customers; much work-in-process will result in increased costs, delays to customers and inability to respond to new customer requirements and work-in-process will convey how well the production/operations area is performing. As Hutchins (1988) states:

> in the Japanese factory the only time that work is lying idle would be between cells. In the West, this would happen between every operation, so resulting in something like six times the quantity of work-in-progress in many cases. (p.21)

Materials will typically account for 60 per cent of the cost of goods sold in cars and will be as much as 85 per cent of costs for PCs (Author's analysis of selected companies costs). This represents a major absolute cost (actual expenditure expressed as a monetary value) and it is clear that overhead costs, including stock-holding, should be kept to a minimum. As we shall see, under just-in-time approaches the aim is to have stockless production. Traditional reasons for holding inventories are shown in Table 6.1.

Many of the reasons given in Table 6.1 are, however, no more than excuses for either bad in-house performance or poor buyer–supplier relationships. Similarly, work-in-process and finished goods inventories tend to act as covers or buffers for possible failures. If finished goods inventories are held in order to 'supply the

Table 6.1 Traditional reasons for holding inventory

To act as a buffer between different operations
To allow for mismatches between supply and demand rates
To allow for demands which are larger than expected
To allow for deliveries which are delayed or too small
To avoid delays in passing products to customers
To take advantage of price discounts
To buy items when the price is low and expected to rise
To make full loads and reduce transport costs
To provide cover for emergencies

Adapted from Waters (1992)

good product quickly to the consumer', then action should be taken to ensure that speed is improved within the in-house process, rather than keeping finished goods, due to the current process being incapable of rapid response. In addition, keeping finished goods in inventory in high-tech markets is dangerous, due to rapid product/component obsolescence. Admittedly, there are industries which are seasonal or extremely erratic and where the threat of obsolescence is low, in which case holding raw materials and finished stock makes some sense. This approach makes little sense in the car, computing or telecommunications industries, however. For example, when Apple introduced its Power PC-based units, the company automatically made $700 million of inventory obsolete. Holding stocks, therefore, will often not add value but will always add cost.

6.6 ABC analysis

ABC analysis can play an important role in the strategic management of materials. The ABC approach, sometimes called the Pareto analysis, or 20:80 rule, will provide a useful snapshot of the costs of materials for a completed product. Another use of the ABC analysis is to plot the amount of usage of a particular item, beside the unit cost. Both of these factors – unit cost and rate of usage – are vital in managing materials. In terms of costs, the 20:80 rule suggests that 80 per cent of the overall cost of a finished product will centre around 20 per cent of the components of the finished product and these components will be vastly more expensive than other components in the finished product. This can then be used for all items of inventory, an analysis of the overall costs of materials in terms of costs and usage rates. The ABC analysis will tend to reveal the trends shown in Figure 6.3.

The importance of this analysis goes beyond the numbers themselves to highlight the need for greater strategic management approaches, especially for

Figure 6.3 ABC analysis.

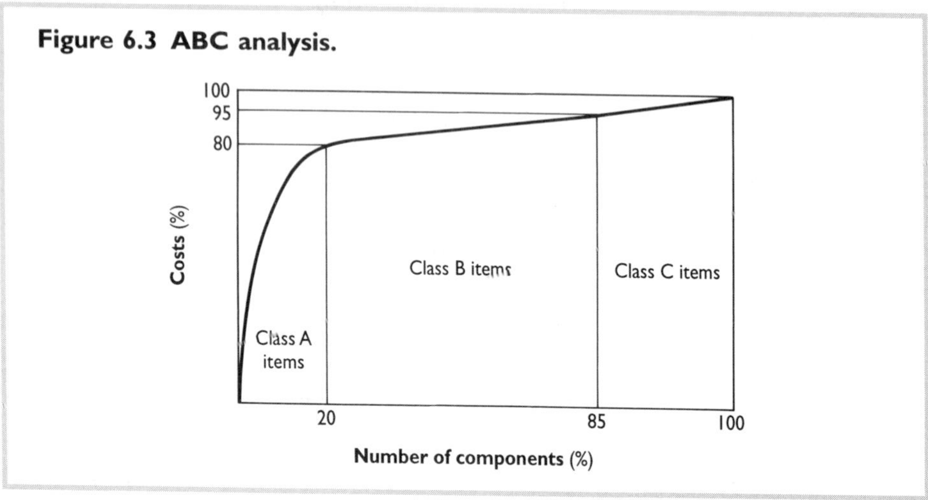

the class A items whose costs will be considerable. Class A items demand that great care and attention is needed. This in turn will demand that the buyer–supplier relationship for class A items is close. Class B items will also be of importance and again merit close supplier relations with class C items needing less strategic involvement than the other two categories.

6.7 The economic order quantity (EOQ) model

If ever a model showed the quick-fix approach to manufacturing it was the economic order quantity (EOQ) model. Although still used in firms, the case against it has been well stated over a number of years, for example Burbridge (1964). The formula was a means of determining the magical balance between having too much stock and having no stock at all. A number of elements are put into the formula and then a figure is determined which if used will supposedly strike the magic balance. The completed formula is shown in Figure 6.4 and a discussion of how this formula is obtained can be found in many other texts, but is not particularly relevant for our discussion on the strategic importance of materials management.

There are however major problems with the EOQ formula, which are listed in Table 6.2.

The points raised in Table 6.2 can be probed further:

1. **The ordering cost** In the EOQ formula, this is seen to be constant, regardless of:

   (a) the distance in placing the order,

Figure 6.4 The economic order quantity formula.

The EOQ formula is given as: $\sqrt{\frac{2AB}{C}}$

Where:

A = Annual demand
B = Variable ordering cost
C = Variable holding cost

For example, A = 12 000 units per year; B = \$20 per order; C = \$10 per unit per year

$$\text{EOQ} = \sqrt{\frac{2(12\,000)(20)}{10}}$$

$$= \sqrt{48\,000}$$

$$= \underline{219.09}$$

(b) the mode of communication (phone, fax, EDI) and the time spent in placing the order,
(c) the salary cost of the particular people who placed the order.

2. **The cost of stock-holding** Trying to determine this value is for all practical purposes impossible. Waters (1992) suggests that:

   The usual period for calculating stock costs is a year, so a holding cost might be expressed as, say, £10 a unit a year. (p.36)

Another approach is to charge a percentage (25 per cent for example) against the actual cost of a bought item. A £100 item, therefore, will have a storage charge of £25. The problem with this is that holding an item for any period, particularly

Table 6.2 Problems of the EOQ formula

1. All costs are known and do not vary – demand for an item is also similarly known and will not vary
2. As a result of point 1 above, both the unit cost of an item and the reorder costs are fixed and do not change according to quantity
3. There is only one delivery for each order – this is fine on an as-required basis for JIT but under the EOQ approach this one delivery means that the buyer will incur stockholding costs until the materials are actually required and then decline over a period of time. The delivery will not necessarily act as a driving force to speed up its use and even if it did, it might merely encourage forcing a material onto a work area before it is required. This will create a bottleneck and act to increase work in process

if the item is a high-tech component, will run the risk of obsolescence, which makes the unit itself redundant. Moreover, trying to work out a standard time that an item might be expected to be in stock is, at best pseudo-scientific, and at worst becomes a means of providing an overhead cost on a unit component in order to fund another major overhead cost, warehousing.

However, the main problem with this is that it enforces a scientific management approach to what is clearly a complex, dynamic and volatile business world where demand can be erratic and where reaction to satisfying this change is the key, not the adherence to a fixed order number-per-material-type approach. The EOQ approach is alien to just-in-time management, which seeks to pull the exact number of materials or components to a particular workstation only when it is required and not before. The EOQ formula encourages buffer stock and endorses a just-in-case mentality rather than a just-in-time approach (discussed later), whose benefits go far beyond mere stock-holding reduction. We saw earlier how ABC analysis can be a simple, but powerful, means of managing materials; the ABC analysis also serves as a final nail in the coffin to the EOQ formula; the EOQ formula will provide a figure which will often be too high for class A items. Costly class A items will be bought in, often in large numbers, and then stored in preparation for manufacturing which means that an on-cost in terms of stock-holding will come into play. In addition the EOQ figure, provided above, reveals how ridiculously unrealistic the EOQ number can be for class C items, for example asking for 219 screws, nuts and similar items from suppliers, when purchase of these items will often have to be made in terms of packs of 500 or more! Finally, the EOQ approach provides examples of buffers in materials, which as we shall see later is wasteful. Under EOQ, the buying patterns emerge in the firm, as seen in Figure 6.5.

From Figure 6.5, the following points emerge:

1. The manufacturing firm carries safety stocks just in case there are problems, either with production/operations performance or, just as alarming, with supplier capabilities; this will bring a cost of storage, together with possible problems such as damage, obsolescence (in high-tech industries) and inventory will take up storage space.
2. The lead times between order and receipt are often long; this tends to reveal that the buyer–supplier relationship is poor – the supplier will receive sporadic purchase orders from the buyer and little long-term planning is provided for the supplier.
3. The buying company (manufacturer) typically buys large numbers of materials, the number having been derived from the EOQ formula which as we have seen is suspect.

Clearly, this situation is unsatisfactory for both manufacturer and supplier; the manufacturing company is buying in bulk and storing inventory (with all the problems that this entails), whilst the supplier has no certainty of demand from the buyer and little or no loyalty exists between manufacturer and supplier.

Figure 6.5 Materials usage under the EOQ approach.

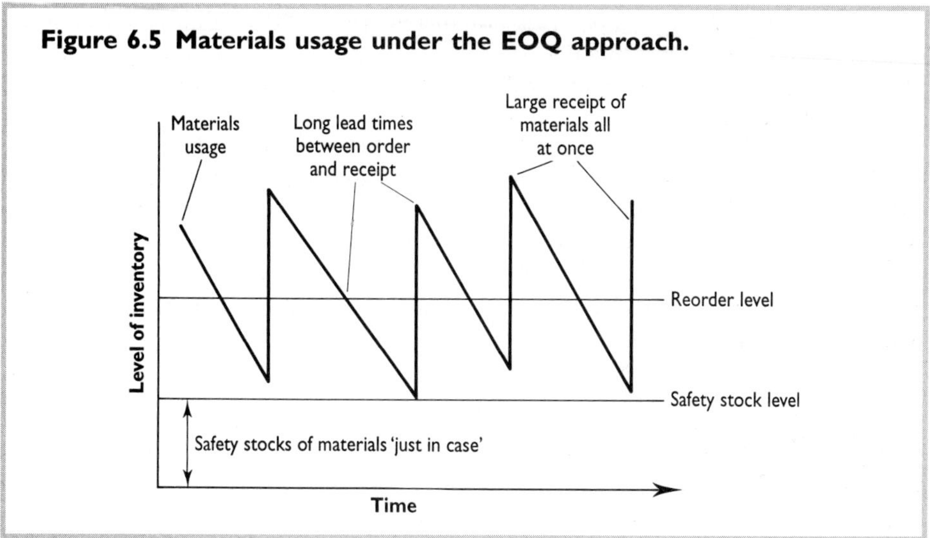

6.8 The development towards a strategic/holistic approach

What has developed in recent years is a move away from tactical buying to a strategic approach, brought about essentially in three ways:

1. The manufacturing firm has to move towards closer relationships with suppliers and see them as strategic partners.
2. The manufacturing firm has to have far greater clarity, in terms of volumes to be produced in a certain period of time. It also must know design data in full for each product that it will manufacture in a particular period.
3. The production/operations capability has to be such that materials are not bought in excess, just in case there are failures; instead, all forms of rework, waste and scrap will be reduced to avoid the need for excess or buffers of materials.

As we shall see later, these three areas have provided a massive challenge to the 'traditional wisdom' of manufacturers and many firms struggle to achieve success in both internal and external requirements.

The holistic impact of materials management is summarized by Lee and Schniederjans (1994):

> Implementing a new inventory system takes more than a commitment from the inventory manager. It takes a commitment from the entire organization, from purchasing to shipping and from top management to the workers at the shop floor level of the organization. (p.323)

Materials management will undoubtedly be influenced by and impact upon other major areas of production/operations management, most noticeably automation, quality management, product design, process design and scheduling. In addition, all stages of the supply chain will be affected by materials management. A number of management approaches to inventory came to light in the 1960s, particularly materials requirement planning (MRP) and manufacturing resource planning (MRPII), together with just-in-time management. With these developments has come the increasing awareness of materials management in terms of strategic significance and holistic scope. Just-in-time (discussed later) can be implemented only when an awareness of and commitment to the strategic factors are in place. A model of the growing strategic importance of materials management is shown in Figure 6.6.

Figure 6.6 The development of the holistic importance of materials management.

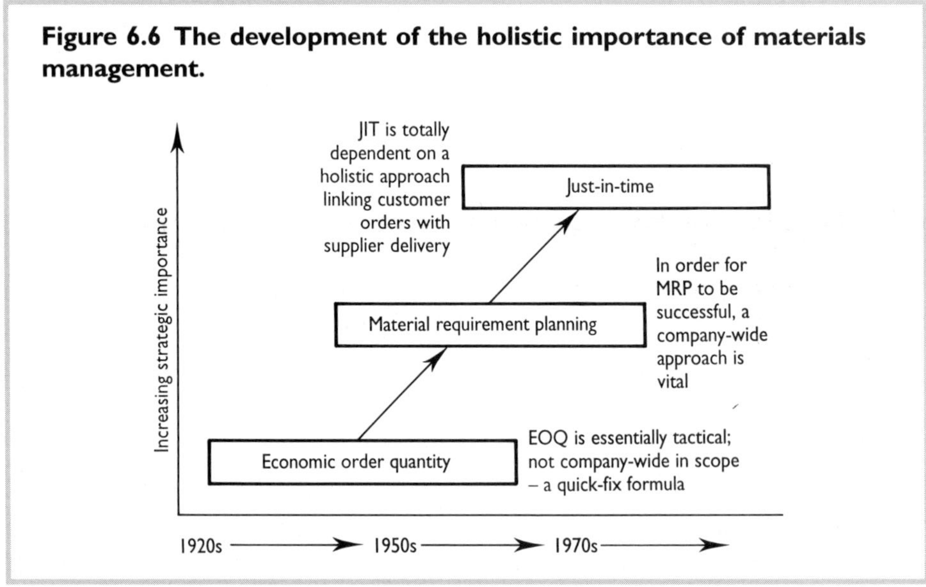

There has been a move away from tactical approaches to materials management and the two major areas of strategic advancement MRP/MRPII and just-in-time, are discussed in the following sections.

6.9 MRP – where operational and strategic levels begin to meet

MRP is a computerized approach to materials management developed in the United States during the 1960s and 1970s and it was hailed as a major breakthrough in the management of materials. The importance of MRP was outlined by Karmarker (1989):

> Penetration of MRP methods into manufacturing has been substantial, especially in industries characterized by complex bill of materials, large numbers of open orders, and many needs for materials coordination among plants, vendors, and customers. (p.125)

Essentially, the major ingredients of MRP are quite simple, involving questions such as:

1. How many products are to be made?
2. When do these products need to be made?
3. What is the finished product composition in terms of materials and components?
4. What are the numbers and types of components and materials currently in stock?

A figure is determined (by subtracting the answer to question (4) from the answer to question (3) to then ask:

5. How many items have to be ordered from suppliers?
6. What is the lead time for suppliers and consequently when do orders have to be placed?

The apparent simplicity of the questions listed above belies the huge complexity of running MRP. In many markets, and in particular automobiles and computing/telecommunications products, the product variations for models will be extremely wide. This, in turn, means that the calculations to determine all of these variations will be a massive task. However, as Adam and Ebert (1992) rightly state:

> The dynamic nature of the MRP system is a vital advantage. It reacts well to changing conditions; in fact it thrives on change. (p.541)

The MRP reporting system will provide two types of report:

1. **Regeneration** This is when the weekly, major MRP report will provide a complete record.
2. **Net change** This is an exception report, or a list of changes since the last report. This is obviously smaller than the major regeneration report.

The basic calculation undertaken in MRP is shown in Figure 6.7.

In simple terms the calculations for materials are as follows:

1. Gross materials requirements = number of finished units to be made × components and materials for each finished product.
2. Materials to be ordered = total (gross) requirements – stock – stock currently on order.

The factor of time is also vital here; the lead time for each item has to be known in order to pull the materials from suppliers.

Figure 6.7 The basic MRP calculation.

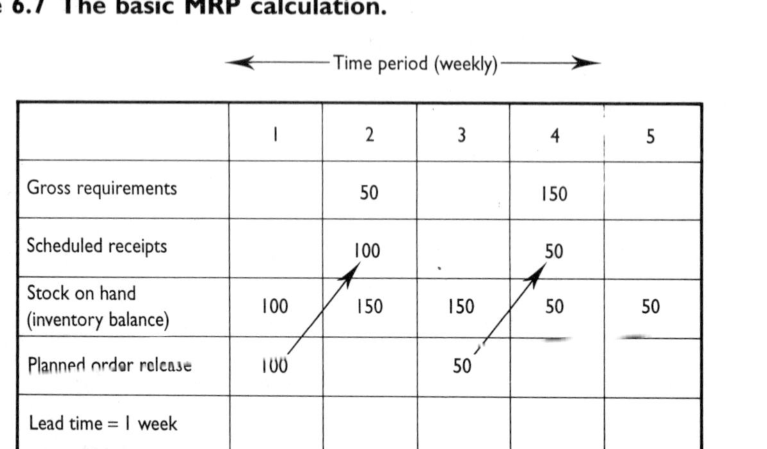

← Time period (weekly) →

	1	2	3	4	5
Gross requirements		50		150	
Scheduled receipts		100		50	
Stock on hand (inventory balance)	100	150	150	50	50
Planned order release	100		50		
Lead time = 1 week					

Some systems make a distinction between 'scheduled receipts' and another feature called 'planned receipts' not listed above. For the sake of simplicity, the above example assumes that the 'planned order release' requested in one period becomes the 'scheduled receipts' in the next

It should be obvious that for MRP to work properly an holistic approach must be made; in order to know gross requirements there has to be close contact between production and marketing departments; similarly, purchasing, far from being *reactive* to MRP, are vital in advising the manufacturing firm of suppliers capabilities in terms of quantities and delivery for a particular time period.

6.9.1 The master production schedule

A major feature of the MRP system is the master production schedule (MPS), which is a statement of products to be built within a given time period. Toyota, for example, tends to have a monthly fixed time period, or 'bucket' as it is sometimes called which will then serve as a build requirement both within its plants and for suppliers who are provided with this fixed monthly plan. At Toyota, the master production schedule is used, which is a feature of MRP:

> We can handle detailed specifications on a 10-day basis for domestic shipments. We can even handle some modifications in specifications on a daily basis. Monthly planning enables us to respond to orders quickly while maintaining a steady level of production throughout the month. (*Just-in-Time Production*, Toyota Motor Company, p.18)

Nissan UK has the same approach; it provides a five-month forecast and then fixes a one-month period which is the commitment to suppliers.

Once the master schedule is in place each product is 'exploded' into a hierarchy of parts and bills of materials are listed. Using the MPS, the MRP programme then calculates the total numbers of components required for each product. The parts explosion is linked to the product structure in terms of levels of composition, as shown in Figure 6.8.

Figure 6.8 Product structures of MRP.

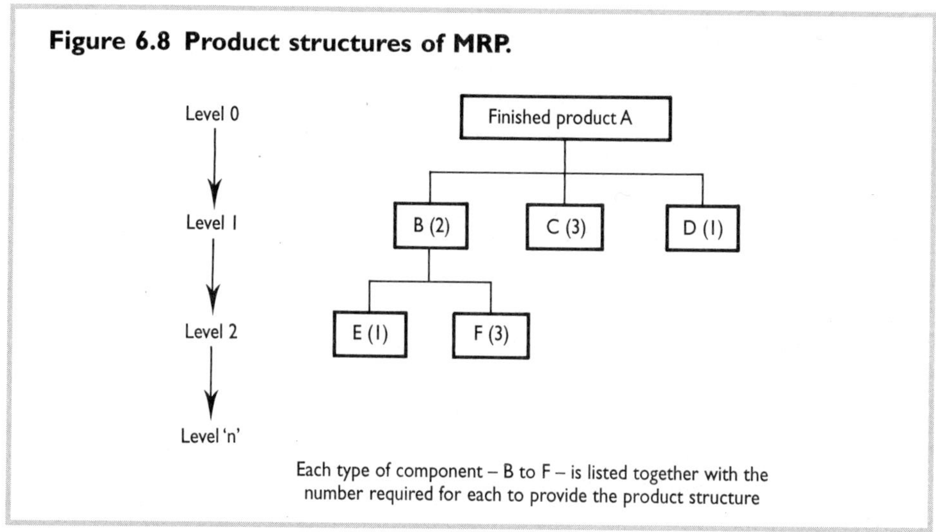

Each type of component – B to F – is listed together with the number required for each to provide the product structure

The MPS shows how vital it is for the firm to have an holistic approach; a viable MPS can only be made possible by close relationships between production/ operations, marketing and purchasing personnel. If this does not take place, the MPS will be meaningless; stock-outs of materials and components will tend to occur and delivery capabilities will be threatened. A diagram showing the links between all of the basic components in MRP is shown in Figure 6.9.

6.9.2 *From MRP to MRPII*

MRP evolved into MRPII which, in essence included MRP and added other management ingredients, such as tooling, routing procedures, capacity availability and man-hours requirement. MRP is therefore a subset of MRPII, as shown in Figure 6.10.

In practice, plant managers will sometimes refer to MRP when in fact the system they have is MRPII; the terms have become almost interchangeable, although there is a difference between them, as discussed earlier.

Luscombe (1994) points out that there has been harsh and, generally unfounded criticism of MRP:

Figure 6.9 Key ingredients to MRP.

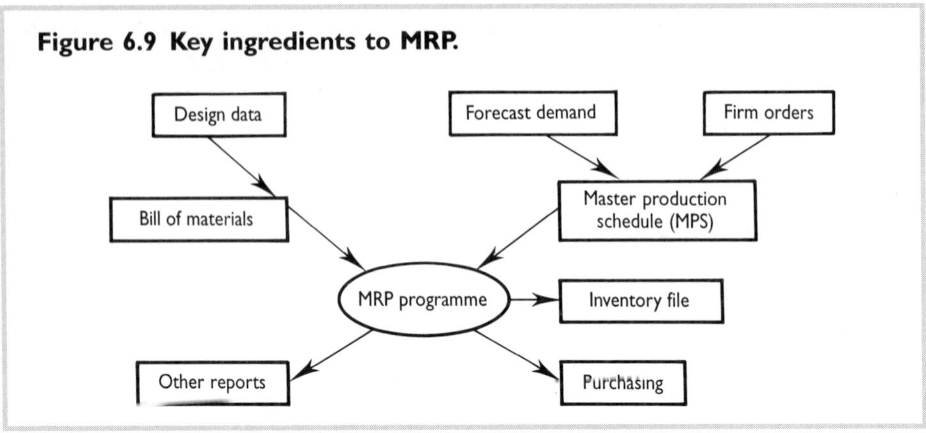

> One article referred to 'disillusionment with existing MRPII-based production planning tools' another stated that MRP II implementation methodologies 'belong to a different era' whilst a third offered reasons why 'so many large-scale MRP II systems failed. (p.123)

However, as Luscombe (1994) suggests:

> Those who abandon MRPII in search of some form of instant-response, shopfloor-driven system are likely to be disappointed, as they ignore the realities of manufacturing as reflected in both MRP II and leading Japanese production systems. (p.123)

Figure 6.10 MRP and MRPII.

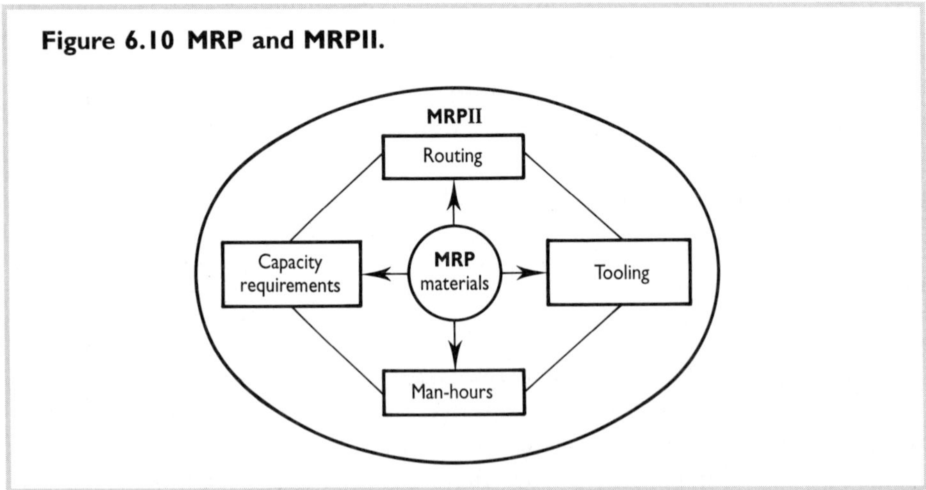

A major exponent of MRP is Oliver Wight (1982), whose works act as a useful manual for would-be users of MRP. Interestingly, a number of the requirements to be classed as a class A user of MRP show the holistic importance of materials management in MRP. Wight's twenty-five point check list, where a firm has to score 23 or over to be classified as a class A user, includes the following: initial education of all employees (not only hands-on production/operations staff); a continuing education programme; regular meetings with key staff in all functions (including production, marketing, finance and engineering); MRP to be understood by key people in all functions; and MRP to be used for financial planning, which will require good understanding of the system by financial personnel. There should therefore be much better cohesion between departments when MRPII is in place. However, as Schroeder *et al.* (1981) found, what *should* take place and what actually *does* take place are not always the same thing; in their survey of around 1700 firms using MRP, they found problems of communication between departments, including the production/marketing interface. However, the most pressing problems were in the lack of education for personnel, and poor top management support. Once again, it would seem that the lack of strategic importance on materials management by senior managers becomes a key reason for failure. When there is a strategic and holistic approach, a closed-loop system becomes a reality, as in Figure 6.11.

6.9.3 Advantages of MRP

With successful implementation, a number of benefits should be realized under MRP, as in Table 6.3.

In addition, MRP should facilitate better relationships with suppliers because in theory all lead times are known and therefore unreasonable delivery requirements are not made on suppliers. Admittedly, shorter lead times are preferable, especially when MRP is used alongside just-in-time, but that has more to do with an ongoing pursuit of improvement in delivery performance via relationships with suppliers, than as a reflection on MRPII itself.

6.9.4 Problems of MRP

There are perceived problems with MRP. One of the main factors is that it should present a learning opportunity for firms over a period of time when the system is often bought in as a means of solving inventory problems quickly. The time factor in implementing MRP is discussed by Hill (1985):

> The creation of data bases and the installation and tailoring of MRP systems to the particular manufacturing company is time consuming with the result that they do not normally bring any significant result in the first two years of their development. (p.194)

Although a two-year period is not long in terms of strategic thinking and change, the problem is that for some managers, whose sole criterion is short-term and

Figure 6.11 MRPII: the closed-loop system.

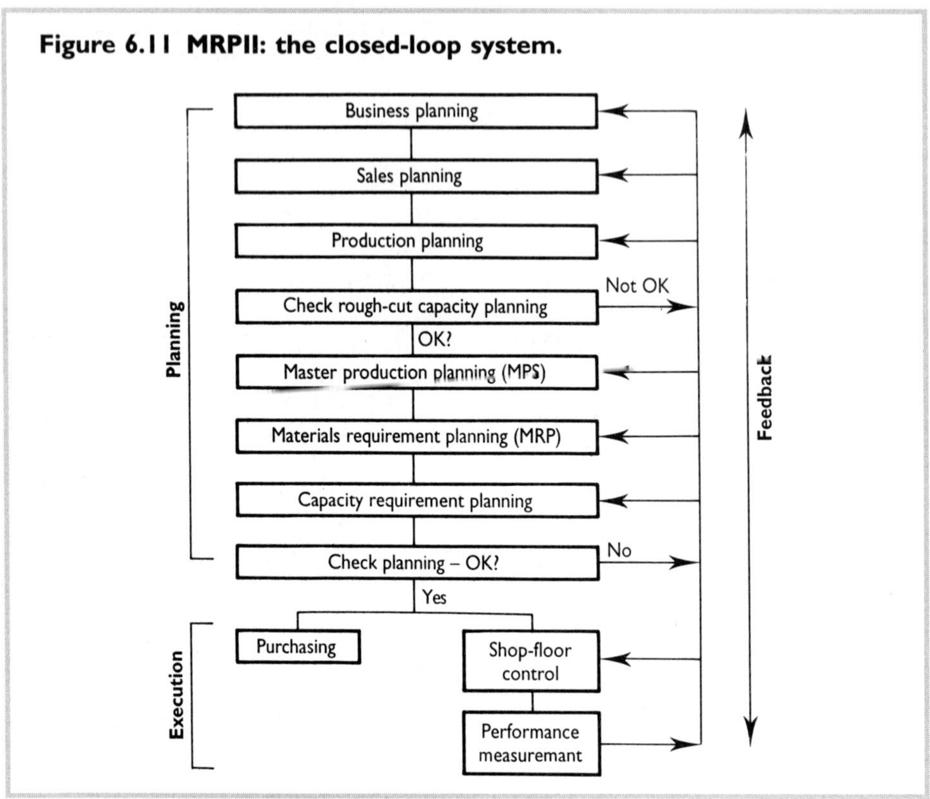

Table 6.3 Potential benefits of MRP

- Reduced stock levels
- Higher stock turnover
- Increased customer service, with fewer delays caused by shortages of materials
- More reliable and faster quoted delivery times
- Improved utilization of facilities as materials are always available when needed
- Less time spent on expediting and emergency orders

From Waters (1992)

financial in approach, a two-year period is a lifetime. Table 6.4 reveals some of the perceived problems with MRP.

The main criticism of the system is that ironically, using MRP might create

Table 6.4 Potential long-term problems with MRP

- Planning and implementing MRP can take years – although off-the-shelf software packages are available, in reality each firm must have an individual, tailored approach if the system is to be successful
- Data entry and maintenance take up much time – even if the reports are 'exception reports'; detailing changes from the last MRP run, this will still take up much time
- Data integrity is essential – this calls for a holistic approach which involves all major functions within a firm: this should present an opportunity; often, it will be the cause of failure: the inability to provide accurate forecasts of supplies and sales, engineering data which is incorrect and so on

work-in-process inventory. Materials or components that have been ordered in due to the MRP calculations might be pushed onto a particular workstation before they are required. However, this has more to do with the management of the scheduling and plant, rather than a criticism of MRP itself. The other problem is that it can be extraordinarily difficult trying to determine the application of materials per level of products, particularly when the range of product variations and models is high. Also, MRP tends to think in terms of grouped time periods or buckets and buys the materials in to suit; this is not exactly just-in-time, although it is hugely preferential to traditional methods of purchasing, including EOQ formulas and the like.

6.9.5 Resolving problems of MRP

There is nothing to stop MRP being used as the planning system, then for the tools and techniques of JIT to be used to actually pull the materials only when needed. At any rate, there must be some sort of master plan for a given time period in order for the firm to know what is to be made in a particular time. MRP can therefore be used as an exhaustive management tool by which numbers of products and, consequently, subcomponents can be determined and tracked throughout the process. MRP should not be used to push components or materials onto a workstation before they are required. Advocates of JIT (and critics of MRP) have stated that MRP is inclined to do this but, again, this has more to do with management's failure in terms of using MRP, rather than the system itself. MRP can provide a discipline so that key areas such as MPS, bill of materials, lead times with suppliers and other data integrity are reliable, accurate, relevant and known to all parties, which is essential to any well-run management information system.

MRP encourages an holistic approach within the firm itself. As Waters (1992) states:

> The introduction of MRP needs considerable changes to an organisation and these require commitment from all areas. (p.279)

The MRP system can also serve to highlight business performance problems with delivery speed and reliability. As Schmenner (1990) suggests:

> Not only can an MRP system detail what should be ordered and when, but also it can indicate how and when late items will affect other aspects of production. It can signal ... how tardiness will alter the existing production schedule. (p.487)

Since delivery speed and reliability are crucial in many markets, it is clear that MRP can play an important role in achieving these market requirements. MRP also becomes a powerful ally to just-in-time management. As Karmarker (1989) states:

> MRPII ... initiates production of various components, releases orders, and offsets inventory reductions. MRPII grasps the final product by its parts, orders their delivery to operators, keeps track of inventory positions in all stages of production and determines what is needed to add to existing inventories. What more could JIT ask? (p.125)

The answer to this question is twofold:

1. Much better internal quality control systems to enable JIT to become a reality.
2. A strategic vision with suppliers – A vision of shared destiny between them rather than the buyer versus supplier relationship that pervades in much of Western manufacturing.

Both of these factors are discussed in depth in the section on just-in-time. Before then, though, a comparison with a previous diagram is pertinent here; we saw earlier how the EOQ formula created buffer stock, long lead times and other non-added-value factors. Under MRP/JIT approaches, a buying pattern tends to emerge for the firm, as in Figure 6.12.

6.10 Overview of just-in-time

Just-in-time (JIT) is probably one of the most misunderstood management terms. To some firms in the West, the thought of reducing costs, via inventory reduction, is appealing. However, in order for JIT to be successful, firms need to move away from short-term cost-cutting ideas to a long-term view of continuous improvements. This sounds like the approach of TQM discussed in Chapter 5; TQM is an integral part and prerequisite for JIT to be successful in manufacturing plants. Just-in-time management is therefore not simply an inventory reduction exercise. In fact, simply reducing stocks will in the first instance create major problems. Shingo in Zipkin (1991) is quoted as saying:

> Stock reduction should not become an end in itself, however, since cutting stock blindly may cause delivery delays ... Rather the conditions that

Figure 6.12 Materials usage under MRP/JIT.

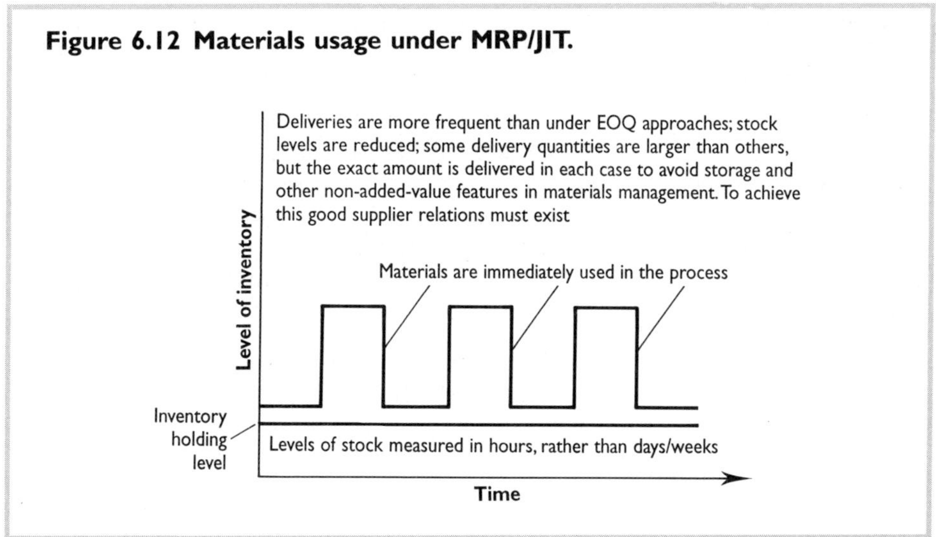

> produce or necessitate stock must be corrected so that stock can be reduced in a rational fashion. (p.44)

Just-in-time is a complete shift away from traditional Western manufacturing. Hutchins (1988) states how:

> JIT is part of a fundamentally different approach to management which when fully developed will help to create a totally new industrial culture. (p.11)

Harrison (1992) shows how this fundamental change works in Japan:

> In Japan, JIT has developed into a total management system from marketing through to delivery. It has diffused through suppliers and distributors. It has provided Japanese companies with a formidable competitive advantage over their Western rivals. (p.24)

The impact upon the UK and European car industry is described by Turnbull *et al.* (1992):

> Changes in the relationship between motor manufacturers and their suppliers are likely to have a particularly profound effect on the UK and the rest of Europe ... altered contractual relations represent the most thorough-going organizational change the industry has yet seen since Sloan's reforms in GM in the early 1920s. In the UK, these changes coincide with major investments by Toyota, Nissan and Honda, the three major Japanese motor manufacturers to whom the current transformation of the industry can be largely attributed. (p.48)

In many firms in the West, materials are bought in batches, then pushed onto workstations regardless of whether the particular station is ready for the components; under JIT, components will be requested only when the workstation is ready to receive them and operators pull the materials to a workstation only as required. Buffers or excess of any type, inventory, space and so on play little or no part in JIT; if buffers exist at all, it will be in far smaller quantities than in former approaches to materials management, based on just in case methodology; the rationale here is to have excess inventory just in case there are problems with quality, component failure, vendor problems, machine breakdowns and so on. The just in case approach has buffers which cover problems:

> The buffers used . . can be either physical (for example inventories, buffer stocks and multiple sourcing) or temporal (such as the allowance of generous lead times between processes). (Turnbull *et al.*, 1992)

Just-in-time is a very simple idea which has been extraordinarily difficult for many companies to implement.

Zipkin's (1991) statement is pertinent here:

> a storm of confusion swirls around JIT. Ask any two managers who have worked with it just what JIT is and does, and you are likely to hear wildly different answers. Some managers credit JIT with giving new life to their companies; others denounce it as a sham. (p.40)

The essence of JIT is that the exact number of components will arrive at a workstation exactly at the time required and in JIT, the supply of materials will exactly match the *demand* of materials both in terms of quantity and time.

Although just-in-time management approaches emanated from Japan, it is clear that the techniques have been transferred with varying degree of success, discussed later in the chapter, to the West.

JIT in Toyota developed out of market conditions in Japan which were not consistent with the mass-production systems of the West:

> Japanese demand for automobiles in the 1930s, when Toyota started making cars, was hardly enough to support the economies of mass production. Management at Toyota recognized they would have to find ways to achieve those economies with small volumes of production. (Toyota Company Information, *Toyota Production System*, p.4)

Thus JIT became an essential, integrated part of the Toyota system, a move away from mass-production, with all of the typical buffers, quality problems and so on, to a highly synchronized approach to materials management. The most prominent applications of JIT are in the automobile and high-tech industries. Although it would be too simplistic to make rigid distinctions between automobile and high-tech industries in terms of their use of JIT, what we can say is that some broad distinctions are evident, as shown in Table 6.5.

Table 6.5 Basic JIT applications for automobile and high-tech industries

Automobiles	*High-tech industries*
JIT is used both to reduce direct costs (amounts of materials used) and to reduce indirect costs – rework and scrap. The requirements of JIT have ensured that process quality has also been greatly enhanced. Other benefits include reduced floor space and labour costs. Much evidence points to greater morale through teamwork, involvement and skills enhancement	JIT is used to ensure that obsolescence of components does not occur. In the PC segment, JIT is seen as absolutely central to reducing costs in a market which is dominated by price wars. Greater productivity is evident (similar to automobiles) and morale is improved; JIT allows much speedier response to customer requirements

6.10.1 Internal factors in just-in-time

For many companies just-in-time will present a massive challenge to the way in which the firm will operate its business. These factors will include both internal and external factors; the internal factors will include an obsession with quality, getting it right first time, because JIT cannot tolerate rework and scrap, since only the exact amount of materials will be pulled to satisfy the component requirements for a particular workstation. The shift from push to pull manufacturing is one of the biggest problems. What JIT does is to force the company to perform to high levels within all of its operations, as Table 6.6 shows.

One of the main factors in just-in-time is in the elimination of waste, resulting in measurable benefits, not always centred on costs- areas such as flexibility, rapid response to customer requirements, innovation and delivery speed and reliability.

The categories of waste include overproduction, waiting, excessive transportation, the choice and management of the process itself, volumes of stock and defective goods.

As a firm becomes leaner in its approach, waste must be attacked and reduced:

> Lean producers ... set their sights explicitly on perfection: continually declining costs, zero defects, zero inventories, and endless product variety. (Womack *et al.*, 1990, pp.13–14)

The Japanese have insisted that in their plants there should not be idle time, waiting or buffers; the Japanese terms for these are:

Muda – Waste.
Mura – Inconsistency by machines or workers.
Muri – Excessive demands upon workers or machines.

Table 6.6 The effect of JIT on operations

	Traditional manufacturing	*JIT/enlightened approaches*
Quality	Acceptable levels of rejects and rework – an inevitability that failures will occur A specialist function	Right first time, every time Constant, on-going pursuit of process improvement Everybody responsible for ensuring quality
Inventory	An asset, part of the balance sheet and, therefore, part of the value of the firm; buffers necessary to keep production running	A liability, masking the operational performance by hiding a number of problems
Batch Sizes	An economic order can be determined to show the balance between set-up time and production runs	Batch sizes must be as small as possible, aiming toward a batch size of 1
Materials ordering	Determined by the economic order quantity	Supply exactly meets demand – no more no less, in terms of quantity; delivery is exactly when required, not before and not after
Bottlenecks	Inevitable; shows that machine utilization is high	No queues – production is at the rate which prevents delays and queues
Workforce	A cost which can be reduced by introducing more automation	A valuable asset, able to problem-solve, who should be supported by managers

When there is little buffer inventory, these three factors become prominent. Conversely, these three factors are disguised by holding amounts of inventory. Holding inventory at any stage can serve to cover poor operational performance and reducing inventory will in the first instance cause these problems to surface, which will then focus the firm in having to make improvements in production/ operations areas, as in Figure 6.13.

Interestingly, when these problems appear the strategic importance is revealed. Instead of a quick-fix, tactical approach, buying more stock to cover problems, the firm must take strategic measures: continuous improvements in-house to reduce stock levels, coupled with strategic alliances with suppliers to enhance delivery, innovations and reduce total costs.

Elimination of waste can have dramatic competitive improvements; for

Figure 6.13 Manufacturing problems hidden by inventory.

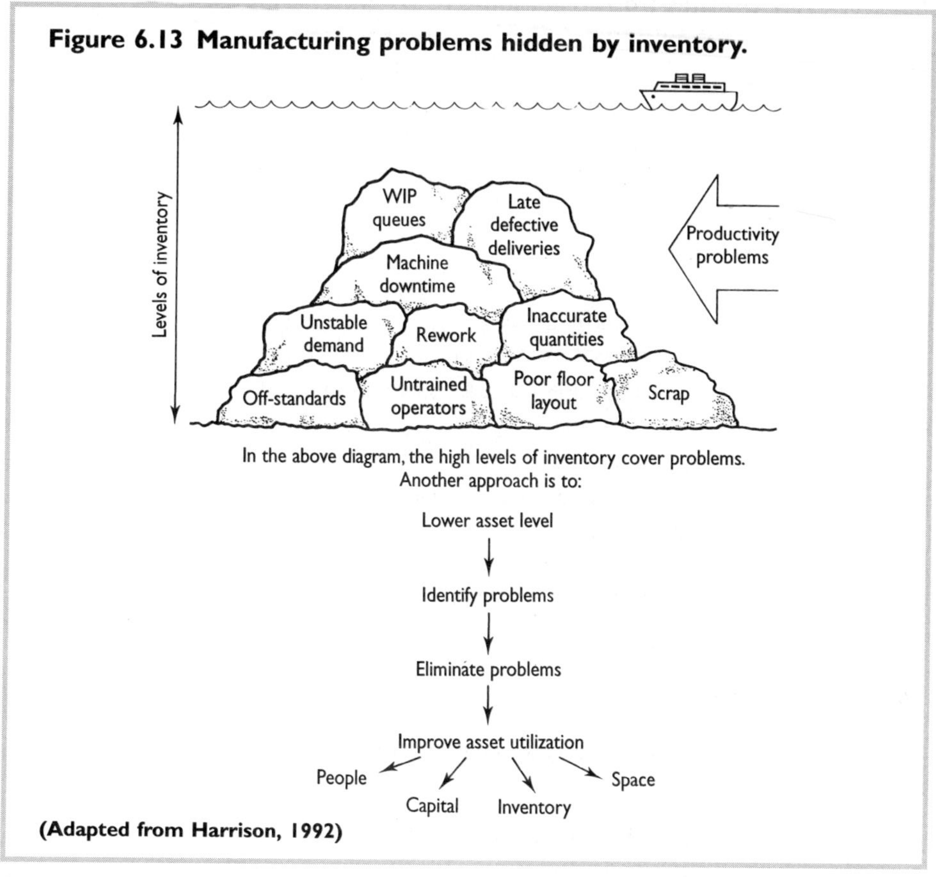

(Adapted from Harrison, 1992)

example, in the telecommunications industry the manufacturing plant of Tellabs, a $200 million products firm, reduced cycle time from two weeks to five days. This has been realized by a company-wide commitment dating back to 1987. Similarly AT&T's Omaha, Nebraska plant reduced inventory levels by 30 per cent and cut manufacturing cycle times by 50 per cent in a two-year period between 1989 and 1991.

6.10.2 Overview of external factors in just-in-time

As well as the internal requirements for JIT, there are also external factors; a major failure of some Western companies in terms of implementing just-in-time is their inability to forge long-term, strategic partnerships with their suppliers. This is vital and is discussed in the next section. However, linking both internal and

Table 6.7 Key changes from traditional to JIT purchasing

	Traditional manufacturing	*JIT*
Lot sizes	Large; just in case, covering several weeks production	Small; JIT for daily production
Delivery	Not linked to manufacture, often erratic	Synchronized for production
Number of suppliers	Several – used to play off one against another	Few, often single-sourced
Purchasing agreements	Short-term; threat of withdrawal from buyer	Long-term and 'certain' Often exclusive agreements
Nature of buyer/ supplier relationship	Stressful, little dialogue; win/ lose scenario	Mutual commitment; constant exchange of communication; win/win approach
Pricing	Tricks on both side; changing and volatile	Fixed by mutual agreement
Proximity	Physical proximity is irrelevant	Physical proximity is vital

Adapted from Lamming (1993)

external factors together several factors emerge in terms of requirements for just-in-time, as in Table 6.7.

The last factor presented a challenge to Toyota in its plants in both the United States and United Kingdom:

> Logistics were a special challenge in implementing the Toyota Production System in North America. That is because the distances between plants and suppliers on the North American continent tend to be far greater than we were accustomed to in Japan . . . the mixed load format we developed at our plants in Kentucky and Ontario enabled us to achieve short lead times . . . despite the vast distances. (Toyota Company information)

By contrast, Turnbull *et al.* (1992) noted how:

> In Japan . . . it has been noted that Toyota has had much more success with JIT than Nissan precisely because Toyota's suppliers are closer and more geographically concentrated than are those of Nissan. . . . Nissan UK, however, is moving towards a spatially concentrated production process (in the UK) . . . having acquired land far in excess of its own requirements which can then be rented to suppliers. (p.166)

The problem of logistics is eased to some degree at least by electronic data interchange between buyer and supplier. Information will be speedy and, just as important in JIT, accurate between the supplier and manufacturer.

6.11 Electronic data interchange (EDI)

Although there are benefits to both buyer and supplier, especially in terms of accuracy and speed of information, achieving the full benefits of electronic data interchange (EDI) is still a challenge for many manufacturers. A Department of Trade and Industry report in the United Kingdom found that:

> only 26% of commercial communications between suppliers and their customers were conducted using EDI, with 26% of firms reporting no EDI activity at all in this respect. (Lamming, 1994)

EDI is a part of manufacturing technology, an information system and a communications instrument, vital when there is a reliance on outside suppliers. EDI is increasingly being seen as a condition for doing business with large US and European corporations. The biggest push behind EDI is coming from big US manufacturers; in 1990 IBM told its suppliers that it would expect them to have EDI by the end of 1992. General Motors requires every firm to which it writes six cheques or more in a year to have EDI. EDI is not simply for accounting, though; it becomes an invaluable tool for advising suppliers and involving them early in the schedule. Using EDI, Compaq transmits manufacturing forecasts to suppliers for a nine-month period and then updates weekly on a rolling forecast basis.

Ford's shared database with one of its suppliers, Dana Corporation, allows Ford's just-in-time manufacturing process to run smoothly and to save time, inconvenience and money. Moreover, Ford has expanded EDI to support its payment process to suppliers. By paying for shipments upon receiving electronic confirmation that the supplier's goods had arrived, Ford eliminated a sizeable amount of its accounts-payable function, as well as invoices. Another example of advanced EDI techniques is Motorola's schedule-sharing arrangement, which allows the company's suppliers to examine Motorola's inventory databases.

6.12 The strategic development of buyer–supplier relationships

6.12.1 An overview of the car industry

There has been a marked increase in attention on buyer–supplier relationships since the 1970s. This has come from the purchasing/operations side (Carlisle and Parker, 1991; Lamming, 1993) as well as from a marketing point of view (Ford, 1984; O'Neal, 1989).

Part of the reason for stronger buyer–supplier relationships has been the increasing concentration of the firm on what it does best, rather than being responsible for all activities in the supply chain. In this way, a company can concentrate on its core strength or competence. What this means though is that greater dependence upon suppliers is then a requirement of the firm.

For Toyota, the closeness of buyer–suppler relationships is not confined to Japan:

> Scores of suppliers throughout Europe have contracted to supply parts and materials to our new passenger car plant in England and to the Toyota engine plant in Wales. We are working with many of those companies and with other prospective suppliers to develop and implement European versions of the Toyota Production System. (Toyota Company information)

In short, the importance of buyer–supplier relationships has increased because of the move away from vertical integration, which had been central to some industries including cars. For example, nearly all the parts for the Ford Model T were owned by Ford, including the steel mill. Abernathy (1978) reports how GM was innovative in subcontracting out supplies, in the 1930s, in contrast to Ford. However, as Lamming (1993) points out, 'Later GM was to mimic Ford's policy of total vertical integration' (p.9). In the car industry, there has been a vast move away from the need for the manufacturer to own all areas of the supply chain. In 1994, Toyota produced only 20 per cent of the value of its cars, whereas GM produced 70 per cent and Ford 50 per cent. Chrysler's comeback has much to do with the link with suppliers – the firm produces 30 per cent of the value of the cars it sells.

The buyer–supplier relationship is a major challenge for manufacturers in terms of their ability to think strategically. As Burt (1989) suggests:

> Managing suppliers is thus no longer a task for old-style purchasing managers. Strategic manufacturing is becoming a partnership between the big corporations that preside over design, assembly, and marketing of finished products, and fewer, smaller, smarter suppliers – often single-source suppliers. (p.127)

Although financial measurement is only one of a number of areas of competitive performance criteria, it is noticeable that the buyer–supplier partnering strategy helped Chrysler to achieve net earnings of $723 million in 1992, compared with a $795 million loss in 1991. As importantly, the strategy played a major role in the company's new line of cars in 1992, the Chrysler Concorde and the Dodge Intrepid, and was then used as the basis for the innovation of the Neon. By 1994, Chrysler's purchasing department had received over 5900 cost-saving ideas since it launched its supplier cost reduction effort (SCORE) supplier programme in 1989. Over 60 per cent of these ideas have been introduced and this has created more than $400 million in permanent, annualized savings for Chrysler (source: Author's interviews).

Important innovations from suppliers include plastic manifolds for the Neon (a saving of $4 per car) and a die change suggestion which saved Chrysler over $1 million (source: Author's interviews). An important insight is seen in the quote from Stallkamp in Lavin (1993a) when the vice-president of Chrysler stated:

When you start to see your suppliers as the experts, then they become valuable partners instead of a switchable commodity. (p.1)

6.12.2 Buyer–supplier relationships in the computer industry

The approach of buyer–supplier relationship is to create value-added partnerships in a particular industry. This is a major challenge for large, vertically integrated firms. For example, in the computer industry, IBM and DEC are among the most vertically integrated in the United States, capable of making almost every part of their products. They were consistently two of the worst performers between 1990 and 1994. The problem for both companies is the failure to reorganize away from vertical integration to prepare for the remarkable, and ongoing rate of change in the industry.

In the past, the computer industry had corporations such as IBM, NCR, DEC, NEC and Wang, which competed against each other as huge, vertically integrated enterprises. Each produced its own chips and system software, based essentially on its own particular system. Also, each company had its own salespeople to sell its particular computer systems largely to corporate accounts rather than educational and home-user segments. However, the PC changed the whole industry and systems were now built upon a standard computer platform. The systems software for these computers is essentially common throughout the whole industry. The manufacturer, therefore, has to form alliances with two powerful groups within the supply chain – suppliers and software.

About 85 per cent of PCs in the United States use Intel processors and Microsoft's operating system. Motorola's chips, used in Apple's machines, account for the next 10–12 per cent, and various other minute architectures divide up the rest. This means that more than 400 manufacturers link to the Intel-based PC market segment. These chips can be common to a wide range of manufactured computers; NCR uses Intel chips in all of its products, from palmtops to mainframes. NCR, like many other manufacturers are largely dependent upon the innovation of these suppliers.

The shift from important manufacturer (IBM) to important supplier (Intel and Microsoft) has caused major problems for IBM. In early 1994, IBM signed a deal with another chip supplier Cyrix to reduce Intel's importance; IBM has also linked with Motorola and Apple to form an alliance aimed at attacking Intel. IBM's relationship with Intel is to put it mildly tangled, a combination of supplier, competitor and partner. IBM can make processors using Intel's design, but cannot sell them unless they are part of other products.

In contrast, Hewlett Packard has become even closer in its links with Intel and the two clearly have a shared vision of the future:

The Intel–HP partnership links the world's largest semi-conductor manufacturer and dominant supplier of microprocessor chips with the second largest US computer company, creating a new power axis in the computer industry. (*Financial Times*, 13 June 1993)

This is especially good for Intel, whose former main customer IBM seeks to use more of the Power PC chips for its future products. The alliance means that Intel can expand further into Hewlett Packard's workstations, network services and even mainframes.

Meanwhile, Compaq, like IBM, has tried to move away from Intel as the sole source of supply of chips; another processor supplier, Advanced Micro Systems, has cut into the relationship between Intel and Compaq by producing chips for Compaq.

While many high-tech firms seek alliances with suppliers, not all companies are outsourcing as much as possible; where a firm believes its key competence is in-house, it keeps that competence. Motorola has formed a number of horizontal alliances (for example with Apple), but builds its own cellular phones. However, as the telecommunications and computing industries increasingly merge, it may well force Motorola to depend more on suppliers, rather than go it alone.

A number of companies have deliberately kept away from dependence on suppliers and in the United States, Sun Microsystems has even returned to more in-house processes: Sun, a leading maker of workstations, relied so heavily on outside suppliers and distributors that its own employees were not involved in the manufacturing process at all. However, Sun now plans to make nearly 40 per cent of its circuit boards, up from zero in 1990.

6.13 The development from adversarial to partnership relationships

Porter (1980) pitched the buyer–supplier relationship largely in adversarial terms: the buyer, for example, should pursue the 'threat of backward integration' and 'use of tapered integration' (p.125), according to Porter. In some industries, such strategies may well be the norm or desirable, but in many industries, such aggressive strategies are outmoded and counterproductive. Porter (1990) argues that in Japan's *Keiretsu* (clustering of companies), 'Hard bargaining also occurs between buyers and suppliers, a function of the large number of rivals in most industries and the competitive pressure they face' (p.154). This is countered by practically everybody who has commented on buyer–supplier relationships in the car industry, based on the 'Japanese model'.

Turnbull *et al.* (1993) state that:

> In Japan, the actual contract between motor manufacturer and supplier is based on co-operation, a full exchange of information, a commitment to improve quality, and a recognition . . . that prices can (and will) be reduced each year...bargaining is not simply focused on price per se but on how to reach the target price while maintaining a reasonable level of profit for the supplier. (p.51)

That is not to say that the relationship is based on complacency and ease, as a result of the partnership deal having been made. Rather, demands are made on the supplier, but these are made achievable as a result of the Japanese buyer helping the supplier to improve its business in terms of lower cost and faster delivery.

McMillan (1990) summarizes how:

> 'Japanese industry is characterized by close and extensive links between manufacturers and parts suppliers. According to . . . (MITI) Japanese manufacturing industry owes its competitive advantage and strength to its subcontracting structure. (p.39)

Much has been written on buyer–supplier relationships, sometimes pertaining to a particular industry (Lamming, 1993) or providing general insights into developments (Carlisle and Parker, 1991). It is clear that major developments have taken place, particularly in automobiles and high-tech industries. In particular, the buyer–supplier relationship, which has traditionally been adversarial, has now in many cases moved to a partnership agreement. The partnership approach is summarized by Schonberger and Knod (1991):

> In the partnership approach, the idea is not to change suppliers. The rule is: stay with one, in order that it may stay on the learning curve, get to know the customer's real requirements, and perhaps participate with the customer on product and process improvements. (p2.91)

The benefits of buyer–supplier collaboration is stated by Carlisle and Parker (1991):

> Co-operation between industrial users and sellers is a far more powerful strategy for making them both more profitable in the long term than any adversarial approach yet devised. (p.5)

However, in order for buyer–supplier relationships to be strong there has to be considerable trust between both parties. Sako (1992) suggests that three types of trust need to be in place:

1. *Contractual trust* – Which is the adherence to formal, legal promises.
2. *Competence trust* – That either side is capable to provide what has been promised.
3. *Goodwill trust* – Which borders on ethics; trusting that appropriate behaviour will ensue.

6.13.1 Developments in the car industry

A number of close, buyer–supplier relationships exist in the car industry. For example, when Rover began its TQM programme, it pledged to work closely with suppliers; it has over 700 suppliers and the strategy was to work with them to enable them to meet Rover's RG2000 specifications, which includes BS 5750. The relationship between Rover and its suppliers is 'open book' on costs and profits. Rover, for their part, pledge to help suppliers to be profitable and to grow with

Rover over the long term. However, development of the buyer–supplier relationship for Rover was a strategic partnership and the learning process was emerging over a decade, as shown in Figure 6.14.

Similarly, Ford awards its key suppliers with a 'Q1' quality rating, which signifies that Ford no longer has to inspect parts from these suppliers. General Motors has a 'Mark of Excellence' award for their suppliers and Nissan has its own 'Quality Achievement Award'. Chrysler has abandoned competitive bidding and no longer provides detailed, written specifications for many parts. Instead, it depends on suppliers to design and build components and to keep their own costs down as a means of improving supplier profitability.

Figure 6.14 Developments of buyer–supplier relationships within Rover UK.

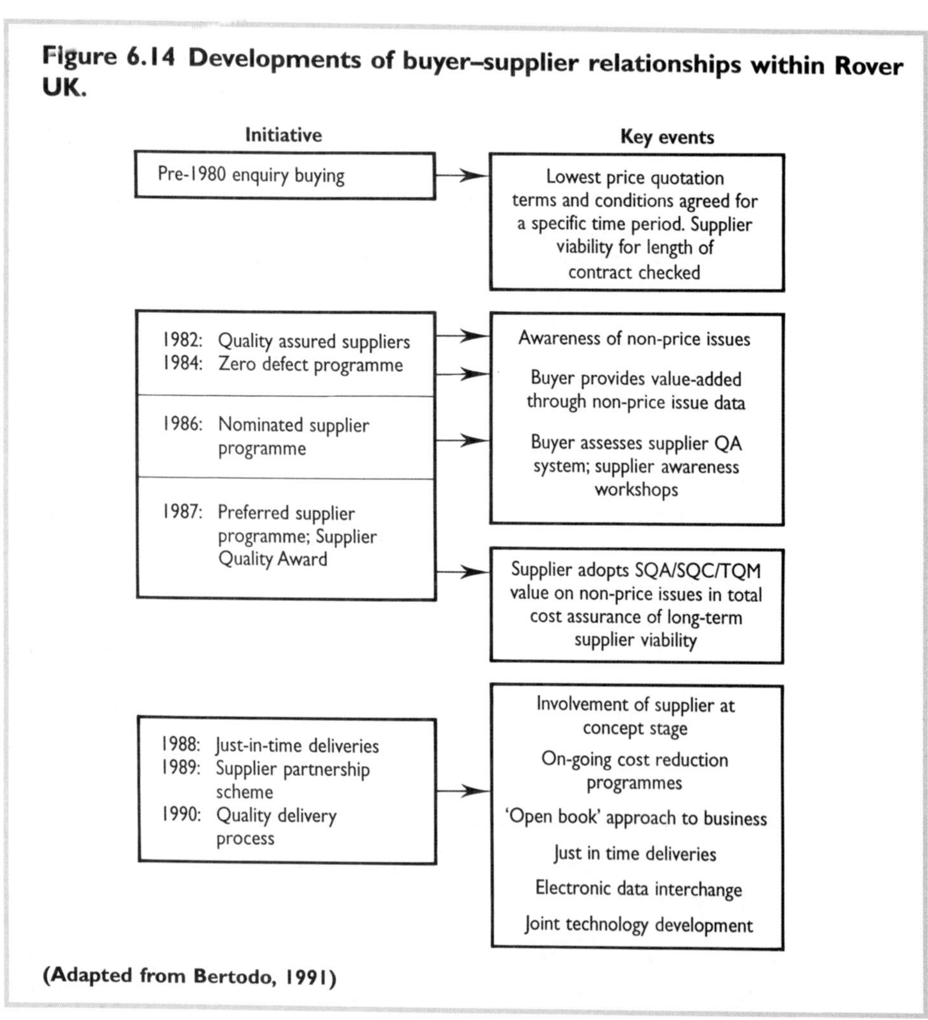

(Adapted from Bertodo, 1991)

Lamming (1993) offers a model which shows developments in the car industry. The Japanese model is seen as an advance upon traditional Western approaches still exemplified by GM. Lamming argues, that there has been development over a period of time, which can be traced as follows: 'traditional' (pre-1975), 'stress' (1972–85), 'resolved' (1982 onwards) and 'Japanese' (1990 onwards). An adaption of this model is shown in Figure 6.15.

This model provides a useful framework in terms of historical developments of the buyer–supplier relationship in the car industry. It is too simplistic though to say that *all* Japanese car manufacturers have progressed with no possibility of returning to traditional buyer versus supplier positions; for example in 1993, Mazda asked its suppliers to reduce their costs by 10 per cent, a similar figure to the GM request in 1992.

It must also be said that this development toward progress from 'stress' to 'Japanese' or 'lean' is neither inevitable, as in some sort of required evolution that all industries will inevitably go through, nor it must be noted is this practice necessarily sought after by some enterprises. General Motors' relationship with its suppliers was considerably worsened in 1992 when, essentially through Lopez (Director of Purchasing), who then left for Volkswagen, GM took up renewed aggression toward their suppliers, insisting that contracts were void and that bidding would take place; all suppliers would have to bid against each other and price would be the determining factor, typically 10 per cent was required as a 'rule of thumb' reduction. Lopez introduced the 'Purchased Input Concept Optimization with Suppliers' programme, a feature of which was that GM staff would scrutinize suppliers, essentially to reduce the suppliers' costs. Lopez's successor,

Figure 6.15 Developments in buyer–supplier relationships.

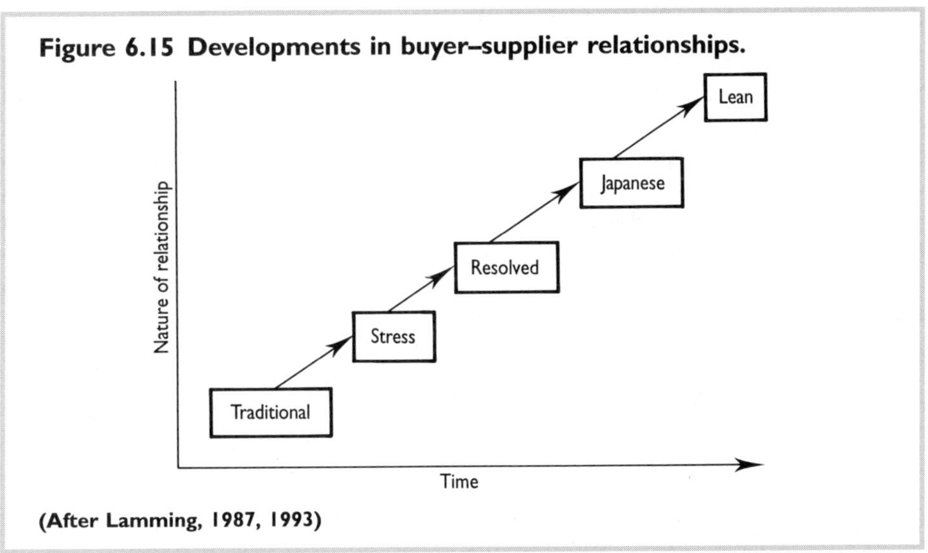

(After Lamming, 1987, 1993)

Wagoner, pointed to the $4 billion in savings gained from suppliers between 1990 and 1993 and was quoted as saying

> We are in favor of partnerships with suppliers, but with very, very high expectations. (*Wall Street Journal*, 9 August 1993, Section B, p.2)

However, while the *Wall Street Journal* raved how 'GM Has Its Most Profitable Quarter' (29 July 1994, p.D2), GM's share of the US market shrunk even further to 33.1 per cent. Clearly, much damage has been done in the relationship between GM and its suppliers who see GM as being only concerned with gaining lowest prices. The non-cost competitive factors could threaten GM; a steel supplier withheld sharing with GM a stamping technique, which would have reduced scrap by 75 per cent, because the supplier feared GM would share the information with a competitive supplier, offering a lower price. The striking quote from the supplier was

> Why should we risk telling them our good ideas . . . At GM there is no certainty. (*Wall Street Journal*, 29 July 1994, p.D2)

Business Week noted how:

> GM's relations with its suppliers remain the worst in Detroit . . . An electronics supplier tells of a $30 part he developed jointly with GM. He says that after he slashed the price to $15, the GM purchasing agent demanded more cuts, citing a $9 bid from a Chinese company that had never made the part in question . . . One parts maker that does $600 million in business with car makers says it is focusing its efforts on selling to GM's rivals. (8 August 1994, p.26)

The same report mentions how GM's lowest bid strategy toward supplies meant that one successful supplier was unable to provide the acceptable quality of ashtrays; this resulted in the delay of the Chevrolet Caprice in 1994. Honda Motors in the United States, unlike GM, does not seek to reduce costs as the focus of their involvement in suppliers' plants. Instead, Honda works with suppliers on process improvements which in turn will reduce costs as well as a number of other key, competitive factors. Palmeri (1992) observes how Honda worked with a supplier of valves, hoses, seals, filters and pumps: a three-month involvement from Honda resulted in a cylinder process being reduced from 19 days to 5 minutes and overall savings amounted to $1.6 million a year.

The 1994 DTI report summarized that:

> communications between vehicle manufacturers and their direct suppliers appears to be generally improved but still not at a level to support such imperatives as effective implementation of electronic data interchange or collaboration on product and process development. (Lamming, 1994, p.5)

CASE A Toyota Supplier

The following is representative of the type of situation that a supplier to Toyota might face. The author conducted a number of interviews with supplier plants and one supplier narrated how Toyota had demanded reductions in costs. The supplier attempted to do so, but failed to see how cost reductions could be achieved without damaging its own business position. When the supplier reported this failure to Toyota, the Japanese response was to send their own engineers to the supplier plant. The plant director stated:

> It was the most incredible thing I've experienced – I would be asked, why I did something in a particular way. I would then explain it and the Toyota engineer would ask: Why? Everything we said was met with one of the engineers asking, why. It drove me crazy to begin with – a series of why, why, why all the time. But when we realized that they were here for our benefit as well as theirs, we were willing to change the way we did things. In under three months we had reduced costs by 20 per cent without hurting our business. They (Toyota) benefit but so do we. Now we always ask the question, Why? before we do anything new in this plant. We also ask it of everything we do anyway, new or not. What a difference. (source: Author's interviews)

6.13.2 Developments in the computing/telecommunications industries

Although IBM in the United States is struggling to reorganize itself in terms of buyer–supplier relationships, IBM's UK plant in Greenock has achieved noticeable successes, due in some degree to the close proximity and involvement of their suppliers. Between September 1992 and October 1993, output increased by 50 per cent; inventory of finished goods declined by 90 per cent, sales increased 42 per cent and, in contrast to other IBM plants, the plant is able to build to order, using just-in-time approaches.

Another example of successful, strategic partnerships in the United Kingdom is evident at ICL; when they had problems with their software supplier, ICL worked with the supplier, rather than seeking an alternative source. Sasseen (1992) reports how this approach enabled ICL to make savings of £160 million, and reduce development time and quality problems between 1988 and 1992.

Although buyer–supplier relationships should ideally be beneficial to both parties, they do not always do so in equal measure or in the same way for both parties. The Hewlett Packard/Canon relationship was not without its competitive caution. Canon (the supplier) was also selling its own printers. When the buyer–supplier relationship began, Hewlett-Packard protected itself by blocking Canon's rights to the 'PCL' software that controls the output of type and graphics and distinguishes Hewlett Packard's printers. In short, the software was the key factor and this key factor was denied to Canon. As a result, although Canon benefited in terms of sales volume of the laser engine for Hewlett Packard's printer, Canon has remained secondary to Hewlett Packard in terms of sales of laser printers. Hewlett

Packard has also managed to produce less expensive inkjet printers which are not dependent on suppliers' involvement.

However, it would be wrong to suggest that Hewlett Packard's relationships with suppliers are strained; its global strategy is to satisfy local supply in each country of manufacture by choosing selected suppliers and working closely with these suppliers (source: Author's interviews). Hewlett Packard is divided into three business groupings and each division operates in an autonomous manner, although commitment to local suppliers is a common feature throughout the corporation.

A cautious approach in the relationship to suppliers is common to many manufacturers in the early stages of the relationship. Although AT&T attempts to forge long-term relationships with suppliers, it is clear that in the early stages of the relationship with their suppliers, a number of checks are made via their 'Vendor Quality Assessment, Vendor Quality Information and Vendor Quality Improvement' processes. AT&T's fourfold approach tends to follow this sequence:

1. Identifying potential suppliers.
2. Assessing capabilities of potential suppliers.
3. Determining approved suppliers.
4. Identifying those suppliers with preferred status. (source: Author's interviews)

Although AT&T do not seek to own their suppliers and are intent on forming partnerships, the early stages of the relationship is like many other firms distant and cautious. However, once suppliers are awarded contracts by AT&T, these are seen as long-term relationships, mutually beneficial to the supplier and AT&T.

There are examples of the buyer versus supplier in the telecommunications industry, though; Selz (1993) reports how one of Unisys' suppliers depended for three-quarters of its $85 million sales turnover on its relationship with Unisys. Unisys sought another competitive supplier, cancelled the former supplier's orders, which caused the supplier to become bankrupt.

6.14 The reduction and consolidation in the number of suppliers

A natural consequence of closer buyer–relationships is that the number of suppliers for each buyer is reduced. Examples of this development are shown in Table 6.8.

In 1992 AT&T began the 'together everyone accomplishes much' (TEAM) approach, which worked with key suppliers but in the process reduced the number of suppliers from 1471 in 1989 to 240 in 1992. This is a dramatic consolidation of the number of suppliers used by AT&T, but is a continuing trend in the car, computing and telecommunications industries, a move to work much

Table 6.8 Reductions in supplier figures in selected firms

Firm	*Current (1994)*	*Before supplier consolidation*	*% change*
Motorola	3,000	10,000	–70
DEC	3,000	9,000	–67
Ford USA	1,000	1,800	–44
GM USA	5,500	10,000	–45
AT&T	240	1,471	–84

source: Author's interviews 1993; 1994

more closely with selected suppliers who are smarter, more flexible and grow with the manufacturer. A supplier may grow in the relationship with the buyer to such a size that a mini-plant may be dedicated to one customer. That does not mean that the supplier cannot do business with other customers and have a number of satellite plants within the overall plant. This is endorsed by Kenney and Florida (1993):

> However, Japanese suppliers and contractors are not exclusively tied to a single customer. Many supply more than one customer. This provides the supplier greater security and stability . . . Nippondenso, an electrical company . . . is still 23 percent owned by Toyota, but now does 40 percent of its business with other firms, and it supplies parts to some of Toyota's competitors such as Honda, Ford, and General Motors. (p.45)

This is supported by McMillan (1990):

> In Japanese manufacturing industry as a whole, only 17% of subcontracting firms deal with a single buyer, 20% have two customers, 26% have three to five customers . . . not surprisingly, the small firms are aware of the bargaining power they gain from having alternatives. (p.40)

6.15 Suppliers and innovation

6.15.1 Supplier innovations in the computing industry

That suppliers 'innovate' in the computing industry is obvious from Intel and Microsoft, whose core objective is continuous innovation.The massive thrust of innovation in the computer industry comes from the suppliers themselves, rather than the manufacturers. The sheer size of Intel, together with its power as a supplier, is remarkable; in 1993, net earnings of $2.3 billion were made on sales of $8.8 billion; these earnings have enabled Intel to spend vast amounts on R&D and other investment:

> (Intel) is spending . . . $1.1 billion this year (1994) on R&D, $2.4 billion on capital investment . . . (and) $750 million for a newly opened chip

> plant in Ireland and is paying $3 billion for two more in New Mexico and Arizona. (*Fortune*, 16 May 1994, p.64)

The nature of the close buyer–supplier relationship is one of shared destiny, where buyer versus supplier is not an issue. Instead, the relationship will develop and be seen as a competitive bond against, where necessary, other buyer–supplier relationships. Bertodo (1991) narrates how this has developed in the European electronics industry:

> The expertise of co-producers (suppliers) lies in the evolution and manufacture of components of high quality and reliability over short time cycles. Low cost and dependable deliveries have characterized their operations ... For these suppliers security of demand has been enhanced by early involvement in the OEM design cycle for new products and hence the opportunity to develop and manufacture components of more advanced design and to a more competitive standard ahead of the competition. (p.41)

Successful alliances with innovative suppliers is hard for other players to emulate. However, because of the power of the supplier in the PC segment this means that PC manufacturers are essentially locked in to the supplier. Intel's chips have become the key ingredient for IBM clone manufacturers, all of whom are locked into this supplier relationship. As we saw earlier, IBM is seeking to circumvent Intel's stranglehold in two ways:

1. Its alliance with Motorola and Apple.
2. Its link with Cyrix, from whom IBM wants to purchase an ever larger number of chips.

What seems to emerge from these alliances is that IBM's strategy appears to be one of reasserting its own power within the industry *against* Intel. Other innovative manufacturers seem less concerned about struggles against suppliers, preferring instead to see suppliers as partners in innovation. There is much evidence that suppliers are vital for innovation in high-tech products. For example, Hewlett Packard involved key suppliers in the development of the Omnibook 400 subnotebook computer. Hewlett Packard has a TQRDCEB evaluation of suppliers, rating them on 'technology, quality, responsiveness, delivery, cost, environment and business condition'. Clearly, Hewlett Packard sees cost as only one factor amongst many, rather than as the sole factor which still pervades in many other firms' supplier selection.

We saw earlier how Hewlett Packard used its relationship with Canon as a means of focusing on a core competence area as far as the printer was concerned: the software linking the printer to the computer. This meant that Canon provided a major innovative component that Hewlett Packard did not wish to design/innovate or even manufacture itself; in forming this partnership, innovation occurred which allowed Hewlett Packard to dominate the global laser-printer market.

6.15.2 *Supplier innovations in the telecommunications industry*

The power of suppliers in the telecommunications industry is shown by AT&T, whose role includes major supplier of equipment to other Baby Bells since the break up of AT&T's monopoly in the early 1980s. AT&T's share of the digital switch market was over 50 per cent in 1994. This was helped by the fact that AT&T makes switching gear as well as transmission equipment, meaning that AT&T can supply entire networks for customers. This has major potential possibilities for AT&T in terms of being a major supplier to the emerging information highway, where AT&T can offer switches, video servers, network software and TV cable hardware.

Buyer–supplier relationships aimed at innovation are common in the telecommunications industry. In 1994, British Telecom (BT) chose five key suppliers – Apple, Alcatel, Oracle, nCube and Northern Telecom – in order to develop the concept of video on demand, an interactive medium where, amongst other offerings, customers can choose videos from a central library via cable to their homes. This is a necessary alliance for BT who know that speed of innovation, together with the likelihood of success, will increase as a result. The alliance is viewed by all parties as a mutually beneficial arrangement for all partners. The alliance also endorses the idea of one cluster forming as a means of competing against and sometimes preventing the formation of other alliances in the industry.

6.15.3 *Supplier innovations in the car industry*

As far as the car industry is concerned, Lamming (1993) speaks of one of the roles of the first-tier supplier in lean supply being investment in and development of R&D leading to innovation. This was not the case under mass-production:

> the mature mass-production supply system is broadly unsatisfactory to everyone concerned. The suppliers are brought in late to the design process and can do little to improve the design, which may be hard and expensive to manufacture. (Womack *et al.*, 1990, p.145)

This is not the practice of Japanese firms, who involve suppliers early in the design process. This is true not only of suppliers in their own country, but also applies in transplant supplier bases. Kenney and Florida (1993) discuss Japanese transplant suppliers investing between $1 and $28 million in R&D. Transplant companies like Bridgestone, Sumitomo, Yokohama and Toyo will undertake such R&D for manufacturers.

Chrysler used 200 suppliers in developing the Dodge Intrepid, Eagle Vision and Chrysler Concorde. The Viper went from conception to market in three years, using seventy-five key suppliers. Chrysler and its suppliers seem to form part of an extended enterprise, depending upon each other. Chrysler engineers now work closely with suppliers during the design stage, with purchasers, engineers, and quality engineers working in commodity teams and managing suppliers. This cross-functional approach has resulted in suppliers finding ways to save the automaker money. Although Chrysler has cut the number of different suppliers it uses, those that remain can expect more business, provided they meet Chrysler's requirements for quality and delivery and can satisfy Chrysler's technology needs.

This provides evidence that the Japanese model is in fact able to be replicated in Western firms. Sometimes this comes from crisis: Chrysler has had to totally change and improve its performance since it nearly went out of business in the early 1980s.

6.16 The transplant suppliers

The Japanese manufacturing transplants in both the United States and United Kingdom are designed to be stand-alone, rather than dependent upon their Japanese base. In addition, the parts supplied to the manufacturers are often from suppliers which are themselves transplants:

> Ohio is home to 65 transplant parts companies, Michigan has 44, Kentucky has 42, Indiana has 41, Illinois has 28, and Tennessee has 30. (Kenney and Florida, 1993, p.128)

The position of transplant manufacturers in relation to suppliers has been made complicated by the political pressure placed upon the Japanese transplants, especially in the United States, where the need to buy American parts has been an important issue. However, not all Japanese transplant firms wish to use US suppliers. Some firms still import from Japan, but continue to use a hybrid JIT system. At Mitsubishi's Diamond-Star assembly plant in Normal, Illinois, all material is delivered to the plant by the daily arrival of 250 trucks, some every 20 minutes. A monthly production plan is set 60 days in advance, establishing the times when parts and supplies are to arrive in Normal from Mitsubishi in Japan.

Other Japanese firms depend on using local US suppliers and of course US personnel in the manufacturing transplants. The following shows some of the complexities involved:

1. Seventy-five per cent of the parts in the Toyota Camry built in Kentucky are from the United States, up from 60 per cent when Toyota started building the car there in 1988.
2. The Honda Accord built in Marysville, Ohio, had 75 per cent domestic content, which then increased to over 80 per cent in later models.
3. Honda is considering building one of its Acura models in the United States for the first time.
4. Japanese companies accounted for about 20 per cent of its total automotive parts sales in 1993, up from 5 per cent in 1988.

5. General Motors' component sales to Japanese car companies amounted to $600 million in 1993, up from $400 million in 1992 and nil parts in 1986.
6. GM's foundry in Defiance, Ohio, supplies 10,000 three-litre engine blocks a month to Nissan Motor Co.
7. Chrysler signed a $1.2 billion contract to supply engines and transmissions for Mitsubishi Motors Corporation's assembly plant in Normal, Illinois.
8. In 1993, Toyota spent $3.3 billion on US parts for its US operations, but only $1.1 billion on US parts for its Japanese operations.

From the Japanese point of view, this has eased potential relationship problems with the United States. For the United States there are both advantages and disadvantages: the Japanese manufacturing plants' involvement with US suppliers means that these suppliers have the opportunity to learn world-class approaches to manufacturing from the Japanese, but transplants add nothing in terms of helping US trade problems; most of the parts that Japanese car makers buy stay in the United States and do not affect the trade deficit.

The Japanese transplants in Europe may well follow the same pattern as those in the United States. As Turnbull *et al.* (1993) suggest:

> it is already clear that the Japanese assemblers are prepared to source pan-European in order to achieve their required supply standards. The 1990s will therefore present component suppliers with a golden opportunity for growth but at the same time subject them to the most competitive environment they have ever faced ... The new model of supplier relations, based on collaborative partnerships ... represents a sharp break from traditional practice in the UK. (p.49)

6.17 The transfer of Japanese practices to Japanese transplants in the West

One of the major questions concerning just-in-time and strategic approaches to materials management is the transferability to Western plants. Schonberger (1986), Kenney and Florida (1993) and Womack *et al.* (1990) suggest that this transfer is possible. Krafcik and MacDuffie (1989) suggest that Japanese transplants have been recreated in the United States, particularly with just-in-time and they argue if US personnel are involved in the running of Japanese transplants, then the transfer to the West is evident.

There is evidence that Honda successfully uses JIT in their US plants and, as we saw in Chapter 5 on quality, Honda believes that the highest quality cars are now made in the United States, not Japan. For Honda's two Ohio plants, Marysville and East Liberty, everything but sequential parts is delivered to a consolidation area where the shipments are broken down and delivered to the plants in the order in which they will be used on the line. In-sequence parts are shipped directly to the plant from suppliers. Mazda's Flat Rock, Michigan, plant uses a similar system, scheduling deliveries both directly to the plant and through a sequencing plant. Parts are delivered from the sequencing centre to the plant every 30 minutes.

It would seem, therefore, that some Japanese firms have fully succeeded in transferring their approaches to materials management to the United States.

In Nissan's UK plant, reduced levels of inventory have been achieved and are now equal to that of the Japanese plants:

Year	Inventory days
1990	3
1991	2
1992	1.66
1993	0.97
1994	0.9

(adapted from Martin, 1994, p.304)

Martin (1994) points to others' evaluation of Nissan in the United Kingdom, how 'The cars, made in England by Englishmen under British management, using parts supplied mostly by European manufacturers are at least equal in quality to those made by Nissan in Japan' and 'Nissan's British factory is regarded by the company as one of the best it has' (p.314).

Since the plant opened in 1986, Nissan's local car content has risen to 80–85 per cent. Nissan has dispensed with quality checks on suppliers; there are only 400 defects in every million and work-in-progress is minimal.

There is evidence therefore that the transplants have been successful using local human resources and suppliers. Although the industrial make up between Japan and the United States and United Kingdom is entirely different, this has not prevented successful plants being created in both the United Kingdom and United States.

6.17.1 The transfer of Japanese practices to Western firms

The question, though, is, will Western manufacturers be able to emulate Japanese practices, especially in JIT? This depends entirely on each case. Although Womack *et al.* (1990) were critical of General Motors, there is evidence that particular divisions in GM have adopted Japanese practices: the Buick plant in Flint, Michigan has reduced in-plant inventories, so that inventory levels range from under 1 hour to 16 hours maximum. Suppliers successfully deliver parts around a 20 minute delivery window and Buick uses 30 per cent of the floor space used by other car plants. Buick's supplier relationships are good, in contrast to other GM divisions.

In the computer industry there are examples of success in JIT in Hewlett Packard, Dell and Compaq. Each of these have in-house process and product quality as the core of their operations and rightly see this as the precursor to JIT.

In addition, these particular enterprises clearly see strategic partnerships as central to their business success.

Conclusions

As we saw earlier, just-in-time is far from being a simple cost-reduction exercise; it is a massive challenge to many Western manufacturing firms in terms of how these firms will conduct business both internally through its production/operations capability and externally in the firm's relationship with suppliers. Partnerships, especially in the supply chain, are strategic issues for world-class firms. For some manufacturing firms, there is a reluctance to form strategic buyer–supplier relationships. Relationships, if they exist at all, are cautious and sometimes volatile, where the (still) large manufacturing giants reluctantly join forces with suppliers, whilst always looking either to hurt the supplier, in terms of imposing cost reductions, or by always being in search for alternative suppliers. With this approach, the manufacturing giants seem more concerned with asserting power over suppliers, rather than developing mutually beneficial relationships. This short-sightedness by power-motivated manufacturers may yet serve as the biggest single cause of their decline. They will pay by having large inventories and, because of their suspicion of sharing developments with suppliers, will be slow to innovate. It is clear from the turnaround of fortunes at Chrysler that there are massive benefits to be gained in forming technological partnerships with suppliers to ensure speedy and successful innovation. A reluctance to form such strategic partnerships will cause delays in innovation and ultimately decline in business performance for some of the large, slow-to-learn giant manufacturing enterprises.

Summary

- **The management of materials is one of the major contrasts between the Japanese and Western approaches to manufacturing, although there is evidence that many Western firms are improving in the area of inventory management.**
- **Materials must be seen as a company liability, rather than as an asset, in that huge costs will often be associated with purchase of inventories in manufacturing firms. This means that cash flow and capital can be threatened.**
- **Materials can, if managed badly, serve as a means of covering problems, both in terms of production/operations and poor supplier performance.**
- **Quick-fix purchasing formulas (such as EOQ) do not provide any strategic advantage for the firm.**
- **The firm must concentrate on improving production/operations performance in order to avoid a just in case approach. In this way,**

materials costs will decrease and, just as important, the firm's capabilities in terms of delivery reliability, rapid response and flexibility will be greatly enhanced.

- **Material requirement planning (MRP) and manufacturing resource planning (MRPII) can be powerful means of controlling materials. However, MRP should not be used to 'push' materials through the production system; rather, MRP is a management planning system where all components can be planned in advance for a particular time period.**
- **Just-in-time is part of world-class strategic manufacturing. However, JIT is not simply about inventory reduction; it is a complete shift from traditional push approaches based around production of large batches (made to stock). Instead a pull system based upon make to order for customers becomes the focus of production.**
- **A vital feature of just-in-time is the buyer–supplier relationship. The traditional buyer versus supplier approach makes little sense; instead, the manufacturing firm must concentrate on focusing on key suppliers and forming strategic partnerships with them.**
- **Partnerships with suppliers will have benefits in addition to reduced costs; close supplier relationships will enhance innovation and improve new product design and implementation.**

CASE Sun Microsystems

Sun was founded in 1982 and is the world's leading manufacturer of computer workstations. In 1994 Sun had over one-third of the market share for workstations. Initially, Sun employed the industry standard, UNIX operating system, and designed systems to operate with other vendors' products. It also licensed its SPARC (RISC processor) to other manufacturers. Sun was able to offer a low-cost system alternative to the major computer manufacturers. One major development was in modifying its own Solaris operating system allowing it to run on both Intel and Power PC chips.

Sun concentrates on what it does best, namely, designing semiconductors, developing software and selling workstations. It has formed manufacturing partnerships with Solectron and Texas Instruments. The relationship with suppliers is critical; customer-specific configurations have to be pulled through the manufacturing system and speed of response to customers is vital. This delivery capability, coupled with the low-cost strategy, has been successful for Sun, as illustrated in Figure 6.16.

However, rising sales and profits are not the only criteria. Sun has been able to rapidly introduce new products. In 1993, it completely renewed its system, software and service product lines in this intensely competitive environment, at the same time retaining an exceptionally strong financial position. Fiscal 1993 revenues grew 20 per cent from the previous year to a record $4.3 billion.

Sun operates in an industry marked by rapidly changing technology and increasing

Figure 6.16 Sun Microsystems sales and profits: 1989–93.

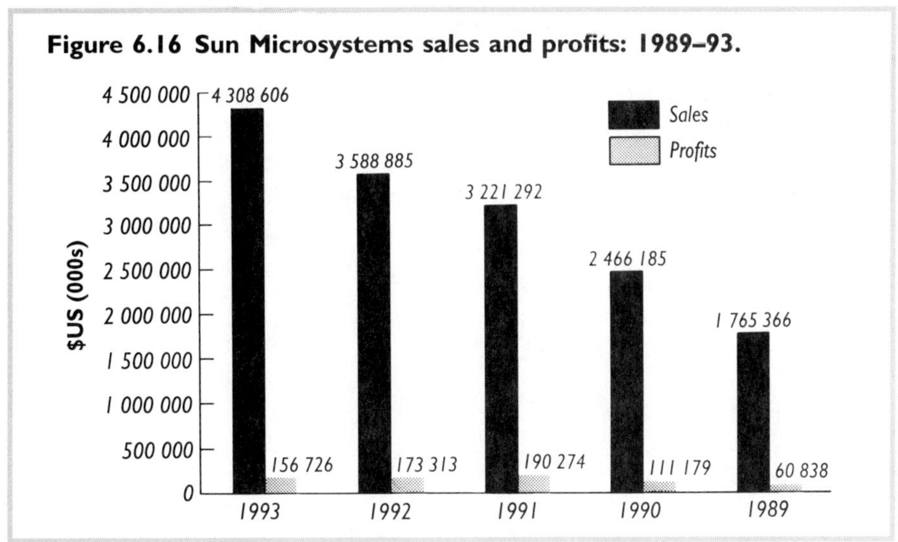

competition, consolidation and globalization. Competition from DEC, IBM and Hewlett Packard has remained strong. Sun's future will depend to a considerable extent on its ability to rapidly and continuously develop, introduce and deliver at volume new products that offer customers enhanced performance at competitive prices. As the 1994 Company Report noted:

> The development of new high-performance computer products is a complex and uncertain process requiring high levels of innovation from both the Company's designers and those of its suppliers, as well as accurate anticipation of customer requirements and technological trends. Once a hardware product is developed, the Company must rapidly bring it into volume manufacturing, a process that requires accurate forecasting of both volumes and configurations, among other things, in order to achieve acceptable yields and costs. (*Sun Microsystems Company Report*, 1994)

The report went on to state that it was increasingly dependent on the ability of its suppliers to deliver advanced components for the timely introduction of new products. The buyer–supplier relationship has markedly improved in a very difficult market in which to plan with any certainty.

The Company's customer order backlog on 30 June 1993 was $160 million compared with $350 million and $450 million, at 30 June 1992 and 1991, respectively. This was improved largely as a result of gaining faster response times with their supplier base.

The importance of suppliers was clear:

> The failure of any of these suppliers to deliver components on time could result in a significant adverse impact on the Company's operating results. The production of

> sufficient quantities of advanced components on a timely basis entails both design risk and manufacturing risk. The inability to secure enough components to build products, including new products, in the quantities and configurations required, or to produce, test and deliver sufficient products to meet demand in a timely manner, would adversely affect the Company's net revenues and operating results. (*Sun Microsystems Company Report*, 1994)

Sun has managed to avert this threat. Sun's product lifecycles now average twelve months and it continues to spend around 10 per cent of revenues in developing new products. Bringing these to market has been made possible only by a strategic relationship with its suppliers.

7 Strategic human resource management

7.1 Introduction

The changing role of human resource management presents a major challenge to many manufacturing firms in the West. The association of manufacturing processes with repetitive tasks and poorly motivated workers has changed to a great degree. This is largely due to an understanding of Japanese manufacturing practices, both in Japan and in Japanese transplants in the West, where workers are far more involved in the management of production/operations, in contrast to the more traditional Western approaches. A motivated, highly trained workforce must form the backbone of any would-be world-class manufacturer. The lack of a skilled, trained workforce accounts in part at least for the decline in manufacturing capability on a national level, particularly in the United Kingdom and United States.

The need for innovation, new idea generation, flexibility and inventiveness comes essentially via the human input, not machinery. As Lazonick (1991) observes,

> the enterprise must plan its human resource needs not only to facilitate the production and distribution of existing products, but also to generate new processes (and) . . . new products that will permit the *long-term stability and growth of the enterprise.* (p.78) (italics added)

7.1.1 The failure of past approaches to human resource management

In the 1980s, a number of Western manufacturing firms invested vast sums of money in technology, one aim of which was to reduce or replace labour costs. We need only look at the limited or sometimes nil improvements in the performance of the plants in which vast amounts of expenditure took place to realize that automation by itself, is not the road to everlasting manufacturing success. Instead, massive reorganization is the only solution for many manufacturing firms, whose structures and methods are now obsolete in comparison with world-class organizations. The reorganization includes a recognition of the importance of human resources as a key input to world-class strategic manufacturing, as well as the abandonment of traditional top-down approaches to management. This is summarized by Hayes and Jaikumar (1988) when they talk about the importance of human resources in new technology:

> Traditional managerial attitudes, manifested in top-down decision making, piece-meal changes and a 'bottom-line' mentality, are incompatible with the requirements and unique capabilities of advanced manufacturing systems. Until their attitudes change, companies will be slow to adopt the new technologies, and those that do will run a high risk of failure. (p.79)

7.1.2 *Learning from Japanese human resource management*

The rediscovery of the importance of human resources to world-class manufacturing is highlighted by Kanter in Erikson and Vallas (1990):

> the speed of workplace reform in the United States was significantly increased after the discovery of the importance of certain human resource management practices in Japanese firms. (p.381)

The difference between Japanese and Western manufacturing was highlighted by Keller (1993):

> One of the main factors that distinguished the Toyota Production System from Fordism was the amount of responsibility and individual control given to workers. In the West the assembly-line worker was a cog in a large machine . . . At Toyota . . . each worker was trained for a variety of jobs which they performed in teams . . . They were expected to think about how the tasks, parts, or equipment could be improved. (p.162)

Clearly, training was a major factor here, but it was not the only one; a culture of worker–manager respect and trust was also a requirement for the enlightened approach to succeed.

Gleave and Oliver (1990) point out how Japanese manufacturers have seen human resources as a core area which helped to shape their manufacturing strategy:

> The major Japanese corporations appear to have succeeded in engineering a good 'fit' between their manufacturing strategy and their human resources strategy. They have manufacturing systems which are highly efficient but which require highly supportive employee attitudes and behaviour. (p.55)

Hutchins (1988) observes how this employee involvement is something which has been learned by the Japanese. The challenge for Western firms then is that they need to learn or relearn lessons which have not been adopted:

> it is obvious from (Toyota) that near total harmony has been achieved between workers and management, managers and other managers, workers and other workers. Contrary to popular opinion, this harmony is not the result of some genealogical feature inherited by the Japanese. (p.131)

7.1.3 The worker versus manager problem

In contrast to the Toyota example, it would appear that one of the problems for Western firms is in the division between managers and workers – indications of this division may be subtle but telling. For example, in the UK BBC TV programme, *Tom Peters – Business Evangelist* (1990), Peters mentions how in a typical company annual report, a number of photographs will appear showing the company's staff. He notes how absurd it is that managers' photographs appear with the manager's name alongside (the name is spelt correctly and a middle initial is given) whereas, by contrast, technicians/operator staff photographs appear without their names. What may appear to be almost anecdotal evidence is, nonetheless, quite telling in revealing the ingrained, differing perception toward status within the firm. This worker–manager divide crippled much of the UK's manufacturing in the 1970s and did severe damage to manufacturing plants in the United States. A major starting point for any would-be world-class competitor then, is to ensure that industrial relations are good. This goes beyond the normal approaches of appropriate pay, fair hours and decent working conditions. In addition to all of these very basic requirements is the need to foster extremely good relationships within the whole firm. The worker–manager divide has to be replaced by harmony at all levels. One of the best ways of doing this is in empowering the entire workforce by training, backed up with the assurance that good ideas for process and product improvements will be listened to and rewarded if implemented. Such an approach forms the basis of quality circles, which were discussed in Chapter 5.

7.2 An overview of key areas in the firm's human resource audit

A number of key areas have emerged in human resources management in the 1990s, including:

1. *Downsizing of numbers of the workforce within many firms.* As we shall see, this is a major factor which has had an affect on many firms, especially in the United States. It may be seen – in a cynical sense – as simply getting more for less. Alternatively, it may be seen as a requirement to compete in terms of speed, innovation and costs. What it must not be though, is a short-term mechanism or excuse to cut costs; as we shall see such short-sightedness seems to have become common in many firms, in the name of re-engineering.
2. *Reduction in the number of levels of the management hierarchy.* This puts greater responsibility on operators to be more managerial in approach. This adds to the point about innovation cited above; levels of bureaucracy will often stifle creativity and innovation; reducing levels of hierarchy will in turn tend to encourage innovation.

3. *Empowering operators in order to elicit process and productivity improvements from the workforce.* This is a particularly difficult task in the light of the downsizing mentioned above, which may be taking place simultaneously with the empowerment of those who remain in the workforce. Training the workforce is obviously a key factor here and is discussed later. Handling downsizing *and* encouraging empowerment of the remaining workforce is particularly difficult and demands the very best of managerial skills.
4. *The role of managers changes from 'policing' to 'facilitating'.* This clearly changes traditional approaches, the 'us and them' mentality between workers and managers, and calls for good managerial skills in areas such as communication, motivation and leadership.
5. *Organizational learning has become a major feature.* There are a number of ways in which a firm might learn and these are discussed later in this chapter. The *means* of learning may influence the speed and extent of learning for the firm.
6. *The firm sees itself as an extended enterprise by way of alliances (both vertical and horizontal) with other firms.* Many firms have moved away from the idea of having to own all of the areas in which the business is operating. Instead, many firms are focusing on their core strengths and do not own other assets which do not add value for the firm. This provides a better means of innovating via partnerships, rather than the firm depending entirely upon its own capabilities. In terms of vertical linkages, the extended enterprise is where a series of value-adding partnerships within the supply chain takes place. This means that there will then be a number of firms which together will be more effective in their chosen markets than if they had tried to do everything as individual firms. In addition, many firms are forming horizontal joint ventures with strategic partners. Sharing in terms of processes, R&D expenditure and effort and new product development are typical motives for such alliances. The alliances also become a core means of organizational learning. Rover's link with Honda, for example, was a major source of learning, enabling Rover to greatly improve its manufacturing capability.

7.3 The importance of human involvement in production/operations

In some firms, there seems to be a major difference between the theory and reality of worker participation in management. *The Economist* summarized this well:

> giving workers responsibility for improving the methods of manufacture is now a proven means of boosting productivity, unleashing the practical knowledge of the shopfloor. One problem is coaxing the knowledge forth from hesitant workers. Another is getting management to react to it . . . many workers say that managers ask for their ideas but do not listen to

> what they come up with. So they have stopped bothering to make suggestions. ('Knowing who's Bosch', *The Economist*, 27 February 1993)

Hutchins (1988) mentions how in 1986 Toyota received 2.6 million improvement ideas from its 60,000 workforce, and 96 per cent of these ideas were implemented. A necessary foundation for such innovation was harmony between managers and workers; firms need to embrace this before launching ideas for continuous improvement and other worker participation schemes.

There is evidence that Western firms are capable of harnessing this human energy and intellectual labour mentioned above; at Rover's Land Rover plant, manufacturing cells comprising sixty people are self-managed. Each team deals with scheduling, production, quality issues and identifies training needs. The participation rate for new ideas is four per employee throughout the plant, whereas 'On a standard British suggestion scheme, one in 10 employees hands in one proposal each year' (*Personnel Management Plus*, April 1993, p.14). At Rover suggestions are supported by a scheme called 'Rise', which stands for recognition of involvement schemes for employees. Each suggestion scores points, which are then accumulated and rewarded. In addition to this monetary award, other recognition is clearly evident; teams can nominate employees for a trophy or certificate for their participation and innovative ideas.

At GM's UK plant, Vauxhall, teamwork suggestions resulted in savings of £5.3 million in 1993 alone, compared with £900,000 in 1990.

Another example of harnessing suggestions at every level comes from Ford. In 1992, it started a comprehensive new suggestion plan aimed at gaining participation from the company's workforce world-wide. The plan, called the continuous improvement recognition system (CIRS), means that individual workers, hourly and salaried, and members of cross-functional teams are awarded points every time their suggestions for innovations are approved. Employees are free to make any suggestion, job-related or process-related. Points which are awarded for suggestions may be redeemed for merchandise. Suggestions which claim to save over $500 must be approved by departmental committees and, in order to speed up this process, the committees themselves can earn points by responding quickly. In addition to monetary awards, an important aspect of CIRS is recognition, so Ford produces a Video of the Month that highlights the efforts of a successful work group and runs stories about individual and team achievements in its in-house publication. To refer back to Peters' anecdote, Ford's videos and in-house publications mention the names of all cited employees, both managers and workers.

7.3.1 The enigma of human resources and the quick-fix solution

One of the enigmas of the traditional behaviour of Western manufacturing firms is the easy readiness with which they will downsize the workforce. A possible criticism of re-engineering is that it seems to have been interpreted (although not necessarily intended by the authors) as licence to cut costs by sacking staff. This approach is strange, because direct labour costs will typically amount to only 10 per cent of costs in key businesses, such as the car, telecommunications and computing industries. This cost is a fraction of the total, far less than the huge costs associated with materials and bought-in components for these products. This provides one of the biggest clues to traditional manufacturing; firing people takes little or no skill and can be demoralizing for both the sacked employee and for those who remain in the workforce. Admittedly, there are those firms who have 'job clubs' and other supportive ideas in order to help staff who are exiting to find new jobs; however, firing is essentially a quick-fix solution. In contrast, Japanese firms have been loath to fire personnel, including Japanese transplants in the West.

A strategic view of the workforce takes commitment, passion and a long-term view of human resources in areas such as training and empowerment. The traditional view sees labour as a cost, rather than as a major asset; an enlightened view sees the workforce as the most important asset in terms of new ideas, flexibility and innovation. The strangest enigma of all is that many Western firms are seeking to relocate in areas where labour costs are cheaper; Japanese transplants, by contrast, are appearing in Western countries and using the local workforce to produce world-class products. Enigmatic indeed!

Keller (1993) notes how the joint venture between GM and Toyota (NUMMI) had seven fundamentals. Of these, five were directly related to human resource management:

1. development of full human potential,
2. building mutual trust,
3. developing team performance,
4. treating every employee as a partner,
5. providing a stable livelihood for all employees. (Keller, 1993, p.166)

The importance of these human resource policies should be clear. Such an approach will undoubtedly foster a working environment in which new ideas for innovation and continuous improvement are likely to be common. Such an approach has brought major benefits for Toyota.

Rover's relationships with the unions and workforce in the late 1980s yielded significant gains in performance. Rover management proposed that a new deal be struck between the company and its 35,000 employees in 1991. These proposals included:

1. Single-status terms and conditions.
2. A greater emphasis on teamworking and continuous improvement.
3. Full flexibility.
4. Job security.
5. An integrated manual/staff grade structure.
6. Streamlined trade union arrangements.
7. An updated procedure agreement.

Both the Rover and Toyota examples read like textbook human resources, which any manager has either read or can easily read. The key seems to be that Japanese and enlightened Western manufacturers do these things, whereas the traditional Western manufacturer either forgets to do them or is suspicious of such soft approaches in the first place. Such forgetfulness was evident in GM's closure of its Tarrytown, New York plant:

> When Bob Stempel announced in early 1992 that Tarrytown would be among the plants scheduled for closing, there was stunned disbelief among the workers, followed by outrage. It was as least the fourth time in GM's recent history that a particularly motivated group of workers tried to save their jobs by doing exactly what management asked, only to see the company fail them. (Keller, 1993, p.186)

There may well be occasions when a firm might have to make reductions. However, the rush to downsize which has taken place in the 1990s in many US and UK firms highlights one of the major distinctions between Japanese and traditional Western approaches to manufacturing. In short, Western firms have often seen people as the first area in which to reduce costs; in doing so, these firms reveal short-sightedness and tactical approaches, rather than having a strategic vision of human resources in manufacturing.

7.4 Three major manufacturing eras and their effect upon human resources

Manufacturing has evolved over time, passing through the following three major eras:

1. **Craft manufacturing** Where workers were largely skilled and, sometimes, owners of their own, small enterprises relative to later larger firms. These small enterprises would create customer-specific products, often with small volumes for each product in, essentially, job shop/very low-volume batch production.
2. **Mass manufacturing** Three changes took place between craft and mass-production:
   (a) *Workers became largely deskilled and work itself became narrow in scope, repetitive and specialized.*
   One of the main criticisms levied against the Taylorist approach to manufacturing was that an increasing amount of job specialization occurred. With this specialization came lack of flexibility, the inability to be able to transfer from one operation to another. Subsequently, over a period of time the specialization often served as the basis of demarcation by unions, largely as a means of securing numbers of jobs within the firm. At the beginning of the century there were advantages of specialization and, to some degree, it was appropriate. Over a period of time, however, this over-specialization became a major source of unrest; strikes, high labour turno-

ver and general mistrust between workers and managers pervaded much of industry in the West in the 1960s and 1970s.

(b) *A major feature of mass-manufacturing was the emphasis upon manufacturing efficiencies gained by greater dependence upon machinery to transform inputs into outputs.*

In essence, machines replaced human endeavour. The move from the highly skilled craft era to a largely, deskilled, machine-oriented approach to manufacturing had enormous implications. This change affected society in general level to some degree, and was lamented by a number of artists, for example, Charlie Chaplin in the film, *Modern Times* and by many writers (see DH Lawrence's poem *Work*, for example). Another writer said:

> men can taste little solace in life, of the sort that skilled handwork used to yield to them . . . In what was once the wheelwright's shop where Englishmen grew friendly with the grain of timber and with sharp tool, nowadays youths wait upon machines. (Sturt, 1923, p.78)

(c) *Products became 'standardized', dependent on high-volume manufacturing.*

A focus upon standardization and economies of scale to be gained by volume was now in place, as opposed to variety of the craft era. Ford's comment that the customer could have 'any colour of car provided it is black' aptly summarized the resource-driven (rather than customer-driven) approach by manufacturing firms in this era.

3. **Post-mass (current) era** As we shall see in Chapter 8, the author is loath to use the term 'lean manufacturing' as an appropriate umbrella term to describe the current era. Instead, the term 'strategic manufacturing' is preferred and the rationale for this term is discussed then. However, other terms such as 'world class manufacturing' (Schonberger, 1986), 'the Fifth Wave of Manufacturing' (Bessant, 1991), 'Mass Customisation' (Pine *et al.*, 1993) and 'Flexible Specialization' (Piore and Sable, 1984) are differing terms to describe basically the same era, which includes at least the following traits:
   (a) *A greater customer-driven approach from the firm, rather than the former, product offered, or resource-driven mentality of the mass-production era.*
   (b) *An obsession with quality, in support of the former point.*
   (c) *Much greater reliance upon human resources as a central means of achieving innovation and flexibility required in markets, which are now more unstable than ever before.*

The three eras and their effect upon human resource management are illustrated in Figure 7.1.

In addition, the current era of manufacturing has been altered and influenced by the higher levels of education than existed before. This has had a major influence, as Kanter in Erikson and Vallas (1990) observe:

Figure 7.1 Human resources from craft to strategic manufacturing.

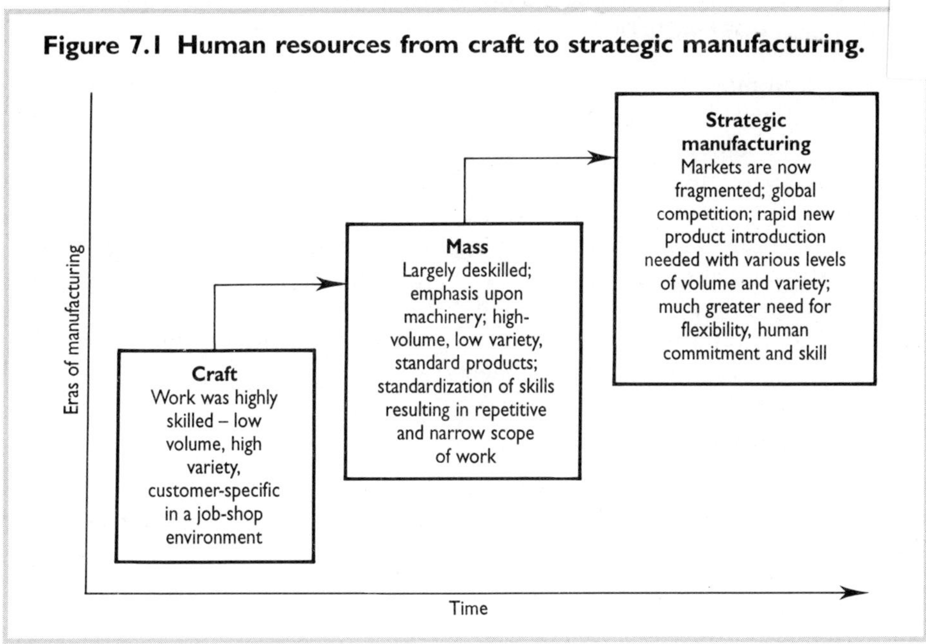

> The new workforce has more education, at all levels; expects a greater voice in decisions at work; and wants opportunities beyond the job to use skills. At the same time, the new workplace is characterized by a requirement of higher levels of employee effort and mechanisms to stimulate this effort. (p.283)

It is too simplistic to think of Toyotism or strategic manufacturing as disguised or clever exploitation of workers by managers. Instead what is now possible is a highly developed, mutually beneficial approach to work, far in advance of any worker–manager divide which was a feature of the mass-production system. The new approach brings a highly trained teamwork approach and a return to self-management in operations, which were features of the craft era. This means that managerial responsibility will become part of the everyday work of production/operations staff. Self-management, often in teams, makes the practice of close supervision by managers redundant. As Kenney and Florida (1993) suggest:

> Team-based organization of work also resulted in the combination of task and resulting production efficiencies. Japanese workers are multiskilled and perform more than one job. Workers also do most direct quality-control activity and preventive maintenance on their machines, resulting in significantly lower rates of downtime. (p.37)

7.5 Relevant human resource theories for production/operations management

There are a number of well-written books on human resource management and this discussion is not meant as an alternative, or challenge, to those books. However, it would seem that human resource works do not often apply ideas specifically to manufacturing firms. This in itself is an interesting omission, because much of the work undertaken by social scientists between 1940 and 1970, which human resource texts often cite, centred on manufacturing firms. In these classic studies, a number of areas were explored, including leadership and motivation theories, some of which are directly relevant for manufacturing firms in the 1990s. A number of these theories provide useful insight into production/operations human resource management.

7.5.1 *The management grid*

An interesting and relevant theory is that of Blake and Moulton's (1985) managerial grid. In this grid, a particular management style can be plotted against two areas:

1. A manager's concern for production.
2. A manager's concern for people.

A score can be awarded from 1 (low) to 9 (high), as shown in Figure 7.2.

What may at first appear to be mutually exclusive considerations (concern for people versus concern for production) instead becomes an indicator of how a manager performs in *both* areas. The two areas are not mutually exclusive; indeed in world-class manufacturing the two gel as inseparable requirements. Concern for production in terms of volume, variety, cost, flexibility, delivery speed and reliability can only be achieved by satisfying the concern for people in terms of training, levels of responsibility, empowerment, safety (including secure employment) and suitable remuneration. The real-life application of this managerial grid theory is that the world-class manufacturing plant must have managers who score a '9' for both concern for production and concern for people.

7.5.2 *Adair's task, individual and group needs*

Another useful insight into management behaviour is provided in Adair's (1973) linkage between three needs:

1. The task.
2. Needs of individuals.
3. Group needs.

Again, these may at first appear to be three mutually exclusive areas. Instead, in world-class practice, the need of the individual, team and task requirements are fully met simultaneously. Both employer and employee win in doing so. The firm

Figure 7.2 The production/people grid.

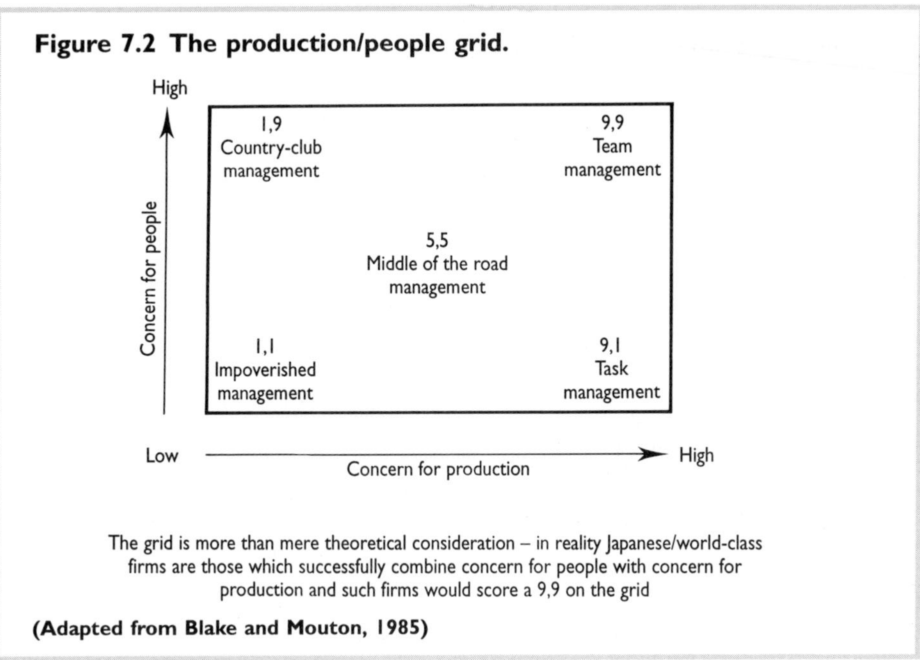

The grid is more than mere theoretical consideration – in reality Japanese/world-class firms are those which successfully combine concern for people with concern for production and such firms would score a 9,9 on the grid

(Adapted from Blake and Mouton, 1985)

will become competitive, and will certainly not be competitive if these three needs are not met.

Adair (1973) proposes a simple model to illustrate the importance of linking individual and team needs with task requirements, as shown in Figure 7.3.

7.6 Motivation theories

A number of motivational theories have been proposed by various writers to describe ways of motivating personnel. A criticism levelled against these theories is that they are offered with very little context. However, whilst some of this may seem to be too theoretical, the theories do provide insight into real-life manufacturing in the 1990s and we need to be aware of them. A short discussion of the relevant motivation theories for production/operations management is offered.

7.6.1 McGregor's theory X and theory Y

Although this might be criticized as too much of a generalization, it would probably be fair to say that traditional Western human resource management in manufacturing firms falls under McGregor's (1987) theory X types. X types are

Figure 7.3 Combining three key needs.

The three areas could, initially, be almost mutually exclusive. The task for the would-be world-class company is to be clear of the task, to develop individuals through training and empowerment, and then to work as a cohesive group, especially in cross-functional teams. This seems to be a key area of Japanese/world-class human resource policy, increasingly embraced by Western firms

(Adapted from Adair, 1973)

those managers who feel the need to direct staff; such managers believe that staff *need* to be directed because workers are inherently lazy and lack self-motivation. In contrast, Japanese approaches have been much more under theory Y type of management, which places far greater faith in the inherent capability and motivation of people and enlists ideas, suggestions and innovations from workers themselves.

With the era of deskilling of the workforce under mass-production, came an attitude to workers which was very much theory X in approach; workers were perceived by managers as lazy, lacking motivation to any degree and therefore needed to be controlled by managers themselves. Theory Y managers, in contrast, see workers as capable of taking responsibility and making potentially greater contributions than under the theory X mentality. It is clear, as we shall see in this chapter, that the theory Y approach is the most appropriate to managing production/operations staff in the 1990s and beyond.

In the UK BBC TV programme, *Tom Peters – Business Evangelist* (1990), Peters offers a provocative challenge; he encourages managers to try and find out what staff are doing *outside* work hours. He says that in the United States, from a sample of ten staff, nearly all will be involved in artistic or creative activities outside of work hours, 'which is to say that 99% of people are creative, vigorous, loyal, committed, caring and energetic . . . apart from the eight hours they work for you (managers)'. This is dramatic stuff, and may be too simplistic, but it is worthy of note.

It is a strange and curious phenomenon, though, that much of this potential creative input is often diminished by the attitude of managers who think that workers have nothing to offer. At the very least, workers' ideas should be encouraged. Japanese practice has clearly demonstrated that using this creative energy in the workplace is a very powerful means of gaining continual improvement in all areas of the business. This has to be good for the firm as well as the individual worker, who then feels part of the firm and cares how it performs, particularly when this involvement is rewarded with recognition and, often, substantial monetary bonuses for efforts.

7.6.2 Maslow's hierarchy of needs

Maslow's (1954) *Hierarchy of Needs* is often discussed in management textbooks. In this theory, Maslow states that there is a hierarchy, or levels of motivation, ranging from basic physiological needs up to 'self-actualization' – the need that a person has to achieve his/her full potential. The model has been criticized in terms of its applicability. Also, the question of how a person moves from one level of need to the next is difficult; whether a person can leapfrog from social needs to esteem needs, for example, is open to debate. The model provides a useful snapshot of psychological needs and is appropriate to our strategic understanding of manufacturing. A useful way of viewing the model (Figure 7.4) is that, in the past traditional approaches meant that, with the deskilling of the workforce under mass-production, came the inability of the workforce to move up beyond social needs. The two higher levels, esteem and self-actualization, seem to have been the prerogative of managers. However, as we shall see, this has changed to some degree, to where a more enlightened approach to managing the workforce means that workers are far more involved and given greater managerial responsibility than before, thus moving into the higher levels of Maslow's hierarchy.

In the past, the assumed position of front-line operators (particularly in the more repetitive line and continuous process operations) was largely at the bottom three levels. Work was essentially a means of earning a living and the tasks were mundane, repetitive and the same job could be undertaken throughout the entire time of a person's employment with the firm. At best, the front-line operator might experience the social element of the hierarchy model during work, but only then within limits. Any ideas of esteem and self-actualization would be achieved only through activities outside of the workplace. This links with Peters' comment that front-line operations staff are often creative outside of workhours because this potential creativity within the workplace is sometimes stifled by managers.

What has developed in the current era of manufacturing has direct relevance to the Maslow model; factors such as job rotation, quality circles and improvement teams, job enlargement and job enrichment have all come into play and have greatly improved morale in many firms. In addition, there have often been financial rewards for workers in terms of stock ownership and other bonus-related pay schemes, formerly linked to only management positions. The basic model is shown in Figure 7.4.

Figure 7.4 Maslow's hierarchy of human needs.

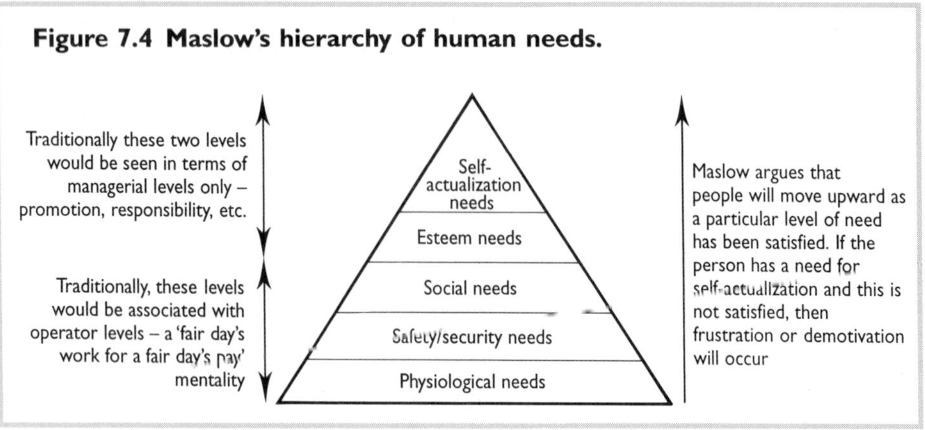

Maslow did not specifically tie the levels of motivation to organizational tiers, but such an association is valid under the traditional approach to manufacturing, where shop-floor operators were deskilled. The task for managers in would-be world-class firms is to encourage responsibility and self-actualization within all levels of the firm.

7.6.3 Linking motivation with conflict

Japanese management practices have viewed employees as valuable assets rather than disposable liabilities. This has a number of major benefits, including the constant innovation from new ideas from production/operations staff. In Maslow-like terminology, because lower needs have been met (in terms of secure employment), production/operations and engineering staff feel at ease and therefore offer suggestions on an ongoing basis. This security, resulting in continuous ideas for improvement, links into Japanese R&D practice:

> Japanese R&D benefits from long-term employment and low turnover. In fact, a recent study found that nearly three quarters of Japanese engineers had only one employer during their entire career. (Kenney and Florida, 1993, p.62)

However, as Pascale (1990) observes in his research on Honda, there is a constant tension within the organization. It is Honda's practice to deliberately bring together a group who are not initially expert in a particular area of problem solving. The idea is that in this way bias is overcome from people who are too close to the problem. The same sort of open conflict is encouraged by Motorola. For example, Motorola has an 'intelligence department', whose job it is to report on the latest developments in technology, gained from conferences, journals and other data. This information then provides material for often heated discussion on future scenarios for the company, together with decision-making on areas such as new product development and R&D expenditure. Motorola *encourages* dissent and open discussion. Also, each employee can file a minority report if he/she feels that their ideas are not being supported and these reports reach senior levels within Motorola. In this way innovation is encouraged, regardless of whether an immediate superior supports the idea. Production/operations staff are encouraged to dispute with their superiors and with each other at regular, open meetings. Ideas are always welcome; if this means clashing with others in the process, then this is seen as inevitable and certainly not problematic (source: Author's interviews).

We have to be careful with conflict, however; a culture of mutual trust must be present within the organization before open conflict occurs. It seems that not all organizations have such trust: *Fortune* magazine narrates how at IBM:

> the system came to encourage infighting and discussion to the point of paralysis and beyond..much of IBM devolved into a collection of fiefdoms based on product, job function, or geographic location. By the time (CEO) Gerstner arrived . . . 'they were all shooting at each other, not at the enemy'. (3 October 1994, p.40)

7.6.4 Linking theories with real life

The conclusions from research on leadership and motivation theories are summarized by Erikson and Vallas (1990):

> We can say . . . that the more autonomous and self-directed a person's work, the more positive its effects on personality; and the more routinized and closely supervised the work, the more negative its effects. And we can say, finally, that those results hold for both women and men and for workers in socialist as well as capitalist industrial economies. (p.2)

This means that empowering workers becomes a requirement to compete in a business environment which calls for constant change, flexibility and innovation from staff at all levels of the firm. Part of the new approach is that workers become their own supervisors, free from the policing role often associated with supervisory roles. A telling quote comes from Peters (1987) who cites O'Toole's observation on the difference between Japanese and US supervision:

> O'Toole . . . in a study of 'span of control', has observed that it averages one supervisor to ten nonsupervisors in the United States. The Japanese ratio runs 1:100, often 1:200. Not surprisingly, O'Toole concludes: 'In general, American workers appear to be oversupervised'. (p.356)

Again, an important distinction is evident here; under traditional approaches to manufacturing, heavy supervision was a feature; under enlightened approaches to manufacturing, this need disappears. This means that theoretical ideas of self-actualization and esteem become connected to real-life practice of responsibility and greater autonomous management.

7.7 Charismatic leadership or company-wide effort?

One of the interesting features of much of the business media is that, when discussing the performance of a particular company (which may have many thousands of employees), the focus still seems to remain upon the personality traits of the CEO. It is as though the military analogy of strategy, discussed in Chapter 1, includes the heroic figure of the charismatic general (CEO/MD) leading 'the troops' from the front. Thus, in the mid-1990s it was Palmer at DEC, Gerstner at IBM, Eaton (after Iacocca) at Chrysler and Smith at GM who, if the business press is anything to go by were charged with almost single-handed responsibility for the fate of the enterprise. For example, the following recounts a speech by Apple's CEO:

> a single spotlight beats down on Michael H. Spindler, the new CEO of beleaguered Apple Computer inc. . . . 'I didn't have to be CEO', says the 51-year old executive. Suddenly, his eyes, tear up. His voice wavers, and he delivers a last sentence, his fist raised to the roof 'The reason why I made this . . . decision is: We can win this'. (*Business Week*, 3 October 1994, p.66)

This is deliberately dramatic and the atmosphere is easy to imagine. Similarly, other stories of charismatic leadership are evident in the business world. For example, Lavin (1993b) narrates how, when the newly appointed CEO of Chrysler gathered scores of senior managers for an announcement of Chrysler's financial performance for a particular quarter, the leadership style quickly became apparent:

> After patting them on the back, Mr. Eaton rattled off snippets of press accounts of Chrysler's turnaround. Then came the kicker: The accolades had been written in 1956, 1965, 1976 and 1983. At least once a decade, Chrysler had sprung from its deathbed to a miraculous recovery. 'I've got a better idea,' Mr. Eaton told his managers. 'Let's stop getting sick . . . My personal ambition is to be the first chairman never to lead a Chrysler comeback.' (p.1)

There is no doubt that such a psychological ploy by Chrysler's CEO was clever; similarly Apple's CEO's speech was undoubtedly stirring stuff and may well serve to motivate employees at Apple. Stories similar to those cited above of other CEOs are common in the media. Just how much the business press has influence is not the point here; it is representative of how in many Western firms the mentality is that hierarchy, together with dynamic, charismatic, 'John Wayne' type leadership is often seen as a requirement. Little attention is given to the fact that if Apple does improve upon its performance, it will depend upon harnessing human capability at *all* levels within the firm.

The major problem with the overreliance upon the CEO is that there is the presumption that the person at the top is the expert and knows best. Such an approach does not encourage involvement and commitment to change at all levels. Keller (1993) tells how CEO Roger Smith behaved at GM:

> Smith totally controlled the flow of information to the board. He alone set the agenda for each meeting and avoided answering questions with any real depth. For example, when board members expressed concern about the quality of GM cars, Smith peppered them with magazine reviews and fragments of articles that showed individual vehicles in their best light. (p.37)

However, the performance of the firm is dependent upon the aggregate capability within all areas; much of this capability will centre around the performance of production/operations staff, on whom areas such as process and product quality, speed, flexibility and delivery capability will all depend. Leadership in firms will be judged not by the words of a particular individual CEO attempting to show his/her charismatic qualities in front of a group of managers in an artificial setting. World-class firms depend upon leadership which is able to harness the creative energy of human resources at every level within the firm.

7.8 Remuneration for production/operations staff

A major challenge for many firms is in how they must restructure their remuneration packages for production/operations staff. In the past, one of the major distinctions between operators and managers was in the different ways each was paid. Managers tended to be paid salaries, whereas operators were paid wages which were subject to a number of variables, including overtime (based upon hours spent, not effort or output necessarily, at specified rates), shift premiums, individual bonuses linked to results, possible group-sharing bonuses (also results-oriented) and special allowances. The effects of these differing types of pay are shown in Figure 7.5.

There are strengths and weaknesses in all three. The first two, for example, are easy to administer, provided that output levels are agreed between workers and managers. The problem with time rates is that people are simply being paid to turn up and there is no link to the quality of output/performance. Piece-rate schemes are essentially linked to mere volume – again, process quality is ignored, and the need to do it right first time may be sacrificed for sheer output, regardless of the quality of the output. Clearly, pay for performance cannot be limited to mere quantity of output, especially if piecemeal rates encourage poor process quality performance in the name of increased productivity. A major feature of such schemes is that they tend to be based on individual or sometimes small team efforts rather than company-wide approaches. In the 1990s, many schemes are moving toward a company-wide performance approach.

Figure 7.5 Traditional types of remuneration for operators.

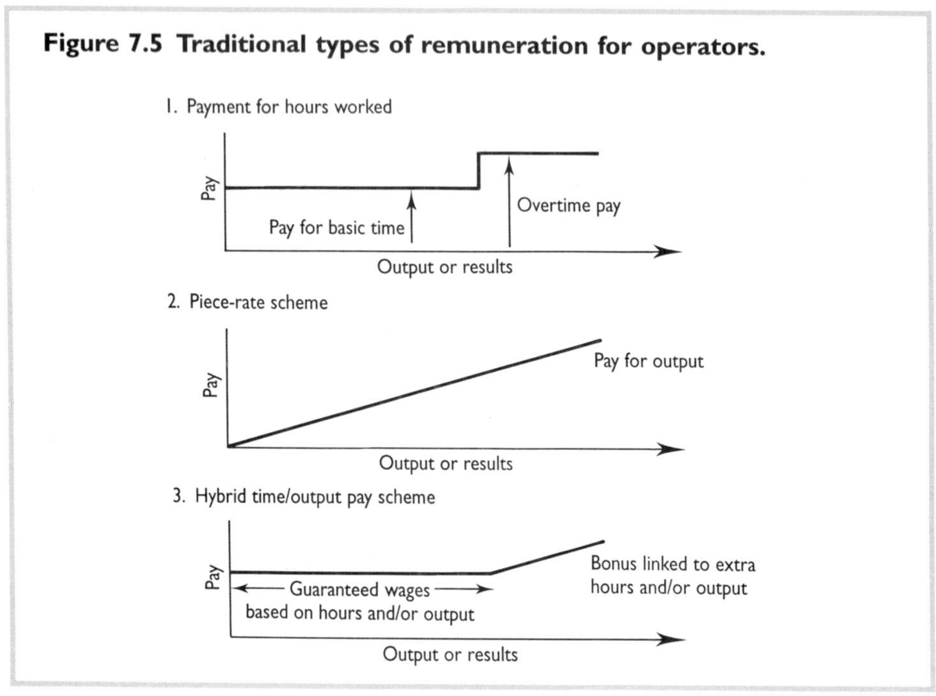

7.8.1 *Company-wide remuneration schemes*

A number of schemes have been attempted over the years which shift the emphasis away from individual performance to company-wide performance. Included in these past schemes were the Scanlon Plan, where the benefits gained by increasing production would be shared between workers and management. Another scheme was the Rucker Plan, which was more concerned with sharing the reduced savings that could be gained from added-value. This was a means of reducing the cost of sales, thus increasing the margin between price and cost. Both plans were more than remuneration plans; they were, in fact, a means of encouraging management/worker co-operation, provided that the levels of increased output (Scanlon Plan) or increased added-value for the firm (Rucker Plan) were reasonable, achievable and agreed by all concerned. The Scanlon Plan, devised in the 1930s, was hailed as a major reason for the turnaround at the Empire Steel and Tinplate company in the United States. The plan called for sharing of rewards gained from productivity improvements. The rewards were then shared between the company and the employees. With this came the change in attitudes that such a plan brings: a move away from turning up and producing to attitudes suggesting improvements in processes. Developments in employee involvement and financial rewards have been made in many industries.

7.8.2 Requirements for company-wide schemes

Clearly, suspicion cannot exist if these plans or hybrid schemes based on them are to be successfully implemented. If employees are to buy into the idea of changes from traditional piece-rate or time-based schemes to remuneration based upon company-wide schemes, there has to be a shared vision at all levels of the firm. As Hamel and Prahalad (1994) warn, however:

> Such an atmosphere is not easily created when top management pays itself 75 or 100 times as much as front-line employees. (p.143)

This has nothing to do with any politics of envy. The point is that if a company-wide scheme is to be introduced, then a sense of fairness must be present in order for the scheme to succeed. Part of the challenge is to move away from pay for status, especially if this is only connected to hierarchy position, rather than results. As Kanter (1989a) observes:

> Status, not contribution, was the traditional basis for the numbers on people's paychecks. The paycheck was a critical element in reinforcing corpocracy. (p.230)

The need to move away from this approach was, she suggests, largely by the recognition of poor US performance against Japanese competitors. However, the repercussions of this change are enormous, as summarized by Kanter in Erikson and Vallas (1990):

> When a merit pay system creates wide enough ranges, it is entirely possible that paychecks can reverse hierarchical statuses, with subordinates being paid more than their bosses . . . The impact of a system like this on productivity and entrepreneurship can be considerable . . . The boss is thus forced to move from a relationship of authority to one that is more collegial (and) if some of the authority of the hierarchy is eliminated, so is some of the hostility of hierarchy. (p.285)

An interesting case is Lincoln Electric in Cleveland, Ohio, where a hybrid system is in place: piece-rate systems (seen by some as representing the old ways of remuneration) are linked to overall year bonuses and stock purchase plans. As Dilworth (1992) states:

> The employees at Lincoln Electric are among the highest paid factory workers in the world in their lines of work. They are also among the most productive . . . The Lincoln system has achieved some results that many companies should find worthy of serious study. (p.288)

Another example is evident from Lexmark International, to whom IBM sold its printer division. Lexmark International changed its way of managing human resources. Teams were formed to make the production lines more efficient and, most importantly, to eliminate as many quality problems as possible. Alongside this change came the opportunity for everyone who worked for Lexmark to be on an incentive plan that included stock options and bonuses.

7.9 International comparisons of hours and wages

There are major differences in the number of hours typically worked in one country compared with another. In addition, there are wage differentials which provide some interesting insights. For example, Britain's manufacturing base has been eroded despite relatively high hours worked and relatively low wage requirements (Table 7.1).

Table 7.1 Typical hours worked per year by country

Country	Hours
Japan	2088
Britain	1989
USA	1957
France	1646
Germany	1638

Source: *Economist* (21 December 1991)

The differences in hours worked in Germany and Japan is clear from the Table 7.1. However, both countries can boast a number of world-class competitors, which seems to indicate that long hours are not the sole reason for such performance.

Britain's national productivity increased in the 1980s, but this was due to the shrinkage in the amount of employees involved in manufacturing. The reason for the decline in manufacturing base cannot be attributed to its hourly wage structure, which is considerably less than both Japan and Germany, as shown in Table 7.2. The figures in Table 7.2 are illustrated in Figure 7.6.

7.10 Organizational factors

The major changes in terms of how firms have reorganized in the 1990s include:

1. **Flatter organizational structures** where layers of management are reduced and in effect managerial responsibility is dispersed throughout all levels, including production/operations staff. For example, there are four job classifications for production workers at Nissan and NUMMI, three at Honda and Toyota and two at Mazda.

Table 7.2 International comparison of wages in the car industry

Country	*Figures are DM per hour*	
	Total wage cost	*Gross hourly wage*
Germany	49.62	28.50
Japan	41.83	34.29
Belgium	37.90	20.00
USA	37.56	26.64
Sweden	37.07	20.82
Netherlands	31.81	17.67
Spain	27.77	16.68
France	27.39	15.05
Italy	27.18	12.85
UK	25.56	18.67

Source: *Financial Times* (2 February 1994)

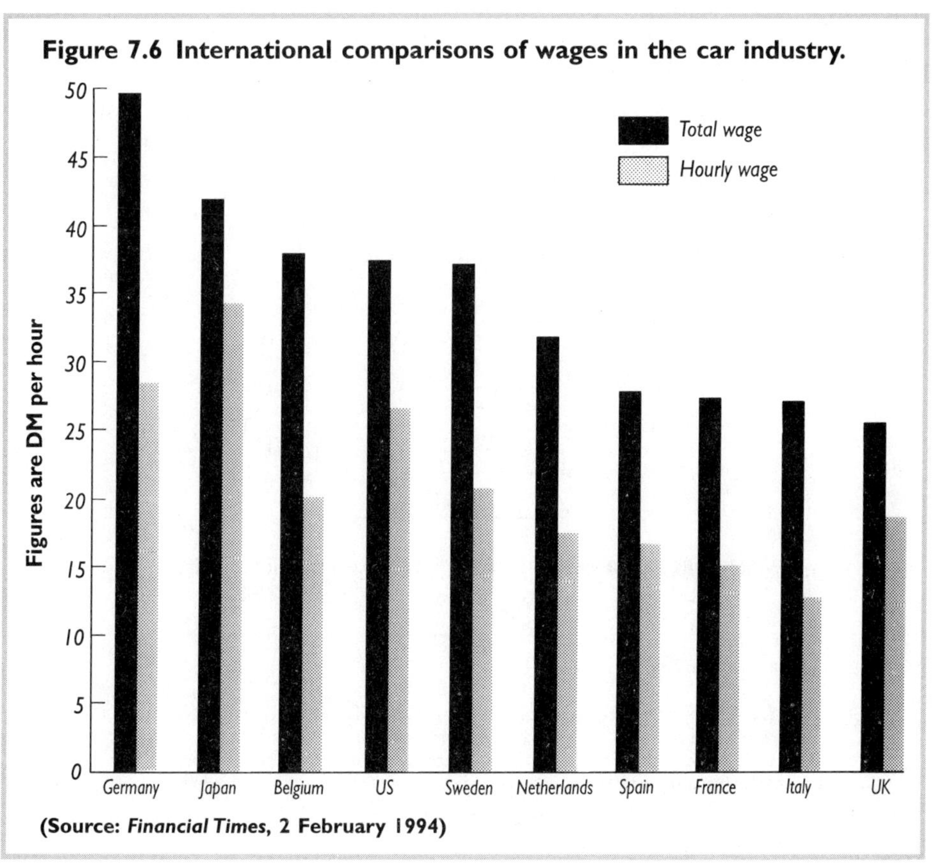

2. **Much more focus** In terms of how divisions are arranged, with far greater specific market/product responsibility given to particular divisions.

Both points are crucial to our understanding of how the role of production/operations has changed and will continue to change, with greater emphasis on self-managed responsibility. These changes are shown in Figure 7.7 and discussed in more depth below.

7.10.1 Flatter organizational structures

The distinction between American and Japanese styles of organization is highlighted by Dertouzos *et al.* (1989):

> In contrast with their Japanese competitors, American firms have several extra layers of hierarchy arranged as an organizational tree. To communicate with one another, people working in different departments often have to go up the tree to their lowest-level common superior and then back down. In Japanese firms the hierarchy has fewer levels and it is layered rather than strictly treelike: people in one layer generally know and can easily communicate with people in the next-higher and next-lower layers, regardless of departmental boundaries. (p.97)

Harari (1992) uses the term 'fat organizations' in terms of levels of management between CEO and operator and showed how General Motors had twenty-two

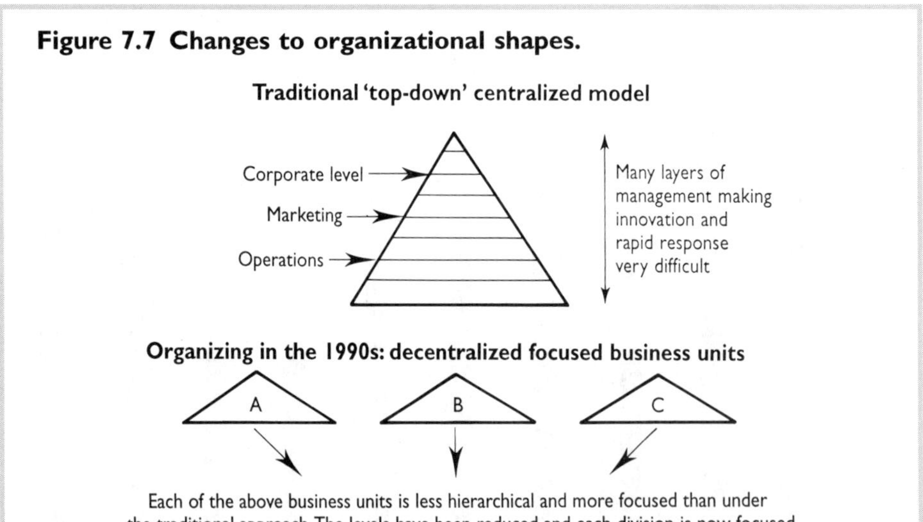

Figure 7.7 Changes to organizational shapes.

layers of management, Ford had seventeen and Toyota had only seven layers. Harari (1992) argues that a fat organization leads to too many people who can say no to innovative ideas and proposals that seem too risky. Managers in a fat company feel that they need to justify their position by smothering those below them with excessive hierarchical control.

We should be careful to note here, though, that flattening hierarchies does not necessarily mean reducing the number of staff. Massive restructuring via downsizing will often leave the firm with demoralized staff and the firm will be more anorexic than lean in its make-up. What the firm can do is to retrain staff and use them in other areas of the firm.

At New United Motor Manufacturing Incorporated (NUMMI), where assembling of GEO Prisms and Toyota Corollas takes place, production is based largely on teamwork and other organizational initiatives which GM has learned from the Toyota Production System. There have been no forced redundancies at NUMMI. There are only two job classifications and workers enjoy frequent job rotation, which reduces the amount of repetition. Training on an ongoing basis is an essential feature for production/operations staff and 100 per cent of the workforce at NUMMI receives training. Workers are called 'associates' and regular meetings take place in order to review production process and to make improvements. Staffing and materials sourcing decisions are made by teams, rather than by a personnel or purchasing function.

There are indications that progress seems to be made at other GM plants, though not as impressive as the NUMMI plants; GM's Cadillac division has reduced job classifications to 7, each with its own payscale; teams of workers are evident throughout the plant, responsible for their own training. The same type of arrangement occurs at GM's Saturn plant where most of the 5000 employees are divided into sizes of 6–15 work teams.

7.10.2 Organizational focus

The firm has to organize itself to best meet the needs of customers in markets which are constantly changing and fragmenting. This presents a great challenge to the traditional approach, where most of the power decisions were formerly made by a centralized corporate headquarters.

Increasingly, functionally organized, geographically arranged structures are not appropriate for the 1990s. Instead, many firms have focused by organizing around specific product or market groups. This emphasis on focus is one of the most stark contrasts between traditional organizational structures, with corporate headquarters making decisions and passing these down to divisional areas, and the more enlightened approach, which is much more focused in approach. At the same time, this change to greater divisional responsibility will enable a firm to be flexible, highly responsive and rapid in its approach to new product developments. The enlightened firm moves away from the paranoia of controlling assets to doing what it does best, concentrating on its core competence. A requirement for doing so, of course, is much stronger links with other firms, both vertically and horizontally.

Failing to organize in this way caused problems for Ford, whose 'world car' the Ford Mondeo/Contour/Mercury Mystique, cost $6 billion to develop (four times the cost of Chrysler's Dodge/Plymouth Neon) because of the expensive, complex co-ordination between UK and German engineering groups. Ford seems to have learned from this development, and has now attempted to realign its organization along world product lines.

Business Week pin-pointed DEC's failure to focus as a key strategic weakness. Like IBM it has been caught in too may areas, resulting in $4 billion losses between 1990 and 1994:

> Dozens of interviews . . . suggest that by radically refocusing on fewer businesses, the company can once again prosper. The best bet . . . is for the company to focus intensely on select markets such as manufacturing where it has always been strong and retains a solid base of customers, and give up on where it remains weak. In the same article, Harvard's Ross Kanter is quoted as saying: It is much better to focus in areas where there's a clear advantage (9 May 1994, pp.27,28)

Digital Equipment (DEC) is said to be structuring product-specific business units in such areas as components, storage products, PCs and multivendor systems integration. DEC's business groups would be serviced by a horizontal group, which is likely to include engineering, production/operations, sales and services. The new structure will theoretically enable the business units to go outside DEC for products or distribution channels. Like all manufacturing firms, DEC has first to focus on customers, then match capabilities with customer needs, either alone or in joint ventures with other firms. If not, in the words of *Business Week*:

> Why sell when you don't know who your customer is? It's a question that continues to vex . . . (the) shrinking computer giant (DEC). (9 May 1994, p.29)

In July 1994, DEC announced the abandonment of its matrix management organizational structure, which had been in place since 1964. DEC also sold off its disk drive, tape drive, solid-state disk and thin film heads business to Quantum Corporation in an effort to sharpen the corporate focus.

This development in terms of how manufacturing firms focus their efforts has reaped benefits for companies, sometimes on a divisional-specific rather than company-wide basis. As Hinterhuber and Levin (1994) point out:

> The development of the nineties is the return to the 'small unit thinking', the clearest example of which is the recent decision of IBM to break up into smaller units focused on their market segments with minimum control from significantly reduced headquarters . . . In comparison with its competitors, IBM is a highly vertically integrated company in possession of a large part of its value-added chain . . . High integration results in a large

> asset-base (50–60 per cent of sales for DEC and IBM) and thus in low flexibility and inability to focus on the essential. In contrast both Apple and Dell concentrate on their competencies and possess a relatively small asset-base (some 20 per cent of sales). (pp.45–46)

IBM has enjoyed much faster speed-to-market developments since its PC efforts became much more focused. New models in 1994 were being developed at a rate of six months, rather than over twelve months in 1991.

The product focus has brought major breakthroughs for Chrysler, whose Dodge Intrepid, Chrysler Concorde and Eagle Vision mid-sized cars were all developed in the same way, in product-focused development teams. The cars were brought to market in 39 months, as compared to the 55–60 months taken for the former 'K-Cars'.

7.10.3 Core competencies

Coupled with the concept of organizational focus is that of determining a firm's core competence; the firm must decide what its strengths are and to focus on this as a means of competitive advantage, rather than being involved in all areas of the firm's business activity. Core competencies are discussed here, because much of the firm's competence will depend on the skills, abilities and learning acquired by human resources over a period of time. Competencies are not limited to human resources. Hamel and Prahalad (1994) define core competence as:

> a bundle of skills and technologies rather than a single discrete skill or technology. As an example, Motorola's competence in fast cycle time production . . . rests on a broad range of underlying skills. (p.202) and a core competence is also a tapestry, woven from the threads of distinct skills and technologies. (p.214)

A number of important issues are involved in the idea of core competencies:

1. *Core competencies provide a competitive advantage*

   > a core competence should be difficult for competitors to imitate. And it *will* be difficult if it is a complex harmonization of individual technologies and production skills. (Hamel and Prahalad, 1990, p.80)

2. *Not surprisingly, then, it is a strategic issue, vital to CEOs*
   Prahalad and Hamel (1990) state that CEOs will:

   > be judged on their ability to identify, cultivate, and exploit core competencies. (ibid, p.81)

3. *Core competencies reveal learning in the organization*

   > Core competencies are the collective learning in the organization, especially how to coordinate diverse production skills and integrate multiple streams of technologies. (ibid, p.82)

4. *Core competencies provide opportunities, rather than limitations for the firm* The authors cited NEC in terms of the firm's chosen core product, semiconductors, and how this would allow them to compete in both telecommunications and computing industries. Concentrating on a core activity actually becomes a means of developing this capability into a number of possible applications.

Tampoe (1994) suggests human resource management must form part of the organization's core competence because 'the basis of competitive advantage is moving from capital, natural resources to human capital' (p.67).

Clearly, human resource management must be a key core competence for any world-class manufacturing firm; without it, the firm will be threatened. New ideas for innovation, new products, continuous improvement and so on come from harnessing this creativity from humans, not via machines or technology.

7.10.4 Downsizing and restructuring

The common theme in many UK, European and US organizations has been twofold:

1. A more focused organizational approach (discussed earlier).
2. Downsizing the workforce.

Downsizing has become a major factor in the shape and reorganization of firms in the West. A major effect of downsizing will be on the employees themselves, who feel demoralized.

As Hamel and Prahalad (1994) state:

> In 1993, large US firms announced nearly 600,000 layoffs – 25% more than had been announced in a similar period in 1992 and nearly 10% above the levels of 1991, which was technically the bottom of the recession in the United States. (p.6)

Business Week's feature – 'The Pain of Downsizing' – is pertinent here:

> The sight of so many bodies on the corporate scrap heap is sparking a corporate debate – about profits and loyalty, and about the benefits and unforeseen consequences of layoffs. Critics . . . believe massive downsizing has become a fad, a bone to throw Wall Street when investors begin baying for cost-cuts. (9 May 1994, p.61)

Downsizing in US firms has been dramatic; AT&T shed 140,000 between the deregulation of 1984 and 10 years later; IBM reduced its headcount by over 100,000 between 1990 and 1994, and General Motors shed over 70,000 within the same time period. In 1993, Amdahl downsized 13 per cent of its workforce, because of reduced demand and eroding prices of its mainframe computers. Amdahl said its planned staff cuts were part of a streamlining strategy that would slash manufacturing capacity by 25 per cent and help keep the company in line with demand. In 1994, DEC fired its number two executive and stated it would shed 20,000 jobs within a two-year period. DEC has shed 6000 jobs in Europe (*Financial Times*, 7 March 1994, p.21).

The point to this is that downsizing, or whatever managerial term may be used to mean reduced staff costs, can be a quick-fix solution and is no substitute for long-term strategy. By contrast, Simison and Williams (1993) observe how Honda see such layoffs as out of the question; when Honda planned to cut its productive capacity in Japan by 20 per cent in the mid-1990s, reducing employment by 3000 workers, it did not layoff. Instead, Honda completed the transaction by reduced hiring, together with training the workers and transferring them to other jobs. Clearly, then, in Honda's Japanese plants, human resources are seen in terms of strategic value and worth, rather than as an instant means of cost-cutting.

This strategic approach is also evident in the Japanese transplants; Nissan's UK plant did not force redundancies on the workforce when production declined in 1993. Instead, it simply did not replace those persons who left or retired. The firm did offer a six-month severance package for those who volunteered to leave. This is in direct contrast to much of the enforced downsizing in many firms.

7.11 Training

Training has been seen as one of the fundamental differences between Japanese and Western manufacturing. There seems to be a major distinction between traditional and enlightened approaches when it comes to training:

1. *Seeing training as a cost (traditional), rather than an investment (enlightened)* – Put simply, Japanese companies, including Japanese transplants in the West, see training at all levels as an investment and not just a cost, which has tended to be the Western approach. Rogers (1993) illustrates the differences between GM and Honda toward training; when General Motors decided to eliminate 38,000 jobs, it used part of the $600 million fund collected to pay for worker training for the departing employees. When 800 positions were threatened at Honda of America, the company decided to train the workers. When Honda cut production of its Accords by 11 per cent in early 1993, no layoffs took place; workers were provided with 5 per cent more training time.
2. *Failure to train at all levels* – Enlightened approaches see the need for company-wide training at all levels, including senior executives; one of the most startling of surveys on training undertaken by the Institute of Directors in the United Kingdom in 1994 revealed that more than 90 per cent of UK directors had not been involved in any training or development activity since their appointment at director level (*Personnel Management*, December 1994). It was as if they had risen above training needs by virtue of their position.

7.11.1 *National importance of training*

Kanter (1989a) spells out the national importance of training:

> Corporate education programs should be a matter of national interest, for they are an important extension of secondary and higher education. Not only do they help companies improve their competitiveness – a matter of public concern – but they also ensure that the labor force remains employable regardless of the fates of particular units of particular companies. (p.366)

The contrast between various countries is noted by Dertouzos *et al.* (1989):

> In one group, including the United States, Sweden and Britain, formal education institutions provide most of the specialized skills that are used in work, and on-the-job training provides little beyond quick task-related instruction . . . In contrast, . . . in countries such as Japan and West Germany, on-the-job training is heavily relied on to develop general as well as specialized skills. (p.83)

Compared to Europe and Japan, training of US shop-floor personnel is inadequate, according to studies by the Educational Society for Resource Management, cited in Vallens (1993). The typical US manufacturer spends $150 a year per employee on training. A report from the American Society for Training and Development showed that most companies in the United States do not offer any type of training:

> Just 15,000 employers – a mere 0.5% of the total – account for 90% of the $30 billion spent on training annually. (*Fortune*, 22 March 1993, p.62)

Leading global companies in other countries, by contrast, spend between $2000 and $3000 a year per employee. According to estimates by the Hudson Institute, the United States must upgrade by at least 40 per cent the skills of 25 million workers by the end of the century or face further economic decline. The same warning has been stated by Lazonick (1990) who also talks of the need for reorganization within firms:

> If U.S. industrial firms hope to match the recent economic successes of their Japanese competitors, then they will have to provide shop-floor workers with the skills required by advanced technological systems, and they will have to build new structures of work organization to ensure that workers use these skills to further enterprise goals. (p.23)

Foley *et al.* (1993) link the role of training to the introduction of new process technology and warn that:

> Skill shortages in a nation's workforce can act as a barrier to the introduction of new technologies and lead to a reduction of a nation's competitiveness . . . There is sufficient evidence to suggest that skill shortages . . . have constrained technological advance in the United Kingdom. (p.131)

The strategic commitment to training in Japanese firms was mentioned earlier. Such a commitment contrasts with the practice within many Western firms. In the United Kingdom, for example, training in firms often becomes dispensed with when short-term profitability is threatened:

> since the commitment of British firms to training is not high, anything other than basic or minimal training may be seen as expendable when profits are squeezed. (Foley *et al.*, 1993, p.136)

7.11.2 Training as a means to competitive advantage

In their study of German and British plants Sorge and Warner (1981) found that training in German plants enabled German plants to have greater flexibility and enabled greater productivity levels to be gained over British plants. Dertouzos *et al.* (1989) comment:

> in Japan and West Germany, patterns of in-plant training and rotations provide continuous retraining for workers at all levels. Rotations create a multiskilled, flexible workforce prepared for change by creating a mind-set for learning. (p.91)

This rotation between departments takes place at managerial levels, as well as shop-floor operator levels. This is a key feature to Japanese and German approaches to manufacturing: there is the ability amongst managers to see strategy in a more holistic approach than other Western competitors who are often guilty of departmental myopia:

> In Japan and Germany, training by rotation is still widely seen as an essential broadening experience. As engineering and business professionals in these countries move into management posts, their rotation through assignments in marketing, production, research, finance, and new product and new-process development *gives them broad knowledge of the firm's technical and manufacturing capabilities*. (Dertouzos *et al.*, 1989, p.98) (italics added)

One of the major repercussions of continuous training across functional barriers is that employees understand and value each other's contribution. This will undoubtedly enhance the strategic planning capability of the firm. The use of Japanese-style management practice was studied by Oliver and Wilkinson (1992) who in their survey of sixty-eight UK-based firms found that a key element was the use of managerial rotation in firms in order to gain a wider vision of the firm's activities.

This means that the likelihood of the firm being pulled into directions where it does not have the manufacturing capability to compete will be reduced and probably will not occur at all, because there is bonding between manufacturing capabilities and marketing departments to better serve market requirements. This cross-functional approach also helps to enhance the speed and success of new product introduction:

> The Japanese emphasis on teamwork and quality gave them advantages over American firms. In the United States poorer teamwork between product-development and manufacturing activities often contributed to delays in bringing new products to market. (Dertouzos *et al.*, 1989, p.219)

Clearly, then, training is seen by world-class companies as a key means of breaking down departmental barriers within the firm. These firms see a holistic view, with all departments focused on achieving corporate objectives as a central feature.

7.11.3 Training in Japanese transplants

As we saw earlier, the training offered by Japanese firms tends to be cross-functional and functional specific.

Vallely (1993) discusses how Nissan UK trains its supervisors, based upon its Japanese approach: supervisors' responsibilities range from recruitment, training and communication to morale building, quality and line balancing. Nissan job-rotates all of its employees up to management level to widen their experience and avoid boredom or complacency. Each of Nissan's supervisors is responsible for a group of manufacturing staff. A new supervisor goes through a development process with staff that involves:

1. Company induction.
2. Department induction.
3. Company-wide initial support modules.
4. Running the job.
5. People management.
6. Initial technical training.
7. Job-specific technical modules. (source: Author's interviews)

There is no single best way to train. In Germany, the approach to work is linked to the education system, which has a multitrack design with technical and university alternatives. This is not the case in Japan, which depends much more on ongoing training to enhance skill levels, rather than depending on high skill levels brought about by the education system, which is the case in Germany. An interesting comparison of practices is provided by Mueller (1992), who researched Japanese and German car plants. An outstanding characteristic of the German plants was the focus on the skilled worker in the production system of a manufacturing plant. The Honda plant in Swindon (UK) represents an entirely different production system from the German system; Honda UK's emphasis is upon on-the-job training, allied to other factors such as single status, good working conditions, participation in teams, self-development and job flexibility. The Japanese route to skill development, which relies on continual training, on-the-job for production/operations staff, is evident in Japanese transplants in the

United Kingdom and United States (source: Author's interviews). Such an approach is, in itself, strategic in nature, as Lazonick (1990) points out:

> Japanese management has taken responsibility for the development of shop-floor skills and . . . has integrated shop-floor workers into the long-term evolution of the enterprise. (p.23)

As we saw earlier, this is in opposition to the attitude of many Western firms, whose long-term vision of the workforce is, at best blurred and more often blinded by short-termism.

An important distinction in terminology is highlighted by Lazonick (1991): the United States (and Britain) tend to categorize types of jobs in terms of 'unskilled', 'semi-skilled' or 'skilled'; in contrast, the Japanese use these same terms to describe the progress of a worker as he/she progresses during their time of employment within the organization. This is more than mere labelling – it is a major clue in which workers are seen as either skilled or non-skilled (the traditional Western approach), as opposed to the view that any worker can become skilled over a period of time. Such an approach has at its centre continuous investment in the workforce as a strategic requirement.

7.11.4 Training in US firms

We saw earlier how training in many US manufacturing firms was generally inadequate. However, there are many firms that do train and state their commitment in company reports:

> We focus on the benefits of teamwork and provide employees with opportunities and resources that encourage team building . . . through the use of extensive internal training . . . we remain an organization that is continually learning and evolving. (*Dell Company Report*, 1993)

Training within Dell is for all personnel at every rank. Part of the culture is allowing casual dress in the firm and the training t-shirt has been a simple, but powerful means of promoting the continued need for training at Dell.

Ford's CEO, Poling, stated that manufacturing process quality improvements of 65 per cent between 1980 and 1988 were due mainly to the employee involvement programmes and this was made possible only after extensive training was in place.

Motorola has its own 'University' and has formed partnerships with a number of other institutions; it was also very involved with the creation of the course on quality at Midwestern University. In 1990, Motorola was spending over $200 million on training (around 1.8 per cent of revenues). This had risen to 4 per cent by 1994 (source: Author's interviews). Every employee had to dedicate at least five days to training and education. This training also extends to key suppliers. Such action within Motorola is recognized by other organizations:

> The intimacy between education and business strategy is tighter at Motorola than anyplace I know. (AT&T's vice-president in *Business Week*, 28 March 1994, p.158)

Motorola believes that every $1 it spends on training brings $30 in gains within three years; since 1987, costs have been reduced by $3.3 billion. This has not come from downsizing, but by simplifying procedures and reducing all waste, the ideas for which have come from training (*Fortune*, 22 March 1993, p.62). We saw how Motorola has become one of the examples of world-class process quality in its production/operations capability (see case study in Chapter 5). Motorola see training as an essential means of performing to such high levels.

7.12 Organizational learning

A key area for organizations in the 1990s is in their ability to learn. Learning may be described as the:

> process by which repetition and experimentation enable tasks to be performed better and quicker and new production opportunities to be identified. (Teece *et al*, 1990, p.16)

The literature on learning has been quite prolific in the early 1990s. However, the concept is not new and the role of organizational learning was explored as long ago as Lewin (1947) who spoke of three stages:

1. *Unfreezing*. A recognition that the existing approach is not appropriate or best practice.
2. *Changing*. Where experimenting with new ideas comes into play.
3. *Re-freezing*. When the new patterns of behaviour become the norm.

This unfreezing or unlearning element is mentioned in Cyert and March's theory of the firm (1963) when they talk of 'A theory of long-term behaviour in organisations must contain a theory of how organisations learn, unlearn and re-learn' (p.56).

Japanese learning is well documented and the human relations factor within the firm is paramount for this to take place. Pucik (1988) states how Japanese firms have open information flows which facilitates learning and:

> The policies guiding the management of human resources at all levels and functions constituted a vital part of such learning infrastructure. (p.81)

Kenney and Florida (1993) observe how Japanese firms learned from their Western counterparts:

> Clearly, Japanese industry benefited from contact with and learning from U.S. Fordism. (p.9)

This learning was, of course, as much in terms of what was *not* appropriate as what was transferable and useful for Japanese practice. Japan was learning from and improving upon the standard mass-production methods. However, this did not mean a complete abandonment of all things Western.

Allen (1993) refers to how, as far back as 1971, Mitsubishi Motors were able to learn from Chrysler UK:

> The fact that Mitsubishi still uses these same techniques, no doubt in a significantly developed form, is a tribute both to the quality of the original concepts and to Japanese competence in adapting and improving what they learn from other people. (p.33)

Learning is something which an organization may or may not do but, as Garvin (1993) suggests:

> A learning organization is an organization skilled at creating, acquiring, and transferring knowledge, and at modifying its behavior to reflect new knowledge and insights. (p.80)

He further suggests that learning organizations are adept at five activities:

1. problem solving
2. experimentation with new approaches
3. learning from their own experience and past history
4. learning from others
5. efficiently (and speedily) transferring this knowledge throughout the organization. (p.81)

Learning from the firm's own experience and learning from others demand that the organizations make time to reflect on this learning in order to reinforce and confirm what has been learned *before* transferring this learning throughout the entire organization. Learning in all of the ways cited above is a feature of world-class manufacturing firms. These firms learn quickly and effectively; they also learn quickly from mistakes and failures, then use the intellectual capability from their trained workforce to rectify the situation. Such learning then manifests itself in competitive areas such as lower cost, enhanced delivery speed and reliability, higher levels of process quality and speedier new product development.

A brief discussion on how firms actually learn is appropriate here. A useful model is Kolb's learning cycle.

7.12.1 Kolb's learning cycle

Kolb (1976) suggests that learning will have profound importance for managers:

> Today's highly successful manager or administrator is distinguished not so much by any single set of knowledge or skills but by . . . his ability to learn. The same is true of successful organizations. Continuing success in a changing world requires the ability to explore new opportunities and learn from past successes and failures. (p.21)

Kolb offers a useful four-stage cycle of learning, incorporating:

1. Concrete experience.
2. Observations and reflections.
3. Formations of abstract concepts and generalizations.
4. Testing implications of concepts in new situations.

This four-stage approach is shown in Figure 7.8.

Like all models, there are some caveats; for example, the size and length of time taken to complete the cycle will vary according to an individual manager and firm. In addition, times will vary in moving from one phase of the learning cycle to the next. However, the model is not a purely academic offering; instead it is offered for pragmatic reasons. Kolb suggests that:

> learning should be an explicit objective that is pursued as consciously and deliberately as profit or productivity. Managers and organizations should budget time to specifically learn from their experiences. (p.30)

However, as Garvin (1993) observes:

> few companies . . . have established processes that require their managers to periodically think about the past and learn. (p.85) . . . There must be time for reflection and analysis, to think about strategic plans . . . Only if top management explicitly frees up employees' time for the purpose does learning occur with any frequency. (p.91)

The implications for production/operations learning are enormous, including *at least* the following:

1. **Quality improvements by learning** Clearly, 'learning by doing' is central to continuous improvement in process and product quality; one of the key roles

Figure 7.8 Kolb's learning cycle.

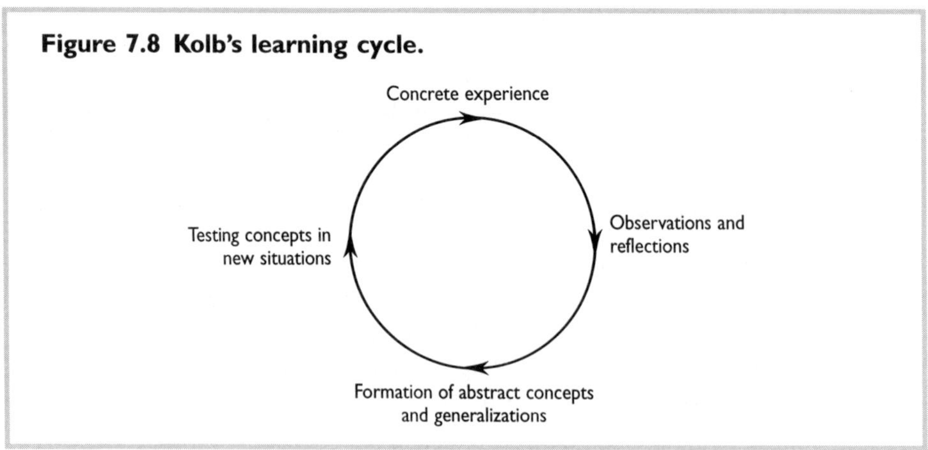

for quality circles is that what has been learned in one area is then transferred into other appropriate areas.

2. **Product innovation** The process of product introduction has changed enormously from the traditional sequential function-to-function approach to the more enlightened cross-functional development. Clearly, then, the process of new product development can become an organizational-wide learning opportunity.

7.12.2 Divisional-specific learning

The role of learning in relation to size of the company is difficult to establish. Much will depend upon how quickly knowledge is passed within the firm, which may have different divisions, and may be geographically dispersed. When each division has division-specific products and processes, the transfer of learning from one to another is difficult. For example, it is clear that GM has learned from the NUMMI alliance; it is *not* clear, though, if the changes in the Oldsmobile, Chevrolet and other divisions will develop as a direct result of learning from NUMMI. The likelihood is that because of the enormous differences, not least the thousands of miles between California and Detroit, the learning has come from means other than focusing on the NUMMI effort. What could be learned from the NUMMI plant and applied in other GM plants is the following:

1. The NUMMI plant is an old GM plant, where automation is *not* a central feature.
2. 85 per cent of the workforce were from GM's laid-off workers in Fremont 3. Within two years, the NUMMI plant was as productive as Toyota's plant in Takaoka and more productive than any other GM plant.

Progress in quality performance via learning has taken place within other General Motors factories, particularly in the Saturn plant. The plant was noted for its process technology, although for GM the major advance was in its management of people; at Saturn, over 160 work teams were created in largely autonomous roles. Each team is responsible for hiring, process control (including licence to stop the production line) and payment consists of base salary, plus bonuses related to quality performance.

Similarly in the Buick Division, the amount of defects of the LeSabres was 180 per 100 cars in 1987, which was reduced to 80 defects per 100 cars in 1991; this matched Honda's quality levels.

However, the opportunity to learn from NUMMI and to emulate this throughout all GM plants is still not fully grasped:

> headquarters in Detroit failed to build on these ... insights. In fact, despite the success of its own Saturn plant, GM has fumbled the transfer of lean manufacturing into the heart of its operations. Many plants are still poorly laid out, carry excess inventories, and have large areas where just

assembled cars must be repaired before they are shipped. (*Business Week*, 20 December 1993, p.67)

7.12.3 The transfer of learning between divisions

Firms can learn from other firms; alternatively, where there are separate divisions within the firm, a firm can learn from one of its own divisions. For instance, the redesign of the Honda Accord owed much to Japanese and American engineers, formerly centred on their own country's approaches, to work together in order to co-design, learning from each other in the process. In doing so, the Accord used 50 per cent of parts common to other Honda cars, an increase of 20 per cent on the previous Accord, bringing savings of $9 billion.

When Xerox costs were greater than those of its competitors, Xerox turned to its own Japanese subsidiary – Fuji Xerox – in order to learn better operational capability; Xerox regained market share, even at the lowest end where price was the deciding factor.

Firms learn not only from one division to another but within one specific area of one division. For example, GM's Pontiac Grand Am plant has piloted lean approaches to one area in the belief that this will then spread to other areas of the same division. Productivity in the new cell is three times that of the older mass-production line only 50 feet away. A focused cell within a larger plant can be a powerful means of learning. For example, Pirelli Tyres in Carlisle, UK, piloted a just-in-time cell in one particular area rather than putting the whole plant on just-in-time. Learning from the cell then spread to all areas of the plant.

7.12.4 Learning from doing and failing

Learning by failure is true of both product innovation and process performance and has been clearly evident at Honda:

> Not all of Honda's development efforts have been unmitigated successes but the company seems to learn rapidly from each of them. Indeed, the capability of learning seems to be a significant part of Honda's overall success in development (Hayes and Wheelwright, 1992, p.55)

Hamel and Prahalad (1994) observes how:

> Honda makes a mockery of the experience curve. There's no lockstep relationship between accumulated volume and productivity improvement; it's the relative efficiency with which a firm learns from each additional experience that determines the rate of improvement. (p.165)

This has massive strategic importance; alluding to Pascale's (1984) case study on Honda, Whittington (1993) concludes that:

> the success of Honda in the American small motorbike market was born not of deliberate manipulation of the experience curve, as Classical

> theorists have claimed, but of dogged commitment to an overall goal and readiness to learn. Despite failure with their large bikes, Honda persisted until, almost by chance, their small bikes took off and a new successful strategy suddenly emerged. (pp.33–34)

This persistence is a key issue for Japanese and world-class manufacturing firms. It reveals an ability to look strategically at markets, focusing on particular market segments, persisting in attacking these segments and supporting this determination with manufacturing capability. Failure thus becomes a learning opportunity, a necessary part of the pursuit of long-term goals of the firm, rather than an organizational weakness. *Response* to failure is the central feature. This is endorsed by Garvin (1993), who writes:

> A study of more than 150 new products concluded that the 'knowledge gained from failure (is) often instrumental in achieving subsequent successes . . . In the simplest terms failure is the ultimate teacher. (p.85)

The scope of learning from failure depends upon the firm's ability to react; Apple was able to recover quickly from the failure of the 'Lisa' in 1983 to launch, only one year later, the Macintosh. However, it took IBM seven years to relaunch the PC into the home market (the PS1) after the failure of the PC Junior in 1983. However, the success of IBM's 360 computer series was dependent upon learning from the Stretch computer's failure. Like the success of Honda's motorcycles discussed earlier, the IBM 360 success was due to the fact that learning occurred by chance rather than by careful planning.

7.12.5 Learning from alliances

A significant part of the firm's learning process is learning how to behave in alliances. This includes the terms and definition of acceptable behaviour, together with the amount of commitment (both in terms of time and amount of energy and effort) that a strategic partnership will demand. The commitment will undoubtedly be enhanced if both parties perceive benefit from the agreement. The readiness with which firms will abandon partnerships (e.g. Rover, discussed below) suggests that learning how to behave in partnerships is a challenge for many a would-be collaborating firm.

Dodgson (1993) suggests that learning in collaboration will need to develop for three reasons:

1. The bargaining power of parties will change over time.
2. Original reasons or motives for entering into the partnership may change or become obsolete (Harrigan, 1986).
3. The initial focus of attention may be on inappropriate sets of issues.

Dodgson (1993) also mentions that three areas of learning are: learning about the partner, learning about the task of the partnership and learning about possible outcomes.

7.13 Collaboration

Collaboration and partnerships have been seen as an important factor in strategic planning and implementation. Partnerships occur in order to develop products (IBM, Motorola and Apple), to share technology, to learn from each other (NUMMI) or any other reason which might be perceived as mutually beneficial for the two or more parties involved in collaborating. The nature of collaboration tends to fall into two key areas:

1. **Vertical collaboration** Where firms within the supply chain share technology and form long-term strategic partnerships; technology development with suppliers will be one of a number of reasons for this type of alliance.
2. **Horizontal collaborations** Where firms within the same, or related industries gain access to each others' market segments or other mutually beneficial arrangements.

What is clear is that both types of alliance/collaborations are central, in many industries, for differing reasons.

Collaboration between firms can often be very specific. For instance, Hewlett Packard and Canon's collaboration in the laser-printer segment is mutually beneficial; Hewlett Packard provides the software, micro controllers and marketing; Canon provides the core of the ink-motor mechanism. However, the two companies are fiercely competitive against each other in the lower end ink-jet segment.

Kanter (1989a) offers a six 'I' framework for the success of collaborative partnerships:

> The relationship is *Important*, and, therefore, it gets adequate resources, management attention, and sponsorship; there is no point in going to the trouble of a partnership unless it has strategic significance
>
> There is an agreement for longer-term *Investment*, which tends to equalize benefits over time
>
> The partners are *Interdependent*, which helps keep power balanced
>
> The organizations are *Integrated* so that the appropriate points of contact and communication are managed.
>
> Each is *Informed* about the plans and directions of the other
>
> Finally, the partnership is *Institutionalized* – bolstered by a framework of supporting mechanisms, from legal requirements to social ties to shared values, all of which in fact make trust possible. (p.173)

Pekar and Allio (1994) state that:

> over 20,000 US alliances were forged between 1988 and 1992, a phenomenal increase from 1980 to 1987 when only 5100 were created. (p.54)

They continue by saying, though, that:

> This appearance of progress, however, conceals some hidden problems. Many managers expressed difficulty in . . . shifting from a control mode of thought to a business building and co-operating mentality. (p.54).

Hinterhuber and Levin (1994) in their analysis of collaborations suggest that, 'Solid and continuous relationships...are not in the nature of American business culture' (p.52); the same can be said for the United Kingdom whereas such relationships are common in Japan. Again, the learning opportunity is enormous and, perhaps necessary in manufacturing companies, where dependence upon horizontal and vertical partnerships will continue to play a major role in many industries.

7.13.1 Collaborations as a means to gaining competitive advantage

It would appear that vertical collaborations are an essential means of improving competitiveness, measured in terms of speed of new product development, a factor which is critical to high-tech industries and becoming a vital factor in many other industries. Due to the inability of any one firm to go it alone, particularly in R&D activity which may be international in intention, firms are in a sense, forced to enter collaborative partnerships. As Ohmae (1989) suggests:

> in a complex, uncertain world filled with dangerous opponents, it is best not to go it alone . . . Entente – the striking of an alliance – is a responsible part of every good strategist's repertoire and Alliances . . . are important, even critical, instruments of serving customers in a global environment. (pp.143–144)

The complexity and uncertainty of markets seems to be a common motive for entering into collaborations. To what extent such links with other firms are truly collaborative is one of the key areas of understanding the failure of traditional approaches derived from short-termism in some Western firms. The long-term view has certainly brought success to Western firms; Ohmae (1989) comments how it took Hewlett Packard two decades to progress in their link with Yokogawa Electric:

> All along, the objective was simply to do things right and serve customers well by learning how to operate as a genuine insider in Japan. (p.149).

However, such long-term strategies are exceptions, rather than the rule in many Western firms, whose short-termism will often override strategic vision. We only have to consider the sale of Rover to BMW as a prime example. Honda needed to learn how manufacturing would operate in UK sites and the alliance preceded the creation of Honda's own plant in the United Kingdom. The amount of learning that Rover has enjoyed from Honda has been enormous and not limited to process improvements, although these have been dramatic in terms of process quality, buyer–supplier relationships and so on. In addition, product innovation has been a major feature of Rover's learning.

However, the approach here, clearly, was that the owner company, British Aerospace, which had paid a bargain price for Rover, was then able to sell it off to a competitor, BMW, without fully taking on board (or even ignoring) the problems that this would undoubtedly bring to Rover's strategic partnership with Honda. This is in stark contrast to the Japanese approach to alliances: Snowdon *et al.* (1991) comment how:

> Japan's alliance success has reflected its ability to make a quick start and maintain a strategic view. The Japanese in their alliance activities seem to have been particularly good at combining these two characteristics. Perhaps there is something in the Japanese thinking process here which Westerners can learn from. (p.130)

Snowdon *et al.* (1991) further note how:

> Almost 80 per cent of major automotive alliances involve one or more Japanese partners ... In a survey by Booz, Allen ... 74 per cent of Japanese CEOs think alliances are effective, while only 4 per cent think they are dangerous. In the USA the respective numbers are 17 per cent and 31 per cent. (p.123)

The Japanese clustering of firms around which technology is often shared – *Keiretsu* is a means of massive collaboration and learning between firms.

Conclusions

While it is too simplistic to be prescriptive about a one best way for human resource management, it is clear that Japanese manufacturing has been seen as a benchmark for many firms in the West. Therefore, there is much that can be used in terms of organizational learning for manufacturing firms in the West:

> If organizational principles and management are the root cause of competitiveness, then Japanese success is replicable. In fact various elements ... such as TQC, JIT production and teamwork have been introduced outside Japan, either in transplants of Japanese companies or by non-Japanese firms. Successful application ... outside Japan tends to silence those who emphasize the cultural uniqueness behind Japanese production. The purely cultural view cannot explain the apparent success of Japanese subsidiaries in the United Kingdom and elsewhere. (Sengenberger, 1993, p.19)

The transfer of Japanese practice to Western plants can only be realized if a strategic view of human resources is in place. This is far removed from many firms who still see human involvement in manufacturing as a necessary evil rather than as an absolute requirement in order to be a world-class manufacturing firm. Being such a firm can only come about if the worker/manager divide, which has ruined much manufacturing performance in the past, is replaced by a combined, holistic view. This change of view is one of the greatest and perhaps hardest learning opportunities for many manufacturing firms.

Summary

A summary of the chapter may be made by contrasting traditional and enlightened views of human resource management.

	Traditional views	Enlightened views
Attitude to workers	Detached – workers must be told what to do and closely supervised to ensure tasks are completed	Integrated – management are visible but operators are themselves 'managers' of the process
Ideas for change	Derived from managers only	Operators are close to the process and are therefore in a good position to see areas for improvement
Staff numbers	Downsize at will; workers are dispensable and an easy way to reduce cost	Have a human resource strategy; which is long-term; recognize that human resource is a major asset; concentrate on reducing costs in all forms of waste
Training	A cost – therefore spend as little as possible. Work is then made routine and repetitive; besides if workers are trained they will leave	An investment – a requirement for worker involvement and awareness in order to make continuous improvement in all processes
Remuneration	Based upon status rather than contribution; managers have salaries, workers are paid wages, based (to some degree) on output only	A mixture of base pay + individual contribution + team performance + stock ownership + profit sharing. Some workers may earn more than managers
Automation	Use as much as possible to replace workers	Use alongside workers – automation cannot invent, suggest or innovate ideas, these come from humans

Alliances	Suspicious and arm's length; stay in only as long as they provide short-term benefits; try to go alone as much as possible	Involved, committed and beneficial for two or more parties; a requirement to compete; form horizontal and vertical partnerships and see them as strategic in nature
Learning	Not an explicit factor for the organization	Explicit and necessary – providing, itself a core competence – the ability to learn from all experiences (not just positive ones) and to improve and innovate processes and products as a result of this learning

CASE General Motors

General Motors is the biggest industrial enterprise and the largest producer of cars in the world. World-wide factory sales of vehicles were 7,146,000 units in 1992, up 1.9 per cent from 1991. However, GM has seen its domestic market share erode since 1979, losing out to both domestic and Japanese competitors. After the huge profits gained in the 1980s, GM suffered massive losses in the early 1990s. Its CEO, Stempel, resigned in 1992 before being asked to leave. GM's problems came before him, though, and his term in office, a little more than two years, was hardly enough time in which the massive giant could be turned around.

His successor, John Smith, made a number of pledges in the 1993 Company address:

'We must get profitable.

We must satisfy consumers with better products.

We must grow the business in future years'.

GM moved from a goal of 'market share with profitability' in North America to 'profit first', with less emphasis on market share. It can be seen from Figure 7.9, that the decline in profit was alarming.

The priority was clear for GM; it had to become profitable and it saw the main means of doing so in the reduction of employees. One of the most striking comments was given by CEO John Smith:

> Where once we had about 13,500 employees in our corporate central office, we now have about 2,300 people. Each business sector now has accountability with clear responsibility and authority for results. (*Company Report*, 1993)

In the report, Smith asked for further commitment and loyalty to the company from its employees. Smith was honest enough to say that:

> GM is hard-pressed to ask for loyalty and commitment from its employees. Here in

Figure 7.9 General Motors sales and profits: 1989–92.

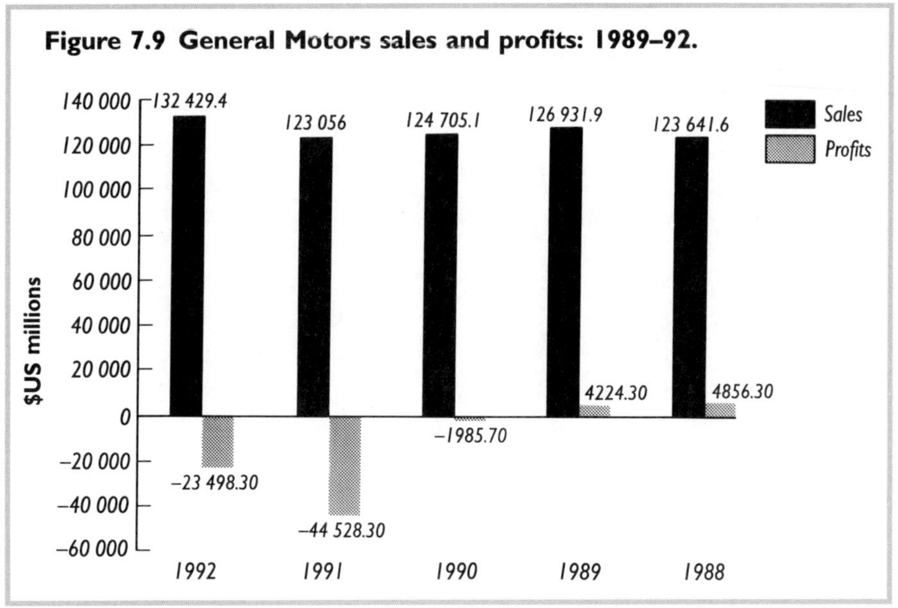

> the U.S., we've had to reduce the number of our hourly employees by over 125,000 in the last eight years, and our salaried employees by about 50,000, mainly by early retirement programs. And it's not their fault we're not competitive. It's our fault for not responding quickly enough to competitive pressures. We regret we cannot replace these people. But we had no choice if we wanted to regain competitiveness. Nevertheless, we need – and I ask for – the support of our employees to get our North American business profitable. Our goal is to grow and offer new opportunities for our employees. But before we can do that, we must be competitive in our productivity and total cost structure. (*Company Report*, 1993)

Part of the challenge was to work closely with the United Auto Workers (UAW) union which had become disillusioned by the constant downsizing from GM since 1986. The company shed 12,000 salaried jobs in 1992, and a further 10,000 in 1993. In addition, GM estimated that up to 10,000 hourly workers took early retirement offers in early 1993. In 1992, GM announced plans to sell or close two dozen North American operations employing 60,000 people. The company had already stated in 1991 it planned to shed 74,000 employees by 1996. The decline in employee numbers is illustrated in Figure 7.10.

However, downsizing was not the only answer to GM's human resource problem. A change of culture had to take place, a move away from the worker/manager divide that had been a problem. CEO Smith's statement that it was 'our fault' (senior managers) went some way to being honest and employee-oriented; much damage had already been done to industrial relations over the years. In the 1980s, Ross Perot, a former director, had often stated that GM should 'Get rid of the 14th floor', referring to the plush executive suites at

Figure 7.10 The decline in employment at General Motors 1986–92.

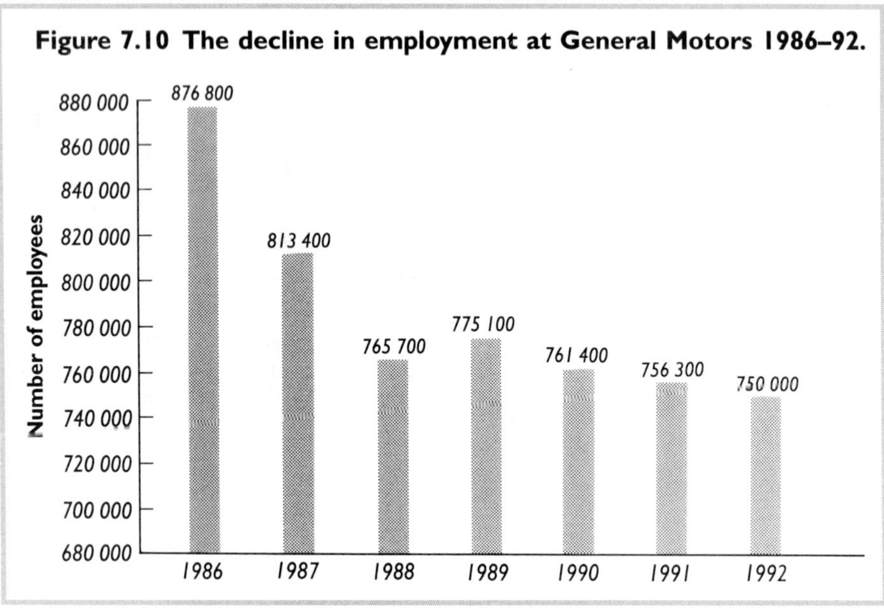

the top of General Motors' Detroit headquarters. Perot had wanted GM's managers to work alongside the people who actually make cars, production/operations staff, which is one of the key features of Japanese management. When Perot left, a corporate disaster took place at GM. Roger Smith, the CEO prior to Stempel, spent $80 billion on efforts to automate GM's factories, only to see the firm's share of the American market tumble towards 30 per cent. By the time his successor realized that GM would never again sell every second car in America, as it had done in 1982, it was too late. Stempel could not stop $6.5 billion in losses during 1990 and 1991. After failing to slim down GM fast enough and facing a third successive year of enormous losses, Stempel lost the confidence of the Board.

Once Stempel had gone, two important developments took place in addition to all of the downsizing. First, GM focused its activities much more by divesting businesses that were not core areas; Hughes, an aerospace company, and EDS, the computer firm which Ross Perot had founded, might be divested in the future.

Second, considerable efforts were made to learn from each other's divisions. The NUMMI alliance between GM and Toyota was one plant from which much could be learned. The other was the Saturn plant. In 1993 the plant ran scores of Oldsmobile executives through courses on Saturn's customer-focused approach to manufacturing. Learning from other divisions makes good sense and illustrates some commitment to strategic human resource management.

The decline in GM's performance since 1979 has been staggering. Despite protectionism against the Japanese in the 1980s and having vast amounts of cash reserves, GM managed to lose out in market share and profitability. The decline was slow, but the reaction in 1992 was swift, resulting in massive amounts of downsizing. *The Wall Street Journal* summarized the position with two telling quotes:

> 'To give Stempel only two years to patch up the hole in the bottom of this ship, I don't think it's fair,' said Steve Featherston, president of United Auto Workers Local 1999 at GM's assembly plant in Oklahoma City. Added Dick Long, president of another UAW local in Pontiac, Mich.: 'They gave him just two years to fix what Roger took 10 years to screw up.' (*Wall Street Journal*, Tuesday 27 October 1992, Sec. A, p.3)

8 World-class strategic manufacturing

8.1 The current position

The decline in the manufacturing base in many countries in the West since the 1960s is clearly evident particularly in Britain and America. Many thousands of jobs have been lost in a number of key industries and the United States and United Kingdom are intent on concentrating on service industries. However, this change of policy (from manufacturing to services) has not been deliberate, but has been forced on both nations as a result of their inability to compete against other world-class nations whose manufacturing capability has often been superior.

The reasons for this decline were explored in Chapter 2, but other points are worth summarizing here. The key failures include:

- Downgrading the importance of manufacturing at societal/government levels.
- Failing to sufficiently educate school students in technical/commercial areas.
- Business schools teaching quick-fix management tools, rather than providing a strategic framework.
- Failing at national and company level to invest in appropriate management development and training.
- Failing at company level to view manufacturing in terms of strategic importance.
- Having a view of the business which is governed essentially by short-term financial criteria.

At societal/government levels, there has been little enthusiasm to inject life into the manufacturing base in both the United Kingdom and United States, the supposed wisdom being that jobs that have been lost in manufacturing will be replaced by services. This simply will not happen. In the United States, manufacturing jobs accounted for 33 per cent of all workers in the 1950s; this fell to 30 per cent in the 1960s, 20 per cent in the 1980s and by 1995 the figure was lower than 17 per cent. The implications of this decline have been explored by a number of writers. One of the most powerful discussions is in the book, *America: What Went Wrong?* (Barlett and Steele, 1992).

Both the United Kingdom and United States have failed to produce a sufficient number of world-class managers; the result of this is the same for both countries, although the causes are different. For example, although there are differences in the education systems between the United States and United Kingdom, the result has been largely the same: producing graduates who are often ill-equipped to manage firms to world-class requirements. The national debt in the United States is testimony to poor management in a number of areas, both public and private, over a period of time and this has been matched by the decline in manufacturing performance.

In the United Kingdom, a number of studies were undertaken in the 1980s of British managers. One of these by Handy (1987) found that fewer than 25 per cent of British managers had either a degree or professional qualifications. Moreover, management training was generally poor, with many managers receiving no training during their career. However, as can be seen from the decline in manufacturing performance in the United States, degrees and professional qualifications are not by themselves sufficient.

Peters (1986) rightly points out that the increase in the number of business school graduates, MBA qualifications and business school publications in the United States has happened at exactly the same time as the decline in the performance of many of its industries. Simply throwing money at education, training and management development, therefore, would be as foolish as the previous 'wisdom' of spending vast amounts of money on automation which took place in many firms in the West during the 1980s. Instead, there has to be a combined effort between governments, companies and education institutions if the situation is to be improved. The present position is illustrated in Figure 8.1.

It is because of this short-term approach that decisions are made which attack the manufacturing base of countries. Two telling examples of this short term, essentially financially driven approach are evident in British practice in the 1990s.

1. Apricot computers was sold off to Mitsubishi in 1990. By doing so, Britain lost its only major hardware manufacturer in one of the highest growth industries in the world. The other British company, ICL, is largely owned by Fujitsu. Apricot's manufacturing division was sold off in order to allow the service and software elements of the business to survive. Mitsubishi have taken over Apricot's manufacturing operations and have been successful.

2. As we saw in Chapter 1, British Aerospace sold off Rover to BMW in 1994 and, in consequence, Britain lost its last volume manufacturer of cars. By no stretch of the imagination can British Aerospace's original purchase of Rover be seen as *strategic*. Rather, it was an 'ideal' model for financial markets, an asset bought at a low price and sold relatively soon after for a major profit. The sale was made with little consideration for other stakeholders in the business, in particular, Honda's involvement as a strategic partner. Honda had contributed in a major way to the alliance and had been fundamental to the transformation at Rover.

The implications of the Rover decision are not yet known, Japanese firms may be loath to enter joint ventures with British firms in the future, for example. In the longer term, BMW might decide to manufacture in Germany, rather than in the United Kingdom. BMW may also decide to source components from German suppliers, thus eroding the supplier base of UK components companies. Both of these moves would be extreme, of course, but BMW decides the future of Rover and its stakeholders. The importance of various stakeholders in the car industry is summarized by Keller (1993)

> On the scale of global business, carmaking is so vast an enterprise that it requires its own infrastructure, which includes energy, technology, electronics, computer programming, and engineering as well as every kind of science, and a wide variety of systems and materials ... In order to build

Figure 8.1 Root causes behind the decline in manufacturing performance.

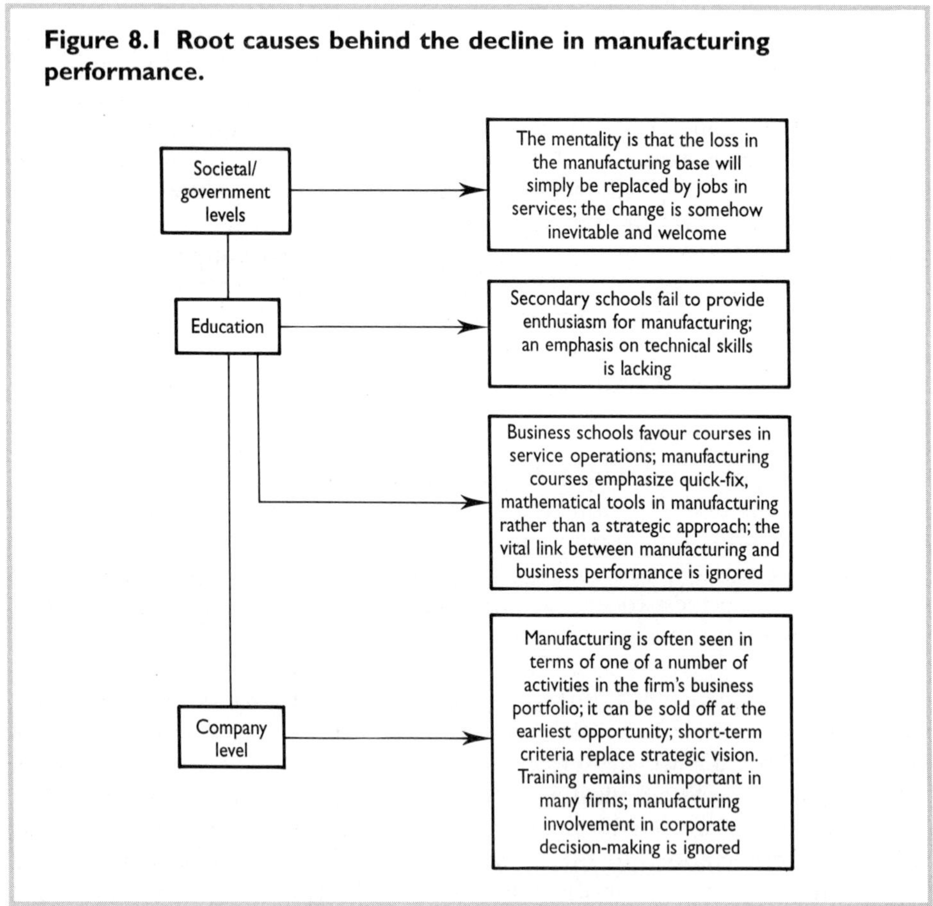

> a car, massive resources and talents must come together, comprising a substantial percentage of a nation's economy. Without the car, many industries could not survive. (p. 2)

All of the factors listed in Figure 8.1 have come into play to some extent and together have served to erode the importance of manufacturing. The net result of this is that many firms are not equipped to compete in markets which have greater competition and which are global more than ever before.

8.2 Overview of markets

Many markets in the 1990s are noted for their volatility, rapid change, reduced product lifecycles and increased speed of new product introductions. Peters (1987) aptly uses the phrase 'chaos' to describe the current era. More important than these characteristics, however, is a fundamental shift from a 'product-offered' to a 'customer-driven' approach by the firm towards its customers. This approach has to be undertaken by the firm if it is to stand any hope of competing successfully in markets. For the manufacturing firm, then, it is vital that all efforts, processes and infrastructure are geared to meeting customers' needs. This means that processes now have to be flexible and capable of producing high volume at the same time. Such an approach is central to the firm's manufacturing strategy:

> In today's turbulent competitive environment, a company more than ever needs a strategy that specifies the kind of competitive advantage that it is seeking in the marketplace and articulates how that advantage is to be achieved (Hayes and Pisano, 1994, p. 77)

8.3 The importance of globalization

A major development in recent years, which should become clear in the firm's business audit, is that of globalization. Globalization means that a firm can have a presence in a number of areas throughout the world. It does not mean that a company will seek to produce a standard product and then sell it around the world. Rather, the firm that is global will seek to provide particular products for particular requirements in specific geographic markets. Another feature of globalization is that there has been an increase in the number of countries represented in many industries. Examples of the extent of globalization in three industries are provided in Table 8.1.

Globalization provides opportunities for new market developments. Much of the future growth of the car industry, for example, will be outside of current markets (Western Europe, North America and Japan) and will move into other areas of the globe, including South Korea, China, Thailand, Latin America and Eastern Europe. Sales in Asia (excluding Japan) are expected to triple by the year

Table 8.1 Examples of global competition in three industries

Computers; office equipment	*Electronics*	*Automobiles*
IBM (USA)	Hitachi (Japan)	General Motors (USA)
Toshiba (Japan)	Matsushita (Japan)	Ford (USA)
Fujitsu (Japan)	General Electric (USA)	Toyota (Japan)
Hewlett Packard (USA)	Samsung (South Korea)	Daimler-Benz (Germany)
Canon (Japan)	Siemens (Germany)	Nissan (Japan)
Digital Equipment Corp (USA)	Sony (Japan)	Volkswagen (Germany)
Ricoh (Japan)	NEC (Japan)	Chrysler (USA)
Apple (USA)	Philips (Netherlands)	Honda (Japan)
Unisys (USA)	Daewoo (South Korea)	Fiat (Italy)
Compaq (USA)	Mitsubishi (Japan)	Peugeot (France)

Source: *Fortune* (25 July, 1994)

2010. Part of the growth is forecast for China, which until recently held little opportunity for Western manufacturers. In the 1990s, however, a number of car firms, including General Motors, Ford, Toyota, Mercedes-Benz, Volkswagen, Peugeot and Daihatsu, were targeting China. New car sales in China increased from 78,000 in 1990 to 430,000 in 1994 and the *Financial Times* (4 October 1994) forecast that this number would rise to over 1 million sales by 1999. Car production in China is likely to increase from 44,000 in 1990 to more than 700,000 by the year 2000. Similarly, car production in South Korea could increase by more than 1 million units from 1.5m in 1993 to 2.6m in 1999. Estimates for car sales are illustrated in Table 8.2.

The way forward for the manufacturing firm intent on globalization is either to export directly into other countries, or to set up manufacturing facilities in these countries. The Japanese have favoured creating transplants. By doing so, they have created strong strategic positions in key markets in Europe and the United States. Their approach has been to strengthen their position by offering employment to the host countries (sometimes in unemployed areas – Nissan's Sunderland plant in North-East England, for example). Japanese transplant manufacturers have become even more secure in their position by creating an 'architecture' or infrastructure around the new transplants. This includes sourcing local suppliers (to some degree at least), thus providing further support to the host countries' employment.

8.3.1 Global alliances

Although the car industry is exceptional due to its size, it is nonetheless representative of the trend in globalization that is taking place in other industries. Due to the increasing amount of globalization in many industries, many firms will need to form global alliances. Very often this will mean creating alliances with

Table 8.2 Estimates of global car production: 1993 to 1997 (000s)

Country	*1993*	*1994*	*1995*	*1996*	*1997*
World	33,134	35,253	36,377	38,042	39,903
West Europe	11,450	12,181	12,743	13,692	14,362
Germany	3,194	3,215	3,306	3,425	3,638
Italy	1,890	1,858	1,948	2,075	2,191
UK	1,778	1,978	2,074	2,236	2,303
France	1,721	1,989	2,051	2,184	2,302
Spain	743	849	867	1,056	1,054
East Europe**	1,334	1,366	1,472	1,550	1,675
Turkey	443	252	287	331	420
North America	9,441	10,245	9,950	9,779	10,150
US	8,702	9,424	9,044	8,822	9,147
Japan	4,199	4,203	4,398	4,628	4,780
Asia Pacific****	2,848	3,155	3,509	3,831	4,027
South Korea	963	1,072	1,167	1,256	1,315
China	430	481	618	758	791
Latin America	1,867	2,051	2,058	2,216	2,404
World (net)*	33,887	35,059	36,554	38,550	40,203
West Europe	11,372	12,102	12,847	13,823	14,206
Germany	3,794	3,946	4,085	4,310	4,391
France	2,836	2,996	3,138	3,332	3,384
Spain	1,505	1,661	1,776	1,801	1,808
UK	1,375	1,433	1,565	1,840	1,918
Italy	1,117	1,213	1,314	1,457	1,558
East Europe**	1,800	1,780	1,920	2,100	2,294
Turkey	348	234	258	297	378
North America	7,329	7,961	7,968	7,758	8,042
US	5,982	6,745	6,750	6,463	6,660
Japan	8,499	7,942	8,266	8,723	9,018
Asia Pacific***	2,807	3,154	3,542	3,914	4,342
South Korea	1,512	1,791	1,962	2,150	2,389
China	241	216	335	451	563
Latin America	2,214	2,423	2,339	2,603	2,651

* Excluding traceable double counting
** Including Commonwealth of Independent States
*** Excludes Japan
Source: DRI World Car Industry Forecast Report – August 1994 in the *Financial Times* (4 October, 1994)

other companies with which the firm may have had little or no contact before. In the 1990s and beyond, however, forming such alliances seems almost to be a necessary feature if the firm is to be successful.

The need to form alliances in the Computer Industry is discussed by Intel's CEO, Grove (1993):

> The European market is a morass of conflicting standards. Europe is full of country-based computer companies, with virtually no pan-European capabilities to supply them. For Europeans themselves, the notion of unifying the computer market is probably exceeded in difficulty only by the issue of a common currency. In Japan, many computer products are incompatible with those of the largest single market, the U.S. This has significantly slowed their penetration in this country. In the mid-1980s, people like me were fearing that Japanese companies would take over the U.S. PC market in no time. Meanwhile, the Asia-Pacific region, especially Taiwan, has become a major supplier of PC subsystems. Asia-Pacific companies somehow manage to supply PCs cheaper than most others, despite labor (their only apparent advantage) being only a small part of the cost of a system. As a result, the region came from nowhere and surpassed Japan as a producer of computers for export. This further complicates an already complex global transition. (Grove, 1993, p. 10)

It is because so many alliances are being formed between American and Japanese high-tech companies that in the future global competition will not only rest upon one nation against another. Instead, competition will centre upon the ability of one combined international grouping or clustering of firms against another. For example, the Canon/Hewlett Packard alliance is countered by the Seiko/Epson (America) venture. Apple has formed a number of alliances with Japanese companies, including Sharp and Sony, for hand-held computers and laptops. The result of such alliances is that it is becoming increasingly difficult to establish the national origins of many computing/telecommunications products. For example, Apple's Macintosh PowerBook 100 laptop was conceived and designed by Apple, further engineered by Sony, then made by Sony in San Diego.

8.4 The strategic response to markets

8.4.1 The demand placed upon production/operations management

Although many alliances will be formed, this does not negate the importance of internal production/operations efforts. In fact, such alliances will provide a valuable means of process and product technology learning between partners. As we saw earlier, one of the key traits of many markets is their volatility and rapid rate of change, demanding flexibility from the manufacturing firm. This flexibility places much greater importance upon human endeavour and commitment than under the former mass-production approach, as we saw in Chapter 7. Human resource capability from production/operations staff now becomes a key means to achieve world-class capability. If markets were stagnant and manufacturing simply about producing high-volume/low product variety then, perhaps automation would have been the answer. However, as we saw in Chapter 4, automation has not by itself proven to be the way forward for manufacturers. This is because markets are now fragmenting into smaller segments and volume has given way to variety, with new product and process development taking place continuously.

Porter's (1990) statement that, 'In fact, standardization and automation are seen by many Japanese companies as the only way to achieve very high quality levels' (p. 410) simply does not gel with the facts. For example, the NUMMI alliance between GM and Toyota has little automation relative to other US plants at the request of the Japanese. The management focus here has been centred on massive investment in developing human resource potential and the commitment to process quality through learning. If the best practice perceived by the Japanese was standardization then clearly they would have adopted the Ford mass-production model of large volume and scale economies centred around a very limited range of products.

The rate of new product introductions, together with the variability and range of models around a particular design, shows that the Japanese have *not* seen standardization as the means of competing in the car industry. Instead, constant new product introduction derived from inventiveness at all levels has been the approach by the Japanese. Their manufacturing capability has been the key factor here, based upon human resources, who are able to deliver wide ranges of products in varying volumes.

This capability provides a powerful means of gaining competitive advantage. Whittington (1993) narrates an example of this at Honda:

> when Honda was overtaken by Yamaha as Japan's number one motorbike manufacturer, the company responded by declaring 'Yamaha so tsubu su!' (We will crush, squash and slaughter Yamaha!) There followed a stream of no less than eighty-one new products in eighteen months. The massive effort nearly bankrupted the company, but in the end left Honda as top dog once more' (pp. 69–70)

Clearly, this response could only be made possible by a strategic commitment to winning against competitors, based upon using to the full the creative ideas and innovations from staff at all levels within Honda. This moves away from old ideas of manufacturing of repetitive, dull processes; instead the need is to fully use the creative energy, imagination and commitment from production/operations staff as a source of constant innovation and improvement in the business.

This enlightened approach to manufacturing is well summarized in the following:

> At the core of the new model of innovation-mediated production stands a set of fundamental changes in the organization of work at the point of production – a 'new shop floor' – which is geared toward harnessing and mobilizing intellectual labor. Both the factory floor and the R&D lab

> become a source of continuous innovation, productivity improvement, value creation, and capital accumulation. (Kenney and Florida, 1993, p. 303)

8.4.2 *Focus and flexibility*

A common theme throughout the book has been that of focus. It has been emphasized throughout that the world-class strategic manufacturing firm focuses in a number of ways including:

- Focusing on specific market segments in which it can successfully compete and deliberately avoiding other segments.
- Focusing on its manufacturing core competence and forming strategic alliances with other organizations in order to satisfy the market segment requirements.
- Focusing within its own manufacturing plant.

As we saw in Chapter 4, it is vital that a manufacturing firm focuses its plant in order to satisfy particular market requirements. This means that world-class plants will often have a number of focused cells of manufacture, each dedicated to satisfying particular customer needs. However, it must be kept in mind that the term 'focus' is not meant to diminish the importance of flexibility. Focus does not mean *fixed*. Focus simply means organizing in a way that makes some sense of the rapid changes that will be needed in order to satisfy various customer needs. Flexibility is clearly a key requirement for any world-class manufacturing firm. The need for flexibility comes as a result of market requirements which are now more volatile and fragmented than ever before. Hayes and Pisano (1994) comment that:

> many elite Japanese companies embarked on an orgy of product proliferation during the 1980s. Sony, for example, introduced 300 versions of its basic Walkman (disclaiming the need for market research it simply introduced a new model and saw how it sold) and Seiko was renowned for its ability to introduce a new watch model every working day. (p. 81)

A focused plant is one that can change rapidly to accommodate new market requirements. This means that the plant can be more flexible unlike the more old-fashioned dedicated line processes that were a common characteristic of mass-production. Flexibility manifests itself in a number of ways, most noticeably in terms of volumes, variety, ranges, product mixes and delivery requirements.

8.4.3 *The task for manufacturing firms in the 1990s*

In the 1990s, all efforts within manufacturing firms must be aimed at meeting customer needs. This means that the first requirement for the firm is to be fully aware of the needs of the markets in which it is competing. The firm must also be aware of business forces that may impact on the firm: these include political, economic, social and technological factors. The firm therefore needs to undertake regular industry analysis and competitive benchmarking in order to remain competitive. It can then seek to determine strategic opportunities and threats for the firm. Figure 8.2 shows this.

At plant level the firm must also clearly understand the competitive position in relation to other competitors. Benchmarking is an excellent way of achieving this, as shown in Figure 8.3.

Benchmarking links with the discussion of competitive profiling and the competitive grid model in Chapter 2. What the model in Figure 8.3 adds is the extent to which performing better or worse than a competitor might be of importance in terms of the competitive advantage that this might bring. This is important, because it will force the firm not only to compare against other competitors, but also to assess the value of the firm's competence and ability in terms of the value to the market itself. For example, being faster than a competitor in delivery speed may bring no competitive advantage if the market's main requirement is low cost.

Benchmarking is most useful when comparing against the very best competitor, rather than simply against another long-standing competitor. This was the case in the US car industry when the big three, Ford, GM and Chrysler, were so intent on out-competing each other that they failed to notice that benchmarking should have taken place in relation to Japanese manufacturers. It is

Figure 8.2 Linking the firm with the business environment.

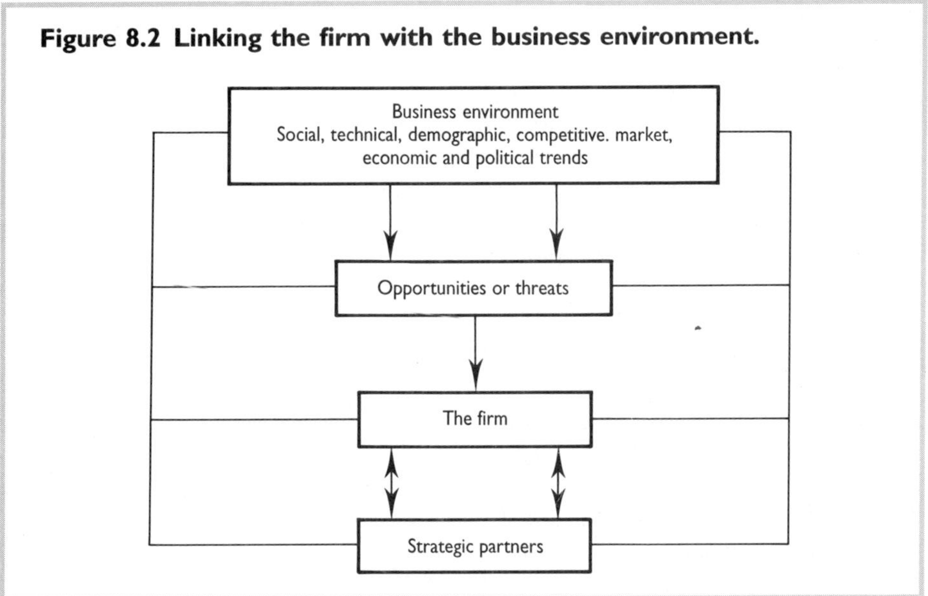

Figure 8.3 Linking manufacturing and marketing to benchmark against competitors.

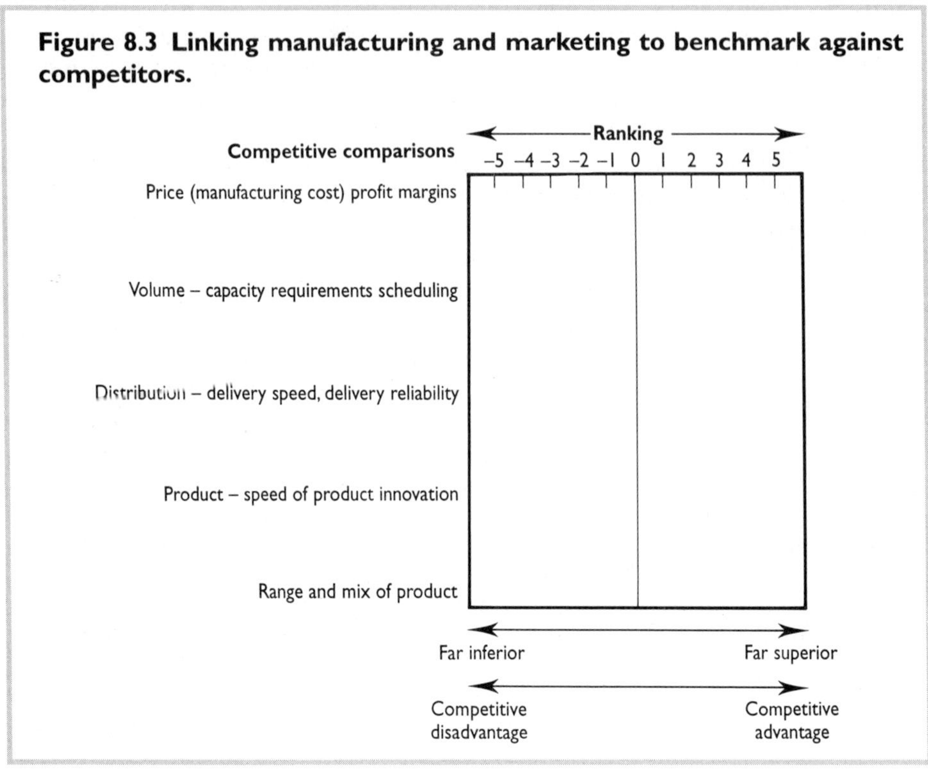

important, therefore, that the firm undertakes *global* benchmarking. In addition to this global scan, a firm might benchmark against unrelated industries. For example, the after-sales service of a manufacturing firm might be best benchmarked against a service organization in an unrelated industry. Clearly, benchmarking ties in with the pursuit of TQM to continuously improve all areas of the business by learning from best practice.

8.5 Describing the current manufacturing era

As we have seen in previous chapters, there have been two major phases of manufacturing in the past. The first major phase can be called craft manufacturing and the second phase falls under the heading of mass-production. The problem for many manufacturing firms is that they remain stuck in the mass approach to manufacturing, when much more flexible and customer-focused systems have to be in place in the 1990s. The difficulties that many firms have in adjusting to this current era is described by Dertouzos *et al.* (1989):

> But the roots of the problem go still deeper. A system of production and an accompanying market strategy were developed by the American industry in the 1920s and perfected over the next forty years. The American success was built on a few simple axioms. The American consumer wanted variety as long as it did not cost very much. Labor was a commodity to be hired and fired as demand rose and fell. Designs were to last for years. Suppliers were treated in much the same way as the workforce; they were both marginal elements of the production system, utilized in boom periods and jettisoned during the troughs. (p. 19)

Clearly, the above approach cannot be appropriate for the current era. We have moved on from the mass era and there is a search for a new paradigm, an umbrella heading which best describes the current era. A number of suggestions have been made, all of which are valid to some degree. For example, the term 'Flexible Specialisation' was offered by Piore and Sabel (1984); the phrase 'Mass Customisation' was put forward by Pine *et al.* (1993); Bessant (1991) speaks in terms of the 'Fifth Wave' of manufacturing, referring to the massive current 'wave' of business, which is linked to technology. Bessant's phrase is useful and insightful; there have been four major industrial 'waves':

1. Before 1830, which was an era of early industrialization.
2. Advances in steam power and railway systems between 1830 and 1880.
3. The era of heavy engineering between 1880 and 1940.
4. The era of mass-production.

Each of these waves overlapped to some degree at least with the next wave and were supported by a number of major innovations. These innovations are not limited to new products, but include new ways of organizing, new process developments, new types of markets and new materials usage. The problem is in trying to tag the present era of remarkable turbulence and change where current innovation, in terms of reorganization, new processes, new products and new materials, takes place constantly and simultaneously. The manufacturing firm has to equip itself to deal with this remarkable rate of change and clearly the term mass-production is not appropriate. The major differences between the mass-production system and the current era of strategic manufacturing are illustrated in Table 8.3.

8.6 World-class manufacturing

Schonberger (1986) talks in terms of 'World Class' manufacturing. This is a term which is easily understood and recognized. It has implications of being 'the best in the world' in terms of production/operations capability. Indeed as Hayes and Pisano (1994) rightly state:

> How can a company expect to achieve any sort of competitive advantage if its only goal is to be 'as good as' its toughest competitors? (p. 77)

In other words, competitive advantage is gained only by being better than

Table 8.3 Contrasting mass and strategic manufacturing

Mass	*Strategic*
Long product lifecycles, measured in years	Short product lifecycles, measured in months
Fixed, inflexible production	Flexible, customer-specific production
Stable, known demand	Unstable, erratic demand which is met by manufacturing capability
Long production runs	Short production runs
Build to stock	Build only to customer order
Short-term management decisions	Strategic management decisions, designed to provide competitive advantage and customer satisfaction simultaneously
Little variety; high volume	Any variety, any volume as required by customers
Firm operates in isolation	Strategic alliances formed to enhance the firm's strategic capability
Emphasis on cost-cutting	Emphasis on cost, delivery, flexibility, quality, design and capability all simultaneously
Unskilled workers	Multi-skilled, highly trained workers
Poor buyer–supplier relationships	Strategic partnerships

competitors. In an era of globalization with major players from all over the world, the term 'world class' is appropriate. It implies the ability of being able to compete in these globally competitive markets. This provides both opportunities and threats. The threat comes via the new entrants which have attacked many markets since the 1970s. The car industry with the attack from the Japanese in particular and more recently the important entrance of the Koreans provides ample evidence of this global competitive threat:

> In an industry where American production used to dwarf that of the rest of the world, Americans now stand third. Europe both buys and builds more cars than America, and Japan builds more. Korean and Japanese imports dominate the low end of the market, and European imports dominate the high end. (Dertouzos *et al.*, 1989, p. 18)

8.6.1 Failing to attain world-class performance

Despite the rhetoric of becoming lean, strategic or world-class, the sad fact remains that many Western firms seem incapable of competing successfully against Japanese players. Two reports confirmed this in 1994:

1. *The 1994 World-wide Manufacturing Competitiveness Study*

The results of a world-wide manufacturing competitiveness study were published by Professor Dan Jones, one of the authors of *The Machine That Changed The World*, and Andersen Consulting. The 1994 findings were based on manufacturing performance and management practices of seventy-one motor components plants in nine countries: France, Germany, Italy, Japan, Mexico, Spain, United Kingdom, United States and Canada.

The study covered production of seats, exhausts and brakes, chosen because they require a variety of process technologies. The researchers consistently found a 2:1 difference in productivity performance between world-class and non-world-class plants. The quality gap was found to be even higher at 9:1 in seats, 16:1 in brakes and 170:1 in exhausts.

Performance was measured by two main criteria: productivity, in terms of annual units of output divided by labour hours; and quality in terms of defects per million parts. Financial measures were not used. Thirteen plants located in Japan, France, Spain and the United States, did achieve both high productivity and high process quality levels, Japan was the best country in terms of productivity, with the United Kingdom well behind. Perhaps surprising to some was that German plants also struggled in terms of productivity, essentially caused by high labour costs and low labour productivity. Japan had a 30 per cent advantage over its nearest rival in quality, the United States, and bigger margins of performance were scored over other countries. The report compared findings of the 1992 and 1994 surveys. The United Kingdom made significant improvements since 1992, but less so than Japan, which suggests that the gap between Japanese and UK manufacturing capability is continuing to widen.

2. *The IBM–London Business School Study*

An IBM–London Business School study, cited in the *Financial Times* (6 December 1994) found that only one in fifty manufacturing sites in four European countries was 'world class', although three-quarters believed they could compete with the best of their international rivals. The report concluded the following:

- Most multinationals are far less globally minded than they think they are.
- They are also much less customer-focused and organizationally flexible than is necessary to win in global markets.
- Many of their attempts to create change were hindered by a trust gap between leaders and employees.

The above studies confirm once again how far behind many firms are in comparison to Japanese performance. Clearly, a complete rethink must take place in many US and European firms if they are to compete in this world-class competitive era.

8.7 Is lean manufacturing sufficient?

8.7.1 Lean manufacturing

One of the most popular terms used to describe the current era is that of lean manufacturing. This developed from the book *The Machine That Changed the World*, published in 1990. The claims of Womack *et al.* are both bold and clear. Ultimately, they claim, the 'lean' message will spread to all manufacturing:

> the adoption of lean production, as it inevitably spreads beyond the auto industry, will change everything in almost every industry choices for consumers, the nature of work, the fortune of companies, and, ultimately, the fate of nations. (Womack *et al.*, 1990, p. 12)

The characteristics of lean production are shown in Table 8.4.

Much of Table 8.4 will seem familiar to those who understand key areas such as TQM, just-in time and so on. Lean production attempts to combine all of these key areas under one heading. The essence of lean is that every form of waste should be eliminated. This waste includes all operations that do not add value. This had been stated by Schonberger (1986) and others before the publication of the lean thesis. However, it is the evidence in *The Machine That Changed the World* that makes it very powerful and convincing. The authors found that there was typically a 2:1 ratio between lean and non-lean producers. For example, lean producers would use half the time that it took to develop a new model, compared to non-lean firms, and the 2:1 ratio meant that in the best lean plants productivity was twice that of non-lean plants. Clearly, much of the content of *The Machine That Changed the World* makes sense and is compelling reading. If firms improve their manufacturing performance by reading it, then this will certainly push the firm in the right direction. There are problems with the lean thesis though, which are discussed in the next section.

Table 8.4 Characteristics of lean production

- Integrated production, with low inventories throughout, using just-in-time management
- Emphasis on prevention, rather than detection in quality
- Production is pulled in response to customers, rather than pushed to suit machine loading or other in-house ideas of scheduling
- Work is organized in teams, using multiskilled workforce problem solving to eliminate all non-added value
- Close vertical relationships, integrating the complete supply chain from raw material to customer

Adapted from Womack *et al.* (1990)

8.7.2 Problems with lean manufacturing

As we saw in the last section the term 'lean' refers to the need to reduce waste in any form in order to provide better levels of process quality and to be more productive. Any world-class strategic manufacturing firm will seek to attack waste in all forms. This will form a central part of its commitment to continuous improvement. Being lean in terms of manufacturing processes is necessary in many ways, but may not be sufficient. The operational capability of Japanese plants owes everything to a completely different strategically minded approach which is alien to many Western plants. This strategic emphasis is not fully explored in *The Machine That Changed the World*. The main problems of the lean manufacturing approach include the following:

1. **The role of the manufacturing function**. The explicit role of the manufacturing function is largely ignored in terms of its contribution (at any stage) to corporate planning. In Japanese plants this role is both central and explicit.
2. **Manufacturing strategy**. There is no mention of an explicit manufacturing strategy which might feed into corporate planning and strategy. Indeed the term manufacturing strategy is noticeable by its absence. A manufacturing strategy which feeds into and forms an essential part of Japanese firms' corporate strategy is a major feature of Japanese business practice.
3. **Seniority of production/operations staff**. Whilst the authors state that manufacturing capability is a key element to success in the car industry, the authors have homed in on the *operational* specifics without addressing the link between this operational performance and production/operations' involvement at senior levels within the firm. It is implied on occasions, but is not seen as one of the cornerstones for current manufacturing. The authors believe that the lean approach is an applicable recipe to Western firms and that this recipe is not confined to the car industry. However, the authors do not state that duplicating Japanese and to some extent best German practice depends, to some degree, on having senior production/operations staff at board level who help set the agenda for both internal and external factors such as:
   (a) the nature, scope and extent of horizontal strategic alliances.
   (b) strategic partnerships with suppliers
   (c) commitment to training
   (d) ongoing, lifetime commitment to quality
   (e) investment in process technology.
4. **Horizontal alliances**. The major role that horizontal partnerships must play in manufacturing firms, particularly in view of ongoing globalization in the 1990s, is not an explicit feature of lean production. The authors do discuss the importance of vertical relationships as a means of achieving lean supply, but do not discuss the vital importance of horizontal partnerships in lean production. This, therefore, omits a major feature of current and future challenges to

manufacturing firms, that of strategic partnerships with other firms in similar, or related, industries. This is a telling omission and gels with the mentality of some manufacturers who see themselves as lean and, therefore successful although these firms have failed to form strategic partnership agreements. Such partnerships will increasingly play a vital part in the future of manufacturing. On this point it is important to remember that Rover would claim to be lean if the criterion for being so is that contained in *The Machine That Changed the World*. Rover would argue that:

(a) their supplier base is a fraction of what it was
(b) new product development now matches the Japanese in terms of the amount of people used
(c) cross-functional teams are involved in concurrent engineering to speed new product developments
(d) the time to new product launch matches the Japanese (thirty-six months)
(e) just-in-time systems are now fully in place.

However, the strategic future of Rover will be decided by its owner, BMW. Rover's leanness will count for nothing if, for whatever reason, BMW decides to manufacture from Germany in the future. The operational characteristics of lean production are necessary to compete in the 1990s and are a vast improvement on how Rover used to perform. However, these improvements came about only because of the strategic alliance with Honda; these operational measurements were achieved only as a result of Rover's strategic horizontal alliance.

5. **The lack of strategic emphasis**. The major difference between Western firms, some of which are now lean and Japanese firms is that an integral feature of Japanese mentality is the ability to think strategically. That is not to say that operational factors are secondary, but that these operational factors and capabilities seem to naturally follow on from a mind-set which sees long-term strategy, including horizontal strategic partnerships, as central. In doing so, Japanese firms seem to learn faster and also respond to occasional failure more easily. In addition, response to opportunities becomes more rapid, even if the original strategic plan may have been modified. We saw in Chapter 1 how Honda was able to succeed even if, as some claim, this had not been the direct result of deliberate planning.
6. **The emphasis on cost**. It may be argued (in defence of the lean thesis) that the actual term lean has simply been misunderstood by companies themselves who have used lean alongside another current business term 'business process re-engineering', which also seems to have been misunderstood, as a justification for slashing costs, particularly in areas directly related to manufacturing. General Motors, for example, believes that it has become leaner by virtue of its attack on its suppliers since 1993, when its then Director of Purchasing, Lopez, was still in post. In fact, Lopez used the term lean to describe his approach to suppliers. Although cost is undoubtedly a major competitive factor in many

> market segments, it stands alongside other, equally important, major factors such as delivery speed, delivery reliability, flexibility and rapid product innovation, which are not necessarily served by reducing costs. It will be interesting to see if GM's slashing of suppliers' costs will adversely affect their ability to involve suppliers strategically in areas such as new product development and other process improvements. GM's short-termism (resulting in a return to short-term profits) may well be offset in the long-term.

In defence of the authors, it may be argued that the term lean has been distorted by some firms as a quick-fix solution and, even more alarmingly, as licence to dramatically downsize to demonstrate a firm's leanness. In doing so, some firms are becoming more anorexic than lean. By downsizing to such a degree in their efforts to become lean, firms could lose the greatest potential asset for change and innovation: the human factor. The amount of downsizing has been dramatic in the 1990s and, in some cases, the staff who are left within the manufacturing firm are demoralized. Admittedly, in the past, giant US corporations were hugely overstaffed and this had massive detrimental effects upon the firms' ability to innovate, especially in new product development; Carroll's (1993) discussion on IBM is full of insight here.

However, it is not the need to downsize which is the most critical factor here; the attitude toward production/operations staff is the most telling factor. A valuable control case here is Nissan UK, which despite some difficulties in the 1990s did not force staff to leave and instead spent even greater amounts of money on training and equipping production/operations staff to be able to compete even better for the future. Downsizing occurred at Nissan only in terms of not replacing staff who had retired or who had decided to leave. Another case would be Honda in the United States, which similarly invested heavily in production/operations staff in order to equip them for the ongoing rapid changes in the car industry. No downsizing took place in Honda's US plants.

8.7.3 Lean supply

Although the above section was critical of the sufficiency of the lean production concept, the term lean supply seems to be wholly appropriate, if by that it is meant that many firms are:

1. Drastically reducing the supply base to fewer, better, suppliers.
2. Forming strategic alliances, or buyer–supplier relationships within the supply chain where the nature of the alliance is long term and both parties benefit, not necessarily in equal measure.
3. Suppliers form tiers (similar to those in Japan), whose role will include research and development and involvement at early stages with new product development and innovation.

Figure 8.4 From lean to strategic manufacturing.

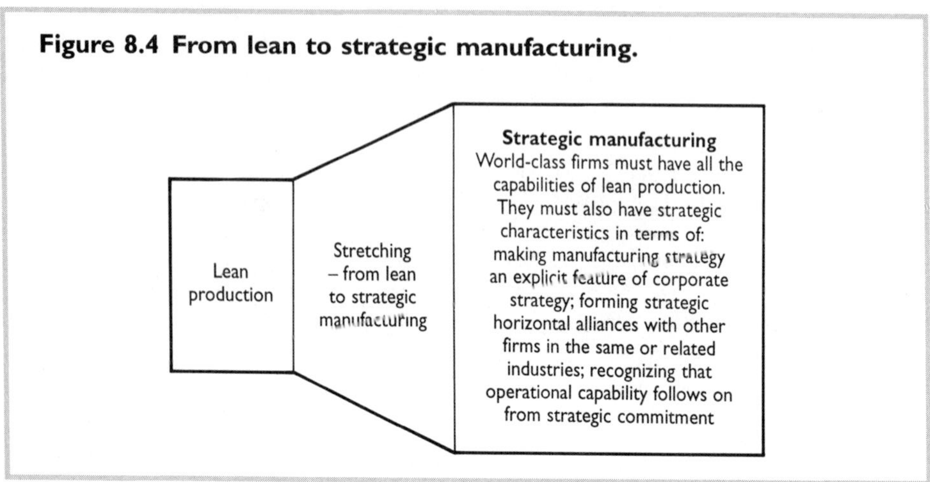

8.7.4 Stretching lean to strategic manufacturing

As stated earlier, the operational characteristics of lean production are valid and any firm would do well to emulate them, but such characteristics must be placed in a strategic setting. In a sense, strategic manufacturing will incorporate the process capability found in lean production. In essence, the concept of lean must be stretched to be included in a wider framework of strategic manufacturing, as shown in Figure 8.4.

8.8 Defining strategic manufacturing

Throughout the book the term strategic manufacturing has been used. The reasons for this include the following:

1. Strategic means having a long-term view of the business rather than the quick-fix mentality which has clearly pervaded in much of Western manufacturing. There is no coincidence that this short-term approach has served to erode much of the manufacturing base of many countries in the West, with Britain being a noticeable example.

2. The term strategic is also used in the military sense, as we saw in Chapter 1. This means that the firm has to be fully aware of all market opportunities and plan strategies which will out-perform their competitors. The successful firm will then target those market segments in which it can compete and at the same time, deliberately avoid those market segments in which it cannot. Part of the strategic planning process is in deciding both where and where *not* to attack in a particular segment.

3. Strategic also means that the firm will support itself via partnerships with other firms. Such partnerships can either be horizontal, especially in joint ventures for developing new technology or vertical, forming strategic partnerships with other firms in the supply chain.

The essential ingredient of strategic manufacturing is that the firm will see its production/operations capability as a core competence. It will not see manufacturing as simply one of a number of businesses within the firm's overall portfolio, ready to be sold off at the earliest opportunity. This distinction is one of the main differences between some Western firms and their Japanese competitors. We saw earlier how Rover had been sold off to a competitor and how Apricot Computer's hardware division had been sold off to Mitsubishi. The Apricot example is difficult to reconcile with a firm claiming to have a strategic commitment to manufacturing.

8.8.1 Characteristics of strategic manufacturing

In addition to ideas associated with the term strategy explored above, the phrase strategic manufacturing means that the firm has to be world-class in all that it does. This criterion refers to all of the specific areas covered in the text. A quick resumé is appropriate here:

1. *Corporate strategy.* Strategic plans are distinct from tactical plans in two ways; first, by the seniority of those persons involved in corporate planning; second, by the time horizons, which are longer than those under tactical decisions. All decisions made at this level should be aimed at providing the firm with sustainable competitive advantage. A glaring omission in many Western firms is the absence of senior manufacturing/technology personnel who might be involved in shaping the corporate vision of the firm.

2. *Manufacturing strategy.* It was noted that manufacturing strategy in many Western firms is often a reaction to corporate plans which have already been decided. This means that manufacturing strategy is very often reactive, rather than proactive. However, we need only look at the content of manufacturing strategy to realize that it should form a central part of corporate strategy in the firm. Decisions will include investment in technology, expanding into new plants and adding capacity, strategic buyer/supplier relationships, the extent of joint ventures with other firms, the extent of vertical integration, and so on.

3. *Product innovations.* Speed of new product introduction is another key requirement for the strategic manufacturing firm. In essence, the major shift has come from the change in the traditional function-to-function approach to a more integrated approach in developing new products. New product development is often enhanced by the involvement of strategic partners whose input is encouraged from early stages of product development.

4. *Process technology*. We saw in Chapter 4 that many Western firms have invested in technology only as a means to reducing the cost of labour. In other words, the investment has been seen as yet another quick-fix solution to a business world which is more complex and dynamic than ever before. The strategic manufacturer invests in technology as a means of enhancing the firm's competitive performance, not to downsize the workforce. Investment in key technologies like flexible manufacturing systems is a strategic commitment and the conviction for doing so must go beyond short-term financial considerations.

5. *Quality*. Quality has been one of the major competitive weapons of Japanese firms and this has been particularly evident in the car industry. The danger for firms is that they might see quality as a management fad rather than a way of life. The firm has to be committed to continuous improvement in all that it does. For the strategic manufacturing firm, this means improving in areas in which it already excels. A non-strategic manufacturing firm would give up on quality as soon as it achieves recognition in the form of ISO ratings or British Standard Certification or some other award. The strategic manufacturing firm knows that customers ultimately decide whether the firm's product is a quality offering. The strategic manufacturing firm will be on a never-ending pursuit in all areas of the business in order to satisfy customers.

6. *Materials management*. Strategic manufacturing firms are those who form strong buyer/supplier relationships with chosen partners. As we saw in Chapter 6, some Western firms attempted to form such partnerships, only to weaken the relationship as soon as short-term financial pressure came to bear on them. Such firms will undoubtedly pay the price for a short-term approach in comparison to strategic manufacturers, which will enjoy competitive advantage in the long term. This advantage will come about by improved delivery performance from their suppliers, together with many ideas from them for process and product improvements. For the strategic manufacturing firms just-in-time is central to their materials management process. This will be supported by other approaches such as MRPII. Materials management is not simply about knowing tactical equations such as the EOQ formula. Rather, strategic materials management recognizes the enormous importance of materials in terms of cost, delivery speed, delivery reliability and other competitive factors.

7. *Human resources*. In many Western firms, downsizing the workforce has become an obsession. Some firms have justified this under the title of 'Re-engineering'. However, what this reveals more than anything else is a return to the view of human resources as a cost rather than any major input to improving the firm's competitive position. Ideas for innovations, new products, improvement of processes and so on can only come from human imagination, passion and commitment to improve the business, not from machines. However, the amount of downsizing in many firms is alarming and one of the major problems is in how

to motivate those staff who remain in the firm. Another challenge for manufacturing firms is in maintaining strategic partnerships or alliances with other firms. This again is a human factor, which demands a strategic vision coupled with passion and commitment to ensure that the alliance will bring rewards for both parties.

8.8.2 Examples of strategic manufacturing

The strategic manufacturing firms are those who look to the future and invest in it. Examples of firms doing so include the following:

1. **Compaq** Compaq has invested $90 million in order to double its capacity at its Singapore manufacturing plant. This added capacity forms part of the plan to be the world's leading PC manufacturer. A further $11 million was injected into its manufacturing plant in Scotland to enhance the manufacturing capabilities there.
2. **Dell** Dell Computers doubled the size of its manufacturing plant in Ireland as part of its long-term strategic positioning in Europe.
3. **Nissan** Nissan expanded its capacity in its Tennessee plant by 1.7 million square feet in order to allow a further 200,000 vehicles to be manufactured there.
4. **BMW** In addition to its acquisition of Rover, in order to strengthen its European presence, BMW announced that it would create a $400 million factory aimed at making 30,000 vehicles in 1995, rising to over 70,000 by the year 2000.

The above examples clearly show the strategic intents of those companies which see their manufacturing capability as one of the core areas of their business. Although they come from different industries, the common link is clear: a strategic commitment to competing in their chosen markets.

8.8.3 Strategic manufacturing in the Japanese transplants in the UK

Some of the most striking examples of strategic manufacturing come, not surprisingly, from Japanese companies, in particular with the investment in their transplants. In the United Kingdom, Toyota, Nissan and Honda between them will account for one-third of the UK's annual car production by the year 2000, by which time they will have spent a total of £2.2 billion on their UK facilities and will be employing 10,000 people. Nissan is already committed to 300,000 vehicles in production and this capacity could reach 400,000 by the end of the decade. Honda has committed to 150,000 cars by the late 1990s, but this could rise to 200,000. Toyota has already reached its phase-one production rate of 100,000 cars a year of just one car, the Carina, and will be producing 200,000 cars or more in its UK plant by the end of the decade.

Nissan, which won the Queen's Award for Exports for three years in succession, emerged as the leading UK car exporter in 1993, ahead of the Rover Group,

Ford and Vauxhall. The Japanese transplants accounted for three of the top six places as UK car exporters. 74 per cent of Sunderland's output was exported.

Honda announced plans to increase the capacity of its Swindon plant by 50 per cent to 150,000 a year by the late 1990s. This will raise direct employment by 500 to 2,500 and lift Honda's total investment in the Swindon facilities to £700 million.

Clearly, the above examples are those where future manufacturing capacity has been envisaged and where a manufacturing strategy is in place to ensure that the vision is implemented. The problem for many firms is that no such manufacturing strategy exists. We therefore need to see how manufacturing strategy helps the firm to become strategic.

8.9 Becoming strategic: linking corporate, marketing and manufacturing strategies

The implications of having an explicit manufacturing strategy go way beyond rhetoric, in terms of greater communication, involvement, motivation and willingness to change from those who are already involved in the process of corporate planning. For example, in research undertaken by the author, in over sixty manufacturing plants in the United Kingdom and United States, the following factors emerged:

- Where manufacturing personnel are involved in the strategy process, performance in manufacturing is greatly enhanced, particularly in product innovation.
- Where manufacturing personnel are involved in helping to form strategy, the transfer to plant level is greatly facilitated.
- Where manufacturing play a vital role in shaping corporate strategy, organizational learning is enhanced.

These are clearly important considerations, which seem obvious to Japanese manufacturers but remain a major stumbling block to many Western firms. If the firm wants to change, it must understand its current position in terms of how it formulates strategy. Key questions for those involved in corporate strategic planning are provided in Table 8.5.

The details in Table 8.5 provide a general overview of the corporate planning process. We then need to understand the content of the current marketing strategy. Key questions for this are given in Table 8.6.

At the same time, there has to be an analysis of the content and scope of the current manufacturing strategy within the firm, as shown in Table 8.7.

Some of the questions in the check list for manufacturing strategy deliberately replicate those contained within the list in corporate strategy (Table 8.5). This will then test the consistency highlighting the differences between the two. These tables are not meant to be exhaustive, merely indicative of the sort of questions

Table 8. 5 Key questions in determining current corporate strategy

- Does an explicit corporate plan currently exist?
- If so, what is the time period envisaged in the corporate plan?
- Which functions are involved in the strategic planning process?
- What is the seniority of persons involved in devising the plan?
- Is the planning group a permanent group or does a more fluid, ad hoc, basis exist?
- To what extent are manufacturing involved? – this would range from no involvement at all to a leader role – leading and defining the business plan
- How is the corporate plan communicated to others?
- Is there a mission statement and, if so, is it for internal, external or both internal and external purposes?
- Are the following areas part of the corporate plans ?

Vertical integration decisions	Yes	No
Make or buy decisions	Yes	No
Adding to existing plant capacity	Yes	No
New facilities – location decisions	Yes	No
Increasing volumes of existing products	Yes	No
Adding totally new products to existing markets	Yes	No
Entering totally new product markets	Yes	No
New process technology	Yes	No

Table 8. 6 Key questions in marketing planning and strategy

- How many businesses compete against the firm/division?
- What is the percentage of sales revenue gained from products launched in the last 5 years?
- What is the percentage of products envisaged from sales in 5 years' time?
- What is the ranking of perceived competitive factors for the firm? (e.g. price, delivery speed, delivery reliability, product quality, regular and rapid product innovation)
- What is the product life of the firm's product offerings?
- Which of the following categories best describes the products?
  - Low volume/low variety
  - Low volume/high variety
  - Multiple products/high variety
  - High volume/low variety
  - High volume/high variety and product change

Table 8.7 Understanding the firm's current manufacturing strategy

- Does the firm have an explicit manufacturing strategy?
- If YES how long are the time horizons in the strategy?
- How often is the manufacturing strategy reviewed?
- To what extent are production/operations involved in new product development?

Original concept	Always/sometimes/never
Initial design	Always/sometimes/never
Screening	Always/sometimes/never
Business analysis	Always/sometimes/never

- Are the following areas part of the manufacturing strategy?

Vertical integration decisions	Yes	No
Make or buy decisions	Yes	No
Adding to existing plant capacity	Yes	No
New facilities – location decisions	Yes	No
Increasing volumes of existing products	Yes	No
Adding totally new products to existing markets	Yes	No
Entering totally new product markets	Yes	No
New process technology	Yes	No

Is production/operations aware of the firm's marketing strategy? Yes/No
If Yes, do production/operations performance support the firm in the following:

Process choice	Yes	No
Manufacturing systems	Yes	No
Materials management	Yes	No
Quality capability	Yes	No
Manufacturing lead times	Yes	No
Cost	Yes	No
Delivery speed	Yes	No
Delivery reliability	Yes	No

that might be asked. For the would-be world-class manufacturing firm, those questions should provide insight into the following:

- How a firm currently plans its corporate strategy.
- If a firm *has* an explicit manufacturing strategy.
- If the firm does have a manufacturing strategy, how central this is in developing corporate strategy (reactive or proactive).
- If similar time-frames exist between manufacturing and corporate strategies.
- Determining the current position of manufacturing within the firm and, more directly, why manufacturing might be relegated to a functional role, even though the firm is in the business of manufacturing, as opposed to the business of providing services.

Figure 8.5 Integrating marketing and manufacturing strategies.

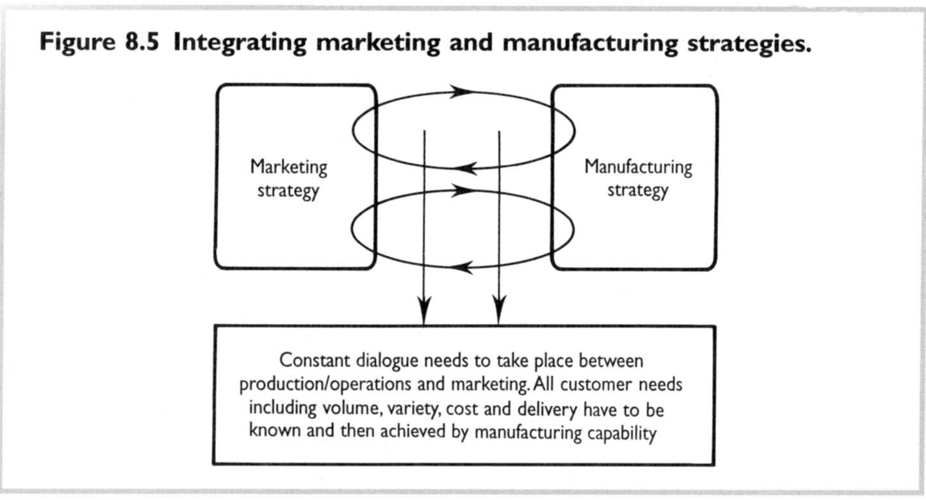

- How the link between manufacturing and corporate strategies helps to define relationships with other strategic partners, both in terms of horizontal alliances and vertical, buyer–supplier relationships.
- How manufacturing presence at senior levels of the firm helps in the transfer of the strategy process to plant level.

The corporate, marketing and manufacturing strategies should link and complement each other. Having senior production/operations staff at corporate level will help to ensure that this takes place. Manufacturing strategy must be constantly reviewed as new information comes to light. In particular, regular feedback from customers should be sought in order to improve performance; the world-class firm seeks continuously to improve all areas of its business and, clearly, customer feedback is a vital input to this. Once this feedback and other pertinent data – details of competitors, new technology and so on – come to light, there must be constant dialogue between marketing and production/operations, as illustrated in Figure 8.5.

Conclusions

This book has emphasized the strategic importance of key areas of production/ operations management for the firm: product management, process choice and technological investment, quality, materials management and human resources. This strategic emphasis is often lacking in many firms. The present era is one of market turbulence and change, for which many firms are not prepared. It is argued that lean production is perhaps a feature of manufacturing practice on the

Figure 8.6 A transformation process model for strategic planning in manufacturing companies.

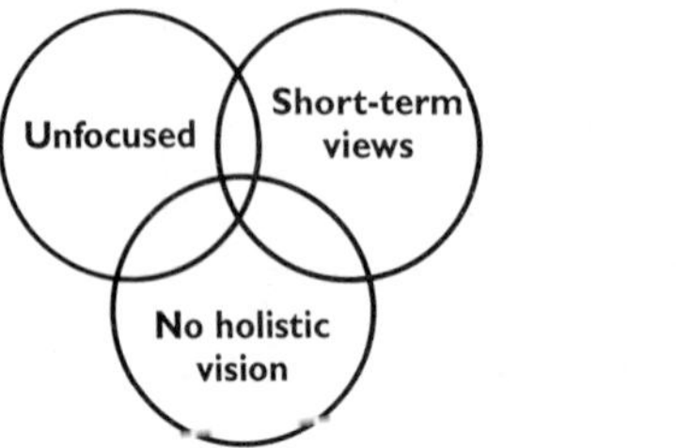

From this... The Traditional Model **To this... The Enlightened Approach**

The transformation process will not be an easy one for many firms, driven by short-term mentality and financial criteria only. First, the firm must clearly decide on its core business and markets (focus). This focus is developed in-house so that plants are in turn, focused (and flexible) at the same time. It must then have a strategic commitment to competing in these markets, rather than having a short-term view. Resources must be allocated and reinvestment in plant and new technology must take place. The firm must have a holistic view which takes on board the other stakeholders in the business – especially suppliers, employees and strategic partnerships

operational level, but that a strategic view must also be in place for the firm. This demands a commitment to manufacturing investment and human resource development in the plant, together with long-term strategic partnerships with other organizations. It has also been argued throughout the book that the role of production/operations is a key issue in understanding how a firm will shape its strategy. Traditionally, the role has tended to be excluded from the corporate debate. In other words, although the firm will fall under the heading of manufacturing, as opposed to service industry, the decisions at senior level will be made by those outside the manufacturing personnel of the firm. This can distort the strategic approach and vision of the firm and there has to be a change from the traditional to an enlightened approach to manufacturing strategy, as shown in Figure 8.6.

In many firms, manufacturing is placed in a purely reactive and functional role to react and implement corporate decisions already made without production/operations' input and influence. There has to be a change of organizational structure if an enlightened approach is to take place in the firm as in Figure 8.7.

Changing this approach is perhaps the biggest challenge for many manufacturing firms. It is clear from the decline in performance of many Western manu-

Figure 8.7 Transforming the organizational approach to strategic planning.

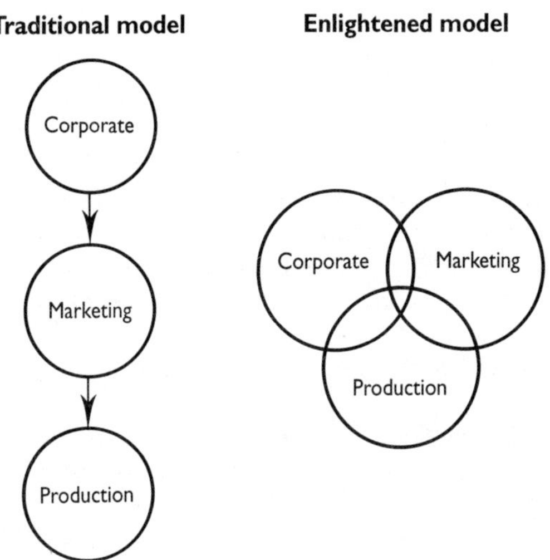

The transformation process from the traditional model of corporate planning to the enlightened model will undoubtedly pose problems and challenges for manufacturing firms. Firms are used to the traditional sequential, hierarchical approach – from corporate to marketing to production personnel. However, this enlightened approach is common to Japanese and other world-class strategic manufacturing firms. Having senior production personnel in place is not enough – these managers need to have good understanding of markets and sound business acumen if the enlightened approach is to be successful

facturing firms that a massive change has to take place in terms of both philosophy and practice. The outcome of this challenge may yet determine the future prosperity of entire nations.

Bibliography

Abernathy, W. (1978) *The Productivity Dilemma: Roadblock to Innovation in the Automobile Industry*, Johns Hopkins University Press, Baltimore, MD.

Adair, J. (1973) *Effective Leadership*, Pan Books, London.

Adam, E. and Ebert, R. (1992) *Production and Operations Management*, Prentice Hall, Englewood Cliffs, NJ.

Adler, P. (1993) 'Time and Motion regained', *Harvard Business Review*, January-February.

Akao, Y. (1990) *Quality Function Deployment*, Productivity Press, Cambridge MA.

Allen, D. (1993) *Developing Successful New Products*, Pitman, London.

Anderson, J., Schroeder, R. and Cleveland, G. (1991) 'The Process of Manufacturing Strategy', *International Journal of Production and Operations Management*, Vol. 11, No. 3.

Argenti, J. (1980) *Practical Corporate Planning*, Unwin, London.

Armstrong, L. (1994) 'New From Nissan: Reverse Sticker Shock', *Business Week*, May 23, p.27.

Australian Manufacturing Council (1990), *The Global Challenge*, AMC, Melbourne.

Barlett, D. and Steele, J. (1992) *America: What Went Wrong?*, Andrews and McMeel, Kansas City, KA.

Bateman, T. and Zeithaml, C. (1993) *Management: Function and Strategy*, Irwin, Boston, MA.

Beamish, P. (1985) 'The Characteristics of Joint Ventures in Developed and Developing Countries', *Columbia Journal of World Business*, Vol. 20, Fall, pp.13–19.

Beatty, C. and Gordon, J. (1991) 'Preaching the Gospel: The Evangelists of New Technology', *California Management Review*, Spring.

Bertodo, R. (1991) 'The Role of Suppliers in Implementing a Strategic Vision' *Long Range Planning*, Vol. 24, No. 3, pp.40–48.

Bessant, J. (1989) 'Flexible Manufacturing; Yesterday, Today, Tomorrow' *in* Bolk, H., Forster, H., and Haywood, W. (eds) *Proceedings of the International Conference on Implementing Flexible Manufacturing*, Amsterdam, 25–27 January.

Bessant, J. (1991) *Managing Advanced Manufacturing Technology*, Blackwell, Oxford.

Bessant, J. (1993) 'The Lessons of Failure: Learning to Manage New Manufacturing Technology', *International Journal of Technology Management*, Special Issue on Manufacturing Technology, Vol. 8, Nos 2/3/4, pp.197–215.

Bignell, V. (ed.), (1985) *Manufacturing Systems*, Blackwell, Oxford.

Blake, R. and Mouton, J. (1985) *The Managerial Grid*, Gulf, Boston, MA.

Boling, D. (1990) 'Bringing It All Together: A Look Inside the 486 Chip', *PC magazine*, Nov. 13, pp.463–64.

Bolwijn, P. and Kumpe, T. (1990) 'Toward the Factory of the Future' *in Revitalizing Manufacturing*, Klein, J. A. (ed.) Irwin, Boston, MA.

Bolwijn, P. and Kumpe, T. (1991) 'The Success of Flexible, Low-Cost, Quality Competitors', *European Management Journal*, Vol. 9, No. 2, June.

Booz, Allen & Hamilton (1982) *New Products Management for the 1980s*, company publication, Booz, Allen & Hamilton, Los Angeles, CA.

Bradshaw, D. (1989) 'A Step Nearer the Design Miracle', *Financial Times*, 19 September, p.3.

British Standard 3138 (1979), British Standards Institution.

Brown, S. (1994) 'TQM and Work Study: Partners in Excellence', *Production and Inventory Management Journal*, Vol. 35, No. 3, pp.34–49.

Burbridge, J. (1964) 'The Case Against the Economic Batch Quantity', *The Manager*

Burn, G. (1990) 'Quality Function Deployment' *in Managing Quality*, Dale, B. and Plunkett, J. (eds), Philip Allan, Hemel Hempstead.

Burt, D. (1989) 'Managing Suppliers up to Speed', *Harvard Business Review*, July-August, pp.127–135.

Business Week, 8 June 1987, p.131.

Business Week, 22 October 1990, pp.84–96.

Business Week, 22 June 1992, p.7.

Business Week, 20 December 1993, p.67.

Business Week, 24 January 1994, p.37, p.88.

Business Week, 28 March 1994.

Business Week, 9 May 1994, p.29, 61.

Business Week, 25 July 1994, p.71.

Business Week, 8 August 1994, p.26; p.54.

Business Week, 3 October 1994, p.66.

Carlisle, J. and Parker, L. (1991) *Beyond Negotiation*, Wiley, Chichester.

Carroll, P. (1993) *Big Blues: The Unmaking of IBM*, Crown, New York.

Chakravarthy, B. and Lorange P. (1991) *Managing the Strategy Process*, Prentice Hall, Englewood Cliffs, NJ.

Chandler, A. (1962) *Strategy and Structure: Chapters in the History of the American Industrial Enterprise*, Irwin, Boston, MA.

Chandler, A. (1992) 'Corporate Strategy, Structure and Control Methods in the United States During the 20th Century', *Industrial and Corporate Change*, Vol. 1, No. 2, pp.263–284.

Ciampa, D. (1992) *Total Quality*, Addison-Wesley, Reading, MA.

Cohen, S. and Zysmann, J. (1987) *Manufacturing Matters*, Basic Books, Inc., New York.

Cordero, R. (1991) 'Managing Speed to Avoid Product Obsolescence: A Survey of Techniques', *Journal of Product Innovation Management*, 8, pp.283–294.

Corsten, H. and Will, T. (1994) 'Simultaneously Supporting Generic Competitive Strategies by Production Management', *Technovation*, Vol. 14, No. 2, pp.111–120.

Crawford, E. (1991) *New Products Management*, Irwin, Homewood, Ill.

Crosby, P. (1979) *Quality Is Free*, McGraw Hill, New York.

Cyert, R. and March, J. (1963) *A Behavioural Theory of the Firm*, Prentice Hall, Englewood Cliffs, NJ.

Dale, B. and Plunkett, J. (eds), (1990) *Managing Quality*, Philip Allan, Hemel Hempstead.

Datta, D. (1988) 'International Joint Ventures: A Framework for Analysis', *Journal of General Management*, Winter, pp.78–90.

Davidson, H. (1987) *Offensive Marketing*, Penguin, London.

Dawson, P. (1993) 'Total Quality Management' *in New Wave Manufacturing Strategies* (1993), Storey, J. (ed.) Paul Chapman, London.

Dean, R. (1974) 'The Temporal Mismatch – Innovation's Pace vs Management's Time Horizon', *Research Management*, May, pp.12–15.

Dell Computers (1993) *Annual Company Report*, Dell Computers, in-house publication.

De Meyer, A. and Ferdows, K. (1991) 'Removing the Barriers in Manufacturing – The European Manufacturing Futures Survey', *European Management Journal*, Vol. 9, pp.22–29.

Deming, W. (1982) *Quality, Productivity and Competitive Position*, MIT Center for Advanced Engineering Study, Cambridge, MA.

Deming, W. (1986) *Out of the Crisis*, MIT Center for Advanced Engineering, Cambridge, MA.

Dertouzos, M., Lester, R. and Solow, R. (1989) *Made In America*, MIT Press, Cambridge, MA.

Devlin, G. and Bleackley, M. (1988) 'Strategic Alliances – Guidelines for Success', *Long Range Planning*, Vol. 21, No. 5, pp.18–23.

Dilworth, J. (1992) *Operations Management*, McGraw-Hill, New York.

Dodgson, M. (1993) *Technological Collaboration in Industry*, Routledge, London.

Drucker, P. (1974) *Management: Task, Responsibilities and Practices*, Harper & Row, New York.

Drucker, P. (1986) 'The Changing World Economy', *Foreign Affairs*, Spring, 1986.

Drucker, P. (1987) *Frontiers of Management*, Heinemann, London.

Dussauge, P., Hart, S. and Ramanantsoa, B. (1992) *Strategic Technology Management*, Wiley, Chichester.

Economist, December 21, 1991, p.38.

Economist, January 30, 1993, p.58.

Economist, January 4, 1992, p.61.

Economist, February 27, 1993.

Economist Manufacturing Technology Survey, 5 March 1994, p.10.

Economist, July 23, 1994.

Edmonson, H. and Wheelwright, S. (1989) *Outstanding Manufacturing in the Coming Decade*, California Management Review, Summer, 1989.

Erikson, K. and Vallas, S. (1990) *The Nature of Work*, Yale University Press, New Haven, CT.

Evans, J., Anderson, D., Sweeney, D. and Williams, T. (1990) *Applied Production and Operations Management*, West Publications, St Paul, MN.

Evered, R. (1983) 'So What is Strategy?' *Long Range Planning*, 16, No. 3, June pp.57–72.

Feigenbaum, A. (1983) *Total Quality Control*, 3rd edn. McGraw Hill, New York.

Ferdows, K., Miller. J., Nakane, J. and Vollman, T. (1986) 'Evolving Global Manufacturing Strategies' *in Operations Management in the 1990s*, Twiss, B. MCB (ed.), Oxford.

Ferry, J. (1993) *The British Renaissance*, Heinemann, London.
Financial Times, 14 May 1991, Section III, p.1.
Financial Times, 17 March 1992, Survey p.v.
Financial Times, 29 October 1992, p.9.
Financial Times, 14 May 1993, Section III, p.VI.
Financial Times, 13 June 1993, p.12.
Financial Times, 2 February 1994.
Financial Times, 7 March 1994, p.21.
Financial Times, 29 August 1994, p.4.
Financial Times, 9 September 1994, p.6.
Financial Times, 2 October 1994.
Financial Times, 4 October 1994.
Financial Times, 6 December 1994.
Financial Times, 5 April 1995.
Fogarty, D., Blackstone, J. and Hoffman, T. (1991) *Production & Inventory Management*, South-Western, Cincinnati, OH.
Fogarty, D., Hoffman, T. and Stonebraker, P. (1989) *Production and Operations Management*, South-Western, Cincinnati, OH.
Foley, P., Watts, H. and Wilson, B. (1993) 'New Technologies, Skills Shortages and Training Strategies' *in New Technology and the Firm*, Swann, P. (ed.), Routledge, London.
Forbes Industry Survey, March 29, 1993.
Ford, I.D. (1984) 'Buyer/Seller Relationships in International Industrial Markets' *Industrial Marketing Management*, Vol. 13, No. 2, pp.101–112.
Fortune, July 27, 1992, p.49.
Fortune, December 14, 1992, p.80.
Fortune, March 22, 1993 p.62.
Fortune, June 14, 1993, p.74.
Fortune, May 16, 1994, p.64.
Fortune, July 25, 1994.
Fortune, October 3, 1994, p.40.
Gaither, N. (1990) *Production and Operations Management*, Dryden, New York.
Gaither, N. (1992) *Production and Operations Management*, Dryden, New York.
Garvin, D. (1983) 'Quality on the Line', *Harvard Business Review*, Sep–Oct, pp.65–75.
Garvin, D. (1987) 'Competing on the Eight Dimensions of Quality', *Harvard Business Review*, Nov–Dec., pp.101–109.
Garvin, D. (1992) *Operations Strategy, Text and Cases*, Prentice Hall, Englewood Cliffs, NJ.
Garvin, D. (1993) 'Building a Learning Organization', *Harvard Business Review*, July–August, pp.78–91.
Gattiker, U. (1990) *Technology Management in Organizations*, Sage, New York.
General Motors Annual Company Report (1993) General Motors, in-house publication.
Giffi, C. and Roth, A. V. (1991) 'Taking Aim At World Class Manufacturing', *Annual Survey of North American Manufacturing Technology*, Deloitte & Touche, New York.
Gleave, S, and Oliver, N. (1990) 'Human Resources Management in Japanese Manufacturing Companies in the UK: 5 Case Studies', *Journal of General Management*, Vol. 16, No. 1, Autumn, pp.54–68.

Grindley, P. (1991) 'Turning Technology Into Competitive Advantage', *Business Strategy Review*, Spring, pp.35–47.
Groover, M. (1987) *Automation, Production Systems and Computer-Integrated Manufacturing*, Prentice Hall, Englewood Cliffs, NJ.
Grove, A. (1993) 'PCs Trudge out of the Valley of Death', *Wall Street Journal*, January 18, 1993, Section A, p.10.
Hamel, G. and Prahalad, C. (1994) *Competing For The Future*, Harvard Business School Press, Boston, MA.
Hamill, J. (1991) 'Strategic Restructuring Through International Acquisitions and Divestments', *Journal of General Management*, Vol. 17, No. 1, pp.27–44.
Hamilton, D. (1993) 'Chokepoints: Computer Makers Face Hidden Vulnerability: Suppliers Concentration; Many of their Crucial Parts and Materials are Made by Just a Few Factories Tracing the PCs', *Wall Street Journal*, August 27, 1993, Section A. p.1.
Handy, C. (1987) *The Making of British Managers*, NEDC Report, BIM, UK.
Harari, O. (1992) 'Imperatives for Deflating the Fat Organization', *Management Review*, Vol. 81, No. 6, June, 1992, pp.61–62.
Harrigan, R. (1986) 'Joint Ventures: Linking for a Leap Forward', *Planning Review*, July–August, pp.2–10.
Harrison, A. (1992) *Just-in-Time Manufacturing in Perspective*, Prentice Hall, Hemel Hempstead.
Harrison, M. (1990) *Advanced Manufacturing Technology Management*, Pitman, London.
Hax, A., and Majluf, N. (1991) *The Strategy Concept & Process*, Prentice Hall, Englewood Cliffs, NJ.
Hayes, R. and Jaikumar, R. (1988) 'Manufacturing's Crisis: New Technologies, Obsolete Organizations', *Harvard Business Review*, September–October, pp.77–85.
Hayes, R. and Pisano, G. (1994) 'Beyond World-Class: The New Manufacturing Strategy', *Harvard Business Review*, January–February, pp.77–86.
Hayes, R. and Wheelwright, S. (1979) 'Link Manufacturing Process and Product Life Cycles', *Harvard Business Review*, January–February.
Hayes, R. and Wheelwright, S. (1984) *Restoring Our Competitive Edge*, Wiley, New York.
Hayes, R. and Wheelwright, S. (1992) *Revolutionizing Products Development*, Free Press, New York.
Hayes, R., Wheelwright, S. and Clark, K. (1988) *Dynamic Manufacturing*, Free Press, New York.
Heizer, J. and Render, B. (1993) *Production and Operations Management*, Allyn and Bacon, Englewood Cliffs, NJ.
Hewlett Packard Quality Manual, 1990.
Hewlett Packard Executive Conference, 19 July 1993.
Hill, T. (1985) *Manufacturing Strategy*, Macmillan, Basingstoke.
Hill, T. (1989) *Manufacturing Strategy Texts and Cases*, Irwin, Homewood, Ill.
Hill, T. (1990) *Production/Operations Management*, Prentice Hall, Hemel Hempstead.
Hill, T. (1993) *Manufacturing Strategy*, 2nd edn, Macmillan, Basingstoke.
Hill, T. and Chambers, S. (1989) 'Manufacturing Strategy: Investing To Meet the Need of the Market', *Director*, May 1989, pp.101–105.

Hinterhuber, H. and Levin, B. (1994) 'Strategic Networks – The Organization of the Future', *Long Range Planning*, Vol. 27, No. 3, pp.43–53.

Hobday, M. (1989) 'Corporate Strategies in the International Semiconductor Industry' *in Technology Strategy and the Firm*, Dodgson, M. (ed.), SPRU/Longman, London.

Hofer, C. and Schendel, D. (1989) *Strategy Formulation: Analytical Concepts*, West publications St Paul, MN.

Hutchins, D. (1988) *Just in Time*, Gower, London.

Imai, M. (1986) *Kaizen: The Key to Japan's Competitive Success*, McGraw-Hill, New York.

Industry Week, May 26, 1986. p.16.

Ishikawa, K. (1985) *What is Total Quality Control: The Japanese Way*, Prentice Hall, Englewood Cliffs, NJ.

Johansson, J. and Nonaka, I. (1987) 'Market Research the Japanese Way', *Harvard Business Review*, May/June.

Johnson, G. and Scholes, K. (1988) *Exploring Corporate Strategy* 2nd edn, Prentice Hall, Hemel Hempstead.

Johnson, G. and Scholes, K. (1993) *Exploring Corporate Strategy*, 3rd edn., Prentice Hall, Hemel Hempstead.

Johnson, R., Newell, W. and Vergin, R. (1974) *Production and Operations Management: A Systems Concept*. Houghton Mifflin, Boston, MA.

Juran, J. (1974) *Quality Control Handbook*, 3rd edn., McGraw-Hill, New York.

Juran, J. (1988) *Juran on Planning for Quality*. Free Press, New York.

Kanter, R. (1989a) *When Giants Learn to Dance*, Touchstone / Simon & Schuster, New York.

Kanter, R. (1989b) 'Swimming in New Streams: Mastering Innovation Dilemmas' *California Management Review*, Summer, pp.45–69.

Kanter, R. (1991) 'Managing Change in Innovative Organizations' *in The Quest for Competitiveness* Shetty, Y. and Buehler, V. (eds), Quorum, New York.

Kaplan, R. (1986) 'Must CIM Be Justified By Faith Alone?' *Harvard Business Review*, 64, pp.87–95.

Karmarker, U. (1989) 'Getting Control of Just In Time', *Harvard Business Review*, September–October, pp.122–131.

Kay, J. (1993) *Foundations of Corporate Success*, Oxford University Press, Oxford.

Keller, M. (1993) *Collision Currency*, Doubleday, New York.

Kenney, M. and Florida, R. (1993) *Beyond Mass Production*, Oxford University Press, New York.

Kerwin, K. (1994) 'GM's Aurora Business', *Business Week*, 21 March 1994, pp.88–95.

Knight, R. (1987) 'Corporate Innovation and Entrepreneurship: A Canadian Study', *Journal of Product Innovation Management*, December, pp.284–297.

Kolb, D. (1976) 'Management and the Learning Process', *California Management Review*, Spring, Vol. XVIII, No. 3, pp.21–31.

Kotler, P. (1994) *Marketing Management*, 8th edn, Prentice Hall, Englewood Cliffs, NJ.

Krafcik, J. and MacDuffie, J. (1989) *Explaining High Peformance Manufacturing: The International Automotive Assembly Plant Study*, International Motor Vehicle Program, MIT Press, Cambridge, MA.

Krajewski, L. (1987) *Operations Management*, Addison-Wesley, Reading, MA.

Krajewski, L. and Ritzman, L. (1992) *Operations Management, Strategy and Analysis*, Addison-Wesley, Reading, MA.

Lamming, R. (1987) *'Towards Best Practice – A Report on Component Suppliers in the U.K. Automotive Industry'*, IRG Report No. 4, Brighton Polytechnic for SPRU, University of Sussex and International Motor Vehicle Programme, MIT Press, Cambridge, MA.

Lamming, R. (1993) *Beyond Partnership*, Prentice Hall, Hemel Hempstead.

Lamming, R. (1994) *A Review of the Relationships Between Vehicle Manufacturers and Suppliers*, DTI Report.

Lancaster, G. and Massingham, L. (1993) *Marketing Management*, McGraw-Hill, London.

Lavin, D. (1993a) 'Chrysler's Man of many Parts Cuts Costs', *Wall Street Journal*, May 14, Section B, p.1.

Lavin, D. (1993b) 'Straight Shooter: Robert Eaton Thinks "Vision" is Overrated', *Wall Street Journal*, October 4, Section A, p.1.

Lazonick, W. (1990) *Competitive Advantage on the Shop Floor*, Harvard University Press, Cambridge, MA.

Lazonick, W. (1991) *Business Organization and the Myth of the Market Economy*, Harvard University Press, Cambridge, MA.

Lazonick, W. (1993) 'Industry Clusters versus Global Webs: Organizational Capabilities in the American Economy', *Industrial and Corporate Change*, Vol. 2, No. 1, pp.1–23.

Lee, S. and Schniederjans, M. (1994) *Operations Management*, Houghton Mifflin, Boston, MA.

Levitt, T. (1960) 'Marketing Myopia'. *Harvard Business Review*, July–August, pp.45–56.

Lewin, K. (1947) 'Frontiers in Group Dynamics: Concept, Method and Reality in Social Science', *Human Relations*, June, pp.5–14.

Love, J. and Scouller, J. (1990) 'Growth by Acquisition: the Lessons of Experience', *Journal of General Management*, Vol. 15, No. 3, pp.4–19.

Luggen, W. (1991) *Flexible Manufacturing Cells and Systems*, Prentice Hall, Englewood Cliffs, NJ.

Luscombe, M. (1994) 'Beyond Focused MRP II', *Proceedings of the 29th BPICS Annual Conference*, Birmingham.

Magaziner, I. and Patinkin, M. (1989) 'Fast Heat: How Korea Won the Microwave War', *Harvard Business Review*, January–February.

Management Today, 24 January 1994, p.38.

Martin, J. (1994) 'A Practical Strategy for Inventory Reduction', *Proceedings of the 29th Conference of BPICS*, Birmingham, UK, pp.303–314.

Maslow, A. (1954) *Motivation and Personality*, Harper & Row, New York.

McDonald, M. (1993) 'Portfolio Analysis and Marketing Management', *Marketing Business*, pp.30–33.

McGregor, D. (1987) *The Human Side of Enterprise*, Penguin, London.

McMillan, C. (1985) *The Japanese Industrial System*, De Gruyter, Berlin.

McMillan, J. (1990) 'Managing Suppliers: Incentive Systems in Japanese and US Industry', *California Management Review*, Summer 1990, pp.38–53.

Meyers, H. (1969) 'The Great Nuclear Fizzle At Old B&W', *Fortune Magazine*, Nov.

Mintzberg, H. and Waters (1985), 'Of Strategy Delivered and Emergent', *Strategic Management Journal*, July–September, pp.257–272.

Mintzberg, H. and Quinn, J. B. (1991) *The Strategic Process: Concepts, Contexts, Cases*, 2nd edn, Prentice Hall, Englewood Cliffs, NJ.

Mintzberg, H. (1994) *The Rise and Fall of Strategic Planning*, Prentice Hall, Hemel Hempstead.

Mitchell, R. (1989) 'Masters of Innovation: How 3M Keeps Its New Products Coming', *Business Week*, April 10, pp. 58–63.

Mowery, D. (1988) *International Collaborative Ventures in US Manufacturing*, Ballinger, Cambridge, MA.

Mueller, F. (1992) 'Designing Flexible Teamwork: Comparing German and Japanese Approaches', *Employee Relations*, Vol. 14, Iss. 1, p.5–16.

Muhlemann, A., Oakland, J. and Lockyer, K. (1992) *Production and Operations Management*, Pitman, London.

Mundel, M. (1955) *Handbook of Industrial Engineering and Management*, Prentice Hall, Englewood Cliffs, NJ.

Naisbitt, J. (1982) *Megatrends*, Warner Books, New York.

Oakland, J. (1994) *Total Quality Management*, Butterworth–Heinemann, Oxford.

Oakley, P. (1992) *The Role of Launch Planning in the Early Commercial Success of High Technology Products*, Unpublished PhD Thesis, City University Business School, London.

Ohmae, K. (1982) 'Japan: From Stereotypes to Specifics', *The McKinsey Quarterly*, Spring, pp. 2–33.

Ohmae, K. (1983) *The Mind Of The Strategist*, Penguin, New York.

Ohmae, K. (1985) 'Becoming a Triad Power: The New Global Corporation' *in McKinsey Quarterly*, Spring, pp.7–20.

Ohmae, K. (1989) 'The Global Logic of Strategic Alliances', *Harvard Business Review*, March–April, pp.143–154.

Ohmae, K. (1990) *The Borderless World: Power and Strategy in the Interlinked Economy*, Collins, London.

Oliver, N. and Wilkinson B (1992) *The Japanization of British Industry – New Developments in the 1990s*, Blackwell Business, Oxford.

O'Neal, C. (1989) 'JIT Procurement and Relationship Marketing', *Industrial Marketing Management*, No. 18, pp.55–63.

Palmeri, C. 'A Process That Never Ends', *Forbes*, Vol. 150, Iss. 14, December 21, 1992, pp.52–56.

Pascale, R. (1984) 'Perspectives on Strategy: The Real Story Behind Honda's Success' *California Management Review*, 26/3, pp.47–72.

Pascale, R. (1990) *Managing on the Edge*, Viking, London.

Pavitt, K. (1990) 'What We Know About the Strategic Management of Technology', *California Management Review*, Spring, pp.17–26.

Pearce, J. and Robinson, R. (1982) *Formulation and Implementation of Competitive Strategy*. Irwin, Boston, MA.

Pekar, P., Allio, R. (1994) 'Making Alliances Work – Guidelines for Success', *Long Range Planning*, Vol. 27, No. 4, pp.54–65.

Personnel Management Plus, April 1993, p.14.

Personnel Management, December 1994.

Peters, T. (1986) 'The World Turned Upside Down', *The Business of Excellence*, Thames TV, London.

Peters, T. (1987) *Thriving On Chaos*, Pan Books/Macmillan, London.

Peters, T. (1990) 'Tom Peters – Business Evangelist', *Business Matters*, BBC TV, UK.

Peters, T. (1992) *Liberation Management*, Macmillan, London.

Peters, T. and Waterman, R. (1982) *In Search of Excellence*, Harper & Row, New York.

Pine, B., Bart, V. and Boynton, A. (1993) 'Making Mass Customization Work', *Harvard Business Review*, September–October, pp.108–119.

Piore, M. and Sabel, C. (1984) *The Second Industrial Divide: Possibilities For Prosperity*, Basic Books, New York.

Platts, K. and Gregory, M. (1989) 'Manufacturing Audit In The Process Of Strategy Formulation', *International Journal of Production and Operations Management*, Vol. 10, No. 9.

Porter, M. (1980) *Competitive Advantage*, Free Press, New York.

Porter, M. (1985) *Competitive Strategy*, Free Press, New York.

Porter, M. (1990) *The Competitive Advantage of Nations*, Macmillan, London.

Power & Associates (1992) *Quality Survey*, New York.

Powers, T. (1991) *Modern Business Marketing*, West Publications, St Paul, MN.

Prahalad, C. and Hamel, G. (1990) 'The Core Competence of the Corporation', *Harvard Business Review*, May–June pp.79–91.

Pucik, V. (1988) 'Strategic Alliances with the Japanese: Implications for Human Resource Management' in Contractor, F. and Lorange P. (eds), *Cooperative Strategies in Industrial Business*, Lexington Books, MA.

Quinn, J. B. (1980) *Strategies for Change: Logical Incrementalism*, Irwin, Homewood, Ill.

Quinn, J. B., Doorley, T. and Paquette, P. (1990) 'Beyond Products: Service-Based Strategy', *Harvard Business Review*, March–April, pp.59–67.

Reynolds, I. (1984) 'The Pinched Shoe Effect of International Joint Ventures', *Columbia Journal of World Business*, Summer, pp.23–29.

Rogers, A. (1993) 'GM vs Honda: A Morality Tale', *Fortune*, Vol. 127, No. 3, February 8, pp.11, 14 (7–8IE).

Rogers, E. (1983) *Diffusion of Innovation*, 3rd edn, Free Press, New York.

Romano, C. (1994) 'Report Card on TQM', *Management Review*, Vol. 83, January, pp.22–25.

Rosch, W. (1989) 'The Evolution of the PC Microprocessor', *PC Magazine*, January 13, pp.96–97.

Rosenbloom, R. and Cusamano, M. (1987) 'Technological Pioneering and Competitive Advantage The Birth of the VCR Industry', *California Management Review*, Vol. 29, No. 4.

Roth, A. and Miller, J. (1989) *A Taxonomy of Manufacturing Strategies*, Paper presented at the 9th Conference of the Strategic Management Society, San Francisco, CA.

Rothwell, R., Freeman, C., Horlsey, A., Jervis, V., Robinson, A. and Townsend, J. (1974) 'SAPPHO Update – Project SAPPHO Phase II', *Research Policy 3*, pp.259–291.

Rover Purchasing Group (1993), in-house publication.

Sako, M. (1992) *Prices Quality and Trust: Inter-firm Relations in Britain and Japan*, Cambridge University Press, Cambridge.

Samson, D. (1991) *Manufacturing & Operations Strategy,* Prentice Hall, Sydney.

Samson, D. and Sohal, A. (1993) 'Manufacturing Myopia and Strategy in the Manufacturing Function: A Problem Driven Agenda', *International Journal of Technology Management,* special issue on 'Manufacturing Technology: Diffusion, Implementation and Management', Vol. 8, Nos 3/4/5, pp.216–229.

Sasseen, J. (1992) 'Delivering the Goods', *International Management,* Vol. 27, September, pp.72–75.

Saxenian, A. (1991) 'The Origins and Dynamics of Production Networks in Silicon Valley', *Research Policy,* 20, pp.423–437.

Schlender, B. (1991) 'The Future of the PC', *Fortune,* August 26, p.40.

Schmenner, R. (1990) *Production/Operations Management,* Macmillan, New York.

Schonberger, R. (1983) *Japanese Manufacturing Techniques,* Free Press, New York.

Schonberger, R. (1986) *World Class Manufacturing,* Free Press, New York.

Schonberger, R. (1994) 'Human Resource Management Lessons from a Decade of Total Quality Management and Reengineering', *California Management Review,* Summer, 1994, pp.109–123.

Schonberger, R. and Knod, E. (1991) *Operations Management: Improving Customer Service,* Irwin, Boston, MA.

Schroeder, R., Anderson, Tupy, S. and White, E. (1981) 'A Study of MRP Benefits and Costs', *Journal of Operations Management,* Vol. 2, No. 1, pp.1–9.

Selz, M. (1993) 'Some Suppliers Rethink their Reliance on Big Business', *Wall Street Journal,* March 29, Section B, p.2.

Sengenberger, W. (1993) 'Lean Production – The Way of Working and Producing in the Future?', *in Lean Production and Beyond,* International Labour Office, Geneva.

Shores, A. (1990) *A TQM Approach to Achieving Manufacturing Excellence,* ASQC Press, New York.

Simison, R. and Williams, M. (1993) 'Industry Focus: Japan's Car Makers Seek Solutions From U.S. Big Three', *Wall Street Journal,* Nov. 15, Section B, p.4.

Skinner, W. (1969) 'Manufacturing – The Missing Link in Corporate Strategy', *Harvard Business Review,* May–June.

Skinner, W. (1974) 'The Focused Factory', *Harvard Business Review,* May–June, pp. 113–121.

Skinner, W. (1985) *Manufacturing, The Formidable Competitive Weapon,* Wiley, New York.

Slack, N. (1991) *Manufacturing Advantage,* Mercury, London.

Slatter, S. (1980) 'Common Pitfalls in using the BCG Product Portfolio Matrix', *London Business School Journal,* Winter, pp.18–22.

Snow, C. and Ottensmeyer, E. (1990) 'Managing Strategies and Technologies', *in Strategic Management in High Technology Firms,* Lawless, M. (ed.), JAI Press, Boston, MA.

Snowdon, M., Ingmar, Y. and Truc, F. (1991) *Building Capabilities with Strategic Alliances: A Practical Guide,* Booz, Allen & Hamilton, New York.

Son, K. Young, (1990) 'A Performance Measurement Method Which Remedies the "Productivity Paradox" ', *Production and Inventory Management Journal,* Second Quarter, pp.38–43.

Sorge, A. and Warner, M. (1981) 'Manpower, Training, Manufacturing Organization and Workplace Relations in Great Britain and West Germany', *British Journal of Industrial Relations,* 18, pp.318–333.

Starbuck, W. (1993) 'Strategizing in the Real World', *International Journal of Technology Management*, Vol. 8, Nos 1/2, pp.77–85.
Storey, J. (ed.) (1993) *New Wave Manufacturing Strategies*, Paul Chapman, London.
Sturt, G. (1923) 'The Wheelwright's Shop', *in Work and Community in the West* Shorter, E. (ed.), Harper and Row, New York.
Sullivan, L. (1987) 'The Seven Stages in Company Wide Quality Control', *Quality Progress*, May, pp.39–50.
Sun MicroSystems (1994) *Annual Company Report*, Sun Microsystems, in-house publication.
Taguchi, G. and Clausing, D. (1990) 'Robust Quality', *Harvard Business Review*, January–February, pp.65–75.
Taguchi, G. (1986) *Introduction to Quality Engineering*, Asian Productivity Organization, New York.
Tampoe, M. (1994) 'Exploiting the Core Competences of Your Organization', *Long Range Planning*, Vol. 27, No. 4 pp.66–77.
Taylor, F. W. (1947) *Scientific Management*, Harper & Row, London.
Teece, D., Pisano, G. and Schuen, A. (1990) *Firm Capabilities, Resources and the Concept of Strategy*, Working Paper No. 90–8, University of Berkeley, CA.
Thompson, A. and Strickland, A. (1989) *Strategic Management*, 5th edn, Irwin, Homewood, Ill.
Thompson, A. and Strickland, A. (1992) *Strategic Management*, 6th edn, Irwin, Homewood, Ill.
Turnbull, P., Oliver, N. and Wilkinson, B. (1992) 'Buyer/Supplier Relations in the UK Automotive Industry; Strategic Implications of the Japanese Manufacturing Model', *Strategic Management Journal*, Vol. 13, pp.159–168.
Turnbull, P., Delbridge, R., Oliver, N. and Wilkinson, B. (1993) 'Winners and Losers – The Tearing of Components' Suppliers in the UK Automotive Industry', *Journal of General Management*, Vol. 19, No. 1, pp.48–56.
Twiss, B. (1992) *Managing Technological Innovation*, Pitman, London.
Twiss, B. and Goodridge, M. (1989) *Managing Technology for Competitive Advantage*, Pitman, London.
Uttal, S (1987) 'Speeding New Ideas to Market' *Fortune*, March 2, pp.62–66.
Urabe, K., Child, J. and Kagono, T. (eds) (1988) *Innovation and Management: International Comparisons*, de Gruyter, New York.
Vallely, I. (1993) 'Why Supervisors Can with Nissan', *Works Management*, Vol. 46, Iss. 10, October pp.18–21.
Vallens, A. (1993) 'Global Economy May Dictate More Spending for Training', *Modern Plastics*, Vol. 70, No. 11. Nov. pp.19–20.
Verdin, P., Williamson, P. (1994) 'Successful Strategy: Stargazing or Self-examination?' *European Management Journal*, Vol. 12, No. 1, March, pp. 10–19.
Vonderembse, M. and White, G. (1991) *Operations Management*, 2nd edn, West, St Paul, MN.
Wall Street Journal, June 4, 1990, p.9.
Wall Street Journal, March 24, 1992, Section B, p.1.
Wall Street Journal, October 27, 1992, Section A, p.3.
Wall Street Journal, February 16, 1993, Section B, p.9.
Wall Street Journal, August 9, 1993, Section B, p.2.
Wall Street Journal, August 27, 1993, Section A, p.1.

Wall Street Journal, October 21, 1993, Section B, p.1.
Wall Street Journal, January 27, 1994, Section B, p.1.
Wall Street Journal, February 24, 1994, Section B, p.1.
Wall Street Journal, July 29, 1994, Section D, p.2.
Waters, C. (1992) *Inventory Control and Management*, Wiley, Chichester.
Wheelan, T. and Hunger, J. (1989) *Strategic Management and Business Policy*, 3rd edn, Addison-Wesley, Reading, MA.
Wheelan, T. and Hunger, J. (1993) *Strategic Management and Business Policy*, 4th edn, Addison-Wesley, Reading, MA.
Wheelwright, S. and Clark, K. (1992) *Revolutionizing Product Development*, Free Press, New York.
Whitney, D. (1988) 'Manufacturing by Design', *Harvard Business Review*, July–August, pp.83–91.
Whittington, R. (1993) *What Is Strategy – and Does it Matter?* Routledge, London.
Wickens, P. (1987) *The Road to Nissan*, Macmillan, London.
Wilmot, R. (1985) 'Wanted: An Industry that is World Class', *Financial Times*, 26 June.
Wight, O. (1982) *The Executive's Guide to Successful MRP II*, Prentice Hall, Englewood Cliffs, NJ.
Womack, J., Jones, D. and Roos, D. (1990) *The Machine That Changed the World*, Rawson Associates, New York.
Young, J. (1985) 'The Quality Focus at Hewlett Packard', *The Journal of Business Strategy*, No. 3, Winter, pp.6–9.
Zipkin, P. (1991) 'Does Manufacturing need a JIT Revolution?', *Harvard Business Review*, January-February.

Index

ABC analysis, 231–2
Abernathy, W., 252
acquisitions, 22, 27–8, 52–3, 98, 100–1
Adair's needs model, 280–1, 282
Adam, E., 115, 237
Adler, P., 210, 211
Akao, Y., 204
Allen, D., 88, 303
alliances, 5, 274, 307
  in computer industry, 99, 100–1
  global, 320–2, 323
  strategic, 9, 26–8, 63, 337
  see also NUMMI project
Allio, R., 308
Anderson, J., 66
Argenti, J., 19
Armstrong, L., 127
assets, 9, 162, 225
Australian Manufacturing Council, 50–1
automation, 134–5, 140–3, 219, 323
  FMS, 72, 149, 152–8, 164–6, 171, 336
  overview, 160–3
  types, 165–8

backward integration, 10, 23, 26–7, 254
Baldridge Award, 178, 202–3
Barrett, D., 316
batch process, 140–1, 143–6, 149, 151, 153, 154, 157, 219
Bateman. T., 120, 121, 155
Beamish, P., 28
Beatty, C., 53
benchmarking, 69, 325–6
Bertodo, R., 262
Bessant, J., 50, 60, 116, 148, 156, 171, 278, 327
Bignell, V., 50, 58, 152, 154
Blake, R., 280
Bleackley, M., 28
BMW (case study), 38–9
Bolwijn, P., 58, 73, 154, 156
Boston Consulting Group, 2, 31, 32
Bradshaw, D., 124
brand loyalty, 90, 97
Britain, 316–17
  Japanese transplants, 5, 337–8
  national performance, 44–52
Brown, S., 210
buffer stocks, 219, 234, 244, 246, 248
Burbridge, J., 232
Burn, G., 204
Burt, D., 252
business innovator, 119
buyer–supplier relationships, 9, 13–14, 28, 53, 65, 335, 336
  inventory management, 226, 230, 232, 234, 251–60, 267

capacity/capacity utilization, 23, 65
car industry, 290–1, 337–8
  buyers–suppliers, 251–3, 255–9, 263–4
  globalization, 317–21, 328
  inventory management, 225, 227–8, 237, 245–7, 250–3, 255–9, 264–5
  new product development, 84–92, 95–6, 98–9, 108–9, 114–17, 120, 122–32
  NUMMI project, 53, 75–6, 84, 98, 162, 210–11, 276, 293, 305, 323
  quality, 178–9, 182–3, 186–7, 191–2, 195–7, 199, 201, 204, 219–20
  transplants, 264–5, 266, 337–8
Carlisle, J., 228, 251, 255
Carroll, P., 85, 118, 122, 333
cash generator products, 30
Chakravarthy, B., 77
Chambers, S., 57, 76
Chandler, A., 3, 34
charismatic leadership, 286–7
chief executive officer, 286–7
Ciampa, S., 180, 202
Clark, K., 115
closed-loop systems, 131, 241, 242
Cohen, S., 45
collaboration, 98, 308–10
Compaq (case study), 80–2
competitive advantage, 10, 49, 59, 96, 156, 169, 225, 295–6, 319, 325
  collaboration for, 309–10

sustainable, 13, 53, 335, 336
training for, 299–300
competitive analysis, 14–15, 23–4, 32, 60–3, 204
materials management, 228–30
of new products, 88–9, 107
competitive profiling, 69–71, 72, 325
components (design), 126–7, 159–60
computer-aided design, 63–4, 110, 123–5, 164, 166
computer-integrated manufacturing, 153, 158, 164, 173
computer industry, 80–2, 261, 320, 322
buyers–suppliers, 253–4, 259–60
inventory management, 227–8, 237, 266, 268–70
new product development, 84–8, 90–1, 94–7, 99–105, 108–11, 116–18, 120–8
computer numerically controlled (CNC) units, 166
continuous improvement, 4, 52, 191, 201, 202, 212, 225, 275
continuous process, 142–6
Cordero, R., 99, 117, 128
core competencies, 9–10, 225, 295, 335
corporate strategy, 66, 170, 335
issues in manufacturing, 1–39
linking strategies, 41, 44, 338–41
Corsten, H., 10
costs, 23, 59, 96, 124, 169–70, 231–2
emphasis on, 332–3
labour, 163, 169, 229, 271, 276, 329, 336
in materials management, 229–30
of quality, 192–7
of stock-holding, 233–4
craft manufacturing, 71–4, 197–9, 277, 279, 326
Crawford, E., 109
Crosby, P., 189, 191, 203, 210
cross-functional teams, 5, 6, 114–18, 122, 128, 129, 275, 305
cultural change, 122, 187, 200, 212, 220–1
Cusamano, M., 93
customer, 92–3, 319
feedback, 100, 110, 341
requirements, 40–1, 180, 182–3, 186
satisfaction, 65, 125–6, 180–2, 185, 203, 210, 336
Cyert, R., 302

database management, 124
Datta, D., 28
Davidson, H., 89
Dean, R., 168
decisions, 1, 4–7, 10–12, 171
matrices (use of), 29–33
technology investment, 161, 162
demand pull, 153–4
De Meyer, A., 58, 61
Deming, W., 52, 60, 177, 189, 191, 207, 209
Deming Award, 177
depreciation policy, 34
Dertouzos, M., 48–9, 105, 114, 127, 292, 298–300, 326–7, 328
design, 107
CAD, 63–4, 110, 123–5, 164, 166
effectiveness (indicators), 125–7
modular, 127–8
teams, 114, 115–18, 128
deskilling, 198, 212, 277–8, 282–4
Devlin, G., 28
differentiation, 23, 24, 96
Dilworth J., 42, 44, 289
distribution system, 185
diversification, 26, 52
divestment, 25–6, 31
divisional-specific learning, 135, 305–6
Dodgson, M., 307
downsizing, 63, 162, 229–30, 273–5, 277, 293, 296–7, 333, 336–7
Drucker, P., 25, 169, 212
Dussauge, P., 28, 96

Ebert, R., 115, 237
economic order quantity model, 228, 232–5, 243, 244, 36
economies of scale, 23, 88, 96, 127, 153, 278
Edmondson, H., 58, 66
electronic data interchange, 251
employees
empowerment, 65, 197–8, 219, 274, 285
internal customers, 180, 200–1, 210
employment in manufacturing, 45–8
environmental analysis, 17, 18
Erikson, K., 272, 278, 285, 289
evaluating strategies, 33–5, 75–9
Evans, J., 50, 75
Evered, R., 3
exports, 45, 46, 50
external customer, 180
external requirements, 68, 69

factory focus, 150–1, 159–60
failure, 107–8, 125, 306–7
'fat organizations', 292–3
feedback, 11, 35, 37, 100, 110
Feigenbaum, A., 179, 189
Ferdows, K., 58, 61, 63
Ferry, J., 189
Fifth Wave of manufacturing, 278, 327
financial performance measurement, 33–4
finished goods (stock-holding), 230–1
firm–business links, 324–5
firm infrastructure, 7–8, 319, 320
'first-to-market' firms, 86, 121

five forces model, 9, 13–14
fixed position layout, 137
flatter organizational structures, 290, 292–3
flexibility, focus and, 324
flexible manufacturing systems (FMS), 72, 149–50, 152–8, 164–6, 171, 336
flexible specialization, 173, 278, 327
Florida, R., 87, 261, 263–5, 279, 284, 302, 324
focus, 9–10, 40–1, 61–2, 171, 324
  approach to inventory, 224–5
  approach to quality, 187–188
'focused cell', 137–8, 141, 150–1, 159
Fogarty, D., 157
Foley, P., 298–9
Ford, I.D., 251
Ford (case study), 130–2
forward integration, 23, 26, 27
function-to-function approach, 108–11,
functional approach, 6, 137–8, 228

Gaither, N., 163–4, 169, 193
Garvin, D., 51, 75, 106–8, 177, 179, 193, 303, 304, 307
General Electric's nine-cell portfolio matrix, 31–2
General Motors, 312–15
  see also NUMMI project
generic choices, 21–4
Giffi, C., 163
Gleave, S., 272
globalization, 319–22, 323
Gordon, J., 53
Grindley, P., 135, 172
Groover, M., 146, 153, 159, 164
Gross Domestic Product, 45, 47
group needs, 280–1, 282
group technology, 72, 149–50, 159–61
Grove, A., 322

Hamel, G., 10, 12, 21, 48, 162, 187, 289, 295, 296, 306
Hamill, J., 27
Hamilton, D., 227
Handy, C., 317
Harari, O., 292–3
Harrigan, R., 98, 307
Harrison, A., 245
Hax, A., 11–12, 33
Hayes, R., 51–4, 57, 60, 66, 73–4, 76, 77, 89, 93, 110, 112, 126, 143, 272, 306, 319, 324, 327
Heizer, J., 156
hierarchical management structures, 6, 11–12, 273, 290–3
hierarchy of needs, 283–4
high-tech industries, 49, 181, 246–7
Hill, M., 166
Hill, T., 43, 54, 56–7, 67, 76, 143, 146, 166, 168–9, 184, 241
Hinterhuber, H., 294, 309
Hobday, M., 51
Hofer, C., 19
holistic approach, 41–3, 51, 299
  to inventory, 224, 235–6, 238–9, 243
  management, 73–5, 76
  new product development, 111–18
  to quality, 187–8, 201, 204–7
Honda (case study), 38–9
horizontal alliances, 9, 254, 274, 294, 308–9, 331–2, 335
horizontal integration, 27, 52
hours (international comparison), 290
human resource management, 7, 271–315
human resources, 59–60, 336–7
Hunger, J., 3, 19
Hutchins, D., 124, 125, 194, 230, 245, 272, 275

IBM (case study), 175–6
IBM–London Business School study, 329
image/image problem, 55–9, 211–12
Imai, M., 201, 202
imports, 45, 46, 50
inbound logistics, 7, 41
individual need, 280–1, 282
industrial output (comparisons), 47–8
industrial relations, 273, 277–8
industrial robots, 162, 165, 166–8
industry–company relationship, 13–17
innovation, 83, 90–1, 121–2, 305, 335
  failure factor, 104–6
  market developments and, 172–3
  role of R&D, 93–100
  suppliers and, 261–4
integration
  alliance strategies and, 26–8
  backward, 10, 23, 26–7, 254
  forward, 23, 26, 27
  horizontal, 27, 52
  vertical, 26, 52–3, 65, 226, 252–3, 294, 335
internal capabilities, 68, 69
internal customer, 180, 200–1, 210–1, 210
internal development, 22, 98
inventory management, 224–70
investment
  process choice/technology, 133–76
  return on, 33–4, 51, 53–4, 169
invisible earnings, 45
Ishikawa, K., 200
Ishikawa diagrams, 206–7

Jaikumar, R., 53, 272
Japanese approach, 6, 51–2, 114–15, 331

HRM, 271–2, 276–7, 282–5, 289, 292, 299–303, 310
inventory management, 224, 230, 245, 247, 250, 254–7, 261, 263–6
quality, 177–8, 186–7, 189, 191–3, 195–9, 201–2, 204, 206–7, 211, 217
transplants, 5, 265–7, 300–1, 337–8
job processing, 140, 143–6
job rotation, 283, 299, 300
job specialization, 277
Jobs, Steve, 119
Johansson, J., 93
Johnson, G., 5, 10–11, 17–18, 22
Johnson, R., 105
joint ventures, 9, 22, 27, 98, 274, 335
see also NUMMI project
Jones, Dan, 329
Juran, J., 52, 60, 177, 189, 191, 209
just-in-time, 65, 127, 142, 219, 306, 330, 336
inventory management, 230, 233–4, 236, 243–50, 265, 267

kaizen, 127–8, 171, 173, 192, 201–2
Kanter, R., 2, 121, 187, 272, 278, 289, 298, 308
Kaplan, R., 155
Karmarker, U., 237, 244
Kay, J., 2, 10, 104, 105
Keiretsu, 254, 310
Keller, M., 134, 162, 272, 276–7, 287, 318
Kenney, M., 87, 261, 263–5, 279, 284, 302, 324
Kerwin, K., 117
Knight, R., 109
Kod, E., 211, 255
Kolb's learning cycle, 303–5
Kotler, P., 95, 108, 110
Krafcik, J., 265
Krajewski, L., 96, 166, 216
Kumpe, T., 58, 73, 154, 156

labour
costs, 163, 169, 229, 271, 329, 336
deskilling, 198, 212, 277–8, 282–4
Lamming, R., 28, 251–2, 255, 257–8, 263
Lancaster, G., 89
Lavin, D., 252, 286
Lazonick, W., 54, 57, 271, 298, 301
lead times, 115, 234, 235, 244
leadership theory, 280, 285, 286–7
lean manufacturing, 129, 247, 278, 330–4
learning, 90–1, 295, 302
from failure, 107–8, 306–7
organizational, 84–6, 135, 274, 302–7
quality improvement and, 195–7, 304–5
Lee, S., 185, 235
Levin, B., 294, 309
Lewin, K., 302
licensing agreements, 94, 98
line process, 141–2, 143–6
long-term policies, 31, 191–2
Lorange, P., 77
Love, J., 53
Luggen, W., 152, 154
Luscombe, M., 239–40

McDonald, M., 29, 55
MacDuffie, J., 265
McGregor, D., 281
McGregor's theory X/theory Y, 281–3
McMillan, J., 225, 261
Majluf, N., 11–12, 33
management grid, 280, 281
management hierarchy, 6, 11, 12, 273, 290–3
managerial responsibility, 59–60
managers, 273–4, 277–9
manufacturing, 63–4, 124, 127, 337
eras, 277–9, 326–7
image problems, 55–9
investment, 133–76
marketing interface, 111–13
national importance of, 44–52
strategic issues, 1–39
manufacturing strategy, 40–3, 338–41
evaluating success, 75–9
formulation, 64–71
holistic approach, 73–5
key reasons, 59–64
market forces and, 71–3
national importance of manufacturing, 44–52
March, J., 302
market, 33, 71–3, 107, 172–3
–company relationship, 13–17
defining relevant, 32–3
pull, 93–4
requirements, 11, 75, 147, 148–9
research, 109
segments, 17, 23–6, 34, 36, 40, 90, 94, 182, 334
share, 4, 27, 31, 88, 90–1, 94, 163, 169, 186–7
strategic response to, 319, 322–6
marketing, 7, 43, 55–6
manufacturing interface, 111–15
strategy, 12, 44, 145, 147–50, 338–41
Maslow's hierarchy of needs, 283–4
mass production, 71, 74, 147–9, 173–4, 198–9, 326–7, 328
automation, 160–3, 165–8, 171–2
FMS, 72, 149–50, 152–8, 164–6, 171, 336
HRM and, 277–9, 282–3
inventory management, 246, 263
Taylorism, 168, 211–12, 234, 277
Massingham, L., 89
master production schedule, 238–9

materials management, 224–5, 234–5, 246, 265–6
  competitive importance, 228–30
  MRP system, 65, 165, 236–44, 245, 336
  scope of, 226–7
  tactical/functional roles, 228
materials requirement planning, 65, 165, 236–44, 245, 336
matrices (strategic decisions), 29–33
Matsushita, K., 197, 211
MCI's alliances, 99, 100
me-too approach, 86, 96–7
mergers and acquisitions, 27, 28, 52–3, 100, 101
method study, 212–15, 216, 217
Meyers, H., 54
microprocessor development, 102, 103
Miller, J.A., 67
Mintzberg, H., 21, 118
miryokuteki hinshitsu, 92
mission statements, 3, 179
modular design, 127–8
motivation theories, 280, 281–5
Motorola (case study), 222–3
Moulton, D., 280
Mowery, D., 98–9
Muda/Mura/Muri, 247
Mueller, F., 300
Muhlemann, A., 4
Mundel, M., 213

Naisbitt, J., 153–4
needs, 280–4
net change (MRP report), 237
net present value (NPV), 169
new product development, 83–132, 305, 335
nine-cell portfolio matrix, 31–2
Nonaka, I., 93
numerically controlled machines, 165–6
NUMMI project, 53, 75–6, 84, 98, 162, 210–11, 276, 293, 305, 323

Oakland, J., 191
Oakley, P., 118
Ohmae, K., 27, 42, 94, 169, 309
Oliver, N., 272, 299
O'Neal, C., 251
operating strategies, 6–7, 42, 60–1, 170
order-qualifying criteria, 67, 91, 146
order-winning criteria, 67, 91, 146, 169
organizational considerations (new product development), 111–22
organizational culture, 119–22, 271–315
organizational learning, 84–6, 135, 274, 302–7
O'Toole, 285
outbound logistics, 7
overhead costs, 234

p charts, 208
Palmeri, C., 258
Pareto analysis, 231–2
Pareto diagrams, 205–6
Parker, L., 228, 251, 255
partnership approach, 254–60, 335
Pascale, R., 2, 284, 306
patents (role), 94, 98, 121
Pavitt, K., 135
Pearce, J., 77
Pekar, P., 308
performance
  measurement, 33–5
  national (indicators), 45–8
  world class, 328–9
PEST analysis, 17
Peters, T., 90, 106, 118, 129, 155, 273, 282–3, 285, 317, 319
Pine, B., 278, 327
Piore, M., 72, 173, 278, 327
Pisano, G., 51, 73, 319, 324, 327
planning (new products), 118–9
plant layout, 123–4, 135–9, 143, 158
Platt, Lew, 112
Porter, M., 7–9, 13–15, 23, 41, 61, 96, 107, 254, 323
Porter's five forces model, 9, 13–14
portfolio analysis, 29–32, 77, 98
post-mass era, 278, 279, 326–7
Powers, T., 104, 114–15
Prahalad, C., 10, 12, 21, 48, 162, 187, 289, 295, 296, 306
preventive maintenance, 217–18
primary activities, 7
proactive policies, 66–7, 86–7, 335
problem-solving approach, 213
process choice, 110, 137–8, 141–2, 172
  marketing strategy and, 145, 147–50
  product lifecycle and, 151–2
  strategy and, 143–7
process control charts, 181, 207–10
process innovation, 83, 172–3
process layout, 137–8
process quality, 52, 181–5, 194, 198, 203, 208–9, 219
process technology, 92, 98, 109–10, 126, 133, 135, 168–71, 336
procurement (in value chain), 7
product
  champions, 89, 119
  development, 83–132, 305, 335
  innovation, *see* innovation
  layout, 138–9
  lifecycle, 33, 77, 111, 112–13
  portfolio, 29–32, 77, 98
  quality, *see* quality

standardization, 126, 141–2, 153, 198, 278, 323
technology, 92, 98, 126, 144
production/operations, 1–3, 8, 10, 12, 24–6, 35–6, 40–2, 53–5, 60–1, 66
demand placed on, 322–4
HRM theories, 274–7, 280–1
image, 55–9
link to other functions, 73, 74
process choice and, 144–5
remuneration schemes, 287–90
role in product development, 83–132
production/people grid, 280, 281
production planning, 65
production risk (new products), 107
productivity, 47–8, 162, 170, 212, 219, 274, 287–8, 290, 299, 329
profitability, 24, 229
project manufacture, 139–40, 143–6
prototypes, 110, 124, 140, 217
Pucik, V., 302

quality
assurance system, 183–5, 193
awards, 202–3
circles, 198–9, 201, 205–6, 208, 213, 273, 283
control, 179–80, 189, 191–2, 198
costs, 192–7
definition, 179–85
enhancement, 90, 92–3
function deployment, 204–9
improvement by learning, 195–7, 304–5
information management system, 201
management, 197–202, 218–19
measurement, 181–2, 216–17
product, 52, 123, 183–5, 208
quantifying, 216–17
strategic importance, 177–8, 185–8
tools/techniques, 203–9
total productive maintenance, 217–18
see also process quality; total quality management
Quinn, J.B., 20, 21, 117, 118

R charts, 208, 217
raw materials (stock-holding), 230–1
re-engineering, 275–336
reactive policies, 66–7, 86–7, 335
recognition of involvement schemes for employees (Rise), 275
remuneration, 65, 287–90
Render, B., 156
research and development, 49, 284–5
new product development, 93–100
resource allocation, 11, 12
restructuring, 2, 293, 296–7
return on investment, 33–4, 51, 53, 54, 169
Reynolds, I., 28
risk (new product development), 107
Ritzman, L., 96, 166
Robinson, R., 77
robots, 162, 165, 166–8, 170
Rogers, A., 119, 297
Romano, C., 187
Rosenbloom, R., 93
Roth, A.V., 67
Rothwell, R., 105, 119
Rover (case study), 38–9
Rucker Plan, 288

Sabel, C., 72, 173, 278, 327
Sako, M., 255
salaries, 65, 287–90
sales (in value chain), 7
Samson, D., 42, 50–1, 59–60, 76
Sasseen, J., 259
Saxenian, A., 101
Scanlon Plan, 288
Schendel, D., 19
Schmenner, R., 115, 159, 207, 244
Schiederjans, M., 185, 235
Scholes, K., 5, 10–11, 17–18, 22
Schonberger, R., 155, 178, 200, 211, 255, 265, 278, 327, 330
Schroeder, R., 241
scientific management, 168, 211–12, 234, 277
Scouller, J., 53
Scully, John, 119
Seiketsu/Seiso/Seiton/Seri, 218
self-actualization, 283, 284, 285
Selz, M., 260
Sengenberger, W., 310
senior management, 3, 6, 190–1
sequential approach, 110, 113–16, 129, 305
services, 7, 45, 316
Shell directional policy matrix, 30
Shores, A., 197, 211
short-termism, 2, 3, 4, 12, 33, 48–9, 301, 309, 317
Simison, R., 297
Skinner, W., 42, 50–1, 54–5, 57, 59–60, 72, 76, 150, 159
Slack, N., 60, 69
Slatter, S., 29, 32–3
Snowdon, M., 310
Sohal, A., 59, 60
Son, K., 75
Sorge, A., 299
Southern Cosmetics (case study), 147–8
SREDIM approach, 213–14, 216, 217
stakeholders, 1–2, 17–19, 119
standardization, 126, 141–2, 153, 198, 278, 323
Starbuck, W., 85–6
statistical process control charts, 181, 207–10
Steele, J., 316

stock-holding, 142, 230–1, 233–4
Storey, J., 166
strategic alliances, 9, 26–8, 63, 337
strategic analysis, 11
strategic approach
  to inventory, 225, 235–6
  to quality, 187, 188
strategic audit, 19
strategic business units, 6
strategic capacity, 4
strategic decision-making, 1, 29–35
strategic fit/stretch, 12
strategic manufacturing, 71–4, 199, 278
  definition, 334–8
  process choice/technology, 133–76
  world-class, 316–43
strategic options, 21–9
strategic planning, 19–21, 35, 37
strategic responses to markets, 322–6
strategic triangle, 42–3
strategy, 3–5
  planning/implementation loop, 35, 37
  process choice and, 143–7
  stakeholders and, 17–19
  see also manufacturing strategy
Strickland, A., 11, 19, 90
Sturt, G., 278
subcontracting, 7, 8
substitute products, 13, 96
suggestion schemes, 275
Sun Microsystems (case study), 268–70
suppliers, 171–2, 219, 227, 260–5
  see also buyer–supplier relationships
suport activities/skills, 7, 171
switching costs, 121
SWOT analysis, 15–17, 20, 54, 68, 69

Taguchi, G., 92
Taguchi methods, 217
Tampoe, M., 296
targeting new products, 89–92
task requirements, 280–1, 282
Taylor, F. W., 211–12
Taylorism, 168, 211–12, 234, 277
team approach, 114–18, 128, 260–1
technical innovator, 119
technological capabilities, 172
technological risk, 107
technology, 7, 65
  investment, 133–76
  push, 86, 93–4, 100, 102, 181, 184
  strategies, 41, 96–8
  trading, 98
Teece, D., 302
telecommunications industry
  buyer–supplier relationship, 259–60
  inventory management, 227, 237, 249
  new product development, 84–5, 91, 94–5, 99–102, 104, 117, 121–2, 125
  supplier innovations, 263
theory X/theory Y (McGregor), 281–3
Thomson, A., 11, 19, 90
time factor, 4–5, 42, 43
top-down approach, 271–2, 292
total productive maintenance, 217–18
total quality management, 4, 59–60, 65, 177–8, 185, 187, 195, 200, 326, 330
  case study, 222–3
  evolution/development, 189–92
  inventory management, 225, 244, 255
  work study and, 210–17
Toyota (NUMMI project), 53, 75–6, 84, 98, 162, 210–11, 276, 293, 305, 323
Toyota supplier (case study), 259,
trade figures, 45, 46
training, 98, 122, 208, 272–3, 293, 297–302, 317
transfer pricing, 34
transfer process, 94
transformation process model, 342–3
transplants, 264–7, 300–1, 337–8
trust, 255, 285
Turnbull, P., 245–6, 250, 254, 265
Twiss, B., 94, 133

unemployment, 167
United States, 5, 316–17
  HRM, 282, 285, 288–9, 292, 298–302
  inventory management, 250, 263–6
  new product development, 114, 115
  quality, 177, 186–7, 193, 195–6, 198, 202–4, 210, 216
Urabe, K., 171

Vallas, S., 272, 278, 285, 289
Vallely, I., 300
Vallens, A., 298
value chain, 7–9, 41, 224
value extractors/enhancers, 54
Verdin, P., 12
vertical alliances, 9, 274, 294, 308, 309, 335
vertical integration, 26, 52–3, 65, 226, 252–3 294, 335
Voderembse, M., 67–8
volume manufacturing, 110, 278

wages, 65, 287–90
warehousing, 234
Warner, M., 299
Waters, C., 21, 233, 243
Watson, Thomas, 85
Western manufacturing
  HRM, 271, 275–7, 281–2, 310
  inventory management, 224, 230, 263–4
  Japanese transplants, 265–7
  see also Britain; United States
Wheelan, T., 3, 19

Wheelwright, S., 52, 54, 57–8, 60, 66, 74, 76–7, 89, 93, 110, 112, 126, 143, 306
White, G., 68
Whitney, D., 107, 123, 124
Whittington, R., 1, 306–7, 323
Wickens, P., 55, 57
Wight, Oliver, 241
Wilkinson, B., 299
Will, T., 10
Williams, M., 297
Williamson, P., 12
Womack, J., 115, 128, 178, 195, 247, 263, 265, 266, 330
work-in-process, 230, 243
work measurement, 215–243
work study, 210–17
worker-manager problem, 273, 277–9
worker participation, 275
world-class strategic manufacturing, 13, 41, 198, 271–2, 278, 316–43
World-wide Manufacturing Competitiveness study (1994), 329

X charts 208, 209, 210, 217

Young, J., 75, 182

Zeithaml, C., 120, 121, 155
Zipkin, P., 244, 246
Zysmann, J., 45